DEMCO

MacArthur's War

KOREA AND THE UNDOING OF
AN AMERICAN HERO

STANLEY WEINTRAUB

THE FREE PRESS
New York   London   Sydney   Singapore

A Division of Simon & Schuster Inc.
1230 Avenue of the Americas
New York, NY 10020

THE FREE PRESS and colophon are trademarks
of Simon & Schuster Inc.

Designed by Carla Bolte

Manufactured in the United States of America

10   9   8   7   6   5   4   3   2   1

Library of Congress Cataloging-in-Publication Data

Weintraub, Stanley
     MacArthur's war : Korea and the Undoing of an American Hero / Stanley Weintraub.
       p.   cm.
     Includes bibliographical references and index.
     1. Korean War, 1950–1953—United States. 2. MacArthur, Douglas,
  1880–1964. I. Title.
  DS919.W46   1999
  951.904'2—dc21   99-35870
                                               CIP

ISBN 0-684-83419-7 (alk. paper)

FOR MY GRANDCHILDREN

MaryAlison

Sarah Beth

Sofia Rebekah

James Benjamin

Hanna Streed

Isaac Ray

Benjamin Lee

Noah Samuel

Contents

Korea in 1950.

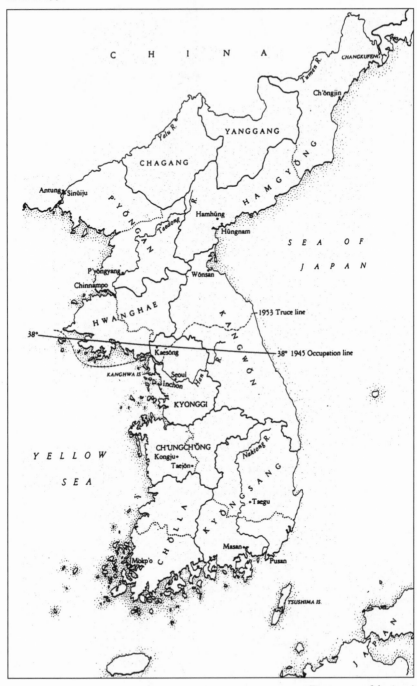

(Department of the Army)

Preface

THIS WAS "MY" WAR. While I have written about other wars, for me Korea is different. I was there.

Blotched with rust and sagging in the water, the weary old ferryboat *Kango Maru* did not look like a seagoing troopship, but it was my ticket to the war. At Sasebo, a naval base in southern Kyushu which we had taken over from the Japanese in 1945, troop trains from Yokohama disgorged us near the docks for the voyage to Pusan and then to replacement depots in the no longer peaceful "Land of the Morning Calm." The water was rough, and in the darkness, the broad deck was awash; below, the lavatory facilities consisted of a large, odoriferous space with dozens of round openings in the floor over which to gingerly squat. By the first light of dawn we were eager for solid ground until the swaying tub approached within a few miles of shore. The fecal stench of Korea, where human excrement fertilized the soil, overwhelmingly more fetid than the fumes arising from the ferry's *benjo,* billowed out to greet us and left us speechless. We hoped it would be a short war.

It wasn't. The three years of conflict cost more than two million lives, yet the line of battle remained largely where the war began, astride the 38th parallel, above which the Russians effected the Japanese surrender in 1945, below it the Americans.

The line had quickly hardened into a Cold War political frontier. A puppet Stalinist regime with officials trained in Moscow or in the Red Army in Siberia set itself up for business in Pyongyang, which became the North Korean capital. Its experienced People's Army would emerge from the tens of thousands of Koreans who fought with Mao Zedong's troops and chased the less than enthusiastic followers of Chiang Kaishek from the Chinese mainland in 1948. South of the parallel, where the American occupation established the self-exiled old nationalist Syngman Rhee in Seoul as president, the Americans and the Koreans outdid each other in incompetence. Washington, however, paid little attention. A finger-like Asian appendage, Korea seemed an insignificant backwater.

Thirty-five thousand American dead in Korea in three years and fifty-eight thousand American dead in Vietnam over twelve years only suggest what followed. Aside from many thousands more wounded in Korea, thousands more were missing in action than in Vietnam. Although the fewer MIAs from the Vietnam War became a political football, the six thousand American missing in Korea remain forgotten. In the American mind the only connection the two wars now have is the abiding embarrassment that neither one was won. Yet Korea at worst was a draw, a limited war that reached its minimal objectives, whereas Vietnam was a defeat without precedent. The leading world power was humbled by a peasant people thought of as barely civilized wards of the colonialist French. Both wars, nevertheless, were fought to the accompaniment of a quavering trumpet. The sense of a compelling mission was difficult to maintain. Yet in Korea a line was being drawn against Communist expansion; in Vietnam that was a controversial premise. Events would demonstrate that those doubts had substance.

MacArthur's War comes to an end when MacArthur's overwhelming presence vanishes. The war did not end with his exit, although the stalemate he predicted came about. He had warned, and would continue to warn, that there was no substitute for victory, but that truism related to a bygone world in which there were no weapons of mutual destruction.

I deal with the war here in some deliberately simplified ways. All the apostrophes in Anglicized Korean place names and proper names are omitted as of no narrative value. Proper names are offered Asian fashion, surname first, unless the Western style is so familiar (as with Rhee) as to make proper usage appear awkward. Endnote numbers are eschewed as intrusive, as are most footnotes. Extensive backmatter notes, however, cite significant sources. Some of my sources are living participants. They are identified when they permitted me to do so, in both acknowledgments and notes, and I am grateful to them. Soon, such memories, like my own, will vanish unless committed to print or to tape.

Living and dead, veterans of this not-quite-forgotten war are now remembered in a moving memorial on the Mall in Washington in which the nineteen soldier figures are outfitted and equipped better than they ever were in reality. On visits to the memorial, those who were in Korea in 1950–53 often gaze with chagrin at bronze GIs wearing ponchos used then mostly to shroud the dead and bearing walkie-talkie field radios, which most never saw. Yet, somehow, the space evokes their sacrifice; and the names of the nations inscribed around its periphery recall that it was the first international effort to roll back aggression. The nearly forgotten war deserves not to be forgotten. Its first eleven months—MacArthur's War—are remembered here.

S.W.

"Organized resistance will be terminated by Thanksgiving . . . They are thoroughly whipped."

—MacArthur to Truman at Wake Island

"This is the damndest war. We can't win, we can't lose, and we can't quit."

—A lieutenant in Seoul to correspondent Keyes Beech

"If I were God, and I could give you anything you wanted [for Christmas], what would you ask for?"

"Gimme tomorrow."

—*Time* combat photographer David Douglas Duncan and a chilled Marine at the Chosin Reservoir

The Second Coming

ONLY THE SECOND COMING could have upstaged General Douglas MacArthur's return to the United States after fourteen godlike years on the Pacific rim. His sleek Lockheed Constellation, the name *Bataan* painted on its nose only a few days earlier, roared to a stop at National Airport in Washington just after midnight on April 19, 1951. For the first time since 1937 he set foot on mainland U.S. soil, touching in salute the garland of gold braid that was his "scrambled eggs" officer's cap.

The halo seemed even less than his due. MacArthur in 1950 was the senior soldier in the American army—"senior," quipped one junior officer, "to everyone but God."

Despite the hour the Joint Chiefs of Staff (JCS), who had unanimously recommended MacArthur's dismissal from his posts in Tokyo so that he and his extreme views would not be factors in the war in Korea, were on hand to offer him an engraved silver tea service. With them was his oldest rival in the military, now the Secretary of Defense, George C. Marshall—to MacArthur only a desk general.

In unassuming civvies, his lapel unadorned even by a miniature medal ribbon, the balding Marshall was hatless despite the wind off the Potomac. Recognizing a political phenomenon who had aspired to the presidency before, and now might sweep in on a wave of popular acclaim, the majority and minority leaders of both houses of Congress were also at the Military Air Transport Service terminal. Of those in power in the capital only President Harry Truman himself, the failed haberdasher who had sacked MacArthur

I

for insubordination to civil authority, was missing. In a deliberate snub, Harry Truman had delegated Brigadier General Harry Vaughan, his military aide, to be his representative. An old crony who had served with him in France in 1918, in the Missouri National Guard, Vaughan owed his general's star to his poker pal's accidental presidency. ("It was a shameful thing to fire MacArthur," an irate citizen wrote to the President, "and even more shameful to send Vaughan.")

As MacArthur was flying in, the predictable brickbats were flying at Truman. A Baltimore resident suggested that the President "step down and permit MacArthur to replace you." A lady from Washington wrote that MacArthur "has forgotten more about the Far East than those advising you have ever known. . . . Of course, I am not one of your followers—have never voted for you—and will never vote for you." A New Jerseyite confessed, "I voted for you in 1948 and have regretted it since," and deplored the bankruptcy of Truman's business in the 1920s, for his turn to politics had been owed to that. The sixth grade at the Nathaniel White School in Cromwell, Connecticut, wrote to ask why General MacArthur "has lost his job in Korea." A lady in Texas charged, "The Kremlin should give you a 21-gun salute." And a Kentuckian telegraphed, "That you should have relieved MacArthur before now is the minority view here." Complainants are always quick to write, but one of that apparent minority, Harold Russell, the national commander of Amvets, who had been maimed in World War II but returned to win an Academy Award for his role in *The Best Years of Our Lives,* wrote to Truman to express support for the President's upholding of "constitutional lines of authority," for "any lessening of civil power over military power must inevitably lead away from democracy."

The period was then thought of as the early years of the Cold War— which had actually arisen before, and survived through, the hot one of 1939–45. Yet most major and minor states were led by men whose world outlook reflected the less complex political and strategic configurations of not merely a prenuclear age but of the seemingly simpler truths of the Great War of 1914–18.

Fifty-one years into the twentieth century, only one leader making news had no memory of the nineteenth—North Korea's Communist ideologue Kim Il Sung. His political and military indoctrination came courtesy of the wartime Red Army. Winston Churchill and Clement Attlee, who replaced each other at Downing Street in 1945 and 1951, respectively, were born in the era of Bismarck and had fought in the earlier world war. Konrad Adenauer,

"*Der Alte*" to West Germans, was born in 1876, two years after Churchill; Syngman Rhee of South Korea, in 1875. Josef Stalin, born in 1879, had been a mature revolutionary in the first decade of the new century when MacArthur, born in 1880, was already soldiering. Harry Truman, born in 1884, had been only a reserve artillery captain activated in wartime. Now, in April 1951, he was commander in chief over the much-decorated MacArthur, who on his promotion in 1918 was the youngest brigadier general in the American army. Chiang Kaishek, holed up in Formosa (Taiwan) after losing China to the Communists, was already past forty in the late 1920s when he was the dominant warlord in China. Mao Zedong, who led the Chinese Red Army in its takeover of the mainland, was a comparative youngster, born in 1893. Sitting atop the burgeoning Third World as its informal spokesman was Jawaharlal Nehru of India, who was twelve in the year of Queen Victoria's death. In Japan, MacArthur had been looked upon as a head of state himself. Defeated but nominally reigning and at fifty the most junior of the older generation, Emperor Hirohito, to symbolize his subservience, paid a courtesy call upon the general twice a year.

Although anxious Democrats worried about offering a national forum for the deposed hero, Congress had invited America's senior active general, at seventy-one a near-mythic military figure, to address a joint session. Republicans, on the other hand, anticipated something approaching the Sermon on the Mount. The valedictory had been drafted in longhand by MacArthur en route, polished by aides, and typed and retyped. Old-fashioned, rolling phrases came easily to him.

In his suite at the Statler Hotel, the general inserted a few more lines despite the approaching dawn and his appointment in the House of Representatives gallery just after noon. He realized that many millions around the nation, including schoolchildren, were to have that Thursday as a holiday in order to hear him on radio, or to see him on their grainy, flickering new television sets. He wanted his words to be memorable as well as mischievous to the administration that had sacked him.

At 12:13 p.m. Jean MacArthur was conveyed to a reserved seat in the front row of the visitors' gallery; other spectators rose to applaud her. Seven minutes later the floodlights for newsreel and television cameras flashed on, and only then did the Republic's elected lawmakers, knowing now that they could be seen by history, file in. At 12:31, a minute behind schedule, the official doorkeeper cried out, "Mr. Speaker: General of the Army Douglas MacArthur!"

The ovation rivaled that of political conventions, yet subsided when it was obvious that MacArthur, with the calm confidence of an actor practiced before cameras and crowds, was ready to speak.

For thirty-four minutes, in a resonant, slow-paced voice some remembered from radio, when he staged the ceremonial Japanese surrender on the battleship *Missouri* in Tokyo Bay in September 1945, he kept his Capitol and nationwide audience spellbound. "I stand on this rostrum," he began after the traditional acknowledgments, "with a sense of deep humility and great pride; humility in the wake of those great American architects of our history who have stood here before me; pride in the reflection that this forum of legislative debate represents human liberty in the purest form yet devised. . . . I address you with neither rancor nor bitterness in the fading twilight of life with but one purpose in mind: to serve my country."

Pausing for bursts of applause that quieted only when he began anew, MacArthur contended that the real enemy in Asia was China, an imperialist nation in Communist disguise, thrusting across Asia and revealing "the same lust for expansion of power which has animated every would-be conqueror since the beginning of time." Its ideology would solve nothing for the troubled continent, he claimed: "What the people [of Asia] strive for is the opportunity for a little more food in their stomachs, a little better clothing on their backs, a little firmer roof over their heads, and the realization of the normal nationalist urge for political freedom." A UN victory, followed by peace, would bring that closer than would Communism. He made no reference to his earlier views that the Joint Chiefs of Staff felt might expand the conflict into World War III. Instead, he declared untruthfully that although he had been criticized for his strategic ideas about Korea, they were "fully shared" by the Joint Chiefs of Staff. The falsehood won him a cheering, hand-clapping, foot-stamping ovation.

"There are those," he deplored, "who claim our strength is inadequate to protect both Europe and Asia, that we could not divide our effort. I can think of no greater expression of defeat. The Communist threat is a global one. Its successful advance in one sector threatens the destruction of every sector. You cannot appease or otherwise surrender to Communism in Asia without simultaneously undermining our efforts to halt its advance in Europe." Victory had been imminent when the Chinese intervened in Korea, he said, but he had never contemplated invading Chinese territory—something very different from neutralizing it by bombing. The changing facts of war, he insisted, now required eliminating the "sanctuary protection given the enemy north of the Yalu." That meant China. Also, he wanted naval and economic blockades of the Chinese mainland, "air reconnaissance of China's coastal waters and of Manchuria," and the unleashing of Chiang's island-bound forces to return civil war to the mainland. All that meant widening the war, which he did not openly say; at the least it went beyond his appeals to Washington four months earlier to permit him to destroy Chinese "industrial capacity to wage war" and to invite Chiang's restless but ineffective troops to augment UN forces in Korea. He denied that he was a warmonger. "Nothing could be further from the truth." The nation was already at war, and "In war there is no substitute for victory." (Wild applause erupted.) "There are some who, for varying reasons, would appease Red China. . . . History teaches us with unmistakable emphasis that appeasement begets new and bloodier war." He would not settle, either, for a "sham peace"—which, like blackmail, encouraged more exorbitant demands. "Why, my soldiers asked of me, surrender military advantages to an enemy in the field?" He paused for effect; then, dramatically, his voice turning husky, added, "I could not answer." Enraptured, audiences did not pause to imagine occasions when MacArthur might have exchanged views with ordinary soldiers. (A veteran of service under the general wrote supportively to Truman after MacArthur's dismissal that his buddies had a slogan, "Stick with Mac, and you'll never get back.")

In closing, the general reminded listeners that he had served in the military for fifty-two years, having become a West Point plebe in 1899. On April 1, from Tokyo, he had sent a message to Colonel W. E. Crist at the Academy, where he was once its commandant, to be used in connection with celebrations of West Point's 150th anniversary. "As I look beyond those fifty years to the day I joined the long grey line," he wrote, "I recall I then felt as an Army 'brat' [that] the occasion was the fulfillment of all my boyish dreams. The world has turned over many times since then and the dreams have long vanished with the passing of years. . . ." Over the Pacific, in penning his address to Congress, it was tempting to incorporate the lines written for West Point "as I near the end of the road." "When I joined the Army, even before the turn of the century," he told his national audience, "it was the fulfillment of all my boyish hopes and dreams. The world has turned over many times since I took the oath on the Plain at West Point, and the hopes and dreams have long since vanished. But I still remember the refrain of one of the most popular barracks ballads of that day, which proclaimed, most proudly, that 'Old soldiers never die; they just fade away.' And like the old soldier of that ballad,

I now close my military career and just fade away—an old soldier who tried to do his duty as God gave him the light to see that duty. Good-bye."

Had the occasion been a quadrennial party convention, MacArthur might have been nominated for president by acclamation. At the Capitol and at radios and television screens wherever the mesmerizing address was heard, overcome listeners sobbed. Some in the House chamber could be heard shouting "No! No!" Telephones began ringing at newspaper offices to second MacArthur's militancy; the White House switchboard was besieged by calls, most of them hostile and many of them abusive.

A few days later New York City gave the general a huge parade that showered down 2,800 tons of ticker tape and the *New York Journal-American* employed a full-page banner headline, in red ink, "God Bless Gen. Mac-Arthur!" Someone in the crowd shouted, to enthusiastic cheers, "Hang that bastard Harry Truman!" Another excoriated the ex-salesman, "He's not selling shirts: he's selling us!"

From his suite in the Waldorf-Astoria in New York, Herbert Hoover, seventy-seven, described MacArthur to a reporter effusively after the radio address as "the reincarnation of St. Paul into a great General of the Army who came out of the East." In the House chamber Republican representative Dewey Short of Truman's home state announced, "We heard God speak here today, God in the flesh, the voice of God." (In the *Congressional Record,* Short amended his encomium to "a great hunk of God in the flesh.")

Truman, claiming later that he had only read the speech as the hour conflicted with his regular Thursday meeting with Secretary of State Dean Acheson, dismissed the nostalgia for soldiering and the strophic farewell. "There was a lot of carrying on about that speech, and some of those damn fool Congressmen were crying like a bunch of women, but it didn't worry me at all." Truman had read an advance copy of the text, having insisted that Army Secretary Frank Pace get him one, as was the President's privilege as commander in chief. MacArthur remained an active general. "Please, Mr. President," Pace appealed, "it would be very embarrassing for me to ask the general or one of his aides. . . . I'd really rather not."

"Frank," said Truman as if the Cabinet executive were an Army private, "I don't give a good goddamn what you'd rather. I want you to get me that speech and bring it to me. On the double."

"He went and got it, and I read it," recalled Truman. "It was nothing but a bunch of damn bullshit."

Six days later, on April 25, the Senate, more moved than was the President, voted to hold hearings on MacArthur's dismissal and on the military situation in the Far East. As opening witness the general testified for three days. He stumbled into repeated contradictions and found no eagerness among the senators for going to war with mainland China. Public interest in the hearings faded soon after MacArthur left the stand. Newspaper coverage declined. White House and congressional mail began shifting away from MacArthur, especially after widely respected Joint Chiefs chairman Omar Bradley observed to the Senate committee that the general would get the United States "in the wrong war, at the wrong place, at the wrong time and with the wrong enemy." MacArthur would wait until much later to call Korea when he ran the war "Mars' last gift to an old warrior."

For MacArthur, events always took a personal twist, as Civil War historian Shelby Foote claimed to novelist Walker Percy. "Heard a funny joke. General and Mrs. MacArthur were sitting together somewhere and a band began to play 'The Star Spangled Banner.' He took her hand and said, 'Listen, darling, they're playing our song.' " By then MacArthur had moved into the Waldorf-Astoria, where at a great height he would live out his remaining years. His imperious former public relations chief in Tokyo, Major General Courtney Whitney, once his investment adviser in prewar Manila, continued to hand out press releases about MacArthur and Korea to a dwindling number of reporters, several of whom, in an idle hour, composed "The Battle Hymn of the Waldorf":

> Here is the Waldorf-Astoria,
> The home of the rich and the odd,
> Where the press speaks only to Whitney
> And Whitney speaks only to God.

While the war in Korea dragged on inconclusively, Douglas MacArthur began fading away.

Before the Deluge

Persistent intelligence reports that the Communist government of North Korea was up to no good finally pushed General Bradley, chairman of the Joint Chiefs of Staff, on June 20, 1950, to ask MacArthur whether an invasion of South Korea seemed imminent. For two years there had been incursions from the north and attacks from the south. Both regimes indulged in provocative talk and even more provocative intrusions across the 38th parallel, a temporary frontier pending unification, as well as bursts of artillery and mortar fire.

Bradley's query came the day after a "Supreme People's Assembly," which included renegade Koreans from the south meeting in Pyongyang, the northern capital, called once more for peaceful union through free elections that in no case were intended to be free. President Syngman Rhee of South Korea, who ran the country as his personal fiefdom, had long called for elections on terms similarly intended to be propaganda exercises. Now Rhee worried—although hardly enough—about the meaning of an order from Josef Stalin that Red Army military advisers should withdraw from Kim Il Sung's forward units. Although that could have suggested an easing of tension, Russian-language battle plans had already been translated into Korean. In the previous nine months the Soviets had furnished planes, heavy artillery and tanks from the stockpiled materiel that had undone the Japanese in Manchuria in the summer of 1945. The Soviets had also instructed the North Koreans in their use. Stalin now did not want to chance having any Russians become prisoners of war, and his advisers were ordered to stay well above the 38th parallel, within access to the Siberian border.

Rhee was encouraged by a visit to the frontier the day before by John Foster Dulles, Secretary of State Acheson's adviser on Far Eastern affairs. Long a Republican stalwart, Dulles, who ostensibly helped to keep Japanese affairs bipartisan, had been in Tokyo conferring with MacArthur on aspects of a formal peace treaty with Japan. The Russians and the Red Chinese remained excluded, the former because Stalin would demand an occupation zone in Japan, the latter because the Communist regime was unrecognized by Washington, which pretended that the offshore island of Taiwan (Formosa) occupied by the Japanese from 1895 to 1945, was legally China.

What Dulles could see with his binoculars was less significant than an earlier Central Intelligence Agency report in March which predicted a push from the North in June. Even a second CIA finding was discounted in Tokyo because there were always bellicose threats from both sides. Still, Dulles flew from Japan "for a look," and Acheson joked in Washington about the staid, dark-suited Presbyterian elder on a forward parapet overlooking the 38th parallel. That Dulles was there, noted State Department adviser George Kennan, who was puzzled about Russian intentions, might lead the Soviets to think "we were on to their plan."

"Yes," Acheson scoffed, "Foster up there in a bunker with a homburg on."

On the twentieth Dulles had presented his new book, *War or Peace,* to President Rhee, inscribed more diplomatically than accurately by the author to "an outstanding and victorious leader in the world-wide struggle for peace and justice." Korea, he ventured in offering Rhee the book, would play "a decisive role . . . in the great drama which is unfolding." Not as much predicting an imminent hot war as an intensification of the cold one, Dulles, who was a church deacon and reputedly as Presbyterian as predestination, was a Cold Warrior of moral certainty that imposition of the American Way was good for everyone, wherever. "The only guy who has direct contact with God is John Foster Dulles," said one of his detractors, "and if you don't think so, ask him."

From Korea, Dulles returned to Japan for further discussions with Mac-Arthur. At a cocktail party in Tokyo, Dulles seemed unsuspecting in the extreme that a shooting war in the area was close. To a high Finance Ministry official, Takeshi Watanabe, he suggested that Japanese industry should gear up to export such products as cocktail napkins to the United States. MacArthur was just as unaware of impending trouble, having had no warnings from his intelligence staff, and little to concern him but his future after a peace treaty with Japan ended his role there. Nearly five years into his stewardship of the Japanese occupation and fifteen years after he had taken early retirement to become field marshal of the Philippine Army—his unanticipated route to Pacific command in World War II—MacArthur had nowhere to go on the conclusion of his proconsulship in Tokyo but honored retirement—somewhere. With no home in the United States, no circle of Stateside cronies and no interest in anything but his wife, son and reputation, vegetation into honorific corporate directorships loomed, and perhaps a memoir to preempt prying biographers. And perhaps politics.

His shogunate in Japan—the reward for having turned ignominious defeat in the Philippines into glorious victory—had to end sometime, but MacArthur could not figure out how to arrange that, short of being summoned home to run for President. As early as 1944, still in wartime, he had put out feelers to Republicans for a nomination which he would not actively pursue. After the war, in the spring of 1946, Dwight D. Eisenhower, his one-time aide in the Philippines before the war and now his five-star peer, arrived on an official visit. MacArthur gave the general, whom he privately described as the best secretary he ever had, a dinner in the American embassy in Tokyo. MacArthur lived up the hill in the embassy compound, in the stately ambassador's home available because resumption of formal diplomatic relations awaited a peace treaty. None of MacArthur's lunches or dinners for guests were formally elaborate, and few included a Japanese guest. According to one intimate, "Only sixteen Japanese ever spoke with him more than twice, and none of these was under the rank, say, of Premier, Chief Justice, president of the largest university." No alcoholic beverages were served, and the food, someone claimed to journalist Joseph Alsop, "was just what you would expect from a good army mess sergeant."

The pattern, repeated through to Dulles's visit just before the shooting began in Korea, was that all the guests, sometimes as many as thirty, would gather in the entrance hall of the former ambassadorial residence to await the viceroy. Then Mrs. MacArthur (who privately called him "Sir Boss") would announce, "Oh! I hear the General coming." He would stride down the sweeping stairway from their quarters above and kiss Jean (so one of his staff generals recalled) "as though he hadn't seen her for 100 years." After a short greeting "just like he was making a speech," he would lead the assemblage into dinner, and on occasion afterwards invite the men to remain for cigars and the women to join them after coffee for a film—newsreels followed by a light comedy, musical or western. Sometimes his projectionist added newsreel-like footage of Japan shot by American Signal Corps cameramen, affording him celluloid acquaintance with the unvisited island domain he governed. (Films were shown every evening but Sunday—far more often than there were dinner guests. MacArthur preferred to entertain at lunch.) Otherwise he would leave the table and return upstairs via the big curving staircase—for a nap if it was after lunch, or to dip into his collection of military memoirs and histories, from Wellington and Napoleon and Grant to Ian Hamilton on Gallipoli. Mrs. MacArthur remained to socialize until it seemed time to announce that she had better join the general.

The wooded, hilly tract little more than a mile from the Dai Ichi Building, the former insurance company offices from which MacArthur ruled Japan (*Dai Ichi* is Japanese for "number one"), had somehow survived the incineration of Tokyo from the air in 1945. MacArthur lived and entertained in the embassy "Big House" on a prominence that looked north into the city. Ambassador Joseph Grew had resided there from 1932 to Pearl Harbor. It had seven bedrooms, four bathrooms, a banquet as well as a dining room, three salons, a smoking room for gentlemen and a host of service rooms— almost the imperial style of MacArthur's penthouse in the Manila Hotel in the 1930s. A second building to the rear of the embassy included apartments for MacArthur's personal staff and occasional guests.

His social activities in Japan, but for occasionally meeting visiting dignitaries at Haneda Airport, were limited to meals and, on occasion, post-prandial conversation. He went once to the Soviet embassy to mark the anniversary of the October Revolution. He went once to a Bastille Day ceremony at the French embassy. On a day in June he went once to the British embassy in honor of the king's birthday. Jean did the rest.

MacArthur's first marriage had been brief and disastrous. He then married Jean Faircloth on a return trip he had made from the Philippines early in 1937 to bury his domineering old mother, who had gone out to Manila with him. MacArthur was then fifty-seven; Jean was more than twenty years younger—a petite, dark-haired Tennessean active in the Daughters of the Confederacy. Ten months later, in February 1938, she bore the general a son, Arthur, now his companion at seven-thirty breakfasts before the boy went off to be tutored by Phyllis Gibbons and MacArthur turned to the thin English-language *Japan Times* before going off to oversee Japan.

When Eisenhower was in Tokyo, MacArthur invited him into an anteroom after dinner to complain privately about military flourishes that he had heard five-star admirals were insisting upon. Eisenhower agreed that distinctions were wrong and that unnecessary ceremony should be abolished.

"That's all right, Ike," said MacArthur. "Just so long as those Navy sons of bitches don't get ahead of us, I don't care."

What MacArthur really wanted to discuss out of earshot was politics. Next time around, he predicted, either he or Eisenhower would be President. Since he expected to be too busy running Japan to be available in 1948, that made Ike a sure thing.

Perhaps believing it at the time, Eisenhower declared that the military ought to keep out of politics. He had achieved, anyway, all he could possibly hope for or deserve. He had no aspirations for the White House.

"That's right, Ike," said MacArthur, slapping Eisenhower's knee. "You go on like that and you'll get it sure."

Possibly MacArthur was sounding out the competition, for again in 1948 he hoped for a call that would be a draft rather than an inducement to be dragged into a primary campaign, yet he permitted himself to be embarrassed in the primaries anyway. Not only did he refuse to campaign; he refused even to return to the U.S. for so much as a speech or a parade.

In Japan, even after five years into his routine, the general was seldom seen outside his daily practice, which took him by beflagged black 1941 Cadillac the few blocks back and forth from the embassy compound to the Dai Ichi. With few exceptions, he would see little of his fiefdom until, in September 1950, he flew south to southern Kyushu to board a ship for Inchon. His two trips out of the country before June 1950 had taken him once to the Philippines and, in 1948, to Seoul for the inauguration of Syngman Rhee as South Korean president.

From 1945 into 1951, MacArthur never left Tokyo to inspect his occupation divisions. (Instead, his chiefs of staff were accompanied by Mrs. MacArthur.) As assistant deputy G-3 for the occupation army, John "Mike" Michaelis, then only a lieutenant colonel, arranged for his chief to see the troops by running "four or five" reviews of about twenty thousand troops on the Imperial Palace plaza near the Dai Ichi. Michaelis recognized "the absolute necessity for timing down to the very seconds. We knew, for example, that it took exactly so many seconds from the embassy compound where he lived to the reviewing stand. . . . A review took days to prepare. General MacArthur was very courteous about it and very careful to thank us afterwards." But the general never materialized at field exercises, where pampered and poorly trained garrison soldiers could not figure out how to erect tents, break down a rifle, assemble chow wagons or maintain themselves in any way without indigenous assistance. As his chief of staff, Ned Almond, admitted, the state of readiness in Japan was known to be poor, but it was blamed not upon leadership lapses but on the poor quality of peacetime recruits and their disinterest in discipline.

Michaelis, however, was "heartsick" at the condition of occupation troops and their officers. In a policy that did not end with the war, when a transport with peacetime replacements arrived in Yokohama, general head-quarters (GHQ) already had the records, cabled ahead or delivered by courier, of all officers aboard. GHQ, according to Michaelis, kept those it wanted in Tokyo. Rejects were shipped to the Eighth Army. "They were known as 'Reject Ones.' After Eighth Army had completed its screening, the rest were released to corps and became 'Reject Twos.' If corps didn't want them, they became available to divisions and became 'Reject Threes.' " The top prospects remained in Tokyo "sitting up at GHQ four-deep."

Day after day, week after week, disdainful of imperial ceremony, MacArthur claimed, he would arrive at the Dai Ichi about ten-thirty in his MP convoy with radio staff cars at each end. At the entrance white-gloved MPs restrained large crowds of Japanese gawkers as he emerged from his car, accompanied by aides Sidney Huff or Laurence Bunker. The Japanese had been in awe of him since his arrival in 1945 as viceroy. Then their own troops, with fixed bayonets, lined the streets for his motorcade with their backs toward him not to protect the general from the crowds but as a sign of humility. Gazing directly at the godlike Hirohito, it was formerly thought, might cause one to be stricken blind. MacArthur had become the informal new sovereign. Even his license plate was number 1.

Returning salutes at the entrance to the Dai Ichi, he strode inside, usu-ally with his hands clasped behind his back and his corncob pipe, unlit, in his mouth. It was, General (then Colonel) John Chiles remembered, "like the changing of the guard at Buckingham Palace." But that itself changed some-what on May 1, 1950, when MacArthur wanted to blunt a Communist May Day protest by the splinter Japanese party and ordered that the imperial pro-cession cease. Nevertheless, he insisted that his ten-minute drive proceed for a stately twenty minutes, which impelled security-conscious military police to follow his Cadillac at an inconspicuous distance. And the white-helmeted MPs at the big doors continued to perform, morning and evening, what MacArthur's assistant Major Faubion Bowers described as a "parade ballet of thunder and blazes: turning, stepping, snapping to, and saluting in four directions, like Tibetan lamas at prayer."

Inside the building, staff got out of the way but for one occasion when,

Bunker observed, the general entered his elevator and "as far as I know, that's the only time he ever looked up or recognized anybody was there. This one morning as he got in . . . he turned around and said, 'Anybody want a ride?' Of course, everyone just sort of stood back, but one brash young major who had just arrived said, 'Yes, sir.' . . . And this young major [then] said, 'Three, please.' The operator whipped them right up to the sixth floor, opposite MacArthur's office. As General MacArthur got out he turned around and said, 'You got more of a ride than you bargained for, didn't you, young man?' That was a rare occasion."

At about two the general would return to his embassy quarters for lunch with Jean, sometimes also with guests, nap after listening to the three o'clock Stateside news on his portable radio, then return to the Dai Ichi about five-thirty or six, remaining into the evening before his late dinner. Staff on duty since early morning had to remain until he left. Often he would send someone to the window (he didn't want to be seen at it himself) to estimate the crowd waiting for him to emerge. Usually hundreds of Japanese, most with cameras, would be poised to click away as he snapped his hand to the faded scrambled eggs on his cap. (Merle Miller claimed, maliciously, "A man I know who was on MacArthur's staff insists that the general had an enlisted man, I believe a corporal, who did nothing but fray battle caps . . . so they would look as if the general had just stepped out of some firing line or other.")

The atmosphere on MacArthur's office floor was reverential. Few aides entered his small sanctum with its broad expanse of desk uncluttered but for in and out trays seldom holding more than a few papers, and three ashtrays. He had no personal secretary and opened all mail addressed to him. His letters were drafted in longhand on legal-size lined pads, and he ripped off sheets to hand to aides for typing. No telephone intruded. He usually went to his chief of staff's office for business discussions, where he met with his "Bataan gang" of subordinates whose elevated ranks were earned by loyalty and who competed for his attention. His own office, spartan by executive standards, was arranged so that he sat with his back to the windows overlooking the Imperial Palace grounds only a street, a moat and a stone wall away. His visitors gazed into the glare, keeping them at a strategic disadvantage.

While Rightists in American politics considered him one of their own—he had been a Hoover appointee as Army chief of staff, and never altered his contempt for Hoover's Democratic successor, Franklin Roosevelt—in Japan he was considered a political liberal. In civil rights and in social programs he was almost a New Dealer, although in business matters he kept the usual big banking and industrial families who had bankrolled the war against him in power, as well as many prewar politicians, in the presumed interest of stability. Where he was rigidly hard-line was in his doctrinaire anti-Communism. The Japanese press loved him, and the Stateside journalists ensconced in Tokyo were more MacArthur boosters than reporters. Life was as good as it got for Americans in imperial MacArthur Japan, and toadying to the shogun in the Dai Ichi meant preferential treatment in accommodations, amenities, access to exclusive stories and interviews. MacArthur, a veteran newsman on the Tokyo beat recalled, kept his wartime swelled head because the corps of correspondents acted more like publicists for him than as objective reporters. "Attacks he could ignore."

In mid-1950 he was already contemplating the presidential election in 1952. Harry Truman, surprise victor in 1948, was unlikely to run again. MacArthur's relationship with Truman was a roller-coaster of wrath and respect. As late as MacArthur's last year, after Eisenhower had served his terms as President, Larry Bunker remembered MacArthur telling an old crony, "Well, you mark my word, . . . Harry Truman is going down in American history as a far greater President than Ike Eisenhower; he made more decisions on important American problems in a proper American fashion than Ike ever contemplated." In part that might have been sour grapes about Eisenhower's easy grab at the presidency, for MacArthur maintained at least to himself that despite his remoteness from American life, there had been a chance for him until 1952. At the close he thought he was no longer remembered as a war hero, but he remained an icon to conservatives, not least because he was a vocal advocate, still, of Kuomintang legitimacy in China—always a litmus test for the Republican Right.

In June 1950, before there was war in Korea, Dulles—reflecting the mood of influential Republicans—remained eager to have Rhee, with MacArthur's permission, invite several divisions of Generalissimo Chiang Kaishek's unusable refugee troops on Taiwan to prop up the South Korean army. Such an arrangement would go far to commit the United States to defend the island, still called Formosa by Americans, from invasion by Mao's forces already preparing to complete the unification of China. It would effectively reverse American policy, affirmed earlier both by Acheson and MacArthur, that the Pacific defense perimeter plunged uninterruptedly from Japan to the Philippines. If China were a nation, undivided, interference in Taiwan was intrusion into an ongoing civil war.

Mao was less than eager to have Kim's ambitions in a minor appendage of Asia upset his own unification timetable. Visiting Stalin on December 16, 1949, the self-styled "Great Helmsman" had asked for "volunteer pilots and secret military detachments to speed up the conquest of Formosa." Stalin promised only to consider the request, but encouraged Mao to think that he had nothing to fear from the United States. "America, though it screams war, is actually afraid of war more than anything. Europe is [also] afraid of war." For seventeen days during the bitter Moscow winter, Mao waited for offers of assistance, but received only an agreement for a Chinese-Soviet treaty that papered over differences. "I got so angry," Mao recalled in 1958, "that I once pounded the table."

Korea did not yet interest either of them. But Kim soon begged for Stalin's blessing for what seemed, from the Kremlin, a rather chancy enterprise. According to Nikita Khrushchev's memoirs, at the Kremlin late in 1949 Kim explained to Stalin that he "wanted to prod South Korea with the point of a bayonet," anticipating that Rhee's ramshackle and unpopular minority government would quickly collapse. It would only be, he assured Stalin (so Khrushchev reported it), "an internal matter which the Koreas would be settling among themselves."

Rhee had similar ambitions for armed unification, but his lack of the wherewithal made his public bluster seem only that, while inhibiting American military aid beyond inadequate defensive weapons. In March 1950 he had threatened to cross the parallel "even though some of our friends across the sea tell us that we must not cherish thoughts of attacking the foreign puppet who stifles the liberties of our people in the North. . . . We shall respond to the cries of our brothers in distress." Privately, to his American lobbyist Robert Oliver, a Penn State professor of speech, he wrote that June 14 of having his forces take the offensive up to "the Tumen and the Yalu" "to mop up the guerrillas" and the "bandits" led by Kim and drive them into the mountains to "make them starve there."

Although such posturing could have provoked a preemptive strike, Kim knew very well that Rhee's rhetoric was empty while the North Korean People's Army (NKPA), or *In Min Gun*, was real. At most, Rhee, while risking destruction of his nation, might have counted in Machiavellian fashion upon armed American support despite declarations to the contrary. As Kim defied logic, he deployed the *In Min Gun* for war.

Since the likelihood of external intervention seemed small, on January 30, 1950, Stalin signaled to his representative in Pyongyang that it was all right to permit the North Koreans to go ahead as long as Soviet surrogates took the risks. "Such big business regarding South Korea," he cautioned his Korean ambassador, Terenty Shtykov, "requires serious preparation."

That hint referred also to Mao's China, which owed the return of favors to Stalin for wartime assistance. Victory on the mainland had left Mao with thousands of now-surplus Koreans with military experience in China's own civil war, who could be marched across the Yalu and legitimately outfitted in Kim's uniforms. On his part, early in 1950, Kim prepared for war by ordering all civilians out of a two-mile strip north of the 38th parallel. This might have been interpreted by Rhee's or MacArthur's intelligence experts as securing an assembly area to jump off an invasion, but it was ignored.

In Moscow again from late March into mid-April, Kim arranged for additional weaponry, including tanks, with which, he assured Stalin, North Korean troops abetted by fifth columnists could advance into unprepared South Korea nine to twelve miles per day and complete reunification in three to four weeks. According to a classified Soviet memorandum, the operation was scheduled for June 25, after the Russians prepared the plan of attack and delivered the arms, so that the operation could be completed "before the rainy season could ruin the enterprise."

Mistrusting Mao as a more formidable Tito, and worrying, too, that China could become a rival for preeminence in the Communist world, Stalin, in the grip of the postwar paranoia of his declining years, wanted China distracted from ideology. He also feared a post-treaty Japan, from which he was being excluded, worrying that South Korea might become a bridgehead into mainland Asia for a resurgent Japan backed by American atomic weapons. The last American occupation troops had left South Korea the year before, and now that the Soviets had broken the American monopoly on nuclear weapons there seemed no chance that the U.S. would risk ground forces on the Asian mainland. On January 28, 1950, Russian intelligence reported to Stalin that the South Koreans had "little hope of American assistance" and that Truman "would leave Formosa as he had left China." In domestic disarray, the Americans, transfixed by instability in Europe, would do almost nothing in Asia—and what little they might do across the Pacific, some worried, would only weaken them in the West.

Kim arrived in Beijing (Peking) on May 13 after his second journey to Moscow. China remained to be won over, and Stalin had cautioned the ambitious North Korean that he could "get down to action" only after approval from "Comrade Mao Zedong personally." Chinese premier and foreign minister Zhou Enlai pressed for the "personal clarifications of Comrade Filippov"—the code name for Stalin among Communist leaders—and was assured that the Soviets had paid in advance for Mao's concurrence by loyally boycotting the feeble United Nations until Taipei was ejected and Beijing seated. But the duplicitous Stalin had a parallel agenda. China, as diplomatic pariah despite substantial foreign recognition of the regime, was finding its contacts with the West, which Stalin feared, largely blocked. Soviet absence from the UN, then, served also to keep Mao's China out of formal international arrangements. Hostile to the West because of its exclusion, China remained dependent upon a self-serving Russia as its seemingly devoted patron. Stalin preferred it that way.

Zhou and leading Chinese generals conceded Kim's right to his adventure, but wanted to limit their outright support to their continuing return of Koreans who had fought on the Communist side. Mao hoped that the United States, preoccupied with an unstable Europe and woefully understrength in Japan, its only source of troops on the Pacific rim, would concede its weakness and intervene only with pious platitudes.

After four days of wary discussions with Kim, Mao, realizing that saying no was out of the question while their own request to Stalin for two hundred combat aircraft and the pilots to fly them was on the table and crucial to a Formosa campaign, overruled his associates. "If the American army participates," he promised, assuming that there was little chance of that, "China will send armies to support North Korea." Hedging then a little from that he told Kim, "If they cross the 38th parallel, we will definitely come in fighting." It was no secret that of MacArthur's four divisions on occupation duty in Japan, all but one regiment of the three in each poorly prepared division lacked an infantry battalion, and none had any combat experience. Postwar enlistees, GIs were so softened by easy living, even on a private's pay, that few Americans in uniform from Kyushu to Hokkaido would ever again enjoy such a coddled existence or afford pleasures from bargain Post Exchange luxuries to a pick of prostitutes. To the Chinese leadership, Mao's offer seemed safe enough.

Dulles's post-parapet speech in June to Rhee's National Assembly, cleared with Acheson at State, was obviously meant to be heard in Beijing and Moscow as well as Pyongyang. Twice in the century, without being bound by any treaty to do so, Dulles reminded his listeners, the United States had "intervened with armed might in defense of freedom" when provoked by "military aggression." And, he underlined, "You are not alone."

Rhee responded that if the Cold War were lost "by default" it would take "a hot war regardless of cost" to regain the lost freedoms. To the Communists later, both speeches were not empty posturing but part of a plot to initiate a war. A South Korean political defector, Mun Kak-bong, would claim in a broadcast that Dulles had not gone to the 38th parallel, "to pick daisies." He was there on MacArthur's behalf, allegedly to instigate a war to provide Rhee with political support and to create an excuse for protecting Taiwan before Mao's Chinese could occupy their national territory, 121 miles across the strait.

MacArthur's intelligence staff in Tokyo, putting together information from sources in Taipei, found, on June 17 and again on June 23, "undeniable evidence" of a Communist invasion fleet marshaling along the southern Chinese coast near Formosa, a motley collection of junks and sampans realistically of no military use. British intelligence cited reports from Shanghai, which it took more seriously than it should have, that Mao had ten LSTs and nine LSMs docked there for ferrying twenty thousand troops to Formosa. Believing it themselves, alarmist associates of Chiang were concocting fantasy plots to displace him in order to build support for a Formosa which the United States might defend, and Chiang—aware of such undercurrents— began exploring possible routes to unannounced exile in Korea or the Philippines. Yet he had some cards of his own to play beyond offering troops to bolster Korea.

Chiang expected his trump card to be the hawkish MacArthur himself. Charles Willoughby, MacArthur's chief of intelligence since 1939—originally Karl Weidenbach of Germany, a Prussian in manner and sympathy— had told MacArthur on June 15 that a leading Kuomintang general, Ho Shih-lai, begging "absolute secrecy," had informed him that Chiang was willing "to accept American high command in every category and hopes to interest General MacArthur to accept this responsibility, preferably for the entire Far East but specifically for Formosa, and places himself and his people in every governmental level at the disposal of General MacArthur." In Washington at the British embassy, Communist spy Guy Burgess, only the day before the war began, cabled London, perhaps hoping to influence decision making, that "the Soviets seem to have made up their minds that the U.S.A. have a finally-decided policy [not to defend Formosa]. This *we* have never quite come to believe." He was probably referring to the Truman-Acheson position, while realizing MacArthur's strongly held opposite views. Nevertheless, it was already too late to influence the action in both Formosa and Korea, where both heads of state were poor advertisements for the "free world."

No one in the upper military hierarchy in the U.S. trusted Rhee, who *would* go to war if he could. He had been permitted no heavy weapons and only a handful of planes incapable of offensive action. Kim Il Sung had nothing to fear from Rhee but company-level line crossings. What Dulles could not see with his borrowed binoculars as he peered across the 38th parallel were railway lines in North Korea surreptitiously being extended southward almost to the border, roads being reinforced to support Soviet T-34 tanks that had bested Hitler's panzers, and tens of thousands of Koreans with experience fighting for Mao who were en route home across the Yalu in full gear. MacArthur, relying upon Willoughby, downplayed any sense of threat, although on March 10, in his weekly report to Washington, he had passed on a warning that the North might invade the South in June. On March 25 he had changed his mind and no longer expected an attack that summer, and two months later, on May 25, thought an attack was unlikely as no offensive preparations could be perceived. Formosa offered more apparent—perhaps more appealing—cause for concern.

While remaining interested in Chiang's isolated island, which he saw as completing an American-influenced arc including Japan and the Philippines, MacArthur could not be bothered with Korea. He had visited only once, in August 1948, when he had declared, in Seoul, perhaps intending nothing more than rhetoric, that the 38th parallel "barrier" had to be "torn down," and that nothing would prevent "the ultimate unity of your people." If the Communists attacked the South, he promised effusively, "I would defend it as I would California." Before his one trip to Seoul he had complained to Major Bowers, "I wouldn't put my foot in Korea. It belongs to the State Department. They wanted it and got it. They have jurisdiction. I don't. I wouldn't touch it with a ten-foot barge pole. The damn diplomats make the wars, and we win them. Why should I save their skin?"

A year later he assured a visiting congressional delegation in Tokyo that South Korea was "in no danger." The South, he contended, would be invaded only if there were a general Communist offensive against the West. His estimate came as usual from Willoughby, a believer like MacArthur in monolithic world Communism. Willoughby kept the CIA out of his area as much as possible, believed only his own informers and told his boss only what he thought MacArthur wanted to hear. Accordingly, on June 20, 1950, MacArthur replied to Washington that the South Koreans, assisted by KMAG—the U.S. Korean Military Advisory Group—were perfectly capable of taking care of themselves.

Privately, Omar Bradley, who distrusted MacArthur, asked the KMAG commander, Brigadier General William L. Roberts, when in Seoul, only twenty-five miles from the frontier, for his opinion. Although Washington withheld from South Korea's nine divisions of undertrained soldiers heavy mortars, anti-tank weapons and artillery heavier than 105mm howitzers, and furnished no tanks on the grounds that the hilly terrain was unsuitable, Roberts claimed that the South Koreans—"my forces," he called them because he supplied 482 military advisers—could "hold the Commies." Still, the reports of "field agents"—spies—compiled by CIA chief Admiral Roscoe H. Hillenkoetter seemed alarming, at least in Washington, however little was being made of the situation in Tokyo and Seoul. Whatever the history of false alarms at the 38th parallel, the admiral wanted his estimate in the hands of President Truman, Secretary of Defense Louis Johnson (who was proud of his budget-minded downsizing of the military), and Secretary Acheson. Hillen-koetter had copies hand-carried to their offices, and insisted upon signed receipts. One unalarmed person in a very high place despite Washington's skittishness was MacArthur, who did not bother with the CIA. *New York Times* roving foreign correspondent Cyrus Sulzberger noted in his diary for May 18, 1950, that he had come from a "very long talk" with the general at the Dai Ichi. "He is a remarkable physical specimen," Sulzberger wrote. "Although he is a few months past seventy, he really looks like an exceedingly well-preserved man of fifty. I am told he dyes his hair. Be that as it may, he is a handsome, well set up man filled with youthful energy."

As MacArthur lit and re-lit his pipe, and fiddled with a box of matches, he voiced his irritation with what he saw as a Europe-focused American per-spective, leading Sulzberger to observe that it seemed reasonable to believe that if any new war were to break out, it would be there. "I had heard you quoted," Sulzberger began, "as saying there was not much chance of a new world war in the near future."

His reasoning, MacArthur confirmed, was "the changed nature of war." Since scientists had made "mass killing" easy, "war is no longer rationally a means of settling international problems. . . . Both sides lose." Even the pub-lic, he contended, "realizes all too well in terms of the last war that there can be no real victory in a future war." Because of that he saw no "psychological preparation" by any of the major powers for "a shooting war." His evidence was that "many incidents have taken place during the last few years which in the past would have led to war but which have been passed over." People now would not permit a war. "That goes for both sides. That is the basic reason for my belief that war is not upon the doorstep." Russia, he claimed, was "arming defensively" and only talking aggressively. "The Russian," he said, very likely meaning Stalin, was "doing so well under the present nonshooting war that he would probably and logically wish to continue the present successful system. It is a rare thing, in sports or anywhere else, when a man changes a winning combination."

Curiously, MacArthur's own thinking was Eurocentric, for he went on to explain how difficult it would be for the Soviets to support a war in Asia "over a single railway which is being worked to death." Improving the Asian standard of living, he thought, would be the best way to eliminate the causes of war in the area. "I wish," he mused to Sulzberger, "there was more effort to face the fundamental problem of doing away with war. For example, the United Nations should look squarely at the problem of *abolishing* war. Yet the United Nations continually asks for its own armed forces. It talks of *fighting* to maintain the peace. That is a ridiculous anachronism."

Five weeks later MacArthur may have wished that Sulzberger had never visited, or at least taken no notes.

South Korea had held its first general elections in the peninsula's four-thousand-year recorded history on May 30. They had been an orderly affair, relatively, as Rhee had ordered the arrests, as alleged Communists, of only 30 of the 2,156 candidates for legislative seats. Nine were judged to be members of an outlawed party; the others were accused of electoral violence. Still, 121 of the 210 seats in the National Assembly went to candidates opposed to Rhee, an outcome that surprised him and may have caused him to regret the paucity of his arrests. As June began he was a minority president.

Opponents north and south would later claim that Rhee instigated a war in order to unify the country under his jurisdiction, but he had no need to do so, as the Communist North was already planning to do that for him. By early June, Kim Il Sung's army had infiltrated guerrilla units into the South, some arriving as early as March, slipping ashore in small boats. Some forces were composed of as many as six hundred men; one unit of one hundred included thirty-five women, according to a deserter. Their orders were to disrupt transport and communications when the war began. Several days before jumping off, organized units to the north of the 38th parallel were allocated weapons and rounds of ammunition ranging from sixty to one hundred, and, usually, four grenades. Everyone received about two weeks' rations of millet or rice. After that was gone they were expected to forage for food or to seize supplies from dead or captured enemy troops. Further rounds and replacement weapons were also to come from seizures.

Orders from Pyongyang were to begin artillery fire across the parallel at

0400 on the twenty-fifth, to commence attacks at 0525 on the firing of green flares, to pause for a further but shorter bombardment deeper into enemy territory on the firing of red flares, to begin a further charge on the firing of more green flares and to cease firing only if white flares were launched. North Korean People's Army units received Reconnaissance Order No. 1 in Russian on June 18. It was immediately translated by military advisers into Korean.

As the invasion date had neared, the 350 Russian "training officers" had been withdrawn and replaced by a smaller elite of operations advisers under the orders of Marshal A. M. Vassilievsky, a Far East expert who had commanded the Red Army invasion of Manchuria in August 1945. The actual operations documents, prepared by Brigadier General Dolgin, a Soviet Engineer Corps specialist, were given to Chu Yong-bok, an NKPA officer who had translated training manuals into Russian, to turn "6 or 7 documents" into Korean for distribution to commanders across the front. Chu was also given an oath to sign that he would guard military secrets with his life. His hands shook, he recalled, as he turned the pages and realized what they were.

Despite the confusing Russian spellings of Korean place names, he hurriedly rushed out his translations. Then he returned the Russian packet, as ordered, to Dolgin, who "himself burned it to ashes on the spot."

Chu recalled that the orders included instructions for removal of land mines by midnight on June 23, and "river-crossing operations and obstacle-removing operations." Plans were particularized down to the battalion level, at which they were to be supplemented locally by orders to smaller units. Copies of these plans would be captured in the early days of the war.

The least defensible segment of South Korea was the sliver of the Ongjin Peninsula above Seoul, as the 38th parallel had sliced across it, rendering the lower portion indefensible. On June 23, South Korean howitzers and mortars on the peninsula began shelling Unpa, above the line, at ten that night, continuing until 4 a.m. However, the parallel area, west to east, was never quiet after dark, as infiltrators tested border defenses on each side. One young participant observed after an earlier incident, on June 21, "There is a war almost every day along the 38th parallel."

Day One

ALONG THE 38TH PARALLEL the border incidents that had marked earlier months in 1950 had diminished in May. Guerrilla activity in the south also quieted, suggesting an easing of tension. Yet some NKPA forces were already across the parallel, lying low for the open attack to come. Dissatisfied with the apparent stalemate, Rhee ordered new probes across the parallel, hoping to draw pursuit, but these failed. The North needed a pause well north of the frontier to complete what it described within the military establishment as its largest maneuvers yet conducted.

In the South only one of the four Republic of Korea (ROK) Army divisions just below the parallel was in defensive position, and many of its personnel were on home leave to help with the rice and soy harvests. In the North, NKPA maneuvers had been ordered on June 11, with all troops instructed to carry socks, underwear and essential gear for several weeks. All divisions would be involved in the "maneuver exercise," allegedly to prepare to resist an expected invasion. The call-up was classified as top secret—not for discussion back home.

What was no secret north or south was that on June 8, just before the alleged training exercise began, an announcement had appeared in the Pyongyang press that the Central Committee of the United Democratic Front, which claimed to speak for all of Korea, had called for the convening on August 15 in Seoul of a parliament representing both North and South. (The date reflected the fifth anniversary of the Japanese surrender—and thus Korean independence from colonialism.) There was no doubt that Rhee would reject any coalition with the Communists, who since 1917 had a history, wherever they were active, of insinuating a minority party into power. The manifesto seemed intended to score propaganda points or to foreshadow a new government in Seoul. On June 10 in Moscow, the state-controlled newspaper *Izvestia* reprinted the story. No one in the West read anything ominous into the seemingly empty offer. Nor did MacArthur's intelligence chief in Tokyo.

The negligible ROK air force would lose most of its few training and transport planes on the ground to Soviet-made Yak fighter-bombers on the first morning of the war. The largest and most modern ship in the tiny ROK navy was a relatively new patrol boat purchased—as surplus—from the American fleet. Rechristened the *PC 701,* it won, on the first day, the most decisive South Korean action at sea in the entire war. In coordination with the ground war, the North Koreans had slipped two small armed steamers, each with an estimated six hundred troops crowded aboard, down the eastern coast toward Pusan. Given the distances and preparation involved, the operation to seize South Korea's second city, in an area in which Communist sympathizers and guerrillas spirited down during the winter and spring were active, could not possibly have been a response to alleged ROK border provocations.

On a routine check of the "East Sea" (Sea of Japan) coast, an ROK navy gunboat at about 5 a.m. on the twenty-fifth spotted what was apparently a troop transport moving south just off Kangnung, below the parallel, and drove it northward. Commander Nam Choi-yong in the *PC 701* encountered the second enemy transport off Ulsan, northeast of Pusan. He challenged it, received no response, then ran it down, sinking it at close range with gunfire. No survivors were reported. A Communist takeover at somnolent Pusan would not happen—which would make the difference in the war. The port was South Korea's lifeline to Japan.

The ROK army was far larger than the thimble navy, but less ready for action. That June, Mike Michaelis, then on MacArthur's staff, recalled, he and his wife were in Yokohama to see off for the States the departing brigadier general who had been commander of the Korean Military Advisory Group, a former colleague from the 10th Armored Division in France. He had left the ROKs, he claimed, more than ready to handle the North Koreans should any problem occur. "He forgot to mention that he had no artillery, etc." The ROK divisions in reality were "gendarmerie [who] could not stop any kind of offensive." Michaelis equated the picture with MacArthur's imaginative description to Washington before Pearl Harbor of his army of

Philippine Scouts who were "really like Boy Scouts. . . . They just weren't soldiers, period." KMAG itself, to demonstrate American peaceful intentions, was actually under the State Department, and MacArthur had made no noises about wanting the military advisers, who acted as a brake upon Rhee, under his wing.

Pyongyang waited until 9:30 a.m. on June 25, Korean time, five hours after its invasion began, to offer by radio an absurd version of events belied in every detail by NKPA movements and preparatory planning. Four thrusts from the China Sea to the Japan Sea were being accelerated by river crossings behind the confused and retreating ROK troops at the frontier. Kim Il Sung's own voice carried the claim that "The South Korean puppet clique has rejected all methods for peaceful reunification proposed by the Democratic People's Republic of Korea and dared to commit armed aggression . . . north of the 38th parallel." Kim had "ordered a counterattack to repel the invading troops. The South Korean puppet clique will be held responsible for whatever results may be brought about by this development."

In central Korea, just below the parallel at Chunchon, surprised units from Colonel Paik Sun Yup's 13th Regiment were struggling to hold off Russian-supplied T-34 tanks with ineffective American 2.36-inch bazookas and even less effective grenades. Neither did more than mar the paint of the T-34s. Below the 13th, in reserve, were units of the 7th Regiment, depleted by leaves and unready to move up. Their unreadiness was duplicated everywhere across the front.

Kang Sangho, Communist Party chief for Kangwon Province, was ordered the same day to be a political "guidance" representative for South Kangwon Province, which includes Chunchon. On arriving there Kang found no evidence of an attack from the south. Stockpiled artillery shells had been abandoned unfired, while north of the parallel "people were taking care of farms and working. . . . If the South had attacked [the] North, a lot of artillery rounds would have fallen here. . . . That was where my doubts started." Pleased with the initial results, the remaining Soviet officers overseeing operations slipped away. On their vehicle radios they could listen to the charges from Pyongyang that South Korean aggression was being met and repulsed.

The least likely place for the South Koreans to initiate trouble was on the indefensible Ongjin Peninsula, above Seoul, for if they were chased back, they had nowhere to withdraw but the sea. The parallel literally cut the peninsula off from the rest of the country. Yet Soviet UN delegate Jacob Malik, ignoring the NKPA buildup beginning on the eleventh and his own government's complicity in it, would claim that an attack at Ongjin had been planned on June 20 by the South, with "a particularly ominous and evil role . . . being played by General MacArthur, who feels that he is the deputy of God in Asia."

In calling for a reversal of U.S. neutrality toward Taiwan in a statement published on June 14, MacArthur, who had shown no interest in Korea, had been intruding into Asian affairs elsewhere. Washington deplored the general's foreign policy comments but could not take up the issue with him until the shooting in Korea had begun. (Dulles had cabled the text from Tokyo on the day before the NKPA crossed the parallel.)

A year earlier Ongjin had been the location of a major exchange of fire—on the last Sunday in June 1949. In the war that had ended in 1945 with the division of liberated Korea, major attacks had often come on somnolent Sunday mornings—as did the invasion of Russia by the Wehrmacht and the raid on Pearl Harbor. As usual, however, inattention was the Sabbath rule. Most South Korean officials were weekending, and the few top American military advisers were not even in the country. MacArthur's intelligence aides saw nothing unusual. They worried more, because their chief did, about a threatened invasion of Formosa, although Mao's forces had yet to stockpile sufficient landing craft, and indeed had few to deploy.

Thinking less of safeguarding South Korea from invasion than of creating an American commitment to Formosa/Taiwan, MacArthur had been exploring on his own the idea of having Rhee invite Kuomintang regiments to Korea. Washington might have its own foreign policy, but MacArthur felt no commitment to it. That June his feelers toward Chiang were still tentative. In a curious paradox, on the other side of the 38th parallel tens of thousands of surplus troops that had fought Chiang's disorganized forces had been beefing up the green North Korean army. Yet Mao, who was not eager to create obstacles to his absorption of Formosa, had contributed significantly if unintentionally thereby to Kim Il Sung's venturesomeness. A quick strike to take Seoul might topple the unpopular Rhee government, create new facts by uniting the two Koreas and, perhaps, make the promised "national" parliament in August a reality.

As Saturday became Sunday along the 38th parallel—it was fourteen hours in advance of Washington, far across the International Date Line—intermittent rain masked some of the sounds of activity just to the north. Trucks and tanks were being positioned, along with ninety thousand troops, to jump off just before dawn. Nearly half would be concentrated at the hip of the Ongjin Peninsula, where it merges into the mainland just above the town of Kaesong, on the route to Uijongbu and, twelve miles beyond, to Seoul. By dimmed lights the North Koreans were re-laying daringly the final stretch of railway trackage on the line that, before the political division in 1945, had connected Pyongyang with the south. NKPA infantrymen began crowding into ancient, once-Japanese rail carriages for what would be a journey unique in war—invasion by train.

Led by Pang Ho-san, the 6th Division, which would sweep south and east on the first day of the war, was manned largely by Koreans who had fought with the Chinese Red Army. They had the battle experience and equipment which the ROK Army lacked. Ideologically and militarily ready, they were a professional force without equal below the parallel.

In the darkness of predawn Sunday, Chu Yong-bok, asleep with his unit just above the parallel, was awakened by a messenger who told him that a staff officer wanted to see him. The NKPA officer, Choi In, was accompanied by two Soviet lieutenant colonels who had been assigned as military observers. Chu was to translate into Russian messages already being received. The observers would be "very amazed" at the quick breakthroughs and rapid advances, one comparing the successes—despite the much smaller scale of the operation—"with their speedy movement when they drove the German army back from Stalingrad. When I translated this comparison back into Korean, Choi In laughed aloud, clapping his hands."

It was four that Sunday morning when the resident KMAG officer in Kaesong, Captain Joseph Darrigo, was awakened by gunfire that was too close to be the routine provocation. He pulled on his pants, grabbed his shirt and shoes, rushed down the stairs and, with his startled houseboy, raced to his jeep. Small-arms fire pinged against the house. Nearby, in another small house, was the Rev. Larry Zellers, a Methodist missionary. Zellers had seen no signs of military activity on returning Saturday night from a wedding in Seoul. Accustomed to hearing artillery fire at night, he rolled over and went back to sleep. But at about 7:30 a.m. he was awakened by NKPA soldiers moving about outside. Zellers would spend a long war as a POW.

To head south, Darrigo, who was assigned to the ROK 12th Regiment but knew that his first priority was to flee, had to wheel around a crude traffic circle in the center of Kaesong. At the station just beyond it, he saw battalions of North Korean soldiers emptying surreally from a long train that he knew could not have been there. Accelerating, and without headlights, he turned toward the ROK 1st Division headquarters across the Imjin River at Munsan.

Although the materialization of the railway cars left Darrigo certain that he had not witnessed merely another minor incident, raids across the parallel elsewhere along the waist of Korea had not yet convinced some sleepy commanders, if indeed they were with their troops, that something different was happening. The *In Min Gun* moved forward easily. ROK troops, abandoning everything, fled.

Just after 4:30 a.m. the effective if low-level KMAG authority in Seoul, Captain James Hausman, awakened by telephone, arrived at ROK Army headquarters just ahead of the hulking chief of staff, "Fat Chae"—the nearly three-hundred-pound Major General Chae Byong Duk. Whatever else, Chae vowed, Seoul had to be saved. He telephoned south to Taejon, to order the 7th Division to move up to join the 2nd Division at Uijongbu. Artillery was already pounding the town's edges. But Brigadier General Yu Jai-hung, the 7th's commander, could not even locate many of his units. A third of his personnel were on weekend leave, and one of his three depleted regiments was in reserve. The division to which Darrigo had raced in his jeep had an inexperienced and underaged twenty-nine-year-old commander, Colonel Paik Sun Yup, who was also away in Seoul. Darrigo was appalled by the unreadiness and the disorganization.

Two weeks into a three-month senior officer training course run by KMAG, young Paik had been on leave from his unit. After a telephone message from his operations officer that Kaesong had fallen, Paik rushed to the street, halted a jeep at gunpoint and raced to Chae's office. "The streets looked just as they did every Sunday, quiet and deserted," he recalled. ROK Army headquarters, however, was "in a state of bedlam." He pushed past a roomful of officers milling about, and finding Chae, Paik asked whether he should return to his division and command. "What are you yapping about?" said Chae. "Get to your division *now!*" Paik ran to the nearby American compound to find Lieutenant Colonel Lloyd Rockwell, his off-duty KMAG adviser, who had a car. Quickly, Paik had a jeep and a driver—the groggy and surprised Rockwell himself.

Distances to the front were alarmingly near. Paik's 11th Regiment was engaged at the Imjin. From his command post, a house well to the rear, Paik telephoned forward to order whatever units he could reach to fall back to Munsan. In disorderly fashion many were already doing that. Soon at Munsan himself, Paik heard from Darrigo about the stealthy seizure of Kaesong, and learned that his 11th and 13th Regiments were already below the Imjin, firing across the river to keep the enemy from crossing. Reconnoitering across the only bridge for miles, Paik returned and ordered it blown up. (As a contingency in case of invasion, major spans had long been set with explosive charges and detonators.) The plunger was activated, but nothing happened. Communists in the south had already anticipated ROK retreats across Korea.

Rather than improvise a new explosive charge, Paik had his troops fire steadily across the Imjin to keep the NKPA from the approaches. The North Koreans were not the only troops stymied. Paik's fleeing 12th Regiment was trapped on the other side, as were units as far north as Haeju and as far west as the Yellow Sea. Commandeering small fishing boats, and assisted by a few patrol boats from the minuscule ROK navy, some crossed to safety. Most troops, with their equipment, were captured.

Panicked, Rhee began packing to move his government south to Suwon, but paused long enough to telephone MacArthur in Tokyo. It was still before dawn that Sunday morning when a duty officer at the Dai Ichi relayed the call to the embassy residence. Syngman Rhee was on the line, hysterical and demanding to speak to MacArthur, he explained to an aide. Putting the Korean president off, the aide told Rhee to call again later, but the crusty patriarch—he was seventy-five—exploded, "American citizens in Korea will die one by one while you keep the general asleep in peace!"

Madame Rhee rushed to cover the mouthpiece with her palm, as her husband was exhibiting shocking discourtesy, but he snapped at her in a voice clearly heard in Tokyo, "Our people are dying, and they don't want to wake up the general!"

Rhee now had the officer's attention, and the telephone at MacArthur's bedside rang. "General," the aide advised, "we have just received a message from Seoul advising that the North Koreans have struck in great strength across the 38th parallel at four o'clock this morning." And he put Rhee on.

"Had your country been a little more concerned about us," Rhee screamed, "we would not have come to this! We've warned you many times. Now you must save Korea!"

MacArthur had no authority to save Korea, but he promised that he would send, immediately, ten fighter planes, and airlift howitzers and bazookas to halt the Communist tanks. That got Rhee off the phone, and MacArthur, for the moment, did nothing. Nearly nine years earlier, in December 1941, when he had picked up the telephone in his penthouse bedroom at the Manila Hotel and learned of the attacks on Pearl Harbor, he had only sat on the edge of his bed and, although no churchgoer, asked his wife, Jean, for his Bible. Again he experienced, as he would write in his memoirs, "an uncanny feeling of nightmare. . . . It couldn't be, I told myself. Not again! But then [over the telephone] came the crisp, cool voice of my fine chief of staff, [Major] General Ned Almond, 'Any orders, General?' "

The first news the Pentagon received had come from press inquiries. Wire services in Seoul had sent bulletins home. Reporters who got to General Bradley found that they knew more than he did. Defense Secretary Johnson, just back from a Far Eastern mission, was routed from bed by a reporter's call, then sleepily hung up and telephoned Army Secretary Pace, ordering him to get on the matter. At Army headquarters in Washington just after midnight on Sunday, the deputy chief of staff for operations, Brigadier General Thomas Timberman, hastily set up a mislabeled command post, for all that he could do was to relay news from the embassy in Seoul received by the State Department back to Tokyo. MacArthur was momentarily on his own.

In 1941 the predawn call to MacArthur in the Philippines had come from Washington, from then-chief of staff George Marshall, warning the general to take precautions, which he failed to do, leading to the debacle at Clark Field nine hours later. It was late Saturday now, in 1950, in Washington. The Joint Chiefs of Staff, the Secretary of State and others were still uninformed, and Truman was home in Missouri for the weekend. In Tokyo, MacArthur asked Almond to keep him abreast of urgent developments. He wanted time alone to think.

He pushed his feet into his slippers and his arms into a favorite frayed West Point bathrobe. Hearing him pace back and forth, Jean came in from her bedroom to ask what had happened. "Are you all right?" He explained the call and resumed pacing until his son, Arthur, twelve, came in. The general put his arm around the puzzled boy until his mother steered him away.

MacArthur returned his hands to the pockets of his robe and strode back and forth across the room, pondering what he should do without instructions and deciding little. By noon he went off to the Dai Ichi, where a correspondent about to fly home found him and asked whether the balloon was really up and was it worth remaining for the big show. "No," MacArthur advised; it was only "a border incident," probably "a trifle." The ROKs could take care of it, he thought.

As Truman flew back from Missouri, a hurried meeting at the State Department opened, to formulate emergency instructions for MacArthur to do something very limited, perhaps by air and sea, until an emergency meeting of the UN Security Council could be convened, with or without the boycotting Russians.

On Pyongyang radio Kim Il Sung's high-pitched voice carried the claim that the South Korean "puppet clique" had rejected "all methods for peaceful reunification proposed by the Democratic People's Republic of Korea and dared to commit armed aggression . . . north of the 38th parallel." The Democratic People's Republic of Korea had ordered a "counterattack" to repel the invaders. "The South Korean puppet clique will be held responsible for whatever results may be brought about by this development."

In central Korea, just below the parallel at Chunchon, Paik's 13th Regiment, only partially assembled, was thrown back. In reserve behind it were ineffective units of the 7th Regiment of the ROK 6th Division, depleted by leaves and—now—desertions. Those South Koreans who did not scatter immediately could hear on their radios rebroadcasts of Kim's claims of self-defense. In the rigidly censored North, listeners would believe it. Some apologists and revisionists in the West would continue to allege it decades later.

Syngman Rhee, the conspiracy theory went, needed the massive provocation of a North Korean invasion to remain in power, and sucked the NKPA in. It was true that he overspent massively on domestic intelligence activities, largely to root out his rivals, and that the Home Ministry spent almost as much on an internal police force as the Ministry of National Defense spent on the army. The only way that his American supporters had been able to secure votes for economic and military aid for South Korea, called by one congressman a "rat hole," was to link it, after an appropriation bill was defeated in January 1950, to China Lobby aid for Formosa. What Rhee needed now, whatever his sins, was immediate military intervention before the ineptitude, corruption and unpreparedness of his regime left it past saving. MacArthur would confess later that in his case the war was a gift to an old soldier. It was also a gift of a sort to an old nationalist.

Despite MacArthur's confidence and Rhee's panic, little activity was evident from the Dai Ichi. MacArthur conceded by cable to the Pentagon that information he had received indicated that the situation in Korea was deteriorating rapidly. Rhee's government had already fled Seoul and the ROK Army lacked "the will to fight" and the equipment with which to resist. "A complete collapse is imminent." Dulles and his wife were unworriedly sightseeing in Kyoto; his aide, John M. Allison, had returned to the Imperial Hotel for lunch (Frank Lloyd Wright's striking structure had survived the war) to find the foreign editor of *Newsweek*, Harry Kern, drinking green tea in the lobby with a Japanese diplomat. Signaling to Allison, Kern asked whether he had heard about the war in Korea. Allison was stunned. He rushed to a telephone to call the Dai Ichi to reach the sightseeing Dulles.

MacArthur's diplomatic adviser, William Sebald, away in Yokohama for a speech, was, like Dulles, on his way back. A conference of military and diplomatic advisers in the Supreme Commander's office had been set for six that evening. There Allison and Dulles learned that a UN Security Council meeting on the situation had been requested by the State Department. Unable to reach the American delegates on the weekend, John D. Hickerson, the assistant secretary for UN affairs, had telephoned directly to Trygve Lie, the UN secretary-general, with the news. "My God, Jack," said Lie innocently, "that's against the charter of the United Nations." Hickerson had then begun drafting a resolution for the deputy UN representative, Ernest Gross, whom he managed to reach when it was well into Monday, Japan time.

To Dulles and Allison, MacArthur downplayed the emergency, although Dulles was anxious for more news, and for action. Striding up and down his Dai Ichi office in the mucky June heat and intermittently sucking on his long, deep-bowled corncob pipe, MacArthur assured them that the attack was just another, if more violent, reconnaissance in force best handled by the South Koreans as in the past. The North Korean tanks would rumble for their own border before they ran out of gas.

Rhee, he admitted, had got very excited, more than usual, and asked for some fighter planes. MacArthur promised to send them, although the Mustangs would have only psychological impact as Koreans were incapable of flying. (He had said much the same thing about the Japanese in 1941.) There was little he needed to do as yet from Tokyo but retain his freedom of action. "If Washington only will not hobble me, I can handle it with one arm tied behind my back."

MacArthur's chief aides were a silent presence. He had said it all. Although they had no independent information, Dulles and Allison remained unconvinced. They had seen what conditions were like at the 38th parallel and knew that South Korean unreadiness went beyond handling aircraft they had never flown. Returning to the embassy, they rushed a jointly signed cable to Secretary Acheson and his Far East deskman, Dean Rusk. "It is possible," they wired without confidence, "that the South Koreans may themselves contain and repulse the attack, and, if so, this is the best way. If, however, it appears that they cannot do so, then we believe that United States force[s] should be used even if this risks Russian counter moves. To sit by while Korea is overrun by unprovoked armed attack would start a disastrous chain of events leading most probably to world war."

Why Dulles thought a Communist regime in Seoul would bring on World War III, while intervening to keep the repressive Rhee in power would not, suggests the Cold War domino theory—a non-Communist government of any sort was better than any government alleged to be Communist and likely to spread the Red contagion, which could be infectious indeed. (Japan is as close to southern Korea as South Florida is to Cuba.) A Soviet surrogate in South Korea could threaten the American presence in Japan, yet a show of force from that American presence might reverse the invasion. Further, Dulles would contend, the failure to counter Communist aggression without "loss to the aggressor" could "lead to Communist encroachments anywhere."

Since Dulles admired Rhee as a doctrinaire and tenacious anti-Communist, Rhee as paternalistic autocrat was no longer an issue. Nor was the Soviet satellite regime in North Korea. It was Stalin. As Army operations chief (G-3), General Charles L. Bolté, one of the hard-liners in the Pentagon, would put it, "History has [already] proved that negotiating with Communists is as fruitless as it is repulsive." In the case of the Pyongyang government, there was no question of its allegiance to Moscow. To Cold Warriors the war went beyond the confines of Korea.

The next morning—it was still late on Sunday in Washington—Dulles and Allison stopped at the Dai Ichi for news. MacArthur conceded that the fighting, from what he had learned, was more severe and prolonged than he expected it to be, but still within the capacity of the ROK Army to handle if it had any spirit. Naples-born American ambassador John J. Muccio, at fifty a veteran of prewar foreign service assignments in China, had been in Korea since August 1948. The night before the attack he had reportedly enlivened a boring evening by playing strip poker with several embassy staffers, and had not had much sleep when he was awakened with the invasion news and groggily called the State Department in Washington. Then he telephoned MacArthur to request air cover for the immediate evacuation of American dependents by ship, which the general promised to furnish although he thought the haste was premature.

Dulles and Allison went off to a scheduled lunch at the British embassy, then to a meeting with Prime Minister Yoshida Shigeru and another with Japanese labor leaders. Dulles returned to a dinner with the MacArthurs while Allison dined with an embassy official who had as another guest the Australian ambassador, W. R. Hodgson. "Well," declared Hodgson, who was notorious for his anti-American gibes, "I've just had the last conversation anyone will have with Korea. . . . The Korean army is retreating all along the front . . . and the American military advisory group is getting ready to pull out." Hearing that, another guest, NBC Tokyo correspondent George Foster, excused himself to make a telephone call, returning to confirm Hodgson's bleak assessment.

With excuses of urgency, Allison arose from the table and hurried to the American embassy, from which he telephoned to Ambassador Muccio. It was now 10:45 on Monday evening in Allison's time zone, an hour later in Seoul. He could hear in the earpiece of his telephone the sound of fire, and Muccio conceded that ROK resistance was "disintegrating." He had succeeded in keeping Rhee from fleeing the night before, warning him of the panic which would follow that news. Muccio had not yet learned that Rhee and his top officials, with their families, had secretly commandeered two special trains and were already in flight. (Many members of the National Assembly, where he did not have a majority, vowed to stay, only to be murdered by the North Koreans.)

It was impossible that MacArthur did not know how critical matters were south of the parallel. He had intimated as much to the Pentagon. Yet when Allison followed up his call with another to Dulles at their hotel, he learned that a movie had been shown, as was often done after dinner at the embassy residence, and that Dulles had learned nothing new about the Korean situation from MacArthur. Guessing that the general's staff felt under orders not to serve him bad news after coffee and dessert, Dulles telephoned MacArthur anyway, and was assured that he would "get something started." MacArthur would send some LSTs to Korea to evacuate any nervous Americans. If matters did get worse, he predicted, responsibility for Korea would become his, and he would take care of the matter.

On Tuesday morning the twenty-seventh in Tokyo, Allison again telephoned Muccio, reporting that, as previously planned, he was leaving with Dulles on a noon Pan American Clipper flight for Honolulu and Washington. Rhee, he was told, was heading by rail for Taejon, ninety miles south of Seoul. The capital was likely to fall almost unopposed. Muccio was getting out.

Surprisingly, MacArthur turned up with William Sebald at the Imperial Hotel in his Cadillac and accompanying MP jeeps to see Allison and Dulles off. Now, however, he failed to display his breezy confidence of Sunday evening. "All Korea is lost," he said, dispensing with his previous air of denial. All that remained was "to get our people safely out of the country." Allison saw "a completely despondent man."

At Haneda Airport an officer reached them with a message that Army Secretary Pace had called urgently to arrange a telecon with MacArthur at one that afternoon—the previous night in Washington. The Pan Am flight was already running late for departure, and MacArthur, obviously lacking in eagerness to consult with the Pentagon, suggested that the aide report back that the chief of staff, General Almond, would handle the call; MacArthur was still engaged with Dulles. Again it seemed a replay of 1941, with an indecisive MacArthur lacking the will to confront bad news. As they looked on with obvious dismay, Allison and Sebald, with Dulles nodding approval at the body language he recognized, proceeded with a ruse to get MacArthur back to the Dai Ichi.

Shortly a loudspeaker in the VIP waiting room announced the immediate boarding of the Pan Am flight. "Will the Dulles party please board first?" At the gangway MacArthur and Sebald offered handshakes and goodbyes, and when the general's limousine pulled away, Dulles and Allison slipped back to the waiting area.

The flight would be as troubled as was Dulles when the plane finally became airborne. Engine trouble over the Pacific kept the Clipper at Wake Island overnight, long enough to hear a radio report that President Truman would be committing the United States to the support of the reeling South Koreans. Realizing that the President had made the decision although he had no more confidence in Rhee than he had in Chiang, Dulles was overjoyed at the risk-taking. He "completely forgot that he was a Republican," Allison recalled, and regarded Truman—for the moment—as "the greatest President in history." From the standpoint of Japan, Dulles's immediate concern, a Red Korea would bring Communism to the water's edge. The war was necessary. (Visiting the State Department after American military forces had been ordered to Korea, Dulles was told by Undersecretary James E. Webb, "Foster, we made an honest man out of you.")

Acheson, Johnson and Webb met Truman at Washington National Airport on Sunday to update him en route to Blair House, Truman's temporary home on Lafayette Square while the White House living quarters were undergoing renovation. The first orders to MacArthur were out, directing him to do what he could by air and sea until an emergency session of the UN Security Council could convene with, or better without, a boycotting Soviet Union. Truman downplayed the amount of logistical support which Russia might furnish the distant North Koreans. "By God," he declared, "I'm going to let them have it."

In Paris a cable quickly arrived at the embassy office of American ambassador David K. E. Bruce, who had just been glumly discussing with his staff in an unusual Sunday morning meeting the lack of American response to the invasion. The message announced, as Bruce called it, "the President's bold and wise decision" to demonstrate military resolve. He hurried to Robert Schuman, the foreign minister who was energizing postwar European economic cooperation, to tell him personally. "Thank God," said Schuman, his eyes welling with tears as he thought of the craven response at Munich twelve years earlier. "This will not be a repetition of the past."

Bruce agreed. "Whenever we have shown determination and strength in the past," he observed, the Soviets "have halted their activities, and I believe [they] will do so again."

The Telecon War

Top-secret messages in primitive 1950 often utilized teletype. A telecon (teletype conference) from the Pentagon or the White House to and from the sixth floor of the Dai Ichi Building required a coded teleprinter and a screen on each end. Exchanges were often of the question-and-answer variety, preceded by two parallel lists of conferees. On the Washington side, participants ranged from generals like J. Lawton Collins, the Army chief of staff, and his deputy, Matthew B. Ridgway, to mere captains and even civilian representatives from departments like State. "So the whole conversation remains constantly before you," Harry Truman explained, "and is not subject to any of the difficulties which come from talk and can so easily be misunderstood."

Since Truman had no peer in Japan, he left the telecon to subordinates. On the Japanese end, MacArthur seemed at first to regard himself as too mighty to appear. The Dai Ichi telecon room was, however, temptingly close by.

With a fourteen-hour time difference, it was difficult to assemble participants on both ends at times that were not awkward. Heading MacArthur's participants for the first telecon early Monday morning in Tokyo was his imperious G-2, Major General Charles Willoughby.

"What NK units were committed?" was the first query from the Pentagon.

"Ground—especially armor," came the response on the screen.

At first most questions to the Dai Ichi were answered with more optimism than the fudged facts warranted. Korean morale was good; no disorders were reported; the government was "standing firm"; there had been no formal enemy declaration of war but an "all out offensive" seemed to be occurring anyway. That "leading elements of [the] South Korean 2nd Division [were] reported now entering Seoul" was less than good news, for it implied that they had fled south from the frontier and would keep going.

Prior to the next telecon, the UN Security Council, minus the boycotting Russians, had met and called upon all members "to render every assistance to the United Nations in the execution of this resolution and to refrain from giving assistance to the North Korean authorities." This was the legal basis for further American intervention in what the Soviets dismissed as a "civil war" once "naked aggression" from the south seemed implausible.

The President met for dinner at nearby Blair House with a higher level Cabinet and military group than had participated in the first telecon. Dean Acheson led off as Secretary of State. Although Louis Johnson was Defense Secretary, he had little role as he was feuding with Acheson. JCS Chairman Omar Bradley spoke for the services, reading aloud before dinner a radioed memorandum from MacArthur that was more about denying Formosa to the Communists than about defending Korea.

After dinner Acheson dealt with authorizing MacArthur under the UN umbrella to supply South Korea with arms and to evacuate Americans from Seoul—an opportunity to employ air cover and, indirectly, airpower. Air Force Secretary Thomas Finletter asked that they urge MacArthur to use air capability for more than "mere evacuation," and Johnson cautioned that instructions to MacArthur should be sufficiently specific to limit his options.

Truman noted that for external political reasons he was "not yet ready" to name MacArthur publicly as commander in chief for Korea, but wanted him to send "a survey group" to the front to see what might be done. He also wanted an assessment of possible Russian intervention and the likely consequences.

Still another telecon was then in progress, employing lower-level Pentagon staff but this time beefed up in Tokyo by MacArthur's chief of staff, Major General Edward Almond, with the inevitable Willoughby, who offered an "unconfirmed report of Russian military participation"—allegedly "three Russian soldiers emerging from disabled tank." MacArthur very much wanted evidence of overt Soviet involvement, but very likely even the ROK disabling of a tank was fiction. "Demolitions" were being prepared by the South Koreans, the Dai Ichi reported, yet the bridge at Ongjin, it was conceded, had fallen "intact to the enemy." General Chae, MacArthur had already warned Washington, "takes [the] attitude that the fall of Seoul," now imminent, "is [the] fall of South Korea."

With the hint of a major new role for him forthcoming, MacArthur himself headed a high-level group for still another telecon late that Sunday night/Monday morning following the Blair House meeting. "Do you need any further instructions at this time?" the Pentagon asked Tokyo. "No," MacArthur responded. He preferred operating without inhibiting instructions and must have been encouraged by a further Monday morning message from Collins: "The Joint Chiefs of Staff join me in expression of gratitude for superb and timely action by you and your command in support of the United States mission in Korea." Collins might have been referring mainly to the efforts to evacuate civilians, but such vague approbation was certain to suggest to MacArthur that he had freedom of action. He would prove hard to rein in.

As Truman left a Monday morning White House conference to oversee preparation of a release on Korea he paused at a large globe. "Here," he told George Elsey, a press assistant, "is where they will start trouble if we aren't careful." He pointed his finger at Iran. He was worried about the Russians exploiting Korea to divert American attention from other areas. "Korea," he added to Elsey, "is the Greece of the Far East. If we are tough enough now, if we stand up to them like we did in Greece three years ago, they won't take any next steps. . . . There's no telling what they'll do, if we don't put up a fight now."

Truman was still getting contradictory estimates from the Dai Ichi. At the same time, Acheson, also misinformed, was telephoning Senate Foreign Relations Committee chairman Tom Connally that "General MacArthur had the situation well in hand, that we were watching developments closely, and that the approaches to Seoul were well guarded by the forces of South Korea." Despite that optimism, later in the day Elsey noted for a JCS summary that Seoul was about to fall to North Korean tanks, and that the South Korean government had fled. As a result, Acheson convened an emergency meeting of the same group that had met with the President the evening before.

At Blair House, Chiang's island would keep coming up as a problem as well as a solution. MacArthur saw Formosa as an unsinkable aircraft carrier, submarine base and supplier of renewable regiments for employment in Korea which the U.S. needed only to equip. Later, just after his dismissal, he would exaggerate, "I believe that from our standpoint we practically lose the Pacific Ocean if we give up or lose Formosa." Temptingly if vaguely, Chiang had even offered to step aside and let MacArthur be viceroy of offshore China as well as Japan. With an enthusiasm Truman would regret later, he chimed in with an off-the-wall suggestion around the mahogany conference (and dinner) table that Monday night about "taking Formosa back as part of Japan," as the island had been under colonial rule from 1895 until 1945. The scheme would have put Formosa under MacArthur's occupation umbrella, but the consequences with respect to Mao's China might have been dire. (It also ignored the wartime Cairo declaration of 1943 that the island belonged to mainland China.)

Acheson politely noted that "it was undesirable that we should get mixed up in the question of the Chinese administration" of the island or let Chiang supply what would in effect be mercenary troops of dubious quality. Money for Chiang to misuse set Truman off. He wouldn't give the Generalissimo "a nickel for any purpose whatsoever. All the money we had given them [for military uses] is now invested in United States real estate."

"And," added Louis Johnson, although covertly a backer of Chiang, "in banks in the Philippine Islands."

That ended the possibility of a MacArthur shogunate extending to Formosa, but Truman concurred in putting the once-formidable Seventh Fleet, shorn of its wartime aggregation and deployed now in the Philippines, at MacArthur's orders to keep Chiang's and Mao's forces apart. A politically necessary sop to the China Lobby in Congress, safeguarding all that was left of Kuomintang China also freed Red Army divisions for other assignments, a factor that would come to haunt the Truman administration.

Returning to the Korean situation, General Collins summed it up as "bad." The South Korean chief of staff, Chae Byong Duk, "has no fight left in him." Still, they recognized that whether or not Korea would be lost, it was crucial not to give it up by default.

Another telecon, at 10:17 Washington time that night, followed, again with MacArthur present. All restrictions on his action below the 38th parallel were lifted. He was to "clear South Korea of North Korean military forces" if he could. In effect, he was UN commander in chief, but he was to issue no statement about it yet. Immediate publicity, MacArthur countered, was crucial "to keep up the morale of the South Korean Army. . . . Our estimate is that a complete collapse is possible."

Now that the President was authorizing American military power via the Dai Ichi to fight the further spread of Communism, MacArthur looked up from his screen to remark, "I don't believe it!" It contradicted his assumptions about Truman's weak commitments to Asia and suspicions he thought the President had about him. More cautious than his feisty language suggested, Truman was indeed Europe-focused, but State was dominating the early days of the Korean War, in particular Dean Acheson and his hawkish assistant secretary, Dean Rusk, who had been involved in Far Eastern affairs since early in World War II. Between them they would take advantage of the crisis to press for more aid against Communist insurgencies in the Philippines and Indochina. Korea would lead almost invisibly to Vietnam.

Grumbling about the awkwardness of teletype conferences, which took time and sometimes needed to be put on hold to find someone in Washington or Tokyo not in the screening room, MacArthur wanted immediate responses and immediate action. Yet he had long refused to have a telephone in his office in the Dai Ichi. Conferring with him, even one-on-one across his desk, was always on his own terms. He preferred operating through underlings.

Now he had to wait for Washington to issue a release announcing his UN role and the extent of his authority. Everyone was operating in an information vacuum. Truman did not know whether there would be support at home or abroad for what might be a turning point in how international aggression was confronted, or whether Beijing or Moscow would come to the aid of their surrogate if necessary. Defense Secretary Johnson worried about if and where the Russians might respond to American intervention or exploit the opportunity to probe the West's weaknesses elsewhere. MacArthur teleconned that he had no clue as to Soviet intentions, although he thought it "probable" that any such countermove would come against "Japan or South Korea" rather than in Europe. He had spent much of a lifetime pointing to the Pacific rim as the fulcrum of destiny. He wanted that prospect to appear frightening. A Russian presence through the whole of Korea would inevitably threaten Japan, where the Soviets, in 1945 and with MacArthur's enthusiastic assent, had been denied a role in the occupation or in the drafting of a peace treaty. (Stalin had gone to war with Japan only a week before the surrender, on the day of the Nagasaki A-bomb.)

From Willoughby in closing came the query, "In view of coverage this telecon do you still desire telecon slated tonight 10 p.m.?"

"Yes," came the reply from Washington, "[we] may have important decisions for you."

The response from Tokyo suggested that the technically absent MacArthur was actually at the elbow of Willoughby and Whitney, although after years of ghosting the CINCFE's (Commander in Chief, Far East) lines they could echo his rhetoric. "Come over and join the fight," the teletype on the Washington screen read. "We are delighted with your lines of action and this [promised] aid should turn the trick."

On the second day of the war, four correspondents in Tokyo (Keyes Beech of the *Chicago Daily News,* Frank Gibney of *Time,* Burton Crane of *The New York Times* and Marguerite Higgins of the *New York Herald Tribune*) hitched a flight, understanding it was one-way, on a transport sent to Kimpo airfield near Seoul to evacuate trapped American civilians. The three men tried to dissuade Maggie Higgins on grounds of her sex, and perhaps also to limit the competition. She brushed them off. Petite and twenty-nine, she had covered the war in Europe right out of college and was as professional as any of them. Barely two weeks later a "fatherly" general took Keyes (pronounced Kize) Beech aside, warned that they could be encircled by the enemy shortly and suggested that he get "Miss Higgins out of here. The front is no place for a woman."

"I told him," Beech recalled, "that I couldn't agree more but that it was all right for Higgins." He was, a later newsman, James Wallace, recalled, "one of those people who . . . would help the new kid on the block." Thirty-seven, Beech had been reporting from the Pacific since his days as a Marine combat correspondent, and was fearless. But Korea was a new kind of war.

Their pilot's instructions from Tokyo were to swoop low enough to look for Americans. "If we don't see any we get the hell out but fast—the field is in enemy hands." At the end of the strip were two planes in flames—strafed just before the twin-engined C-47, the workhorse of aviation (as DC-3) since the middle 1930s, appeared. About thirty Americans, Higgins wrote, "signaled us with all the intensity of the shipwrecked who fear the rescue ship will pass them by."

On the rubble-strewn tarmac the reporters learned from a KMAG lieutenant colonel that Seoul had not yet fallen, and that some of his military colleagues had returned to their headquarters in the capital. Yet the parking lot at the airfield was packed with abandoned cars, many with keys left in the ignition. Even though firing could be heard, the KMAG officer estimated that the enemy was at least seven miles away. Refugees with babies and bundles trudged southward away from Seoul. Korean soldiers were streaming in every direction.

The correspondents located a car with a key and drove to the sprawling gray building housing KMAG, temporarily run by a colonel who had been vacationing in Japan two days before. Assigned billets for the night, they left to see what was happening outside and encountered General Chae, huge and resplendent in his GI helmet and uniform. With a confidence intended for American newspapers he assured them, "We fightin' hard now. Things gettin' better." Unconvinced, the four retired fully clothed. Things would not get better for Korea nor for Fat Chae.

Not long afterwards at Taejon, after some hairy days escaping south, Maggie and another correspondent, Tom Lambert of the Associated Press, were trying to flag a vehicle for a ride and finally succeeded in slowing down a jeep with "a Korean officer who turned out to be an exceptionally neat, well-dressed fellow who spoke English quite well." Lambert got in the back with the officer while Maggie sat next to the driver. "Say, Buster," Lambert began, slapping his companion on the back jovially, "do you fight in this man's army?"

"Well," answered the officer, whose uniform looked too clean to suggest a combat record, "I plan to. I have just returned from Fort Benning."

"That's fine, Buster," Lambert continued, again clapping him on the shoulder. "And what do you do?"

"I shall reorganize the South Korean defenses," he explained. "You see, I have just been appointed the new Chief of the Korean Army." Major General Chung Il Kwon had only returned from the U.S. on the last day of June.

Almost as soon as the correspondents at KMAG had settled down for the night, an officer burst in shouting, "Get up! They've broken through—we have to run for it." Hastily, everyone did. In a queue of KMAG vehicles from jeeps to trucks they pushed toward the Han River bridge to the south, only to watch it prematurely blown up. In shock, the sixty Americans in the military contingent and Maggie Higgins—the other three reporters had already raced off—watched the orange flames spread toward the hundreds of troops and trucks trapped on the span. If his group stuck together, said Sterling Wright, the KMAG colonel, they might find an alternative route out of the city and across the Han.

In vans, weapons carriers and jeeps they snaked toward the river, in search of a railway span to bump over or a ferry dock. After several futile hours, having found nothing, they crowded together at the riverbank. The sky was brightening toward dawn. Gloomily, Higgins saw her scoop vanishing and captivity, or worse, approaching. "What's the matter, kid?" asked Colonel Wright. "Afraid you won't get your story out? Look, stick by this radio truck and we'll try to send a message out for you if you keep it short."

Retrieving her portable typewriter, she set it on the hot hood of the jeep, and, in navy blue skirt, flowered blouse and bright blue sweater, typed away while passing refugees and retreating ROKs gaped. The message would not go through.

Eager to get across, the Korean soldiers pointed guns at boatmen in midriver and procured passage. Realizing that it was the only way to the other bank, the Americans followed suit. Under fire still far enough away to be inaccurate, they abandoned their vehicles, threw the keys in the Han, and commandeered whatever floated.

Maggie perched on an overcrowded raft with Lieutenant Colonel George Kelley. Overloaded and swamped, and still under inaccurate artillery and mortar fire from the north, it began sinking when close to the opposite side. Everyone swarmed off and waded ashore, slogged through the mud and lay prone in a rice paddy. Maggie was still close to Kelley. "You scared, Maggie?" he asked.

"No," she said, still protecting her portable typewriter. "But how the hell are we going to get out of here?"

A dirt trail over the hills southward toward Suwon was next. Tramping along, single file, they overtook and passed weary troops and tattered refugees, encountering, after four hours, a jeep with five ROK soldiers. Maggie still hauled along her precious typewriter. The KMAG colonel and a Korean officer ordered the jeep stopped and, inviting Maggie with them, squeezed aboard. The grotesque overload failed to last long. ROK stragglers were becoming so disorderly, abandoning weapons and gear as they retreated, that the two officers jumped off to try to reorganize the rabble. In the lightened jeep with five Koreans who spoke no English, Higgins headed toward Suwon to appeal for transportation to retrieve the rest of the KMAG party.

Despite the confusion she found in Suwon, she located the American Advance Command, the existence of which she had been unaware. It meant at the moment the newly arrived Brigadier General John H. Church and a group of officers from Tokyo in clean uniforms, and Ambassador Muccio, who was about to leave for Taejon, farther south. The Agricultural Building was Church's temporary headquarters, and there Higgins mentioned to Muccio the dispatch she wanted to send. Muccio had a message of his own. The correspondents in the area were a nuisance and should go away.

The next telecon did not identify MacArthur as a participant, but it is entirely possible from the dialogue that he was present but deliberately unnamed. "Has your survey party arrived in Korea and, if so, where are they?" Washington asked.

"Survey group now designated Advance Command Group," came the response. "Will arrive Suwon—30 miles south of Kimpo approximately 1800 hours today." No details were given. Tokyo was being extremely cautious, even to the Pentagon, as a Soviet intercept could reveal that the party was headed by the CINCFE himself. At the time—the afternoon of the twenty-seventh in the U.S.—the Security Council was meeting again at Lake Success on Long Island. The Council was to vote on a second UN resolution about Korea in the absence of the Russians, who had again declared the meeting illegal because the actual government of China—Mao's regime—had not been permitted to take the permanent seat still occupied by Chiang's delegate. More strongly than before, the council recommended that members furnish such assistance to South Korea "as may be necessary to repel this armed attack." The vote was seven to one in favor, with Yugoslavia voting no and Egypt and India abstaining.

The Labour government in England had approved the votes of its UN representative when the weekly meeting of the Cabinet was held that Tuesday morning. Korea was the fourth agenda item, but not all Ministers were even certain where Korea was. Prime Minister Clement Attlee asked one of the senior officials sitting in, who advised, helpfully, that Korea lies "between China and Japan." In the Opposition since mid-1945, Winston Churchill approved of confronting Communists in Korea but claimed never to have heard of the "bloody country."

In Korea for the first time, General Church also knew little more about the country, but had reason to learn fast. Fifty-eight, frail and severely arthritic, Church was the ranking representative in Korea from GHQ in Tokyo. Five years removed from the realities of war, he displayed on the jacket of his combat fatigues a chestful of sewn-on campaign and medal ribbons from the last one. MacArthur's appointee to lead the survey mission, he had been a World War II division commander in Europe with a Silver Star for heroism. In Suwon he commanded thirteen officers, mostly lieutenant colonels, and two enlisted men, all of whom had arrived, after many delays, on a four-engine C-54 (DC-4) from Haneda. Largely due to Church's unaltered peacetime priorities, it had not been easy to get off. When the party had arrived at the airfield at 4:00 a.m., some assumed a direct flight. Urgency was indicated. The transport, however, flew first to Itazuke, an air base on northernmost Kyushu once used by the Japanese, from which the Fifth Air Force was directing most of its initial operations in Korea. There, Church announced that he wanted breakfast. Staff cars were summoned to take his group to a leisurely meal at the posh officers' club. (Where the enlisted men breakfasted is unrecorded.) Then Church telephoned Tokyo for an update on his orders, and GHQ informed the general to stand by. Kimpo airport, near Seoul, had been his destination, but it was now threatened by the North Koreans. No backup site had been fixed.

Hours passed before Church was ordered back to Tokyo. When he asked, then, to have his C-54 returned to Haneda, a major at Air Force operations protested. The plane had been scheduled to bring out stranded Americans, and it would go, with or without Church. More hours and more calls later, the Far East Air Force (FEAF) remained firm about dispatching the C-54, although some more unhappy solution by then might have greeted the Americans in Seoul. Finally, Church was advised to await other arrangements, and eventually he would be set down south of Seoul, at Suwon. (The original C-54 left for beleaguered Kimpo, to be escorted by F-80 jets. Given the differences in speed, the jets would not even take off until the C-54 was nearly there.) It was not an auspicious beginning for Church's mission in Korea.

While the United Nations—in effect, Harry Truman—was preparing to designate MacArthur its commander in Korea the next day, Ambassador Alan Kirk in Moscow learned from Andrei Gromyko's guarded language at the Foreign Ministry that the Soviets were "unlikely to commit its forces to Korea." Unaware yet of either event, MacArthur was touching down at Suwon for the first of many flying trips from Tokyo. The Pentagon had authorized posting troops from the 507th Anti-Aircraft Artillery Battalion to protect Suwon for U.S. aircraft, and other soldiers and sailors to secure airfields and docks at Pusan, on the southeast corner of the peninsula, for landing equipment, supplies and men. It was something of a surprise in Washington—as MacArthur intended—to learn that Suwon was being held for the CINCFE himself.

On the twenty-seventh President Rhee, fleeing Seoul with his Austrian wife, Francesca, in the first of two special trains crowded with his aides and his belongings, had intended to go diagonally across the peninsula to Pusan, and then to his summer cottage on the coast nearby at Chinhae. Ordering a pause at the Taegu station so that he could telephone to Seoul, he realized that he had been too hasty and might be charged with undue panic. He had the train return north as far as Taejon and took over the provincial government offices, where he confronted Americans from KMAG and the Seoul embassy and blamed the United States for Korea's plight. Everett Drumright, Ambassador Muccio's deputy, showed him a copy of a telegram intended for KMAG Colonel Sterling Wright, farther north in Suwon: "Be of good cheer." It was signed "MacArthur" and hinted of forthcoming action. Rhee calmed down.

The next morning, Wednesday the twenty eighth, Drumright and embassy aide James Stewart brought Rhee a copy transcribed from shortwave radio of Truman's statement committing naval and air forces to Korean defense. Rhee had the message printed in handbills for distribution and read on government radio. Then Muccio, the usually dapper ambassador, arrived from Suwon, muddy and bedraggled after a Yak strafing of the airfield there. Short of information, State had cabled him to "act boldly." Taking his chances with the talkative, emotional Rhee, he confided that MacArthur would be flying in the next morning to evaluate how best to turn the war around. He would attempt a landing at Suwon. Rhee was enthusiastic.

In Suwon itself, General Church was expected to make preparations for MacArthur's arrival. Harold Noble, the embassy senior officer in Suwon, saw Church "wholly lost within himself. . . . He was suddenly given responsibility in a war that was rapidly disintegrating around him." Knowing little about what remained of the ROK Army, he remarked to Noble "that he would rather have one hundred New York policemen than the whole Korean army." He posted a KMAG radio truck under a tree at the front entrance to a schoolhouse near the airport, and hoped for further news and instructions.

When Drumright and Muccio arrived in Suwon that night they found a message that FEAF planes would begin attacking the North Koreans at 1100 that morning. No one had seen any combat aircraft, nor did Americans in Suwon know how poor flying conditions were over Japan. Drumright and Wright had already spent hours at a small schoolroom table with General Chae and his aide, Captain Sim, urging them to set up defenses on the south bank of the Han before it was overrun. Chae argued that he had to save what was left of his demoralized army by moving south quickly, reorganizing his remnants and waiting there for American help. "Where is this new line?" the Americans asked. "If you retreat too far the war is over." Church was not present. He had no confidence in Chae and preferred to wait for MacArthur. "No member of Church's staff," Noble wrote later, "had any part in it or was aware of it."

Earlier on the twenty-eighth, in Tokyo, MacArthur had summoned four influential representatives of the press to the Dai Ichi and offered them a ride in the *Bataan* the next day to the front. MacArthur didn't merely choose four reporters who happened to be hanging about the Dai Ichi to accompany him. His "palace guard" (as less favored correspondents viewed them) comprised the bureau chiefs of the major English-language news organizations— Russell Brines of the Associated Press, Ernest Hoberecht of the United Press, Howard Handleman of the International News Service and Roy McCartney of Reuters.

MacArthur confided to them that he didn't know whether anything could save South Korea. "In past wars there has been only one way for me to learn such things. There is only one way now. I have decided to go to Korea and see for myself." He didn't yet know where they could land, he added, although he knew very well that his representative there, General Church, had established himself in Suwon, where there was an airfield. To make the prospect more dramatic, he noted that his C-54 was unarmed, and that he could not guarantee fighter cover—although, of course, he could arrange that. "With a great, big, radiant smile on his face," Russell Brines recalled, MacArthur announced, "Boys, we're going to the front. Now, you don't have to go, you don't have to go."

"He sort of said it," Brines told one of MacArthur's biographers, "in a sly way, knowing damn well that anybody who was scared enough not to want to go was too scared to say so. So we joined him the next morning."

Thursday morning in Washington, at a crowded news conference, Harry Truman would be asked, "Mr. President, would it be correct . . . to call this a police action under the United Nations?"

"Yes," said Truman, grateful for the euphemism for the escalating involvement. "That is exactly what it amounts to. We are not at war." Although Truman's tag in the popular mind, the euphemism had come by way of Senator William Knowland of California, often referred to as "the senator from Formosa" because of his outspoken pro-Chiang position. On the Senate floor Knowland had announced in support of aiding Rhee, "The action this government is taking is a police action against a violator of the law of nations and the charter of the United Nations." A reporter had picked it up. No declaration of war would ever be formalized, and Korea was to become the precedent for later shooting wars by executive order.

What MacArthur found was unambiguous war. In fog and rain Lieutenant General George Stratemeyer, commander of FEAF, had arrived at Haneda in advance of his chief to inform the *Bataan*'s pilot, Lieutenant Colonel Anthony Story, and the waiting newsmen, that with the ceiling at zero, he was grounding MacArthur's flight. Story kept the propellers turning. Hundreds of wartime missions in the ensuing months would lift off from Haneda in similar murk, even in heavy snow.

It was not the first flight from Japan in barely tolerable conditions. MacArthur wanted to encourage the South, while discouraging the North, by displays of strength. As a result, flights from Kyushu, which accomplished neither goal, went up despite hazardous visibility on the first day they were authorized. The Fifth Air Force's B-26 light bombers were unavailable, flying continuous (if unnecessary) cover for a fetid Norwegian fertilizer carrier from Inchon, the *Reinholte,* plodding toward Japan with a cargo of refugees. From the base at Itazuke once used by Zeros, Lieutenant Bryce Poe II took off in the "foulest imaginable" weather in an RF-80A Shooting Star to try to find the leading edge of the NKPA forces, the first combat sortie ever by an American jet.

Ned Almond had insisted to MacArthur that other aircraft also go up, whatever the weather, as he "wanted bombs put on the ground in the narrow corridor between the 38th parallel and Seoul, employing any means and [even] without any accuracy." No one yet had grid-overlaid maps of Korea with coordinates to make high-altitude targeting more than guesswork.

Hostile ground fire riddled twelve B-26s near Munsan, just south of the parallel. Crippled, one lost sight of the fogged-in runway at Ashiya on returning and crashed, killing all aboard. In further orders as stupid as they were wasteful, F-80 pilots were instructed to bomb anything above the Han River, 310 miles from Itazuke, and if they ran out of fuel over Japan en route home, to bail out. The jets dropped napalm, using jettisonable fuel tanks as fire-bombs. Other planes made passes over the Han River rail bridges on which the NKPA was attaching wooden decking to permit passage of tanks, trucks and troops. Nothing helped to keep the ROKs from crumbling further.

Arriving at Haneda on Thursday morning in his leather Air Force flight jacket and faded suntans, carrying field glasses and wearing his trademark sunglasses, MacArthur quickly overruled Stratemeyer. The C-54's propellers continued to revolve.

"You'd go up yourself, wouldn't you?" asked MacArthur.

"Yes," conceded Stratemeyer, "but I don't count. You're a different matter."

"We go," MacArthur said.

In the air, he paced the aisle nervously, one of his staff assuring a reporter that it was normal practice. "He'll walk half the way there before we set down." From the *Bataan's* windows could be seen four F-51 Mustangs covering the flight—usefully, it turned out, as a Russian-made Yak fighter-bomber was just pulling away after a raid on Suwon that cratered the field and left smoldering wreckage at the end of the runway. A Mustang peeled off after it while Story swung his C-54 evasively and then came in.

Up from Taejon was Syngman Rhee, accompanied by John Muccio. At the schoolhouse, General Church and his subordinates, now two-day veterans of the war without having gone very far afield, explained what they knew of the deteriorating situation, using maps tacked on a wall and a pointer. Occasionally MacArthur asked a question, pointing the long stem of his corncob pipe toward the maps.

General Chae had not been invited until Noble pressed Muccio to insist upon it, and the hulking Chae stood at one side of the room, spoke a few sentences in his limited English and then had his interpreter take over. Chae then switched to a slow and rather sleepy Korean, explaining that some troops had not crossed the Han into the disorganized crowds of refugees but had seized small boats and headed south along the western coast, landing with what arms they could carry. Few paid attention to his briefing. He was widely blamed for the premature destruction of the Han River bridges and the abandonment of ROK units isolated to their north. (In September, the ROK engineer who supervised the demolition, Colonel Choe Chang-sik, was court-martialed and executed. By then the discredited Chae had been killed in action.)

What was clear from the briefing was that the area between Suwon and Seoul was not yet overrun. While some South Korean soldiers were still retreating to the south bank of the Han, soon the crossers would be the enemy. Americans barely had control of the air over Suwon itself, as the high brass on the *Bataan* had already learned. Six Yaks had strafed the field earlier that morning; jet fighters clearing a path for MacArthur shot down two Yaks which had ventured too close to the airfield. Once the F-80s left, the North Koreans returned and destroyed a transport on the ground.

MacArthur was in the schoolhouse when four more enemy planes attempted to evade patrolling Mustangs circling over the newly arrived C-54, the general's *Bataan*. The conferees hurried outside to watch the more maneuverable Yaks attempt to evade the faster P-51s. Two Yaks went down. The others escaped to the north.

"Let's go up to the front and have a look," MacArthur proposed. To *Life* photographer David Douglas Duncan, the general "seemed buoyant. His eyes possessed that same luminous brilliance I had sometimes seen in the faces of fever patients. The last time I had seen him was when, aboard the *U.S.S. Missouri* in Tokyo Bay, I watched him sign his name to the Articles of Surrender of the Japanese Empire. He was keyed to the same pitch both times."

A battered black Dodge and two jeeps jolted the group, minus Rhee and Muccio, north to the lower banks of the Han River. In the opposite direction streamed refugees desperately hauling whatever possessions they could carry to some unknown destination out of the range of enemy fire. Even more discouraging to the Americans were the trucks teeming with soldiers heading south, many still bearing their unused arms. "There was not one defensive position to be seen anywhere along the road," Duncan remembered, "nor any evidence that the soldiers we saw scattered along the route had any intention of fighting. It was not that they were all turning tail and running away. It was more as though they thought that this chaotic disintegration was happening to someone else's army. We were wildly cheered as we churned up the dust and rolled north. Not because the first car contained MacArthur, but solely because we looked grim and dirty and businesslike, and were driving north."

At one point, Deputy Chief of Staff Edwin "Pinky" Wright recalled, someone in the first jeep ordered a stop to take cover. From another jeep just behind MacArthur's Dodge, Wright leaped into a ditch. Then, looking up and around a tree, he saw MacArthur sitting in the back seat of the car quietly sucking on his pipe. Wright crawled forward and said, "General, don't you think you should get out?"

"Aw, no," said MacArthur. "Those things aren't going to hit me."

As they approached the Han the refugees thinned, but the line of fleeing trucks camouflaged atop by branches and wheeling southward did not. Nowhere was any sign of ROK leadership or organization. A mile from the river the Americans could see artillery fire landing on their side and hear the thump of enemy mortars. At the next intersection MacArthur ordered his car stopped so that he could get out and walk to the top of a rise to look out through his sunglasses at the smoke rising from Seoul, on the other side. At the Yongdungpo crossroads, where one fork turned east toward Seoul, he was given a hasty briefing. It was dangerous to remain, but MacArthur displayed to the admiring Duncan an "absolute arrogance and almost exasperating belligerence" that delighted him. After all, Duncan was a photographer for *Life*.

Seeing a railway bridge still intact and another buckled but usable by foot soldiers, MacArthur put down his field glasses, turned to Stratemeyer and, waving at the spans, said, "Take them out." According to Lowell Thomas's CBS newscast on June 29, drawn from wire service accounts, "MacArthur gave an immediate command—to blast the bridges. Which happened promptly. He had hardly left the hill overlooking Seoul, when huge columns of smoke arose—the bridges [were] destroyed." Nothing from a command level happens that quickly, and despite FEAF attempts long after MacArthur's party had left, the bridges remained viable. Yet accounts wired to American media made what was a rout seem almost like a victory. MacArthur was there. He was taking charge of the war.

MacArthur's return to Suwon was a two-hour jostle through a chaos of refugees and troops, but Thomas claimed to his radio audience on the basis of information received that Koreans were "bucked up." Most soldiers were hastening away from the front, and as MacArthur observed frankly to his chief of staff, Ned Almond, "I haven't seen a wounded man yet. Nobody is fighting." But word had quickly spread among the Koreans that the party that had headed north included Americans who were going to help them, including a general. Ranks of soldiers, before hurrying farther south, stood at attention. Officers saluted; villagers waved and shouted greetings. It was an eerie contrast to the realities of retreat.

The *Bataan* had lifted off from Suwon for safety, circling in a holding pattern to the south. As the group returned to the airfield the C-54 settled down again, its prop wash flattening the soybean fields. Duncan strode over to MacArthur and asked whether he could hitch a ride to Japan to get his film posted to New York. "Of course," MacArthur said. Then it was time to get aloft.

When back in Tokyo, the four wire service pressmen who accompanied MacArthur would file lengthy dispatches. By then the chief himself was in the Dai Ichi telecon room preparing for a conference that would activate the Pentagon before dawn.

Christopher Isherwood read Russell Brines's AP version of the Suwon flight in the *Los Angeles Times* on June 29, scoffing in his diary that it was "an obviously press-agented account of how the veteran diva, General MacArthur, flew to the South Korean war front." Although there was no censorship the correspondents at first reported little that was alarming, clearly intending to stay in the good graces of the general, who would indeed convey them on later flights. Marguerite Higgins, not then one of the favored few, would later write that the exodus from Seoul "provided the most appalling example of panic that I have ever seen." Even MacArthur's courtier, Brigadier General Courtney Whitney, would write, much later, that as the official party proceeded northward from Suwon they saw "the dreadful backwash of a defeated and dispersed army." Intelligence chief Charles Willoughby melodramatically recalled their route as "clogged with retreating, panting columns of troops interspersed with ambulances filled with the groaning of broken men, the sky resonant with shrieking missiles of death and everywhere the stench and misery and utter desolation of a stricken battlefield."

While Willoughby's fiction (ambulances were almost nonexistent) was intended to imply the genuine courage displayed by MacArthur in plunging into the confusion at great personal risk to assess the situation for himself, the AP dispatch suggested that MacArthur was intervening while matters could still be turned around. From the front, Brines wrote for the AP:

> General MacArthur said the hundreds of South Korean soldiers seen along the road seemed to be in good shape and their morale appeared undiminished. Many saluted briskly. Most of them cheered or sang as the General's caravan passed. . . . None in a convoy of twelve trucks returning to the front seemed downhearted. They all cheerfully waved flags. Even most of the hundreds of tired, discouraged refugees trudging southward along the highway stopped and applauded the general.

Most elements of the story spun the facts for consumption in the U.S., where intervention in an already-lost cause was unlikely to go over well. In reality the ROKs had lost nearly half their army and most of their heavy weapons. Some stragglers were returning, and some ROK troops, seeing Americans, had indeed made a show of enthusiasm. But MacArthur saw past the shallow enthusiasm and would tell Rhee that he must have a new chief of staff who would inspire confidence.

It was not fiction when the press contingent reported that as they bumped back toward Suwon they saw more Yaks approaching and shouted warnings to the MacArthur motorcade from their jeep. Vehicles accelerated into the nearest clump of trees, and everyone but the general ran for cover. While the planes buzzed overhead looking for targets, MacArthur sat alone in the black Dodge. Not a shot was fired from above or below, and the enemy planes swung northward while the occupants of the vehicles returned, awed at their stoic chief.

From the mobile relay station outside the schoolhouse, Muccio telephoned to State Department representative in Tokyo, William Sebald, "The Big Boy had a lot of guts and was magnificent." MacArthur was only exhibiting the sense of destiny that had carried him through 1917–18 and later. He was untouchable, not suicidal.

Maggie Higgins's newspaper rivals were already in Suwon. They had been on the Han River bridge approaches in their borrowed jeep when charges intended to deny the span to the Communists exploded. Crane and Gibney had bloodstained undershirts tied around their foreheads. Despite Muccio's warning, the fearless Gibney remained, but Crane, badly cut by flying glass, hitched a ride to Haneda with Keyes and Higgins.

At the Suwon airstrip Higgins had discovered the four-engined *Bataan*.

(MacArthur's party was then returning.) "I was crouched by the side of the windy airstrip typing a quick story on his visit when the general himself appeared." Seeing her, he walked over to say hello and asked whether she wanted a lift back to Tokyo. As it was the only way to file her copy, she accepted, not realizing how hard it would be to get back.

Since MacArthur had given the Tokyo-based newsmen a briefing en route, General Whitney offered, "I'm sure he would like to talk to you now. Why don't you go up and see him?" Slender, blonde and attractive, Maggie made everyone's day, excluding journalistic rivals. Besides, her bylined dispatches appeared in a paper that supported MacArthur's views. And she was personally supportive. Especially gratifying to her was the general's proposal that in the new Japanese constitution women be granted the vote. She also liked the story she had picked up in Tokyo that despite his imperial manner he drew the line at its debasing manifestations. An old Japanese woman had once gotten close enough to throw herself face down before him as he approached the Dai Ichi entrance, to demonstrate her respect. MacArthur, had bent down and raised the tiny lady to her feet, explaining, "Now, now, we don't do that sort of thing anymore."

MacArthur had thought out some possible solutions to the Korean emergency, all dependent upon massive support from the States, but they were not for publication. Instead, he gave Maggie his pep talk for the Pentagon, which belied everything both had seen. "The South Korean soldiers," he declared, "are in good physical condition and could be rallied with example and leadership. Give me two American divisions and we can hold Korea. . . . The moment I reach Tokyo, I shall send President Truman my recommendation for the immediate dispatch of American divisions to Korea. But I have no idea whether he will accept my recommendations." What MacArthur did know, however, was how to preempt the Pentagon and the President. He had done it before.

In his memoirs MacArthur would claim that it was on the knoll overlooking the Han and shattered Seoul that he got his idea for what he called in his penciled notes, perhaps first made on the plane, Operation Bluehearts. Later rechristened Chromite, the notes laid out an amphibious landing above Seoul, with feints elsewhere, to cut off the enemy likely by then to have occupied most if not all of South Korea. No longer walking the aisle of the C-54, MacArthur spent the return flight to Tokyo puffing contentedly on his corncob, conferring with aides and writing notes on a yellow pad in preparation for the next telecon to Washington.

Aboard the *Bataan* as part of the GHQ staff, Stratemeyer urged on MacArthur a more active role than ground support and aerial cover. It was clear from the schoolhouse dogfight that the most effective interdiction was to encounter the enemy a lot sooner. To control the air over South Korea required getting at air bases in North Korea. "How can I bomb north of the 38th parallel without Washington hanging me?" MacArthur asked rhetorically, then decided that his own implied authority as commander in the field during an emergency permitted him to deny an enemy sanctuary. From the plane Stratemeyer radioed to Earle Partridge, deputy commander at FEAF headquarters in Japan, "Take out North Korean airfields immediately. No publicity. MacArthur approves."

Jumping the gun on Washington was obvious insubordination, but MacArthur reasoned that the Pentagon and the President would furnish authorization after the fact, which they did. Besides, "hot pursuit" was accepted doctrine, seemingly appropriate for what had already been labeled a "police action."

Almost everything that MacArthur urged on Washington as a field commander for months thereafter would be rubber-stamped, sometimes after a pause for agonized consultation. Since he seemed on the scene—his dramatic flight to Suwon emphasized that—it was difficult for desk strategists nine thousand miles and fourteen time zones distant to contradict him.

Maggie Higgins's personal interview with MacArthur had riled the palace guard quartet of correspondents, but their anger exploded when she reported that he was planning the bombing of enemy airfields north of the 38th parallel. She could only have learned that, they assumed, on the *Bataan*, where they had been asked on security grounds to keep the decision off the record. Since they could not attack her personally, her alleged breach of confidence was leaked to *Newsweek*, which reported on July 10 that she had "wangled her way" aboard MacArthur's plane and stolen the story. It took weeks for Maggie to learn of the charge, but little time thereafter to send a letter to the editor to deny it. She had been "almost continuously at the front" and "completely shut off from news of the rest of the world," she contended heatedly in *Newsweek*'s issue of August 7. "It is untrue that General MacArthur told me anything of plans to bomb north of the 38th parallel during the plane ride to Tokyo as alleged." She had learned about it "from a quite different source at the front. . . . I had no knowledge whatsoever of any agreement between headquarters' correspondents concerning a security blackout on it."

Her counterattack rubbed in the difference. The accusers were "head-quarters" types. She had been at the front. Two other elements of pride were tacked on to her pique. "I was invited by General MacArthur on the plane through no request of my own." And she was "twenty-nine, not thirty." At the same time that she cabled *Newsweek* to correct its story she wrote an apology to MacArthur for any embarrassment she had inadvertently caused him. "Pay no attention to what your jealous male colleagues say about you," he returned in courtly fashion. "I know them better than you do and they have been harassing me for more than four-and-a-half years." A curious form of harassment, he did not add, as it took the appearance of its opposite.

MacArthur's long report on his mission would urge on Collins, the Army chief of staff, a combat role for ground troops. Americans were already involved by air and sea and, in a very limited fashion, on land as well. In the Cabinet Room of the White House at 5:30 p.m. on the twenty-ninth, only a day before Suwon itself was evacuated, with Church and Muccio jeeping south to Taejon just ahead of the North Koreans, Truman conferred with the Joint Chiefs of Staff on the next moves in Korea. Collins saw no alternative to preserving a beachhead in South Korea while time remained. Army Secretary Frank Pace agreed that no limitations about how to rescue what was left of the peninsula should be put in a directive to MacArthur. Truman believed some reservations were necessary. He wanted only to restore order along the 38th parallel, not to do anything north of it except to "keep the North Koreans from killing the people we are trying to save. You can give the Commander-in-Chief all the authority he needs to do that but he is not to go north of the 38th degree. . . ."

Acheson interpreted that broadly as freedom of action to deter movement in the direction of the frontier, but not "outside of North Korea"—beyond its borders into Chinese or Siberian space. In that regard he noted both the Kirk message from Moscow and the warnings from Red China. There was a Soviet scheme, he thought, to view any attacks on military targets across the Yalu River border with Manchuria as an attack on China itself, "so that the Chinese Communists can have an excuse to enter the Korean dispute."

"That means," Truman suggested, "the Russians are going to let the Chinese do the fighting for them."

From the JCS that evening went a directive to the Commander in Chief Far East in Tokyo which "consolidates, broadens and supplements existing instructions governing your actions with regard to situation in South Korea and Formosa." The CINCFE was authorized to use American naval and air forces to support South Korea. MacArthur could use Army combat and service forces for "essential communications" and "to ensure the retention of a port and air base in the general area [of] Pusan-Chinhae." He could also operate in North Korea against troops, aircraft, tanks, depots, air bases and "other such purely military targets" supporting the invasion of South Korea. He was, however, to "avoid unnecessary casualties to our forces" and take care to "stay well clear of the frontiers of Manchuria or the Soviet Union." As for Formosa, he was to employ naval and air forces only to keep the Chinese Nationalists and Communists from attacking each other. Although the decision to intervene militarily in Korea and to provide additional support to him beyond resources in Japan was "taken in full realization of the risks involved," war with the Soviet Union was to be avoided other than in self-defense.

In effect, MacArthur had all the authority he wanted except on behalf of Chiang, and on his first day back at the Dai Ichi, MacArthur would even expand upon that. His response arrived in Washington at 10:30 p.m. on the twenty-ninth just after Truman's Cabinet had left Blair House and gone home. Although later MacArthur would praise Rhee's government and military far more fulsomely than was realistic, he described his mission to Suwon with graphic pessimism, noting that the ROK Army was "in confusion," had "not seriously fought" and "lack[ed] leadership." They were "incapable of gaining the initiative" and "entirely incapable of counter action." To prevent the enemy from entirely overrunning Korea he required "the introduction of US ground combat forces." If authorized, it was his intention "to immediately move a US regimental combat team" to the area and to build up to "two-division strength from the troops in Japan." Without forces in adequate strength, he argued, "our mission will at best be needlessly costly in life, money and prestige." It would be "doomed to failure."

The telecon began at 3:40 a.m., in the bleak early morning hours in Washington, with MacArthur at one screen and Collins at the other. "There was an eerie quality about this telecon," Collins recalled, "that makes it stand out sharply in my memory. The air was fraught with tension as we assembled in the middle of the night in the Army's darkened telecon room in the Pentagon. . . . We instinctively spoke in hushed voices as the questions, numbered serially, were flashed on the screen, and we pictured in our minds the gathering in Tokyo where answers were being framed that would vitally affect our participation in this strange new war."

Without U.S. ground forces the war would be over in ten days, Mac-

Arthur warned. He now wanted four complete new divisions shipped from the United States, at least two of them immediately. It was an implicit admission that his troops in Japan were understrength and undertrained.

"That is impossible," said Collins.

"Please tell the President that," said MacArthur. At 4:57, Frank Pace, awakened by Collins, telephoned Truman, and before the teleconference closed CINCFE was given authority to move a regimental combat team from Japan "immediately to the combat zone." The two-division emergency augmentation MacArthur wanted was left on hold, but no one doubted that once forces were committed, more would follow. Telecon DA-11 closed from Washington with "Everyone here delighted [at] your prompt action in personally securing firsthand view of situation. Congratulations and best wishes. We have full confidence in you and your command."

Again, consideration was given to procuring divisions from Chiang rather than occupation troops from Japan. After all, Pentagon reasoning went, China (now limited to Formosa) was still the fifth permanent member of the Security Council, and Britain, Australia, Canada and the Netherlands had offered at least token military support. But, George Elsey noted after the White House staff was up and calls had gone back and forth to the Pentagon, "Must be careful not to cause a general Asiatic war." Further, as one skeptical general put it, not only had Chiang's troops performed poorly on their own soil, "The troops were 45 years old. They weren't 25 years old. They had been fighting since '31. . . ."

MacArthur anticipated sweeping American intervention. Authorization came a few hours later in a message from the JCS, "Restrictions on use of Army Forces imposed by JCS 84681 are hereby removed and authority granted to utilize Army Forces available to you as proposed your C 56942 subject only to requirements for the safety of Japan in the present situation which is a matter for your judgment."

That afternoon the Norwegian ambassador to Washington, Wilhelm Munthe de Morgenstierne, reflecting the activist views of his compatriot Trygve Lie, the first secretary-general of the United Nations, visited Acheson at State. The ambassador represented a traditionally neutral nation that had been overrun by contending forces in 1940 and then occupied by the Nazis for five years, an experience which left Norway in 1950 less than doctrinaire pacifist. Five days earlier, with Lie's backing, the UN Security Council had supported, for the first time, an international effort to reverse an invasion. "It was a great moment in history," the ambassador told Acheson.

"I think," the secretary of state agreed, "it is a turning-point in world history."

MacArthur's UN mantle (since 1945 he had been Supreme Commander Allied Powers, or SCAP) remained informal yet inevitable. At 9:39 p.m. on the thirtieth—only 7:39 that morning in Washington, still prior to that meeting at State—he prepared orders for the Eighth Army. His umbrella military organization in Japan was headed by Lieutenant General Walton H. "Johnny" Walker, who had been a corps commander under Patton in 1945. Walker expected to deploy some troops, but perhaps not the division MacArthur targeted, nor to be used as MacArthur directed:

> Move the 24th Division at once to Pusan by air and water. The 24th Division will establish a base at Pusan with a view to early offensive operations. In accordance with the mil[itary] situation it will at once advance a delaying force to the north by all possible means, contact the enemy, now advancing south from Seoul to Suwon, and delay his advance. . . .

Based in Kyushu, the southernmost major Japanese island, the 24th, under Major General William F. Dean, was the closest unit to Sasebo, the likely port of embarkation to Korea via Pusan. Proximity was the key in MacArthur's decision. Dean also had some Korean experience. In October 1947 he had become, for a year, military governor of South Korea until elections established the republic. He knew something of the country. The 24th was understrength, inexperienced and poorly equipped, as MacArthur realized was true of all of his occupation divisions. Nevertheless, one of them had to go. Dean's 19th, 21st and 34th Infantry Regiments were ordered to make ready. Their equipment was World War II leftovers. First Lieutenant Philip Day Jr., executive officer of C Company, 21st Infantry, learned quickly what being understrength meant. Five troublemaker enlistees, court-martialed for "everything from VD to fighting, disobeying orders to showing up late, going AWOL to drinking too much," had been shipped off in handcuffs to a stockade in Yokohama, to be returned from the good life to the States. "You know what happened?" Day recalled. "Someone up there decided C Company could not do without these five thugs and they were shipped back to us." So Dean's division, under Walker's orders, prepared for Korea.

At eleven o'clock in Washington, four hours later, and only two hours after a meeting with the Joint Chiefs of Staff, Truman convened yet another Cabinet session. Many of the participants were exhausted from what seemed like continuous conferences. From a military point of view, the President commented, he preferred to see no public reference yet to American troops in Korea, but their presence was bound to leak out. The White House had to make an announcement. "This is all very delicate," said Truman. "I don't want it stated any place that *I* am telling MacArthur what to do. He is not an American general now; he is acting for the United Nations." On this last day of June in 1950, it was in every sense MacArthur's war.

Bataan II

MACARTHUR KNEW from a report to him on May 30, 1950, that the 24th Division had the lowest combat effectiveness of any of the occupation forces in Japan. Yet it was the easiest of his four understrength divisions to commit to Korea. From Kyushu, where it was located, shipment to Pusan was simple, whether by LST, ferryboat or troop transport. Also, its 21st Infantry Regiment was beginning what was called air transportability training.

With the ROK Army collapsing, MacArthur had little choice but to fly in the first units he could—two rifle companies, some anti-tank teams and an artillery battery. Suwon had already fallen; the division's destination was Taejon, to the southeast. Even so, bad weather forced flights farther south to Pusan, where the main body of the 24th Division was expected by sea. General Church, who had relocated to Taejon, was ordered by Almond to have railway cars at the ready to move troops northward into action from Pusan.

Everything in MacArthur's rule book argued against piecemeal commitment of inadequate troops against superior enemy forces. He could have recommended to the Pentagon *not* throwing his troops in, permitting the peninsula to be overrun while planning to retake it amphibiously (if at all) at an opportune time. But that went against the grain of his militant anti-Communism and his recognition that he had personally abandoned an earlier peninsula—Bataan. And as he had not visited his garrisons in Japan, he seemed to have had no idea how unready they were for any action beyond the fleshpots that had mushroomed around every occupation base.

Having endured Bataan in 1942, where the outcome was catastrophic,

MacArthur was far more sanguine about Korea. While again he expected to be crowded into a corner of a peninsula, Korea's larger area afforded more room to maneuver and included a major port for resupply. Further, he had few concerns about being isolated unless the Russians or Chinese intervened, and Willoughby had assured him that would not occur. As a CIA monograph on the Pacific war would observe, "MacArthur's practice was to not allow intelligence to interfere with his aims, and his history of complaints about Willoughby's reports resulted mainly from their contradiction of his own estimates and preferred courses of action." In the Philippines, his resupply route was eight thousand miles long, and every mile of it hazardous to traverse; he now had in occupied Japan a source of men and materiel only hours away by air, overnight by sea. Japan itself could be a huge support system for Korean operations, from longshoremen on the docks to mechanics in rehabilitated Japanese factories.

Massive problems remained, nevertheless. The ROK Army, already in disarray, had to hold what was left of South Korea. American political will had to back up the requirements of war. And U.S. troops in Japan had to become effective combat soldiers.

Task Force Smith was an overblown designation for the first 406 men from the 1st Battalion, 21st Infantry. Not assigned as one of the now-legendary 406, Lieutenant Carl Bernard was one of two young officers in the 21st Regiment trained as parachutists. At the air base at Kokura he was helping to "load out" Task Force Smith when Lieutenant Colonel Charles Bradley Smith said to him, "Stay on the plane. I've got work for you." In the oppressive heat a warm rain was pelting the tarmac at Pusan when they landed. Undiminished by the whirring propellers of the first C-54s, the fecal stench that every arriving GI would associate with Korea hung over the runway.

As bad weather closed in, some of Lieutenant Colonel Smith's troops, still airborne, were turned back to Kyushu, to fly in the next day and be trucked to a ramshackle train en route north. At Taejon, Smith, a Pacific war veteran who had been a lieutenant (West Point '39) when the Japanese raided his barracks near Pearl Harbor, was interviewed by General Church, who pointed to a place on a map south of Suwon. "We have a little action up here," he said lightly. "All we need is some men up there who won't run when they see tanks. We're going to move you up to support the ROKs."

Smith had no effective weapons against Russian-made tanks, but he did not yet know that. He also had few officers or noncoms with combat experience. Still, his orders were to engage the enemy on sight. Contact with Americans would be psychologically persuasive. The North Koreans might pause to reconsider further advances.

With additional troops, the commanding general of the 24th Division, William F. Dean, flew into Pusan on the evening of July 2, then began moving forward. From Taejon he telephoned cautiously to Doyle Hickey, Deputy Chief of Staff to MacArthur in Tokyo, "This first show must be good. . . . We must get food and bullets and not go off half-cocked." Before long—it would be July 8—Dean, in deep trouble, was appealing, "I am convinced that the North Korean Army and the North Korean soldier, and his status of training and equipment, have been underestimated." By implication he meant American troops, in training and equipment, had been overrated.

More men from the 24th's three regiments—the remainder of the 21st, plus the 34th and the 19th—had been shipped to Pusan by July 5. To bolster the 24th with additional armor, MacArthur ordered a tank company from the 1st Cavalry Division to augment Dean's forces. Piecemeal commitments would continue.

For MacArthur, merely ordering men and materiel to move into combat proved much more complicated than ordering his embassy Cadillac and contingent of jeeps. Logistics outside central Tokyo were little better than primitive. When the 34th Regiment moved by train and trucks to Sasebo, only two dilapidated ships were in Sasebo harbor, the rust buckets *Koan Maru* and *Konga Maru*. Neither freighter had been in use since 1946. Anything seaworthy, even ferries, had to be found. Japanese crews were recruited in the port and vehicles loaded.

With few essentials warehoused, food for the long haul had to be withdrawn from commissaries, and was at best inadequate. A check of stockpiled K rations of World War II vintage showed that the ham-and-egg component had turned black, but the outdated rations were taken aboard anyway. There was no replacement tentage, nor wire, radios, combat boots, spare parts for vehicles and other essentials. Weapons condemned as inoperable in an inspection made in February 1950 had not been replaced. Jeeps could not be offloaded in Pusan because the gantry cranes there had a rated lift of only one ton. The vehicles had to be returned to Sasebo and brought out later on an LST—and then proved to be in such poor state of maintenance that all but one broke down en route to Pyongtaek and had to be abandoned. Even standard tie-down rope or cable was unavailable in Korea, and not carried over with American supplies. Rice-straw rope of unknown tensile strength had to be used to secure equipment to flatcars for the movement north.

Since no one had expected a war, the litany of inadequacies was enormous, escalating as each unit deployed to Korea. Neglect was everywhere beneath the facade of the benign occupation. Once inland, Colonel Jay Lovless of the 34th, with Carl Bernard, broke into a schoolhouse near Ansong, south of Osan, "and tore a large map from a geography book that had the branches of the two roads south of Chonan on it." Even less detailed maps were nonexistent. Although General Dean would quickly replace Lovless with Colonel Robert Martin for alleged command failures, such episodes involving unready occupation troops were inevitable. At 8:16 a.m. on the fifth, the *In Min Gun*, with thirty or more Russian-made T-34 tanks, approached Smith's hastily dug positions just above Osan, eight miles south of Suwon. He now had 540 men including his artillery support. An artilleryman worried that his battery had only six rounds of anti-tank ammunition—one-third of what could be found in all Japan. "What will happen to the guns," he asked, "if the North Korean tanks get through the [ROK] infantry up there?"

"Don't worry," said an officer confidently, "they'll never get that far." The South Koreans, it was assumed, would gain confidence with the Americans behind them, and when the North Koreans discovered that the United States was in the war, they would turn around. But Task Force Smith had no ROKs forward of them. Even the South Korean truck drivers had bolted, one telling Smith through an interpreter, "The war is *that* way. We should be going the *other* way." GIs who could drive were "volunteered" by a sergeant, bringing the contingent within artillery range of the oncoming tanks. At seven-hundred yards, fire from World War II–vintage bazookas smashed against enemy tanks uselessly. Second Lieutenant Ollie O'Connor let two tanks pass him, then fired his rocket launcher against the thinly armored rear of each tank. Damaged, one in flames, they pulled to the side of the road to let the other tanks through. While two crewmen clambered out with hands raised, a third followed shooting, killing the first American soldier lost in the war. (There were already several Air Force losses.)

Another tank would be disabled when GIs went for its treads, but the inefficiency of obsolete American equipment demoralized Smith's dwindling men. Rain came down steadily. Heaving grenades at NKPA troops moving behind the tanks, Smith's troops took hits, scattered and abandoned the field, leaving their immobile wounded behind. A lieutenant, himself seriously wounded, dragged himself past six GIs helpless on the muddy ground. "Lieutenant, what is going to happen to us?" one moaned. With the apology, "This is the best I can do for you," he was offered a hand grenade.

For Carl Bernard, Task Force Smith was "a platoon of strangers" that was destroyed "because we stayed too long in a losing fight." After three days of "prudent walking through the North Korean units to reach our retreating forces," he and "the stragglers I gathered up" separated. He went back to his own L Company of the 21st Infantry. It did little better in its own first fight two days later, "but at least I knew those guys. And we fought smarter because I had learned [that] the anti-tank weapons we had couldn't kill tanks. We lost 85 men dead or missing from a 120-man rifle company."

Ruefully, Pfc. Robert Roy of Smith's heavy-weapons M Company remembered, "Before I fired the first round I counted thirty-five tanks coming down the road. Everyone was shitting their pants. . . . We had no armor-piercing shells, so we tried to stop them by hitting the tracks. . . . Some rounds were duds, some were even smoke rounds. We could see them bounce right off the tanks." By mid-morning several GIs had scurried behind a hill out of the firing and reached for cigarettes. An irate officer yelled down at them, "What the hell are you doing?"

"We're having a smoke."

"You're about to die."

"Yeah," they said, "we're havin' our last smoke."

Brad Smith gave the order to withdraw. They were to destroy their guns in such circumstances, but no one had self-destruct charges to drop into the breech. They abandoned their weapons and "hauled ass." Roy was nineteen. "We were sent over there to delay the North Koreans," he said. "We delayed them seven hours."

Distraught by the unreadiness of MacArthur's troops, Francesca Rhee wrote to her husband's lobbyist and speechwriter, Robert Oliver, on July 14 that the bloodied Americans "are good in the air but have no tactics on land. They only retreat—our soldiers are desperate. They wanted to retreat from Taejon this morning but Gen. Dean and Gen. Walker were called down by the Pres[ident]. . . . The Am[erican]s are no match for the heavy tanks and the tactics of the Reds. . . . The [North] K[orean]s openly say that the Am[erican]s cannot fight on land because they do not want to die. It sounds ungrateful but they do not even know if they face a north K or a S Korean."

Since the Pentagon could not second-guess the estimates and needs of its commander in the area, who also happened to be the most distinguished and most experienced general on active duty, the JCS took very seriously MacArthur's increasingly high estimates of the NKPA's strength and his escalating demands for resources. Only days earlier he had promised to win with one arm tied behind his back. After his flying visit to Suwon, now lost to the enemy, he thought that two divisions and some airpower would be enough. By the time his first forces were committed, and quickly driven back, he had again scaled upward his requests for men and equipment. On July 7 he radioed the Pentagon, "It is now apparent that we are confronted in Korea with an aggressive and well-trained professional army equipped with tanks and perhaps other ground materiel quite equal to, and in some categories superior to, that available here." The NKPA leadership and its tactical skills were "excellent." He now saw that he needed four to five divisions, an airborne regimental combat team and an armored group, even if that depleted other forces. And that, he warned, was "a minimum."

Two days later he radioed that he required even more manpower merely "to hold the southern tip of Korea." In "addition" to everything he had already requested he now wanted "an army of at least four divisions, with all component services, . . . dispatched to this area without delay, and by every means of transportation available." The enemy, he now conceded, was as effective "as any seen at any time in the last war." It was a level of competence he attributed, in what was very likely an invention for him by General Willoughby, to "a combination of Soviet leadership and technical guidance with Chinese Communist ground elements." (The Russians had exited as the war began; the Chinese were not there at all.) "To date," he admitted, "our efforts against his armor and mechanized forces have been ineffective"—a result he attributed to being vastly outnumbered. (He implied the incompetence and uselessness of the South Korean remnants by his silence about them.) At that point his on-the-scene survey had been limited to one visit of a few hours.

MacArthur's time on the ground in Korea in further flying visits would seldom exceed a few hours. He depended upon briefings from senior officers who in some cases should have been relieved sooner than they were. Most correspondents covering the war—and there would be many—recognized that censorship was at first the do-it-yourself variety. One could send home anything, but if something which gave "aid and comfort to the enemy" were published or broadcast, loss of accreditation could follow. Correspondents instead reported stories of valor that implied, as heroism often does, mistakes made at higher levels.

Sometimes, as James Michener, who was there reporting in the early days of the war, recalled, there were local press "conspiracies" to cover up appalling command decisions. "For a while . . . we had a general who was very brave,

very stupid. He would say the craziest things, make the most impossible pre-
dictions. Had we reported even one tenth of what this amazing man said we
could have ruined the entire war. By common consent we protected him.
Possibly we were wrong. . . ."

After the 24th Division, led by Major General William F. Dean, arrived,
Major General William B. Kean's 25th began embarking for Korea on July 9
and was deployed almost at once. It was brought to strength by cannibalizing
the 7th Division and by folding in almost every able-bodied—but not necessarily combat-trained—GI arriving in Japan as a replacement. Major Nat
Wisser observed bakers, clerk-typists and the like arriving in Pusan as replacements for combat units and being evacuated to Japan a few days later as casualties. Pfc. Leonard Korgie, on guard duty at Sugamo Prison in Tokyo,
watching over war criminals, found his name on a list for an escort company
to bring North Korean POWs to Japan. (None were ever shipped out of
Korea.) "Our officers told us to take our dress summer uniforms—we'd need
them in a few weeks for the victory parade in Seoul." He packed his duffel
bag and was trucked to the Yokohama Replacement Depot at Camp Drake
in a group of 150 men and two officers. But there the depot commander
claimed to know nothing of a POW escort unit. He telephoned the Dai Ichi
and reported that MacArthur had said, or had someone say in his name,
"Hell, we're not taking any prisoners in Korea; we're being taken prisoner.
Put them all in the infantry!"

"Wow!" Korgie shouted to a frightened buddy as inexperienced as he
was, "we're going to fight!" He would find himself in the 34th Infantry. The
34th had already been sent northwest on a dusty, dilapidated train with a
sputtering coal-burning locomotive that blackened troops with soot. "We
were the only ones going north," Sergeant Bill Menninger recalled; "the
South Korean Army was heading south." The last car in the ROK train going
in the other direction was a flatcar loaded with land mines, which soldiers
dropped between the tracks. They expected the North Koreans soon, and
intended to leave no usable trackage. The Americans would have to retreat
some other way.

When they detrained near Pyongtaek they had no idea that any friendly
troops were ahead of them. "We found out there were, when some survivors
of Task Force Smith straggled into our lines," Menninger remembered. The
first troops in the area, Smith's informal battalion, had been overwhelmed.
Carl Bernard recalled the disasters of unprepared and underequipped units in
the fighting near Taejon on July 11. A rifle company of the 21st Infantry,

employing ineffective 2.36-inch bazookas—"paint scratchers" to Bernard—against T-34 tanks, lost most of its men, including all its officers and NCOs. Of the other two rifle companies in the action, one had only two officers and two NCOs survive, and the other had all its officers and NCOs killed or captured and ninety-five men lost. One surviving officer was Bernard, who had climbed atop a T-34 only to find a tanker inside opening the pistol port to spin the turret and fire a burp gun to clear the Americans off. "Because I was safe on top, I could hit the [port] chain hard enough with my rifle butt to break it loose and [Lieutenant] Hugh Brown emptied a 15-round carbine magazine through the port as soon as their burp gunner paused to reload. We got the other tank by pouring a five-gallon can of gas on its hot engine compartment. (By the way, the first tank [of three] did not burn by itself. We set it off to make the two others less aggressive.)"

Poor communications made conditions worse. South Korean soldiers and civilians fleeing south would snip and steal lengths of field telephone wire to make backpacks. Field radios had short ranges and needed unavailable replacement batteries. Units cut off would improvise leaders or attach themselves to nearby troops. With little idea of where forces were, and poor maps, airmen flying support missions furnished a rain of friendly fire. Four Royal Australian Air Force pilots on their first mission under UN auspices sprayed bullets and bombs onto an ROK ammunition train at Pyongtaek, well below the *In Min Gun* advance. Nine cars with their locomotive exploded, taking with them the railway station and uncounted hundreds of civilians in the village. An American plane strafing a South Korean position was shot down and the pilot taken prisoner. In the same area other fliers hit fuel dumps, a friendly airstrip, trains, motor columns and an ROK Army headquarters. FEAF aircraft fired on a column of thirty ROK trucks and killed hundreds of soldiers.

After several strafings by Air Force planes, a sergeant griped to Maggie Higgins as they huddled in a roadside ditch, "Why don't those bastards stay at thirty thousand feet or go back to the officers' club?"

Angrily, General Church, still trying to coordinate troop movements from his schoolhouse, telephoned General Stratemeyer in Tokyo to demand that air strikes be limited to the Han River and northward, and MacArthur ordered all ROK vehicles to be marked with a white star on a surface visible from above. Reports from the Dai Ichi described only successful air missions, and even the official Air Force history of the war would omit the continuing embarrassments.

In the chaos that prevailed most of the time wherever the front happened to be, life on the ground without accurate maps was made even more hazardous by air support raids by pilots who also had inadequate charts and only a vague sense of where friend and foe were. Pfc. George Hanrahan, in a three-man tactical air control squad, directed by radio from below the targeting for carrier and land-based aircraft. "I was always in front of our own infantry and dug a slit trench, put out my silk marker panels for identification, and called for artillery smoke to mark the targets. . . . All very exciting but not recommended for a long life. In essence, I was always alone at the front, never had a hot meal, never had a bed. . . . I served all my time in the infantry, really, a function I received no training for."

In Taejon, soon to fall to the North Koreans, Maggie Higgins discovered that her recent companion across the Han, George Kelley, was now temporary rations and fuel officer. She appealed for some C rations and a five-gallon jerrican of gas. She had found a *Stars and Stripes* reporter who had filched a jeep but had no gas for it. Her deal was that she would get a ride to the front if gas could be had. "Her clothes were filthy," Kelley recalled; "she was wearing an army shirt and a pair of Korean pants held up by a grass rope. Her smile was winsome. Of course I gave her what she needed. Later that day she returned alone and very depressed. The *Stars and Stripes* reporter had been killed; Maggie had driven the jeep back without a scratch. She went off by herself, refusing to talk about it. . . . She was a lovely lady and the bravest woman I ever knew."

Following that, thanks to the intervention of Carl Mydans of *Life*, she hitched a ride with Keyes Beech, with whom she would pair for many weeks in Korea. Dirt and desperation and death were everywhere around them that sweltering July, and Higgins was asked again and again by GIs new to war, "Why don't you tell them back home just how useless it really is?" A committed anti-Communist after her postwar reporting years behind the Iron Curtain, she did not agree that it was useless to oppose Communism, but she was not in Korea to argue with frustrated and unhappy GIs.

Riding earlier with Mydans and an Australian reporter for Reuters, she found Colonel Harold "Red" Ayres near Pyongtaek. Newly arrived, he was looking wearily at the bodies of Korean dead amid their burned-out vehicles, hit by "friendly" Australian aircraft. Had she heard of any further reinforcements coming from MacArthur's forces in Japan? "I was just wondering," he said, "whether we would still be around when they got here."

Maggie had first encountered one of the officers with the troops plucked from the occupation, Lieutenant Colonel Mike Michaelis, in France in 1945.

New in Korea after duty under MacArthur in Tokyo, he met his new regiment—the 27th—for the first time on the docks at Pusan, having been reassigned from the Dai Ichi. His executive officer was new, his battalion commanders were new, his staff was new. It was "a complete pick-up unit." Many of his troops were also new, fill-ins from other stations in Japan, augmented by recently arrived recruits. Even his experienced troops had little more than the experience of easeful occupation. General Walker assigned them to reserve, to be thrown in where needed. They did not remain in reserve very long.

A Pentagon-commissioned history would confess some errors by the rushed-in regiments and the inexperienced Air Force personnel, yet blamed the Communists who were not yet there. "So we killed civilians, friendly civilians," *Battle Report* admitted, "and bombed their homes; fired whole villages with their occupants—women and children and 10 times as many hidden Communist soldiers—under showers of napalm, and the [carrier] pilots came back to their ships stinking of vomit twisted from their vitals by the shock of what they had to do." As the North Koreans advanced farther down the peninsula, the authors explained, the "wholly defensible, wholly abhorrent, task of warring against civilians was forced upon the Allied airmen" by the "stealthy" Communist practice of hiding soldiers among refugees. As late as 1999 reports emerged in the press that panicky American troops, often on orders, fired on Koreans clogging vital roads and bridges.

By December, a month when few expected the war still to be ongoing, all but three regimental commanders had been relieved. Yet MacArthur kept ineffective generals on, apparently, because they were there. The official, multi-volume account seldom refers to Major General William Kean, of the ill-starred 25th Division. There are also few references to Major General Hobart R. Gay, commander of the 1st Cavalry Division, which MacArthur had hoped to exploit as an assault force but which had to be thrown into Korea in mid-July to attempt, vainly, to hold on to Taejon. Both were disappointments, a particular frustration to MacArthur as Gay had been General George Patton's executive officer in 1944–45.

Kean had less to go on, inheriting, in his division, the segregated black 24th Infantry Regiment, which had white senior officers and morale as bad as its combat readiness. Writing off Taejon, the Dai Ichi on July 20 downplayed a withdrawal from the city to a position four miles to the southeast. "General MacArthur said that the loss of Taejon would have no special psychological repercussions for the [South] Koreans, and that the city had no special significance."

Task Force Kean, commanded by its senior general and eventually to include the 5th Marines, many of whom had never heard a shot fired in wartime until someone banged away at shadows in their first base camp, was referred to in the diplomatic official Marine history as "distinguished for its informality. Oral orders were the rule. . . ." Similar conditions seemed to prevail across the blunted ninety-degree angle that was the Pusan Perimeter early in August when Edward R. Murrow's outrage was at its most extreme. The distinguished CBS correspondent, first seeing Korea as an Asian Czechoslovakia, where the West had to live up to its slogans or live afterwards in shame, had flown to Pusan with W. L. Lawrence of *The New York Times* on a military plane loaded with canisters of blood. At K-9 air base in Pusan they were met by CBS correspondent Bill Downs, dirty and bearded after days on the line, waving them away with "Go back! Go back, you silly bastards! This ain't our kind of war. This one is for the birds!"

Murrow would call that the best piece of advice he ever ignored. In Tokyo he had visited MacArthur's air-conditioned Dai Ichi and sampled how civilization was returning to Japan. In Korea the best on offer for the press was the omnipresent schoolhouse in Taegu. The colonial oppressor's gift to Korea, it housed correspondents from twenty-four countries, ten to a room on army cots, with indigenous hole-in-the-ground toilets and one busy telephone line to Tokyo. Radio reporters strapped on twelve-pound battery-operated tape recorders to take to the line. By the second week of August twelve correspondents, ten of them Americans, had been killed, wounded or missing in a war with fluid frontiers pressing inward on Taegu and Pusan.

Murrow watched the remnants of a black unit returning. "Their helmets and their clothing were pearl grey from the mud of the rice paddies. . . . They had fought, crawled, and scrambled nine miles across country. . . ." The group was from the 24th Infantry. Virtually none of its men, all black, as well as its officers, both black and white, had any prior combat experience, prompting the highest-ranking black in the regiment, Lieutenant Colonel Forrest Lofton, to refuse to leave Japan for Korea. It would be a disaster, he claimed. Undisciplined, Lofton was assigned instead to maintain the 24th's base at Gifu in central Honshu. (The regimental band also remained to enjoy the good life.) At a sermon to enlisted personnel, a black chaplain had reportedly declared it inappropriate for black Americans to fight an enemy of "color." As their trains pulled out of Gifu, the men expected only a short holiday, and their Japanese girlfriends ran alongside, passing through the windows packets later found to contain drugs. (The Communists had already begun to discover the efficacy of making heroin easy to get for GIs in Korea, and telltale yellowish eyeballs gave it away.)

With Sasebo now crowded with ships and replacements, the 24th had been diverted to the port of Moji, to the northeast, and shipped out on colliers, tankers, fertilizer haulers and ferries, but not before raising hell in the city. "They shot the town up. It was very bad," a cook with the regiment remembered. Military investigators dismissed Japanese reports of rape, robbery and desertion, although disorders continued on the twelve-hour passage to Pusan.

By the afternoon of July 13, all of the regiment was in Pusan, but local dockworkers were on strike and the ships could not be offloaded. Either wages or Communist sympathies were involved, and money issues might have masked ideological efforts to disrupt the buildup. Some units did their own offloading; others forced the strikers to work at gunpoint. As GIs debarked without their heavy equipment, much of it still deep in the holds, they were piled immediately onto trains for the port of Pohang, 110 miles north and directly east of Taegu. Then, with General Dean's 24th Division in trouble, they were moved eighty-five miles west to Kumchon, where they could have gone directly from Pusan. In the confusion, rumors spread that the regiment's white executive officer, Lieutenant Colonel James B. Bennett, already a medical evacuee, had faked a heart attack. He had said openly that he would never go into combat with a black unit.

Moved again, this time by truck, the increasingly leaderless 24th Regiment spent seven hours more on the road, with scant sleep or rations. Its kitchen trucks had been lost or stolen in Pusan. Arriving in Yechon at two in the afternoon of the fourteenth, the regiment was ordered to dig in to protect ROK troops on one side and Michaelis's 27th Regiment on the other. By the next morning they were under fire. The 3rd Battalion scattered, abandoning vehicles and weapons, and a platoon leader, the black Lieutenant William D. Ware, was reprimanded and ordered to move his men forward to their original positions. Twelve days later, trying to protect his men, he died under fire, and was posthumously awarded the Distinguished Service Cross.

Since the chaos should have been apparent as far off as the Dai Ichi, it seemed absurd that MacArthur would try to run the war from Tokyo. Yet even his Eighth Army commander, with troops both in Japan and in Korea, had not been given the authority to take the blue UN flag to Korea and direct operations on the scene. Lieutenant General Walton Walker arrived only on July 12, setting up his headquarters at Taegu. MacArthur's instructions were to withdraw as necessary from indefensible areas, but to safeguard as large a beachhead around Pusan as was possible.

In his memoirs, Truman would downplay the rout of the South Koreans and the disorganization of the early American efforts, claiming that the press "made dramatic news out of this retreat. News stories spoke of entire units being wiped out and exaggerated the rout and confusion. Truth was that a small band of heroic youngsters led by a few remarkable generals was holding off a landslide so that the strength for the counterpunch could be mustered behind their thin curtain of resistance. The fact is that there was more panic among the civilians at home than among the soldiers in Korea."

Informal censorship was proving ineffective. The embarrassing facts, or at least some of them, were crossing the Pacific. The reality was worse than the handouts from the Dai Ichi or at headquarters briefings in Korea. Truman's own carefully chosen words at the time were to retain public support for the war. Some generals were remarkable only for their incompetence, and inexperienced but courageous youngsters should not have been the shock troops to blunt the North Korean sweep south. Yet there were no other troops.

Where there were small victories, the American press made much of them, as when Yechon was temporarily reoccupied on the twenty-first by platoons of the 24th Regiment, an achievement made possible because the town was abandoned and almost uncontested for. Lieutenant Colonel Samuel Pierce Jr., the white commander of the 3rd Battalion, had little idea what was happening as he prudently remained more than two miles to the rear. The success received wide coverage in the good news–starved American press, under headlines like "Negro Troops Score Victory." Much worse news had come the day before, when the commanding general of the 24th Division, William F. Dean, was reported missing in action. He had become separated from his troops when they had withdrawn from Taejon, with division casualties approaching 30 percent. Two days later the 1st Cavalry Division relieved the remnants of the 24th, which had fallen back nearly a hundred miles and lost most of its equipment. (Dean was injured and then captured, enduring the rest of the war as a POW.) In Washington, General Collins privately deplored "the personal involvement of a senior commander in the combat of small units or in one small segment of an action."

Chastised for his impulsive courage—the kind that becomes necessary when things fall apart—Dean at the least set an example that could not be disparaged by the ranks. James Michener reported GIs early in the war telling of a colonel "who made enlisted men dig him a foxhole so deep that not even his ears showed when he was standing up." It got back to headquarters and he was "finished." After the war Keyes Beech reported the "pathetic sight" of a "two-star general" in the summer of 1950 "standing in the middle of a Korean road. . . . He was an old cavalryman. In Europe only a few years before he had commanded a corps of troops that rolled triumphantly over the broad, smooth highways behind armored spearheads in pursuit of a fleeing foe. On this day he stood ankle-deep in dust, thoughtfully slapping his riding crop against his thigh while his green, understrength division fell back around him." His identity was charitably not given, but it wouldn't have mattered. MacArthur kept him on.

As things went from bad to worse in July, there was little good news to write home. It was understandable if outrageous, Maggie Higgins believed, that Colonel Pat Echols, MacArthur's press chief in Korea, considered the media his enemies. Correspondents blamed Echols for being limited to a lone telephone line to the outside, usable only between 2:00 and 4:00 a.m. Despite the racket of reporters shouting into the phone, when away from the front Higgins stubbornly dozed on a table in the room with the phone, waiting her turn.

As the battle for Taejon took its ominous course, she was handed orders to leave Korea. To buck up her spirits, Colonel Richard Stephens of the 21st Infantry, a compact, leathery veteran of the early fighting, assured her that if she couldn't get back as a correspondent, "I'll hire you back for my rifle platoon."

With no one to appeal to, she got on a hospital train headed toward Taegu, and out. By then she had an explanation from Echols, who quoted General Walker as saying, "This is just not the type of war where women ought to be running around the front lines." Since he had been given "the final say" by MacArthur, she left the crowded stinking train at Taegu and telephoned the *Herald Tribune* to confirm that she was in Korea as "a duly accredited correspondent . . . and not as a woman." Of course she was both. As correspondent Bob Elegant would put it years later, "Maggie wasn't above using her little girl's smile and her big girl's body to get the jump on the competition." Her paper quoted her words, afterwards picked up by the Soviet *New Times,* which published a cartoon showing her being evicted from Korea at bayonet point. The caption read "MACARTHUR'S FIRST VICTORY."

A public relations aide to Walker put her on the next plane out; escorting her to K-2 air base were two armed soldiers.

In Tokyo she managed to see MacArthur. "There are no facilities for you in Korea," he explained, backing up Walker.

"Nobody worries about powder rooms in Korea," she insisted.

"The language is bad—unfit for a lady."

"I've already been to the front in Germany," she reminded him. "I didn't need another war to teach me to fill in the dots and dashes in Hemingway's novels. The niceties of language just aren't very important on the battlefield."

With nothing to lose, she reminded him implicitly of his own vow in 1942 to return to the Philippines. "I walked out of Seoul. I want to walk back in."

MacArthur scratched out a cable to go to the *Trib:* "BAN ON WOMEN IN KOREA BEING LIFTED. MARGUERITE HIGGINS HELD IN HIGHEST ESTEEM BY EVERYONE."

She determined, on returning, to forgo coverage of the arrival of the Marines, since most other correspondents, including her *Herald Tribune* rival, Homer Bigart, would be there. Early on her reexplorations of the line she encountered Lieutenant Charles Payne of Task Force Smith's C Company. Of its original 135 men he was one of six left. Payne offered a lesson for her that could be acquired only in the middle of things. "Once we'd accepted death as inevitable everybody calmed down. It became kind of exciting instead of just plain terrifying." It had been exciting, however, only in the memories of the survivors. His "kids" had been "scared" when none of their last-war equipment could stop the first North Korean tanks. "Some died," he admitted. Others were too shot up to withdraw. "One man kept begging me to shoot him."

Payne offered her a gold pen-and-pencil set that his wife had given him, assuming that his luck would run out and he did not want an enemy who looted his body to have them. Months later, he recalled long after Korea, "when I saw a wire service photo of Maggie at her typewriter, I was really pleased to spot my pen and pencil tucked into her pocket."

Although Higgins paired on occasion with other correspondents, her partner after the first weeks of war was usually Keyes Beech, who according to speculation by press rivals shared more than a jeep with her. He owned up to skinny-dipping with Higgins in a running stream, to the entertainment of GIs with binoculars on a nearby hill. "You'd think they'd never seen a woman before," she scorned, splashing about and savoring being, momentarily, clean. (Once they had to interrupt a bumpy journey along a dusty dirt road, to find a venue with nurses, when Maggie announced that she had "the curse," and nothing for it.) Among her rumored lovers was MacArthur, perhaps because he openly flattered her, but nothing was less likely than an extramarital affair for the general, who had little privacy and at seventy enjoyed his uxoriousness.

Mike Michaelis, another rumored lover, scoffed later that "conditions couldn't have been worse" for such things. "The country was filthy. Everybody had diarrhea. . . . The first time I saw Marguerite she was covered with dirt. The so-called road she'd just jeeped in on was two inches of dust. A man's a man; you think about sex. I thought Marguerite might look pretty good if I could get her into a tub, but the opportunities just didn't exist. . . . I rarely saw her when she wasn't surrounded by about fifty guys who just wanted to look at her because she was a woman."

Although eager to visit Michaelis and his regiment again, Maggie almost didn't make it. She and Beech had been invited to an ambassadorial dinner in Pusan hosted by bow-tied John Muccio—a holiday from the war with the possibility of meeting guests who might make a story. Accelerating much too fast from Muccio's temporary embassy, Beech found—or claimed—that his brakes had failed. To avoid a plunge down a steep embankment, he explained, he rammed a concrete pillar. "I chose the gatepost and Maggie hit the windshield." Carried indoors, bleeding, she insisted on surveying the damage in a mirror. "She took a few steps and we caught her before she hit the floor."

Medics arrived with a stretcher, but she insisted on sitting up front in the ambulance, only to collapse as she got out. Beech caught her. The next morning he found her sitting up in bed, hospitalized in a blue MDUSA gown. "Those sons of bitches have stolen my clothes," she complained.

Doctors wanted to keep her down, but she insisted that Beech get her some clothes, which he did from the press billet. By the time that her accident made the rival *New York Times*—but only on page 12—she had slipped out, Beech remembered, "and headed for Michaelis's outfit. She reached his headquarters just in time for it to get hit. It was a hell of a good story. . . ."

Michaelis himself was a good story. Maggie found him in the usual command post of a battered schoolhouse, thirty-three miles west of Pusan, where, the next morning, the former schoolhouse was attacked by small-arms fire. Officers and noncoms rushed out to their units. Reportedly, North Koreans inland were being augmented by a force landed from the sea. In the melee a GI machine gunner went berserk and began firing toward his own men. An officer winged him and settled things down, and as enemy machine-gun crews were zeroed in and eliminated, it turned out that the landing had been by friendly ROKs. In the confusion occurring so often in the war, Koreans of one side were mistaken for the other, and Higgins, who had jumped out of a window, discovered her teeth chattering with fright. Then she experienced something new in her repertoire of emotions, already described by Colonel

Red Ayres—"the cold awful certainty there was no escape. My reactions were trite. As with most people who suddenly accept death as inevitable and imminent, I was simply filled with surprise that this was finally going to happen to me. Then as the conviction grew, I became hard inside and comparatively calm."

She ceased worrying; her teeth stopped chattering; her hands stopped shaking—just in time, as Michaelis materialized to ask, "How are you doing, kid?" Higgins managed a "Just fine, sir."

The *In Min Gun* attackers had been real, but in the darkness it had been even more difficult than usual to tell friend from foe. Not only did North Koreans often conceal themselves as white-coated refugees; they attempted when they could to confuse GIs with captured American arms and gear. Adapting the egalitarian appearances of the Communist Chinese, most NKPA officers below staff level could not be identified by the shiny insignia which made American equivalents prime targets for snipers. If one could get close enough, one could spot an officer by the deference paid him, the burp gun or pistol he carried, rather than a rifle, or the small aluminum pot dangling from his belt for boiling rice. In the armies professedly of the people, officers rarely ate from the communal pots shared by the lower ranks.

When the sector quieted and Higgins prepared to leave with Harold Martin of the *Saturday Evening Post* to file reports in Pusan, she put a carbine in their jeep and asked Michaelis if he had any message for the divisional commander, General Kean. "Tell him," Michaelis said, "that we will damn well hold." Her dispatch would note about the rush of casualties that "one correspondent learned how to administer blood plasma." Michaelis heard of it and wrote to the *Herald Tribune* to identify her and lavish praise on her "selfless devotion." It was published. After that, Maggie recalled, "it was hard for headquarters generals to label me a nuisance . . . as an excuse for restricting my activities."

MacArthur had been trying to promote the feisty Michaelis back to his World War II rank of colonel but the War Army was severely limiting high-level "temporary promotions." "This went on," Michaelis said, "for a series of twelve messages." Each time MacArthur repeated his request. His thirteenth message, dated August 4, 1950, was, "This day I have promoted Michaelis to colonel." (By February 1951 he was a brigadier general and assistant commander of the 25th Division.)

From the Dai Ichi, MacArthur kept a barrage of repetitious messages going to the Pentagon crediting NKPA successes not only to superior Russian equipment and "thoroughly first class" infantry, but also to "a combination of Soviet leadership and technical guidance with Chinese Communist ground elements." Although the *In Min Gun* flew the North Korean flag, he charged on July 9 that "it can no longer be considered an indigenous North Korean mil[itary] effort." But there were no Chinese Communist ground elements other than the NKPA troops who had once fought for Mao but now were in the 4th and 6th Divisions of Kim Il Sung.

State and Defense in Washington were skeptical about making allegations of overt intervention and more concerned about Communist exploitation of UN intervention now that token forces other than Americans were being offered. "For worldwide political reasons," they informed MacArthur on July 12, "it is important to emphasize repeatedly the fact that our op[era-tio]ns are in support of UNSC [United Nations Security Council]." He was asked to identify himself "whenever practicable" as UN commander, or SCAP—Supreme Commander Allied Powers. He was to emphasize in communiqués "whenever facts justify, activities of other countries' forces," and in particular to identify "Asiatic" forces that might join his command. It was also important, the recommendation went on, "to emphasize that this is an invasion from the north." He was to refer to the "North Korean invaders," "Communist invaders," even "international Communist forces"—a description that could only encourage MacArthur as ideologue.

"Considerable harm is being done worldwide," Washington deplored, "by news interviews and eyewitness accounts of setbacks, lost battalions, humiliating defeats, etc. Without yet resorting to censorship, it is suggested that press briefings be given at Hqs to fulfill need for keeping these stories in perspective and reporting with equally colorful details UN or American successes, heroism, etc. You may wish [to] point out censorship [is] avoidable only if reporting is balanced and avoids causing undue harm abroad."

MacArthur in Tokyo would go through cycles of confidence followed by private despair. He was reluctant to sack commanding officers from general on downward who were unable to cope or to lead, but he remained equally reluctant to set foot in Korea when the news was bad, unless he could reinterpret—at least for himself—the bad as good. After his first somewhat risky flight to Suwon, now lost, he had not returned. When he began again what would be more than a dozen fly-ins, he would seldom leave the environs of the airfield. On one occasion he would remain for only forty-five minutes before ordering his plane back to Japan. He would never spend a single night on the ground in Korea. From Tokyo he alternated desperate appeals for more troops with self-congratulatory appraisals of how well his command had performed.

Both were combined in his "Personal for the President" response late on July 19 in an appraisal of the situation. In it he saw the North Korean "chance for victory" as having been "ended." It had depended, he explained, on overrunning South Korea quickly once the Han River had been breached. "This chance he has now lost through the extraordinary speed with which the 8th Army has been deployed from Japan to stem his rush. When he crossed the Han line the way seemed entirely open and victory was within his grasp. The desperate decision to throw in piecemeal American elements as they arrived by every available means of transport . . . was the only hope to save the situation."

Nothing he reported explained the unpreparedness of the troops from his command which had been thrown in, but he celebrated their "skill and valor thereafter displayed in successive holding actions . . . which so slowed [the enemy's] advance and blunted his drive that we have bought the precious time necessary to build a secure base." Although he announced in a telecon to the Pentagon on July 24 that he was confident he could keep a foothold around Pusan, he hardly had much more than that left. Regiments were rearranged along the contracting perimeter, the least reliable of them the black 24th, which seemed to be withdrawing far more rapidly than events made necessary, abandoning trucks and artillery. White and black officers alike appeared to panic, sometimes before their troops did, but the impression which MacArthur did not confide to Washington was that black soldiers needed only a few rounds of fire to impel mass desertions. If jeeps or trucks were not available for flight, they resorted to what was sardonically labeled "organic transportation"—feet. Cases of straggling outnumbered examples of gallantry, but the men were loyal to recognized friends. On July 28 a platoon led by white Lieutenant Leonard H. Kushner was surrounded and Kushner himself was severely wounded. His men needed four hours of fighting to rescue him, but he had defended a number of them in court-martial proceedings in Japan. Kushner returned lashed to the rear of a tank.

Mass departures under fire and even the suggestion of flight gave a new word to the language—*bugout*. The press had used the word although Washington deplored it. Men of the 24th would, unashamedly and ungrammatically, sing "Bugout Boogie":

When the Commie mortars start to chug,
The ol' Deuce Four begin to bug. . . .

When you hear the pitter-patter of little feet,
It's the ol' Deuce Four in full retreat. . . .

After a black lieutenant, Leon A. Gilbert, refused a direct order to take his men back into the fight, he was given the opportunity to change his mind or be charged with desertion under fire, a capital offense. He refused again with a "No, I'll get killed." Colonel Horton V. White, a veteran of World War II service with black units and the commander of the regiment, swore in anger and heaved his helmet. Gilbert would be tried and sentenced to death. In November, President Truman commuted the sentence to twenty years, but the 24th and segregated units in general were finished. On August 1 the 24th was ordered off the line. Truman would insist that the integration orders he had given in 1948 be completely carried out, eliminating second-class service.

Although "bugout fever" in the first weeks of the war was often as irrational as the word *fever* implied, it was also a response to North Korean tactics, which were to follow frontal assaults with flanking attacks, cutting off units and forcing surrenders, then murdering most captives after binding their wrists behind them. Maintaining prisoners required resources and handicapped mobility; it also meant eschewing ideological hatred. Only when a prisoner seemed worth taking for intelligence reasons or when appearances required a show of prisoners did the NKPA move captives north to stockades. Recognizing what could happen to them even if they were not killed in action, soldiers often withdrew in a suicidal hurry, abandoning gear that would slow their retreat. They stripped off clothes—even boots—that might bog them down in flooded rice paddies. And every Korean, whatever the uniform or lack of uniform, could be an enemy—a realization that magnified the panic.

Up with the men, Maggie Higgins refused to run, but sympathized with the urge. "Any human being wants a fighting chance," she wrote some months later. "You don't get that at fifty-to-one odds. In the first skirmishes . . . we paid a high price in the lives of our trained officers because a disturbing number of our troops were reluctant to follow orders and stand pat. It was routine to hear comments like, 'Just give me a jeep and I know what direction I'll go in. This mamma's boy ain't cut out to be no hero,' or, 'Someone really gave old Harry [Truman] the wrong dope on this war. He can find someone else to pin his medals on.'"

The argument to "the average GI" that "these sacrifices were gaining us desperately needed time" was a mockery, Maggie conceded, "if you have just seen your men massacred in what seems a hopeless fight." But Keyes Beech reported her scorn at "bugout fever" when the two correspondents passed a "southbound tank sergeant" and then bore around a bend toward the sounds of shooting. "Hey, lady," the sergeant yelled, "you're headed the wrong way." "It seems to me," Higgins shouted back, "you're the one that's headed the wrong way." It was difficult for Maggie to remember that Johnny Walker had promised her "absolutely equal" treatment but appealed that he'd get "a terrible press" in the U.S. if something happened to her. "So please be careful and don't get yourself killed or captured."

The embarrassments that Ed Murrow observed and could not report included that of the 29th Infantry Regiment, formerly on occupation duty in Okinawa. Understrength and undertrained, it was alerted for Korean duty and promised preliminary shape-up in Japan. Instead, four hundred new recruits arrived on July 20 in Okinawa to be lined up at supply depots and assigned to the regiment's only two battalions. A few hours later they were back on troop transports bound for battle with the rest of the truncated 29th. How they were handled could not have been unknown to MacArthur in Tokyo and Walton Walker at EUSAK (Eighth United States Army in Korea) command. The burly Walker, with his perpetual bulldog scowl, was desperate for men. The *In Min Gun* was trying to force crossings of the Naktong, which would place the Perimeter in jeopardy.

Officers of the 29th protested, one radioing EUSAK that their recruits had only eight weeks' basic training and were totally unready for combat. The assistant G-3 would promise Lieutenant Colonel Harold Mott only three days of further training on landing in Pusan.

On July 24 the understrength regiment debarked in Korea and was ordered immediately to embattled Chinju, west of Masan in the farthermost corner of the Perimeter. With the green troops were rifles and mortars never test-fired and .50-caliber machine guns still packed in heavy Cosmoline grease.

Two days later the 3rd Battalion (there was no 2nd) was ambushed at Hadong, a road junction just above the south coast. To call for air support, troops employed radios that did not work. Planes visible above failed to see them below and flew off. Fleeing across the Kum River under fire, infantrymen of the 3rd shed boots, clothing and weapons. "They hunted us down," a survivor reported, "like they were shooting rabbits fleeing a brush fire." Of the 757 men recorded in the battalion, 313 died and at least a hundred were taken prisoner. The episode receives one bland sentence in the official U.S.

Army history. MacArthur had told the JCS that he was buying time with space. The deployment purchased very little time. "If our center is unable to hold," he had warned the Pentagon, "our perimeter will have to be contracted." It was contracting.

One mobile Army surgical hospital after another, new to Korea, was being strained to capacity. Intended to be sixty-bed facilities, they were overwhelmed and expanded to two hundred beds. Captain Oree Gregory, a nurse with MASH (Mobile Army Surgical Hospital) 8055, a cluster of tents in the Perimeter, wrote in her diary for July 23, "In all my seventeen years of experience I've never seen such patients, blind, or with legs and buttocks blown off. Many died despite skilled surgery." After two more tough days she added, "The July heat was intense and the flies swarming about were green, large and heavy." A month earlier many of the medics had been dispensing aspirin at sick call in well-appointed hospitals in Japan.

MacArthur and Walker hadn't a single MASH when the war began. They existed only on paper. The first ten doctors in MASH 8055 (the 80 meant Eighth Army) left Sasebo for Pusan on July 8, seven days after the unit was activated. Most of its physicians were blanks on organizational charts, yet the war looked far from over. In Washington, Congress recognized the embarrassing deficiency by proposing that doctors under fifty-one be drafted, and by September 1, Public Law 779, the Doctors Draft Act, had become law. Experienced physicians in private practice, however, exerted pressure on Congress to ensure that residents and interns would be drafted ahead of them. After rudimentary basic training the greenest physicians were tagged for Korea, where they received traumatic on-the-job training.

MacArthur flew back to Korea on July 27, landing at Taegu, the only major city remaining after Pusan. Careening in his jeep convoy between battalions under pressure, Walker came to K-2 air base to meet him. The general's mode of travel seemed intended to out-Patton his late boss. Despite the clouds of dust in dry weather and the spattering mud when it rained, Walker's lacquered helmet gleamed and his command vehicles were trim and shiny. His personal jeep displayed black leather seats, and a machine gun mounted in the rear, with attendant gunner. Walker sat in front next to the driver, and brandished a .45 automatic and a repeating shotgun. "I don't mind being shot at," he said, "but these bastards aren't going to ambush me." Walker also had a light command plane, normally used for artillery spotting; however, Captain Mike Lynch, his pilot, would be ordered to fly low enough for the general to shout visible if unheard encouragement to the troops below, and sometimes orders to their officers in the field. Exasperated with bugouts, Walker wanted to appear to be everywhere.

Walker also wanted to appear in better shape than he really was. According to Michaelis, who had first served with him in France, Walker "suffered badly from . . . curvature of the spine, which gave him constant pain. . . . It made life miserable for him and may have altered his facial expression. It gave him a very turned-down kind of a bulldog look."

A few weeks later Walker would tell a division commander in the buckling center of his line, "If the enemy gets into Taegu you will find me resisting him in the streets and I'll have some of my trusted people with me and you had better be prepared to do the same. Now get back to your division and *fight it!*" On July 26, however, he had telephoned from Taegu to the Dai Ichi, proposing that he shift his headquarters to the last possible fallback location, Pusan. With the loss of Taejon on the twentieth, and the NKPA thrusting from the west ever closer to Taegu, Walker wanted to hold a line on the banks of the Naktong River but without, he said, endangering irreplaceable communications equipment. General Almond, taking the call, might have misheard Pusan for Ulsan, a minor port on the Sea of Japan directly east from Taegu. In either case he opposed the move, which he saw as a precursor to a pullout from Korea and possibly "the forerunner of a general débacle."

Walker would sometimes retort to the peremptory Almond, "Is this Ned Almond talking, or is this Ned Almond talking for MacArthur?" Almond, who had one star less than the EUSAK commander, replied that he would consult with MacArthur about the headquarters move.

Rather than put MacArthur on the phone directly to Walker, Almond went to his chief to urge that he leave "at once" to steady Walker. The next morning, the Supreme Commander, who had not been in the war zone for a month, although he was planning a leisurely visit to Chiang in quiet Formosa, flew with Almond to Korea. They remained only ninety minutes— long enough for MacArthur to warn Walker that further withdrawals would not be tolerated. The horseshoe of the Perimeter had to be held at whatever cost to tie up the *In Min Gun* while an amphibious flanking operation was organizing. Walker, in fact, would have to give up his eagerly awaited Marine brigade, about to land in Pusan on loan to him until they were diverted to the amphibious movement. Nevertheless, his weary troops were to prevent a Korean evacuation at whatever price. For Walker it was a walk to the woodshed for a chastising by the chief—arranged by Almond, whom he now disliked even more.

Looking at the situation from Walker's perspective, Michaelis saw EUSAK as a "hideous responsibility. . . . Walker had to defend the Pusan perimeter with very limited troops and with his total reserve being my regiment, which he moved about from day to day, plugging a gap here, plugging a gap there."

On the twenty-ninth Walker met with General Kean and his 25th Division staff (including Michaelis) to inform them what MacArthur expected, and what every soldier in the field was to be told. Other divisions were to get the same message. Notes of Walker's "hold the line" order suggest MacArthur's strong language. "There will be no more retreating, withdrawal, or readjustments of the lines or any other term you choose," Walker said, speaking for MacArthur. "There is no line behind us to which we can retreat. Every unit must counterattack to keep the enemy in a state of confusion and off balance. There will be no Dunkirk, there will be no Bataan, [and] a retreat to Pusan would be one of the greatest butcheries in history. We must fight to the end."

He reminded commanders, based on atrocities reported by the few escapees who had played possum, that to be captured by the North Koreans "is worse than death itself. . . . If we must die, we will die fighting together. Any man who gives ground may be personally responsible for the death of thousands of his comrades."

Coming from MacArthur himself the dramatic language would have meant more than from his surrogate, but officers knew that the Supreme Commander had spent all of an hour and a half in the war zone, and most of that at the edge of K-2 airfield. Still, Walker exhorted, "I want you to put this out to all the men in the division. I want everybody to understand that we are going to hold this line. We are going to win."

The reality was less promising. Also on the twenty-ninth Pfc. Leonard Korgie's L Company (34th Infantry), just before pulling back across the muddy, swirling Naktong, attempted to move forward as ordered, firing as they did. A bazooka team watched its ineffective missiles bounce off enemy targets, a result common since the early days of Task Force Smith. L Company knew it was in trouble, yet at dusk the North Koreans lifted their fire, and the Americans used the respite to dig in on the exposed forward slope of a hill. With nothing to eat or drink all day they were desperately hungry and thirsty, but even more exhausted, and fell asleep once they could crawl into shallow shelters. Soon Korgie was awakened by screams, and saw shadowy figures thrusting bayonets into foxholes. Figures floated toward him, and he fired. They disappeared.

The next morning the surviving infantrymen began taking small-arms fire, and three friendly Mustangs flew over on a strafing run, which only delayed a rain of enemy mortar shells. The heat was intense—"an open oven"—and some GIs risked their lives to get to a small stream, several collapsing before they could be picked off. "We dragged along to the next position a few miles farther south," Korgie recalled. Holding the line as decreed by MacArthur and Walker was empty rhetoric. "Guys, sweat-soaked, shitting in their pants, not even dropping them, moved like zombies." On a hill he saw an officer unknown to him eating from a box of C rations. Fire from North Korean artillery zeroed in, and he heard someone yell, "We're pulling out!" According to official reports the withdrawal across the Naktong was orderly and proceeded smoothly.

A GI version of the phrase imposed on Walker by MacArthur became a Walker signature. Jack Ben-Rubin, then a Merchant Marine officer, recalled helping to shepherd a contingent of the 2nd (Indian Head, from its shoulder patch) Division from Bremerton, Washington, directly to Pusan—troops put together at embarkation who "scarcely knew each other" and who had little combat training. "Many of the men were not displeased to be going to Korea. There were malcontents and misfits who had gladly volunteered rather than face time in the stockade for severe disciplinary or criminal behavior."

Disembarking at Pusan, troops "formed in groups on the dock. . . . General Walker addressed them. He stood erect, wearing a pearl-handled pistol at his side, similar in appearance to General George Patton. He told the men not to look back at the ships that brought them. . . . They were here to stop the North Koreans. They were to stop them on land, or die in the water."

"Stand or Die"

It DID NOT take long for the American press to applaud MacArthur's "stand or die" order to Walker. Hanson Baldwin, military columnist for *The New York Times,* called it from his remote vantage "a well-merited rebuke to the Pentagon." The injunction read differently to Lieutenant Harry J. Maihafer, West Point '49, and fresh out of Fort Benning in Georgia. Maihafer encountered it in the *Pacific Stars and Stripes* on a troop train bound for Sasebo. "It was a message," he remembered, "with very little sales appeal for those of us hurrying to join the team."

He arrived in Korea with five hundred others on the weather-beaten freighter *Yoshiba Maru.* "The ship shuddered and came to rest alongside the Pusan dock. On deck, lined up alphabetically, we waited patiently as someone chalked a number on each helmet. When my turn came, I learned I'd be going to the 78th Medium Tank Battalion of the 24th Infantry Division and that I'd be shipping out by train that afternoon." When he reached his unit he learned that at Taejon it had lost, in a single day, eleven of its seventeen light M-24 tanks to Russian-made anti-tank shells.

Another '49er with him on the troopship, Trevor Swett, reported to the already notorious black 24th Regiment. There, Lieutenant Colonel John Corley, a much bemedaled veteran of World War II, asked if he recalled Stan Crosby, West Point '47. Swett was Crosby's replacement. "I told Crosby the same things I'm going to tell you—and that was a week ago. He didn't listen, and now he's dead. You listen!"

Platoon leaders, company commanders, even battalion commanders,

Corley insisted, had no business leading their troops from forward. That meant certain death. Officers were in short supply, and troops could not be commanded from a rolled-up shelter-half (like the poncho, an improvised precursor to the Vietnam body bag). "It sounded like good advice," Swett thought, although "it was probably something Corley himself seldom practiced." As a battalion commander in a regiment already notorious for bugouts, Corley had to hazard himself as an example, and on September 6 he would be given the entire regiment, the youngest officer with such responsibility in Korea. In January 1950, Army regulations following Truman's order to desegregate mandated assignments of personnel without regard to race, but troops in the occupation had remained segregated.

The 77th Engineer Combat Company, which often accompanied the 24th Infantry, was also a black unit known for straggling, the euphemism which the Army preferred to bugout. The men "were very bitter," said its black commander, Captain Charles Bussey. "They felt they were stupid to risk their lives unduly because when they got home they didn't have the rewards citizenship should have provided. . . ."

Another segregated outfit was the newly arrived 65th Infantry Regiment. In October it would supplement the understrength 3rd Division, which when activated for Korea on August 6 at Fort Benning had only two regiments, the 7th and 15th Infantry, each itself woefully understrength. The Puerto Rican 65th Infantry had been shipped off hastily to the loud protests of soldiers guaranteed at enlistment not to be sent any farther from home than the Panama Canal Zone. So low in numbers that it hardly fit the designation of regiment, it was augmented as it passed through the Panama Canal by troops skimmed from the 33rd Infantry at Fort Kobbe. The post commander offered the 65th's Lieutenant Colonel William W. Harris soldiers he released for reasons he did not need to make public. (They were mostly blacks.) By the time the largely Spanish-speaking regiment arrived in Pusan it had been reassembled from Hispanic Puerto Ricans, black Virgin Islanders, and Japanese and black Americans. Most of its officers were southern whites. Still understrength, it was filled in further with Koreans who spoke no English, then sent into action with the Eighth Army. MacArthur claimed to need whatever units he could field, but the efficiency of the motley regiment was as low as its morale.

New arrivals encountered the poor example of ROK troops whose homeland they were there to rescue. Marginally trained and poorly motivated draftees, the ROKs referred to themselves as *Han-gook-in,* "men of the country called Han." To exasperated Americans who saw them as a lesser breed of human they were just "gooks," whose running away from their war often put EUSAK in jeopardy. When E Company of Corley's 3rd Battalion tried to stop an ROK outfit on the American flank from abandoning its weapons and fleeing, Lieutenant Charles Ellis, E Company's black acting commander, "went down to the Korean captain who was in charge." As Ellis told the Army Inspector General's investigator on September 15, he "asked him why he was pulling out of position. He said: 'Enemy was coming.' I said you cannot fight them if you run. The officer [then] tried to pull his men back into position, but they killed him and continued to run."

Another West Point '49er, Cecil Newman, had been sent to the under-strength 1st Cavalry Division as a company commander, defending Hill 303 (hill designations were their heights in meters) overlooking the Naktong near Waegwan. As an enlisted man he had survived infantry combat in France. In Korea, Newman was gone in a week. Wounded in both legs but alive, Swett lasted a week longer before being evacuated. Corley said he was sorry that he hadn't had a chance to teach him more.

Two days after MacArthur's exhortation to the 25th Division to give up no more ground, delivered for him by Johnny Walker at Sangju, General Hobart Gay ordered his troops to withdraw to positions three miles east of the town. That was not quite what MacArthur had in mind, but he was unavailable. (He had flown that morning to Formosa with an entourage requiring two planes.) On the Kumchon front, other units of the 1st Cavalry, abandoning their heavy equipment, loaded into trucks and moved farther to the rear.

Although MacArthur had nothing to show for the first month of inter-vention but one reverse after another, he had succeeded in drawing the United States into a commitment in Korea that he was sure would eventually turn the tide of war—provided neither the Russians nor the Chinese inter-vened in force and his own troops kept a bridgehead. To deter the Chinese from Korea he lobbied strenuously to have Mao distracted by Chiang in For-mosa. To MacArthur, Formosa would be an essential military base and man-power supplier for the war in Korea, and a hostage in U.S. domestic politics for continued Republican support of the war.

Within the Truman administration there was little support for utilizing Chiang. On July 28, Secretary of Defense Louis Johnson, technically a Democrat but philosophically a Republican, proposed "unleashing" the Nationalists to mine waters between Formosa and the mainland, and to attack Communist troop concentrations onshore. The JCS liked anything that relieved the pressure on MacArthur in Korea, and were ready to approve the proposal—until Acheson persuaded Truman that the United States was fishing for trouble. The compromise solution had been to send a survey team to Formosa to determine what further "defensive measures" might be taken to safeguard the island. Taking that as authorization to see for himself, MacArthur announced on July 31, just after returning from his confrontation with Walker, that he himself would preside over the survey.

Intimidated yet again, the JCS weakly suggested that he send a deputy, but conceded, "Please feel free to go, since the responsibility is yours." The license implied was not lost on MacArthur, who flew off almost immediately, before anyone in Washington foreclosed his opening to Chiang. A month earlier he had been ordered to refer any "proffer of troops" to the State Department, so he included in his entourage no diplomatic representatives and claimed no "political implications" for his visit, although his presence alone was transparently political.

MacArthur arrived in Formosa like a head of state, with a personal party of twenty plus a flock of reporters, aides and secretaries in two headquarters planes. With him were his wife, Jean; General Almond; Vice Admiral C. Turner Joy, commander of naval forces in the Far East; General Willoughby; General Stratemeyer; and General Alonzo P. Fox, Almond's deputy chief of staff. Almost no one of any importance at the Dai Ichi was left behind. While crowds of delighted spectators watched the arrival, six F-80 Shooting Star jets flown over from the Philippines streaked across Taipei.

For two days the general and his top brass closeted themselves with the generalissimo, whom MacArthur described in an airport welcome as "my comrade-in-arms of the last war," although they had never before met. He praised Chiang's "indomitable determination to resist Communist domination," and on departure declared that "arrangements have been completed for effective coordination between American forces under my command and those of the Chinese government." *Time,* a highly visible media backer of every MacArthur move, quoted a "reliable source" in Tokyo—almost certainly General Whitney, who often wrote and spoke for MacArthur—that there was no reason to fight in Korea unless the United States also had the resolve to fight Communism "wherever it arose in Asia." Anything less, would "invite Communism to sweep over all of Asia."

Despite the alleged surrender of "responsibility" by the JCS, MacArthur had no authority to embrace the generalissimo politically, yet he had, as intended, undermined any covert efforts to replace Chiang. Unhappily, Truman on August 4 issued a statement that he alone as commander in chief determined how American military force was employed, and that "the most vital national interest requires that no action of ours precipitates general war or gives excuse to others to do so."

Having mischievously tested his powers, MacArthur responded that he understood "thoroughly" what his limitations were as theater commander, "and you need have no anxiety that I will in any way exceed them." He fully recognized, he said insultingly, Truman's determination "to protect the Communist mainland." Truman wondered who was President and began thinking of sacking MacArthur. Yet any semblance of a bipartisan wartime foreign policy required at least the illusion that it was MacArthur's war.

To soften the obvious estrangement between the White House and the Dai Ichi, a military aid appropriations request would soon go to Congress, defusing, Truman hoped, any allegations that he had failed Chiang. However, the generalissimo remained forbidden to attack the mainland, and what MacArthur labeled his "prompt and generous" offer of troops for Korea remained on hold, where Truman wanted to keep it.

Also unwelcome was the return of the Soviet Union to the Security Council. Stalin's boycott had made Korean intervention possible. Although Korea had the effect of weakening the American presence in Europe, the Soviets wanted their abdicated UN spoiler role back. In what was no coincidence, Jacob Malik resumed his council seat on August 2, the day that the rotation of the chair put the Soviets into it. Acheson discussed the matter with Truman inconclusively. All they knew was that Stalin was up to no good.

On the same day, while MacArthur was in Taipei, a conference of Communist military bigwigs—the Revolutionary Military Committee—was hurriedly convened in Beijing. Although General Su Yu, deputy commander of the Third Army and proposed commander for the invasion of Formosa, was present, the timing was very likely unrelated to MacArthur's visit to Chiang. General Peng Dehuai was to deliver a report on invasion preparations as of July 30, in the Hall of Longevity, a pavilion in the Park of Fruitful Bounty. Advance copies were made available to the delegates.

Peng first dealt with the situation as it was, including the shielding of Formosa by the American Seventh Fleet. (A cruiser and a few destroyers, the fleet was more symbol than reality.) Peng, fifty-two and the second man in the military hierarchy, contended that when the Korean affair was wound up, which he hoped would be soon, the shadow threat of the fleet would be withdrawn. More troubling, he contended, was that China was totally unready in both shipping and amphibious training to mount an invasion, and lacked airpower to support such an operation.

Korea, the conferees realized, could upset even a much-delayed timetable to take Formosa. After the winter to come, and more propitious invasion conditions, would China be involved, instead, across the Yalu? "If we can't send troops to Korea," Mao challenged, "the reactionary forces in the world will become bolder."

"I say we'll need four months to move a sizeable army into Korea," said General Ye Jianying. "The Chairman thinks we can do it in three weeks."

"It will take longer than three weeks," said Peng.

"What's come over the army?" Mao questioned. "Are we recruiting tortoises?"

"It's more complicated than in the old days," Peng explained. An opposed water crossing was far different from a trek across the hills and valleys of the mainland.

The issue of Korea required a follow-up session the next day, in the Hall for the Consummation of the Martial Arts, built four hundred years earlier by a Ming emperor. In the chair was General Zhu De, at sixty-four the commander in chief of the People's Liberation Army. Again it was an intensely hot day, and the participants had trouble concealing their irritability. General Nie Rongzhen, commander of the North China Field Army and the closest military leader to Korea, opened with a briefing reminding listeners of the official line that the war was a defensive response to an unprovoked South Korean attack. His information about the situation now, he noted, had come from Colonel Xu Lixu, the military attaché in Pyongyang, where a Chinese embassy had opened only eleven days before. The past lack of interest suggested Red China's view of North Korea as a Soviet client state.

Colonel Xu reported two matters that General Nie found disturbing. (Had he known them, General MacArthur might have taken comfort in both.) First, the NKPA "counterattack" had slowed almost to nothing. The war was in its sixth week, once considered all the time needed for victory. Second—and he opened another file folder—NKPA losses in men and materiel were high and likely to grow much higher. Communication with the fronts was slow and inefficient. The casualty totals could get much worse. American air attacks on the lengthening supply routes were costly. Losses in transit of equipment and supplies were greater than losses in combat. Even worse were the losses in men—more than 40 percent casualties. Fifty thousand had been killed and wounded, Xu reminded the generals. North Korea could not sustain such attrition; the United States, on the other hand, was populous and productive, and could bleed North Korea into submission even without regaining lost South Korean territory.

Contingency plans, Zhu De urged, were needed in case the battlefront situation deteriorated. Questions arose about whether the Americans might use atomic bombs, and even why China should be involved at all. General Nie reminded the others that Korea abutted upon northeast China and could not be ignored.

"Well, I ask you," Mao proposed, exasperated by the continuing discussion, "are we to take this threat sitting down?"

Su Yu wondered if the problem was only that the NKPA was falling behind schedule or whether the Americans could reinforce the Pusan Perimeter to the point of successful counterattack. "It should be evident," General Nie interrupted, "that the imperialists and their puppets must be driven into the sea before the [North] Korean People's Army finds itself in a prolonged attritional struggle."

An aide interrupted with a bulletin, which he handed to Nie. The NKPA, Nie read, was planning an offensive beginning on August 5 against the southwestern bulge of the Naktong. A murmur of relief spread through the conference room.

If the "stay and die" order, as American troops interpreted it, was grim news, there was better shortly to come. On the afternoon of August 2 the 1st Provisional Marine Brigade, largely troops of the 5th Marines, a regiment of the 1st Marine Division being bulked up across the Pacific for the amphibious operation in planning, entered Pusan harbor. More enthusiastically than accurately, a Korean band on the dock played "The Marine Corps Hymn."

As darkness settled on the port area, four thousand Marines debarked under searchlights, then filed back in some confusion for a shipboard meal. The next morning they left by truck for the forty-mile jolt (there were no paved roads) west to Masan, only seven miles from enemy lines. Stifling dust turned their fresh fatigue uniforms gray.

At Changwon they encamped for a second night in Korea, restless with tension and uncomfortable in the fetid atmosphere. After ten, a shot rang out, very likely accidental, but jittery Marines seized rifles and fired into the darkness. Machine guns went into action. Two Marines were killed and others wounded, one from mistaken identity when challenged. It took five hours to restore calm. Four reporters, three whites (including Ed Murrow) and a black, were also challenged in the darkness, and Murrow was marched off with a gun to his back by what appeared to him to be a raw seventeen-year-old. At a command post, a captain recognized Murrow's radio voice.

"These kids were shooting each other up," veteran CBS radio correspondent Bill Dunn recalled. "Anything that moved they took a shot at. I was disgusted. Jesus, I thought, if these guys are going to fight our war for us, we might as well quit now. Do you know, they went into combat in a few days . . . and the minute they were in combat, they became terrific; they knew what they were doing. But . . . that night I wouldn't have given you ten cents for the whole United States Marine Corps."

With few exceptions, American troops had given the NKPA no cause for alarm, although the timetable for pushing through to Pusan had been upset. MacArthur could have congratulated himself that he had indeed traded space for time, and that his piecemeal employment into combat of companies, battalions, regiments and divisions, as soon as he could get them, and in whatever condition, had paid off. Yet he owed much to the greed of Kim Il Sung and his advisers, who had been trading time for space, detouring south and west to grab thinly defended provinces in which they were held off, if at all, by national police and ill-equipped home guards. Halted five miles short of Masan because two battered American divisions had time to bolster each other, General Kim Chaek of the 6th NKPA Division withdrew to regroup.

An assault on Pusan was still planned, directed through Korea's southern underbelly via Chinju and Masan, but the Americans had shown in costly if indecisive counterattacks protecting Taegu in the north of the Perimeter from the NKPA 3rd and 4th Divisions that victory for Kim Il Sung would not come that way. To make that point clear to his less aggressive generals, Walton Walker had told one of them not to return from the front again unless it was in a coffin. To MacArthur he reported that the 24th Division was no longer capable of fighting and needed rehabilitation in reserve, and that he had equally grave doubts about the 25th Division.

General Kim recognized the depleted state of the defenders after the NKPA 6th Division bent but did not break under counterattacks in the west, and regained what it had lost. Displaying renewed confidence, Kim issued a challenge to his troops just as the Marines were digging in. "Comrades," he declared, "the enemy is demoralized. The task given to us is the liberation of Masan and Chinju and the annihilation of the remnants of the enemy." Now, Kim exhorted, was the time "to cut off the windpipe" of the Americans.

His goal looked possible. Even where the last bridges across the wide, muddy, swirling Naktong were being blown, the thousands of bundle-burdened refugees herded across to theoretical safety—often used by the NKPA as human shields—were a continuing problem. Without food, shelter and a future, they were an additional logistical burden to EUSAK, and clogging the unpaved excuses for roads, they impeded redisposition of troops, tanks and artillery. Yet loudspeakers from Psychological Warfare, mounted on jeeps, tanks and trucks, urged villagers across so that the places in which they had lived for centuries could be bombed and shelled into rubble. No cover was to be left for the invaders.

While the center held, the eastern sector again began to sag under assaults from the NKPA 8th and 12th Divisions. Its 5th Division outflanked an ROK force in the 1st Cavalry area, putting in jeopardy P-51 operations out of the airfield at Yonil, below Pohang on the eastern coast. While the Americans remained, as always, road-bound, the North Koreans were able to move across mountainous terrain with whatever small arms they could carry on their backs, even machine guns and sections of artillery pieces. By August 11 they were at the railway yards at Pohang, and General Earle Partridge, not waiting for approval from MacArthur, who had once declared that he would fight to hold Yonil, withdrew his Fifth Air Force planes all the way to Kyushu.

Ed Murrow, soon to resume his home-based broadcasts, saw the abandoned airstrip, evacuated after American forces had disregarded warnings of an attack from the north. The runway was inoperable, and some of the reinforcements rushed belatedly to the scene already lay buried nearby. He was appalled by the incompetence that squandered courage.

With the airfield now within artillery range, flying time, now from Japan, went from minutes to hours, and in using up precious fuel merely to cross to Korea, the Mustangs could afford little time in ground support before breaking off to return.

To rescue the ROK 3rd Division, Walker on August 15 called in the Navy, which sent Task Force 77, including two carriers, to bombard the coast while a destroyer led four LSTs in an evacuation which continued into the morning of August 17. The hills were pounded until they were stripped of trees and denuded of dug-in North Koreans from Yongdok south almost to Pohang. There the 1st Cavalry had first come ashore without opposition on July 18. Villages along the coast were now reduced to rubble. Since the area neutralized was shallow, the South Koreans were evacuated hurriedly into landing craft, abandoning much of the equipment the Americans had supplied. (So much materiel was being furnished to the enemy by default that the NKPA had begun counting on that factor to mount their war.) Still, 5,800 troops were extricated, 1,200 refugees, the American liaison group and some light vehicles. Offloaded farther south, the ROKs were sent back into action, yet the ostensibly successful withdrawal did more than underline the unreliability of South Korean troops and command failures of American leadership; it foreshadowed to some the ultimate Dunkirk—Pusan.

Despite the continuing incapacity and low morale of South Korean troops, Syngman Rhee maintained a show of confidence in his communications with MacArthur. Even as the ROK 3rd Division was on the verge of destruction and American divisions continued to falter, Rhee wrote to the general about the "grand job" being accomplished by UN forces. "We have inflicted heavy losses on the enemy," he wrote with some accuracy, and "captured large quantities of their weapons," he invented. With more truth he worried about whether Taegu or even Pusan could be held long enough for "American reinforcements . . . to launch an offensive." Although he saw the enemy losing "its advantage of superior weapons," he blamed the continuing losses of ground on its "unlimited manpower resources" and a "ruthless" recruiting system that had even "forced small boys to fight." South Korea had begun with far more potential soldiery than the North, but desertion, capture and loss of population centers—none of which Rhee mentioned—had depleted ROK potential. Rather, he blamed NKPA "tactics of forcing whole town populations to fight for them. . . . In some places, for example, young school boys, some 13 or 14 years old, march to the front while Russian or North Korean officers keep them at gun point. Another example is the fact that we have found the drivers of Russian-made tanks wired to their seats so that they will fight to the death."

In the Yechon sector, he alleged, somewhat more believably, Communist troops forced schoolchildren "to line up in front of them," prompting American and South Korean troops to declare helplessly, "We cannot shoot them." MacArthur had heard Rhee's propaganda before, and knew that the hostage factor was true and that the Korean president was not advocating similar savagery. Rather, Rhee wanted more South Koreans armed, especially potential "guerrilla fighters" in land lost to the enemy. However, whatever side of the line the South Koreans were on, MacArthur realized, their arms would soon be in enemy hands.

Rhee also knew his audience when he moved on to examine Russia's role in the war. The Soviets would not back down "to avoid World War Three," he felt. Russia "will not and cannot stop until she is stopped." The United Nations "should prepare to deal a much heavier blow to remove Soviet influence from Korea." He wanted "firm bases of operation established on the eastern side of the Manchurian border" to provide "great advantage over the enemy when the global conflict begins." Rhee was looking forward to a third world war if it took that to liberate all of Korea. Rhee worried about less war rather than more, anticipating to MacArthur that the UN might sponsor a negotiated settlement to end the war at South Korean expense. Rhee would agree to nothing to which his government had not had a role in mediating. Despite the belligerent tone, he was appealing to MacArthur's militant anti-Communism to forestall a sellout.

Frustrated by the single telephone line from Taegu to get his voice recorded for CBS radio, and by the "communiqué commandos" in Tokyo, Murrow planned to leave in mid-August via Japan. Dai Ichi press relations people spun optimistic accounts for MacArthur and had begun enforcing a headquarters ruling that "unwarranted criticism" of command judgment would earn a ticket home. Murrow intended to get in a last lick. Possibly reflecting MacArthur's own exasperation with the way the war was reported, rumor had it that he had pressured CBS to recall Murrow, for his last broadcast from the field ended with "Correspondents are not supposed to criticize command decisions, but there are responsible officers out here who doubt that we can afford the luxury of attacking in the south when we are so thin on the ground in the northern and central sectors of the front. In spite of our offensive at the bottom of the peninsula, we are still engaged in a desperate defensive action. If we lose the airfields in the north and the center, much of our power, offensive *and* defensive, will go with them."

From a Tokyo studio on Tuesday, August 15, Murrow made his final transmission from the Far East, intending to follow up Bill Lawrence's page-one account in *The New York Times* criticizing the implicit censorship. Murrow had already been sharp about command failures in his last report from Korea, and had got away with it. Now he began, "This is a most difficult broadcast to do. I have never believed that correspondents who move in and out of the battle area, engage in privileged conversations with commanders and with troops, and who have access to a public platform, should engage in criticism of command decisions, or of commanders, while the battle is in progress. However it is now time to cast up an account of the past ten days. For the question arises whether serious mistakes have been made."

Murrow targeted misconceived operations on both ends of the Perimeter. The Eighth Army and 5th Marines "were committed to that push along the southern end of the peninsula to secure the high ground east of Chinju."

(Chinju is as far west of Masan as it is west of Pusan.) "Experienced officers, some of them wearing stars, called it folly. . . . This was not a decision forced upon us by the enemy. Our high command took it because, in the words of one officer who was in a position to know, 'We decided we needed a victory.' "

Pulling no punches, although he named no names, he was referring to the only "high command" there was—the desk commandos in the Dai Ichi. The botched operations were both Task Force Kean's failed counteroffensive in the southwest against the veteran China-blooded 6th Korean People's Division and the bungled defense of the east coast that had led to the costly evacuation above Pohang. In most sectors, Americans, with some Koreans, were now employing more men and artillery than the NKPA, as well as preponderant airpower, yet were unable to hold their ground. Numbers meant nothing, however, when West fought East. The U.S. employed huge quantities of troops in rear support and service functions, thinning out at the front, while the North Koreans, in sandals or sneakers, had few soldiers who did not fight. And North Korean willingness to die was worth extra divisions. Americans still told themselves that they'd be home by Christmas.

Laying out South Korean geography for his listeners' mental map, Murrow explained that in the north the Naktong River defenses weakened as one reached the east coast. Yet, with increasing reinforcements, "For the first time we had power—could hold it in reserve, strengthen the river line, or plug the gaps. . . ." However, "The general commanding the right end of the line up on the east coast . . . replied that the situation was well in hand." Almost certainly Murrow meant the 1st Cavalry's General Gay, who had ignored reports that the North Koreans were coming down behind the hills that protected them from naval gunfire. A relief force sent too late, and in darkness, was ambushed and the airfield under attack rendered useless. "We aren't flying anything from there now. . . . That was one price we paid for the southern offensive. Today a spokesman in general headquarters denied that we had underestimated the enemy strength in the north."

Murrow was broadcasting from Tokyo, where there was only one "general headquarters."

"You will find," Murrow continued sadly, "battle-wise men out in Korea —some with stars and others with sergeant's stripes—who have fought Germans, Japanese, Italians, and North Koreans, who maintain we have gained nothing by this southern offensive and meanwhile have lost that vital airstrip and endangered the center of the line. . . . I met no officer in Korea who believes that we can mount an effective offensive with our present strength."

His informants suggested that it would take eight American divisions, "and after that about six months of hard fighting to see this thing done, assuming that the Chinese Communist troops and Russian air [force] do not join the battle. And yet correspondents here have received cables from their home offices indicating that air-conditioned sources in Washington think the thing can be wound up this fall. To paraphrase the GIs in Korea—that ain't the way it looks from here."

Murrow was not criticizing why the war in Korea was being fought, but how it was being managed and explained. To do that, he conceded, he might have violated directives "from general headquarters" in identifying command failures and in quoting officers on the scene. Then, after predicting that despite the issues he had targeted "we shall stay on that peninsula," he raised further problems that went to the heart of intervention in Korea. He wondered how dispossessed and despairing Koreans moving back after the war to "villages to which we have put the torch by retreating" would view "the attraction of Communism." He questioned whether it was necessary to scorch and burn all that the people we were rescuing had, turning them into beggars and refugees who might then hate the Americans for doing that only to preserve corrupt and authoritarian regimes which happened not to be Communist.

Communist propaganda, a psychological warfare officer had told him, had "made headway." We had to tell the people "what they can look forward to when we have won the war. And then drop that statement in leaflet form on top of them." And, Murrow closed, "a correspondent who shall be nameless" declared, "That will take quite a bit of writing and, when the pamphlet is done, we should drop some on the American people, too."

Possibly the toughest broadcast Murrow had ever made, its text, reduced to teletype, was rushed through CBS offices in New York to news editors, the corporate attorney and the top executives, Frank Stanton and William Paley. On the telephone to Tokyo, Stanton told Murrow that if he insisted on broadcasting his piece, he would have to do it "as a private citizen." It would, allegedly, give comfort to the enemy, and could be used as propaganda by Radio Moscow. Murrow was scrubbed from his own show.

Murrow did not go public. However, the decision leaked out, and the seven hundred correspondents of the Overseas Press Club cabled a protest to MacArthur. It would take more than a month before the story emerged in *Newsweek*. Meanwhile, Murrow remained outspoken. On his first return broadcast he charged that the West, by omission and commission, had handed the Communists the opportunity to capture, and channel, "the surging desire for change, the resentment of foreign domination" and "the language of Asia's aspirations." It was clear to those who didn't merely read the Moscow line into Murrow's words that he was questioning, as would Asians, MacArthur's trumpeted visit to the discredited Chiang and the war to restore the unpopular Rhee. "Korea," Murrow wrote to a colleague, "was just plain hell and convinced me that I have become an old man."

It was easy to become an old man quickly in Korea that August. A medical evac in mid-July, Lieutenant Carl Bernard was back a month later to observe another screwup. A platoon along the Naktong had blundered into a minefield. One soldier had been mortally wounded; another, trying to get to him, had set off another mine and lay wounded under sniper fire. The survivors of the patrol retreated back to Love Company, where Bernard was exec. He yelled at them for abandoning their comrades and insisted they return with him. In the distance they could see one man moving. "If this is a regular field," he explained, "the mines will be laid in a staggered pattern. In other words, if you move in a straight line, chances are you'll set off only one mine. Now I'm going to walk straight toward that wounded man; if a mine goes off, you'll be able to follow okay on that same line."

He took off his boots and most of his clothes. In bare feet, he hoped, he could feel any hidden tripwires. As the others watched nervously, he made it across to the wounded GI and slung him across his shoulders. Shots exploded from the village across the field. Bernard put down the wounded man, unslung his carbine and returned the fire. It became quiet again. Picking up the soldier, he made his way back.

"Let's get out of here, Lieutenant," an infantryman said. Bernard chewed him out. "What are you talking about? You don't think we're going to leave that dead man just lying there, do you?"

Back he went, and carried the body out; then he called for a litter jeep, which never came. They found a Korean farmer who had a wheelbarrow. Bernard gave him his gold Longines wristwatch, won in a shipboard poker game en route to Japan, and a note asking the first American unit the farmer came across to take care of the casualty. (The wounded sergeant was in Pusan on August 8. The farmer went to the coast and got him down on a fishing boat.) With his boots back on, Bernard managed to get back to his command post with the rest of his squad. There, as Lieutenant Maihafer watched awkwardly, the tension drained from Bernard and he began to sob, more and more violently. "Damn it all, Harry," he cried, "why do I have to get this way? Why can't I keep hold of myself and be like the rest of you guys?"

Maihafer found Bernard's "Love Company Rear" was a cluster of huts at the base of a mountain where "six or eight Americans" were loading rations on the A-frame racks carried by Korean bearers high on their shoulders. With the Koreans they trudged up the trail from which they could see the Naktong "flowing serenely several hundred feet below us." The men were a "lean, scruffy bunch," one of whom—a teenage rifleman—called himself Ole John E. Between burrowing "in below grade" to avoid shrapnel from mortar bursts and crawling out of his shelter-half in the pine forest in the rain to relieve his dysentery "twenty one times one night," John E. "didn't have enough sense to be real scared, just a whole bunch confused . . . , especially when I would hear that 'so and so' died during the night from enemy fire. Or that we could expect a lot worse in the nights to come as the [North] Koreans especially seem to attack . . . during the hours of darkness."

Below the Naktong in the west, the 5th Marines had a psychological value beyond their military usefulness. They attempted to live up to their reputation. At Camp Pendleton in California, as they embarked, the commandant allegedly sent the brigade off with "You boys clear this up in a couple of months, or I'll be over there to see you!" It hadn't proved to be that easy. They were fighting disciplined, experienced North Koreans, and had to gain discipline and experience the hard way themselves. Pfc. Arnold Winter discovered quickly how to prepare a foxhole under fire. "I learned to dig a foxhole like you wouldn't believe. I'd dig, and when I'd hear a shell coming in I'd put what part of my body I could in the hole, to save that part. I kept digging, through rocks and roots and everything, until I had a hole big enough to get my entire body in. I could feel the hot wind each time a shell landed close by."

The Marines sent out patrols to draw fire, and once enemy positions were exposed, Marine Corsairs would be summoned by radio to drop napalm, and artillery would follow up. When a Corsair, called in after men had been hit, dropped a five-hundred-pound bomb right in front of their position, Winter remembered, "My ears came out of my head. . . . They were ringing like sirens." Often, the going was "straight uphill. No cover." But he refused to concede that any bravery was involved. "There was the fear of disobeying an order. In the Marines, even an order from a corporal is like an order from a general. . . . And there was also the fear of letting your buddies down. There's an almost unbelievable loyalty among men in a rifle company."

Claiming to be desperate for more troops on grounds that he would soon have to withdraw the Marines to rejoin their division, MacArthur pressed the British to make good their offer of an infantry force. What he wanted much more than their numbers was the appearance of a multi-nation effort, and he preferred troops that spoke English and created no communications problems. When Air Vice Marshal Cecil Bouchier arrived in Tokyo to consult about a British ground force—Commonwealth naval forces were already in action and Australian planes had been flying since the first days of the war—he knew what to expect. On August 10 he reported to the Ministry of Defence in London, "MacArthur's first question was how soon will [the] British brigade go into Korea. I said my personal impression was that the earliest it could arrive was four months time. He said the urgent requirement for now and the immediate future was to get more men into Korea with rifles. At present they are flying in from America five hundred troops a day by chartered four-engined civil aircraft. . . . Gist of his off-the-record remarks was that a little got in fast was better than a lot later."

There were further discussions between General Bradley and British military liaison at the embassy in Washington, notably retired Royal Air Force Air Marshal Lord Tedder. To London, Tedder cabled that "stemming present attack" was crucial for "they are still dangerously thin on the ground," although "they have denuded Okinawa, Hawaii, Puerto Rico and Panama of their garrisons." And he quoted Bradley that "a platoon now would be worth more than a company tomorrow."

With some misgivings—the Ministry of Defence did not trust MacArthur's willfulness—London ordered the 27th Brigade shipped from Hong Kong as the first element in a Commonwealth division, the news arriving in the colony late on August 18, a Friday. Operation Graduate was to be continued with the 29th Brigade and an Australian battalion. The first unit would sail from Hong Kong on August 23, piped out by the band of the King's Own Scottish Borderers.

The brigade docked in Pusan just as the NKPA struck across the bulge of the lower Naktong in the west, above Masan. Harried as usual, Walker failed to meet the senior staff of the brigade, flown into Taegu separately. Apologizing, he told Brigadier Basil Coad, "I want you to know that if you have any difficulties you can get to see me at any time." It would not be that easy. The brigade was to be "looked after" by the 24th Division, but would not go into action until furnished with and trained to use the new 3.5-inch anti-tank rocket launcher which was replacing the useless 2.36-inch bazooka of World War II vintage. When the NKPA forced crossings of the upper Naktong in the hills above Taegu on September 2, Walker abandoned his promise of training and acclimatizing the 27th Brigade and hurried it to the Naktong line on September 4, on the left

flank of the 1st Cavalry, just west of Taegu. The British were still without vehicles, which were to come north from Pusan on flatcars. Shunted off on a siding
to give priority to another train, the equipment remained unavailable.

Lieutenant Geoffrey Norton of the Middlesexers was sent to retrieve the
vehicles, which he discovered had given way to a trainload of eight large ice
cream machines. Coad, now under General Gay and the Cav, found no one
really in charge, with impulsive judgments—one had already switched his sector—resulting in frequent changes of orders. He discovered that MacArthur,
while determining to keep the 1st Cavalry in Japan for occupation duties, had
transferred 750 noncoms from it as replacements for the battered 24th and
25th Divisions. The Cavalry's own corporals and sergeants were often green
replacements. "With very few exceptions," Coad would tell Anthony Farrar-
Hockley, who arrived later as a captain in the 29th Brigade, "the American
staff officers never leave their HQs, even to visit lower formation HQs [closer
to the line], and never in our experience did any staff officer come to look at
any [of our] ground." Higher-ups, however, were very interested in cultivating
the press, "who, in spite of the urgency of the situation, stopped us to take
photographs and then crowded into the Command Post to hear the general's
orders." The brigade's transport finally arrived on September 8.

From late August into early September, Walker also received, via the port of
Bremerton, Washington, Major General Lawrence Keiser's 2nd Infantry Division and more than five hundred Pershing and Sherman tanks, which could
handle the enemy T-34s. The 2nd also brought ashore new motorized anti-
aircraft firing vehicles, although the enemy had few planes to fly troop support.
At an encounter at the bulge of the Naktong, twins from Maryland, Richard
and Vincent Kreps, landed on August 14, lost a half-track to a T-34 and a light
tank to an enemy roadblock. Their stalled anti-aircraft vehicle proved to be a
roadblock of its own. Vincent crawled through enemy fire to the abandoned
gun and got the engine going. Driving boldly through an NKPA position to his
own line, he rejoined the fight and helped drive the North Koreans off.

Regaining lost territory meant confronting the costs of being captured.
Typically, the twins found men from the 2nd, as new to Korea as they were,
wrists tied behind their backs and executed. Encountering each other again
at nearly three in the morning after two weeks off the USS *General Mitchell,*
the Kreps twins, glad to be alive, "forgot about sleeping."

Although MacArthur and Walker kept clamoring for more troops, they
now had almost too many for the crowded Perimeter. As more units and more
materiel arrived, and both Pusan and Japanese ports teemed with resupply

shipments and preparations for the barely secret new operation, MacArthur did more adjudication of forces from the Dai Ichi. Earlier he had assured Stratemeyer and Partridge that they could run their own show, but he stepped in to demand more ground support in place of strategic bombing. In the short run it wouldn't do much to save the Perimeter. On August 14, MacArthur directed B-29s, hardly troop-support aircraft, to dump bombs on enemy positions north of Waegwan for saturation bombing, and on August 16, B-29s hit an alleged troop assembly area with a thousand tons of explosives from ten thousand feet. Later, intelligence could find no evidence that a single North Korean soldier had been killed, and prisoners taken in September declared that none of their units were in the target area at the time. When MacArthur asked for even more carpet bombing—likely only to waste bombs and destroy villages—Stratemeyer persuaded him to go after more definable targets. Had Ed Murrow known of it he would have felt his parting tirade justified.

No bombardments from the air seemed useful anywhere along the front to deter the North Koreans intent on Pusan. The *In Min Gun* knew how to dig in and reappear in places which conventional-thinking Americans assumed were inaccessible to masses of troops. Yet NKPA bridgeheads across the Naktong were eliminated after punishing fighting on both sides. In the east at Pohang and Yongchon the threat to Pusan subsided when the 24th Division, in poor shape and in reserve to regroup, was called back to help. Walker's forces, once too thin to resist the North Koreans, had swelled (with support troops) to 180,000 men, twice that of the enemy, with five times as many serviceable tanks and command of the skies.

The NKPA had long and difficult supply lines, interdicted by day from the air, and had to resupply troops at night, often by primitive means. Yet Walker seemed unable to break out of the Perimeter. Running the war by remote control from Tokyo, MacArthur could not see why.

The Marines in the southwest continued to operate out of the "Bean Patch," a large field near Masan, but began seeing their heavy equipment disappearing in the direction of Pusan, to be reloaded on ships in the harbor, now one of the busiest ports in the Far East. The Marines themselves would be "quietly pulled off the line," Pfc. Winter recalled. "We weren't told anything, but one thing we knew, we weren't going home."

Operation Chromite

MACARTHUR'S PACIFIC WAR strategy from 1942 to victory had been predicated on "leapfrogging" amphibious operations which outflanked and bypassed enemy strongpoints like Truk in the Carolines and Rabaul, just to the east of New Guinea, on the crescent of New Britain. Now, while he threw in reinforcements to save the Pusan foothold, he was planning a breakout that would be coordinated with a landing in force to isolate Seoul from the north. Inchon, on the west coast of Korea just above the lost capital, looked right for an outflanking operation. Concerned aides offered other options on both coasts. Inchon was hazardous. Deep tidal shifts, a narrow channel, broad mudflats and fortified offshore islands made the harbor an unlikely invasion route.

To MacArthur, that was the attraction of Inchon. It would not be anticipated. Further, the only barrier to Seoul beyond Inchon was the Han River, and engineers could cope with that crossing. He dismissed concerns that he courted catastrophe and ordered a plan developed to send Force X on Operation Chromite—the name from an oxide of iron and chromium. No chemist, MacArthur might have been attracted to the symbolism the word suggested, as it combined iron with a steely element known for its luster. He intended it to be his most lustrous achievement.

His island-hopping years from New Guinea to the Philippines had made MacArthur a believer in amphibious operations. Even before Korea, he had brought in Rear Admiral James H. Doyle, who had learned his trade in the central Pacific under Admiral Richmond Kelly Turner, to talk to headquarters people in the Dai Ichi about what MacArthur called "amphibian" war-fare. Many of his replacement officers had served in Europe after D-Day and had no such field experience. Surprised, on a prewar trip, to find Doyle in Tokyo, General Bradley and Secretary Johnson asked the admiral what he was doing there. Bradley "simply looked scornful" when Doyle explained. Appearing before the House Armed Services Committee in October 1949, Bradley had predicted that "large-scale amphibious operations" were an anachronism in a world where wars would be decided by rockets, nuclear bombs and the like—"never [to] occur again." Later, in MacArthur's office with Vice Admiral C. Turner Joy, Doyle mentioned the JCS chief's reaction. "Bradley," said MacArthur, "is a farmer."

Operation Bluehearts, MacArthur's first code name for the risky flanking operation he had rechristened Chromite, was not wishful thinking. As early as July 2 he had asked the Pentagon for men who could operate landing craft and for a Marine regimental combat team. Someone had leaked his interest, for on July 3 a *New York Herald Tribune* column under David Lawrence's byline reported that although MacArthur had no "trained amphibious forces," the Marines at San Diego were "all packed up and ready to sail . . . as reinforcements for MacArthur's troops." Lawrence had seen no orders acti-vating ships "mothballed" in 1946, but assumed as much, as it took "weeks —not days—to transport men and supplies across the Pacific." It should have alerted Moscow if not North Korea.

The next day MacArthur would convene a study group, including Admiral Doyle, to consider an amphibious counterstroke using the 1st Cav-alry Division—conventional infantry despite the historic name, and avail-able to him in Japan. MacArthur proposed Inchon, which was close to Seoul. The day before he had requested 1,200 amphibious engineer troops from the Pentagon to back up a large shopping list for "planned operations from 20 July to 10 August." He had thirty LSTs on loan to the Japanese government for interisland shipping, and asked Doyle to supervise rehabilitating them for Bluehearts. The operation seemed premature as well as risky in the extreme. Still, MacArthur thought that he could improvise a landing as early as July 22 and assigned his G-3 section to work out the details.

Planners with connections in General Charles Bolté's G-3 shop in the Pentagon claimed later that among the many contingency papers circulating even before the war was an operation predicated upon a North Korean inva-sion below the 38th parallel. An amphibious counterstroke at Inchon would land a force behind the enemy which, the plan assumed, had already captured Seoul. The contingency plan should have been no surprise to the Joint Chiefs. Although they might not have been familiar with thinking emanating from the lower levels of the Pentagon, one or two of the Chiefs might have recalled Inchon from studies made late in 1944. Among alternatives to end the war with Japan had been landings on Formosa, the Chinese coast itself, Korea (at Inchon) and Kyushu. "Operations against Japan subsequent to Formosa," JCS 924 dated June 30, 1944—before MacArthur's invasion of the Philippines and early in the planning for the end-of-war amphibious assaults—had included Korea as Appendix B. Among the seaborne alternatives for the outflanking and isolation of Japan was Jinsen, or Inchon. However, an advisory to the President from the Joint Staff Planners (JCS 1388) had warned of "the paucity of good beaches and exits therefrom," and "the rugged terrain back of the beaches."

Korea's proximity to the easternmost edge of Siberia made the Inchon location, even for an immediately postwar "administrative landing," insurance for an American presence above Seoul and in the part of the peninsula closest to Japan. Doyle had been Richmond Kelly Turner's operations officer in the final months of World War II, and, like MacArthur, privy to amphibious alternatives refloated in 1950. Without such detailed earlier data, MacArthur could not have carried out Chromite on such a short fuse.

While the JCS chairman downplayed the likelihood of future amphibious operations, MacArthur's initiative with Admiral Doyle had been followed up by the unpublicized arrival of a planning team in April 1950, still before the war, headed by Colonel Edward S. Forney, who led Mobile Training Team Able of the Marine Amphibious Training Command. Possibly MacArthur was preparing to counter the wrong invasion, anticipating an opportunity to strike at Mao's forces threatening to swallow up Formosa or at Stalin's frustrated designs upon the northern Japanese home island of Hokkaido. (Stalin had intended to invade Hokkaido in August 1945 until he was warned off by Truman, and the Soviets had no occupation role in Japan.) MacArthur would name Forney deputy to Major General Edwin K. Wright when, on July 4, the first American ground contact with the enemy was failing. With MacArthur's Inchon ideas crystallizing, Wright was ordered to put his Joint Planning and Operations Group to work on Bluehearts. (His summons to Forney, the key amphibious expert at the Dai Ichi, propelled him out of an Independence Day party organized by the American colony in Tokyo.) Whether by intuition or luck, MacArthur was strategically on target.

MacArthur's planning staff was assigned an old airplane hangar known as Building AP-1, used by the Far East Command's (FEC) downtown motor pool. To the American military and civilian Japanese doing the refitting into offices, the location might have appeared curious, but the demands of war mobilization had exceeded prime space, which seemed explanation enough. The Korean front was contracting so rapidly, however, that unless MacArthur pumped his intended amphibious troops into Pusan, there would be nothing left to defend. Bluehearts had to be postponed if not canceled. In desperation, as MacArthur's occupation forces were of low combat effectiveness, the Pentagon approved rushing a small, and inadequate, "provisional" Marine brigade, including an air component, to Korea. Yet in continuing interservice rivalry Air Force Chief of Staff Hoyt Vandenberg—the only general whose gold-braided cap rivaled MacArthur's—tried unsuccessfully to strip the Marines of their air support.

From Tokyo, MacArthur continued his campaign to refocus Washington on Asian priorities. The perspective from the Dai Ichi was that the new war in Korea was the flash point of the West's all-or-nothing rivalry with world Communism. "We win here or we lose everywhere," the general claimed. "If we win here, we improve the chances of winning everywhere." It sounded persuasive to MacArthur, but the view from Washington remained that a direct Soviet-U.S. or Chinese-U.S. confrontation in Korea could ignite World War III.

Since the JCS could not merely rubber-stamp each of MacArthur's urgent appeals for troops and equipment—the downsized services had no such wherewithal—Army Chief of Staff J. Lawton Collins and Vandenberg were dispatched for an on-site inspection. Bluehearts had already been put on the shelf, MacArthur explained to them on July 13 before they flew off to Korea, but sooner or later it would have to be reactivated to "envelop"—a favorite term of his—and choke off the *In Min Gun*. Later that day in Korea—because of bad weather they could get no farther than Taegu—Collins got "a better conception of the ruggedness of the Korean mountains and the problems our troops were facing in the field." They returned to Tokyo early on the fourteenth, where Collins and MacArthur held "a simple ceremony atop the Dai Ichi Building" to raise the flag of the United Nations, presented to the command by UN Secretary-General Trygve Lie. Then the discussion about the Inchon operation, renamed Chromite, continued with Collins reiterating the skepticism of the JCS and, especially with respect to the enormous local tides, of the Navy. MacArthur would very likely get little more personnel, Collins cautioned, because there weren't any. "General, you are going to have to win the war out here with the troops available to you in Japan and Korea."

Sitting in also was Admiral Arthur W. Radford, Pacific Fleet commander, who recalled MacArthur responding confidently, "Joe, you are going to have to change your mind."

When the Pentagon generals left for home, MacArthur continued his preparations for Inchon, informing Washington as little as possible. General Lemuel C. Shepherd Jr. of Fleet Marine Force Pacific was already at Camp Pendleton, near San Diego, pressing for the commitment of a full Marine division, and General Clifton Cates, the service commandant, had flown west from Quantico, in Virginia, to meet him. Cates confided to Shepherd about an invitation from NATO, then organizing, to have the Marines mount an Atlantic force. "Clifton," Shepherd urged, "you cannot let me down on this. This is a hot war. We ought to be in it."

Two days after Bluehearts was shelved, Shepherd and his operations officer, Colonel Victor H. Krulak, were in MacArthur's office to discuss employment of the 1st Provisional Marine Brigade, 6,534 officers and men. Troop transports had sailed from San Diego on July 14 and would go directly to Pusan rather than be stockpiled for Inchon. MacArthur wished aloud that he had the entire division, as he had "a job for them to do." On a map, with his long pipestem as pointer, he showed Shepherd and Krulak his "annihilation" plan to end the war.

"Why don't you ask for the [entire] 1st Marine Division, General?" said Shepherd, impressed.

MacArthur wondered whether he could get it, and Shepherd suggested a formal request to the JCS. MacArthur could have the division up to strength by September 1. He scrounged a message pad from General Almond's office—MacArthur kept a clean desk—and drafted the request himself. The politically savvy Lem Shepherd realized that the Marine Corps itself was fighting for its existence. Bradley and the Army hierarchy in Washington saw no need for a separate ground service under the Navy and, through budget cuts, had shrunk the Marines to near-invisibility (74,279 men worldwide at the start of the war). In a letter to a congressman, Truman had even written tartly, "The Marine Corps is the Navy's police force and as long as I am President that is what it will remain. They have a propaganda machine that is almost equal to Stalin's." After the letter was leaked, Truman had to apologize. The Marines would be authorized to send a full division to FEC—less the brigade already shipped.

"I understand," MacArthur radioed Washington in Shepherd's draft, "that a force of division-strength can be assembled by the Marines in a matter of six weeks and be in Japan. I hereby make that request. . . ." On July 23 he explained to the JCS that he was now thinking of mid-September for an "amphibious landing in [the] rear of enemy lines for purpose of enveloping and destroying enemy forces in conjunction [with] attack from south by EUSAK." He indicated no place but added vaguely, "General character of operation was described to CSUSA [Collins, Chief of Staff, United States Army] during his recent visit."

Two weeks later orders were issued to bring the 1st Marine Division to strength within three weeks, using reservists when necessary. Force X was turning from theory into reality. Shrewdly, to co-opt the Washington brass, MacArthur requested for it Major General Clark L. Ruffner, chief legislative lobbyist for the Army, who would become its deputy commander. Collins, ostensibly MacArthur's boss at the Pentagon although lacking one of his stars, and suspicious of every move at the Dai Ichi as self-aggrandizing, might have thought that Ruffner gave the JCS eyes and ears in Tokyo, but he was a MacArthur loyalist from World War II days. Force X would be packed with MacArthur devotees. Directing logistics was Colonel Aubrey Smith, the son-in-law of retired General Walter Krueger, who had commanded MacArthur's Sixth Army during the return to the Philippines. The top slot would go to Major General Edward Almond, the shogun's own chief of staff at FEC. The Joint Chiefs in Washington were not consulted. MacArthur calculated that he could fend off objections by describing it as only a temporary assignment, with Almond keeping his Tokyo post.

Covertly, MacArthur was angling to get Almond a third star. Almond had not been a party to the general's design. As head of MacArthur's staff, he had been arranging for Force X's mission, planned for seventy thousand seaborne troops, and found that a Force was a bureaucratic anomaly. Army regulations required that a unit have a legitimate status in order to be equipped. Since the force would be several times division size, Almond recommended that it be designated a corps. Army practice labeled such units with Roman numerals. "Why not," he suggested, "call it X Corps?"

MacArthur liked the idea. As chief of his staff, Almond urged MacArthur to make the appointment of an X Corps commander a priority matter, for only a month remained to coordinate all aspects of the operation. "I will let you know this afternoon," MacArthur said. Almond assumed that Washington would be consulted. But MacArthur typically consulted no one.

When Almond returned a few hours later asking, "I came in for the name of the person that you selected to command this force for the Inchon landing," MacArthur said matter-of-factly, "It's you."

"This surprises me greatly," said the startled but pleased Almond, "and [it] changes the position of the chief of staff. I cannot hold two jobs at once."

Brushing aside the objection, MacArthur predicted that the Inchon operation would conclude quickly. When X Corps linked up with the Eighth Army breaking loose from the south, Almond could return to Tokyo. In the meantime he could choose one of his deputies to keep the FEC office going. "We'll all be home by Christmas."

Almond, who had no seaborne operational experience, had his orders. He could have from MacArthur whatever components remained in Japan or which he could secure in time from Hawaii or the States. X Corps would be independent of the Eighth Army, whose brusque commanding general, Walton Walker, MacArthur disliked. Walker had not been MacArthur's choice to head the Eighth Army. In 1948, when he came aboard on orders from Washington, MacArthur's attention was elsewhere—on remodeling Hirohito's reduced empire into a capitalist democracy. In any case, the army of occupation was not defending Japan; it was only garrisoning the island. A tank commander in Germany under Patton, Walker continued to mimic his late boss. Sour and unsmiling, chunky, with a belly going to pot, he radiated toughness. MacArthur preferred disciples who fit into his cult, men like Almond, who considered his boss "the greatest man alive." A desk general since 1945, Almond needed a combat command to move up. X Corps gave that to him while keeping total command in Korea with MacArthur.

Collins in Washington was only less astonished than the Joint Chiefs. To create a makeshift army independent of the Eighth Army command was a slap at Walker which would also shortchange him of reinforcements and equipment. In Korea, Walker seethed at the implied division of his command, and confided to a colleague, "I'm just a defeated Confederate general."

Walker had still another major worry. As his headquarters learned from radio intercepts, Kim Il Sung was pressing his commanders in the field to seize Pusan before more American troops could be deployed in Korea. The war might be over and Walker's army hurriedly outloading for Japan while Almond's X Corps, with troops that might have saved the Perimeter, floated impotently at sea.

The Joint Chiefs saw Almond's appointment as a high-handed move to prevent Washington from choosing a Navy or Marine commander of appropriate rank and tested ability from Pacific war days to mount a major amphibious assault, especially one of such likely difficulty. Yet MacArthur had fought not only the Japanese in the Pacific, but also the Navy and Marine hierarchy that had insisted on dividing the oceanic theater of operations in two rather than letting him run the entire island-hopping campaign from near-exile in Australia. He was not about to let the Navy run his new war. The Pacific rim was his.

Wearing both his chief of staff hat and, in effect, his new X Corps patch, Almond convened a planning group that included MacArthur's intelligence chief, Charles Willoughby. On August 12, MacArthur was able to send the Pentagon a new proposal for Chromite. Impressed by its boldness, Truman urged the JCS to "act on it rapidly." Since MacArthur insisted upon an Inchon landing, his G-2 dutifully promoted its feasibility by estimating weak troop deployment there—an understrength regiment of new conscripts, and a coast artillery unit on the harbor approaches. The North Koreans counted on geography more than on soldiery to thwart an invasion force. (However, the *In Min Gun* could rush reinforcements south after a landing.) Navy concerns about weather were also dismissed. It would be typhoon season, but the region had little history of severe typhoons.

When Admiral Arleigh Burke, deputy chief of staff to Admiral Joy in Tokyo, objected to the downplaying of the natural obstacles and proposed to take the Navy's objections directly to MacArthur, Almond intervened. It was his responsibility to deal with the chief.

"No," Burke protested, "somebody has to make a decision. I've got to talk to MacArthur myself." Almond asked him to see the G-3, Edwin K. Wright, who had been a tank commander in Germany in 1945, but Burke insisted, "I have to see the boss man. I think it's important."

Almond would not budge, offering to discuss the problem with MacArthur himself.

"Well, I'm sorry, but I can't do that," said Burke, exasperated. "I'll go back to my office."

When he opened his door he found a message waiting that he could now see MacArthur. Burke returned to explain the impact which the typhoon season could have on the sailing schedule necessary for encountering favorable tides at Inchon. For once MacArthur listened.

"What do we do, Admiral?"

"We sail early."

"All right. Please prepare the dispatches."

"I happen to have them right here."

Although nearly a month remained before departure, the ship movement orders were issued immediately. Without the troop transports available well in advance, the operation might well have aborted.

On July 18 the 1st Cavalry Division, depleted of some of its best non-coms to fill gaps in divisions already in Korea, was landed hurriedly at Pohang, to shore up the shrinking front north of Pusan. That eliminated it from Chromite. MacArthur would also be forced to commit the provisional Marine brigade as soon as it arrived, although he intended to pull it back for Inchon when he could. Still without word on whether he would get a full Marine division, he sent the JCS a fourth request—labeled that way, as if it were an overdue bill. "It is essential that the Marine Division arrive by 10 September 1950," he closed, ". . . there can be no demand for its potential use elsewhere that can equal the urgency of the immediate battle contemplated for it."

On July 23, only four weeks into the war, with the republic only a rump state reduced to two population centers, Taegu, now near the front line, and Pusan, MacArthur offered what he hoped were persuasive plans to Washington. He intended to use the 7th Division and the 5th Marines which he wanted augmented into a full division, in "major amphibious operations" preceded by a proposed (but scrubbed) landing by the 187th Airborne Regimental Combat Team. All units involved would be part of his envisioned X Corps, independent of Walker's depleted Eighth Army, which would break out from the Pusan bridgehead as soon as the Inchon landing was assured.

Squeezed as usual by MacArthur, Walker objected, although he had yet to receive the Marines, "I will not be responsible for the safety of Eighth Army's front if I lose the 5th Marine Regiment!" Still, he knew he had to lose it. There would be no deal with the Marines—or the Navy—unless the entire division participated as a unit.

"Tell Walker," MacArthur agreed, "he will have to give up the Marines."

As always, he promoted his plan by prophesying the dire consequences of doing anything else. "The alternative," he explained to the JCS, "is a frontal attack which can only result in a protracted and expensive campaign to slowly drive the enemy north of the 38th Parallel. . . ." The next day, at a telecon with the JCS, he assured the skeptical Chiefs that "barring unforeseen circumstances, if the full Marine Division is provided, the chance to launch the movement in September would be excellent." At first the JCS did not even ask for details. Won over by his optimism, they turned to concerns about whether the arrival from Japan of the 25th Division to back up the beleaguered 24th Division and the 1st Cav could hold the Pusan Perimeter.

Aside from Marine and ROK and supplementary units, X Corps was to employ the 7th Infantry, commanded by Major General David G. Barr, an Alabaman of fifty-five who had been a second lieutenant in France in 1918 and a staff officer in 1939–45. Since Barr had never been a field general, Almond considered him a liability but inherited him with his division, which had done occupation duty in Japan and was drawn from as a replacement pool for Perimeter defense. When Barr's understrength division was alerted for Chromite one month into the war, it was assigned all the infantry replacements arriving from the States in August—390 officers and 5,400 enlisted men—yet it would not be enough. MacArthur ordered Walker to dragoon able-bodied Koreans to fill his army's gaps. Knowledge of English was deemed unimportant. The order inaugurated the KATUSA (Korean Augmentation to the U.S. Army) program, which had the unrealized ideal behind it of a buddy system. MacArthur was to order KATUSA incorporated into other understrength units and expected reports to him to show that it worked.

Syngman Rhee had watched his poorly equipped and trained troops, even more unprepared than the Philippine constabulary which MacArthur had commanded at the start of the Pacific war, disintegrate in the first weeks of fighting. Still, Rhee was convinced that those which had been re-formed behind the Pusan Perimeter could break loose and rout the NKPA if given offensive equipment and air cover. A month into the war he gave a South Korean captain a message to deliver to Walton Walker for transmittal to MacArthur. Although on July 14, twelve days earlier, Rhee had formally designated MacArthur "command authority over all the land, sea and air forces of the Republic of Korea," he wrote that if the ROK Army were given "artillery and some heavy guns," and General Partridge's FEAF furnished "continued cover," he would order his army forward. The enemy, Rhee contended, had "no reinforcements to support a spearhead which is far to the south and we can push up towards Seoul and cut the main part of the enemy force from behind. We are absolutely sure of success. If we fail to do it now, the enemy will occupy the entire south and not only the lives of the Korean people but of many Americans will be in great danger."

Should the South Koreans not be entrusted with such a flanking operation, Rhee warned, "the major battle will be fought by the U.N. forces when the Soviet reinforcements for the Communist army arrive." (Rhee was obviously appealing to MacArthur's anti-Russian attitudes.) Rhee's defiant message, so a scrawled note at the top from Captain Sim claims, was "not given to Gen. Walker."

Rhee had no idea yet of the amphibious flanking operation which MacArthur was planning with the same objectives in mind, and on his own urged MacArthur to "open a second front" by landing at Inchon. Rhee's troops were already being readied for that operation by the time of his message, but MacArthur did not respond. (Curiously, Rhee was more concerned about Soviet than Chinese intervention.)

For weeks MacArthur had propagandized that the ROK divisions being reorganized were worth reequipping, although earlier they had fallen apart quickly. He blamed their disintegration on the fact that the NKPA was "as capable and tough" as any army he had ever confronted. To buy time to turn the ROK units into fighting men, as he still hoped was possible, he had nearly emptied Japan of American troops. The failure of Chromite might not only lose Korea; it might also put Japan at risk if the Russians took advantage of the defensive vacuum. Both Washington and Tokyo took the possibility much more seriously than did Stalin, who had internal reasons to restrict his adventures.

Aside from MacArthur, the American military thought Inchon the "worst possible place" and the early fall the worst possible time. It was typhoon season almost everywhere in the Pacific rim. The tidal problem at Inchon was daunting. There the tide falls more than thirty feet twice a day. Its dock area fronts a narrow channel between great banks of mud which become exposed as the tide recedes. Periods of high tide determined, daily, when landing craft could be beached. High seawalls which were bulwarks against the tides made disembarking and assault even more dangerous. To put many of the seventy thousand men assigned to Chromite ashore there with their equipment during the brief tidal "windows" under expected enemy fire required an unprecedented feat of timing. By comparison, D-Day in Normandy was a piece of cake.

The field commander of the Marines, Major General Oliver Prince Smith, was convinced, as he told Admiral Doyle, the designated head of Task Force 90, that Inchon was "a terrible place to land." O. P. Smith reached Tokyo on August 22, three weeks from MacArthur's firm invasion date. Both Smith and Doyle thought that the attack should be delayed at least a week and shifted southward about twenty miles to Posung-myon, on the coast west of Suwon. But when Smith made a courtesy call at the Dai Ichi, MacArthur parried all alternatives with supreme confidence. A month after the landings the war would be over.

Further skeptics arrived on the sixth floor of the Dai Ichi the next day for a high-level conference set for 5:30 p.m. Representing the JCS, which had been kept largely uninformed, were Collins, Chief of Naval Operations Admiral Forrest Sherman and Vandenberg's deputy, Lieutenant General Idwal Edwards. From Hawaii came Admiral Arthur Radford, the Pacific Fleet commander, and Lieutenant General Lemuel C. Shepherd Jr., who commanded the Fleet Marine Force—and who, like Smith, was not invited to the conference, although the Marines were to be the primary strike force.

MacArthur was not perturbed, as he opened the meeting, that although Chromite was well along in preparation, it still lacked formal approval in Washington. "Frankly," General Collins would confess in 1952, "we were somewhat in the dark." The lack of details from Tokyo had forced the Army chief of staff into what seemed like commuter status to Japan, where he hoped this time to focus upon Kunsan as a more viable landing site. Much farther south and not subject to extreme tides, it appeared to offer a better chance for a linkup with the hard-pressed Eighth Army. Possibly recalling the plight of Anzio in the Italian campaign in 1944, Collins believed the Inchon bridgehead might wither without what he called "a quick junction" to EUSAK.

Inchon, MacArthur insisted, presented the best opportunity to end the war quickly and decisively. "Now," he told his visitors, "my G-3 will give you the outline plan."

Using a large wall map, Major General Edwin K. Wright took up the briefing. The island of Wolmi-do dominating the harbor, he explained (the *do* was a redundancy, Korean for "island"), would be seized at morning high tide. The Marine assault on the mainland would exploit the evening tide and take the seawall and the docks.

Wary of the amphibious complications, Collins and Sherman wanted the obstacles explained—the high tides, the mudbanks, the narrow and possibly mined channel, the seawall. Wright gave way to Admiral Doyle, the designated attack forces commander. MacArthur sat quietly at one end of the table. "Doyle," Sherman asked, "do I gather that you think this is an impossible operation?"

One account has Doyle responding, "The operation is not impossible, but I do not recommend it." The rigid timetable and chancy weather were factors. For many weeks MacArthur had been insisting on September 15. To count upon maximum water over the mudflats for landing craft, that day furnished a tidal height of 31.2 feet. LSTs needed at least twenty-nine feet. There would not be thirty feet over the flats again until October 11. Every day's delay increased the pressure on the Pusan Perimeter. A delay of a month could be catastrophic.

According to General Wright, Doyle was reluctant although cooperative. "Absolutely not, Admiral Sherman," Doyle is recorded as saying. "As far as the Navy is concerned, nothing is impossible. As a matter of fact, when you realize the strategic implications, . . . it is not only a possible operation but I think it is a very fine operation, strategically. I just want[ed] to bring out the difficulties that we are going to have."

Questions ranged back and forth, one on preparatory naval gunfire. Doyle brought out a gunnery expert on his staff, a young lieutenant commander who debated with General Wright about how many days of fire were necessary. He wanted ten. Even five, said Wright, were unnecessary. "Two days, as far as I'm concerned, is the maximum."

Sherman interrupted to question the length of gunfire support, and the lieutenant commander began, "Well, Admiral, as a gunfire expert. . . ." MacArthur could have had no better, if inadvertent, advocate.

"Young man," said Sherman, "I can tell you more about naval gunfire in ten minutes than you'll know the rest of your life. Sit down." The young officer sat down. "I think," Sherman went on, "two days will be ample, but as a matter of fact I don't see where one day isn't enough. . . ." Turning to MacArthur he added, "We understand the problem now, General, but we would like to hear a little more from you, if you would like to add to it."

MacArthur paused to fill his pipe and then went on for forty-five minutes in a low, deep voice that held his audience transfixed. Yes, he conceded, Inchon was unsuitable as a landing site, the very reason the enemy would not anticipate it, and would assume that any activity in its direction was a feint masking the actual target area. He recalled the surprise victory of General James Wolfe against the French in 1759 when the British scaled the steep riverbank south of Quebec. Moving to the wall map, he pointed to the corner of Korea he held at Pusan, and how taking Inchon would not only outflank much of the North Korean army but make possible the liberation of the capital, Seoul. That would seize the imagination of all Asia, he insisted, always claiming that he could comprehend the Oriental mind. Brushing off Kunsan, Collins's recommended landing site, he demonstrated that it was not far enough up the peninsula to bottle up enemy forces now besieging the Perimeter. Always a master of facts and figures, he went into questions of artillery, railcars, aircraft support and numbers of South Koreans he would integrate into American divisions.

"So he explained all the implications," Wright recalled, ". . . and made it a very beautiful thing." And typically, MacArthur concluded by eliminating any possible attempt to alter decisions he had made on his own. "Of course," he conceded, "the initial stages of this are basically a Navy operation. This pleases me very much because the Navy has never failed me. I know the difficulties, but, believe me, I know it will be perfectly all right and a tremendous success. I hope you gentlemen, when you get back to Washington and talk to the other members of the Joint Chiefs, can come up with a very positive approval, because it would be impossible for us to stop now, anyway."

He had more confidence in the Navy than it had in itself, MacArthur cajoled, yet no confidence that a landing anywhere south of Seoul would succeed. His aim was to envelop the enemy, cut off its supplies and seal off the lower half of the Korean peninsula. He used his favorite rhetorical device, an exaggerated comparison, to emphasize the benefits of Chromite. Any other strategy but his own would be vastly more expensive in lives and very likely to fail. "The only alternative to a stroke such as I propose would be the continuation of the savage sacrifice we are making at Pusan, with no hope of relief. . . . Are you content to let our troops stay in that bloody perimeter like beef cattle in the slaughterhouse? Who will take the responsibility . . . ? Certainly, I will not." Grasping for a peroration, he declared solemnly, "I can almost hear the ticking of the second-hand of destiny. We must act now or we will die. . . . We shall land at Inchon and I shall crush them. . . ." His voice faded to a whisper. "If MacArthur had gone on the stage," said Wright, recalling the scene, "you would never have heard of John Barrymore."

MacArthur not only believed in himself; he knew he was lecturing to his juniors, even his inferiors. He had been a general when they were nothing. He possessed a geopolitical perspective which they could only learn from a past master. None of them wore five stars, as he did. And he was proconsul in Japan. "The prestige of the Western world hangs in the balance," he warned. "Oriental millions are watching the outcome. . . . Asia is where the Communist conspirators elected to make their play for global conquest. The test is not in Berlin or Vienna, in London, Paris or Washington. It is here and now—it is along the Naktong River in South Korea. . . . Actually, we here fight Europe's war with arms, while there it is still confined to words."

Backtracking a bit when Doyle repeated his feeling that Inchon at best was "not impossible," MacArthur promised, "If my estimate is inaccurate and I should run into a defense with which I cannot cope, I will be there personally and will immediately withdraw our forces before they are committed to a bloody setback. The only loss then will be my professional reputation. But Inchon will not fail. . . ." It was, he exaggerated for dramatic effect, a five-thousand-to-one gamble, "but I am used to taking such odds."

Sherman rose to thank him, and Doyle protested any thoughts of withdrawal. "No, General," he said, drawn under MacArthur's spell, "we don't know how to do that. Once we start ashore, we'll keep going!" Someone commented that enemy guns might make the channel impossible, but Admiral Sherman, now emotionally committed, broke in, "I wouldn't hesitate to take a ship in there!"

Mindful of his naval history, MacArthur welcomed Sherman's conversion with "Spoken like a[n Admiral] Farragut!"

The only remaining skeptics were the unrepresented Marines. Since they were designated to mount the assault, they expected to have something to say about how it would be conducted. O. P. Smith of the 1st Marine Division had clashed with Almond even before the crucial meeting to which he had not been invited. Almond had set the agenda and Smith had protested that he needed more time. That was not "our idea of responsiveness," Almond rejoined. With none of MacArthur's celebrated tact, Almond nevertheless acted as his surrogate. At his first meeting with the white-haired Smith, fifty-seven, Almond—who was fifty-eight—had addressed the Marine general as "Son."

Also excluded had been Lem Shepherd, who outranked Almond by a star. By the next day both generals had pressed second thoughts on Admiral Sherman, and all three went to confront MacArthur and press their case for shifting the operation thirty miles south, near Osan, where the water was deeper and the tides less treacherous. But blocking MacArthur's door in the Dai Ichi was Almond, who insisted on talking to them first. Downplaying the Inchon tides, seawall and mudflats, Almond described the amphibious operation as only a mechanical exercise, even though he had never participated in one. Smith and Shepherd insisted on seeing MacArthur, but found him in no mood to change his mind. That the Communists would consider Inchon impossible was enough for him. "For a five dollar ante," he claimed, "I have an opportunity to win $50,000, and I have decided that is what I am going to do." When MacArthur had last played poker is unknown, but the metaphor convinced the Marine generals that they could not shake his confidence in Chromite.

As Collins and Sherman were about to leave for Washington, MacArthur was preparing to activate X Corps, now planned to field 71,300 troops built around the Marines and the 7th Infantry. At a farewell visit to the Dai Ichi, Collins, as a courtesy, asked Almond, "Is there any other thing I could do to aid you in this operation?" Almond pulled open a desk drawer and showed the Chief of Staff a list of about thirty officers he wanted transferred to his new corps. Many had served under him in Italy in 1944–45 as ranking whites in his otherwise black 92nd Division, which had not covered itself with glory. Recognizing the names, Collins found excuses for evading the reassignments, but Almond, knowing he had MacArthur behind him, told Collins, his ultimate boss in Washington, that his "active combat command" should take precedence over other assignments. "I got about a third of my staff list," he later crowed.

Backing down, Collins had betrayed again the awkwardness of the post-war military hierarchy in dealing with a prewar chief of staff who had become an icon while they were junior officers. MacArthur's top appointees were, from Washington's perspective, shadow MacArthurs. That the abrasive Almond, according to his own X Corps second-in-command, "could precipitate a crisis on a desert island with nobody else around," suggested the problems he would have with the Marines.

Once back at the Pentagon, Collins and Sherman briefed the other Joint Chiefs and, out of range of MacArthur's persuasive rhetoric, teletyped him on August 28 to keep options open:

> We concur after reviewing the information brought back by General Collins and Admiral Sherman in making preparations [for] and executing a turning movement by amphibious forces on the west coast of Korea, either at Inchon in the event the enemy forces prove ineffective, or at favorable beach south of Inchon if one can be located. . . .

In July, MacArthur had told Collins and Vandenberg that if Inchon was unworkable he would strike at Haeju or Chinnampo, both *north* of Inchon, but the JCS was warning him here to operate south of the 38th parallel.

The response was less than a full vote of confidence in MacArthur, but the Chiefs knew that at the very least Admiral Doyle, an expert on amphibious operations, would be in charge of the landings, and that the 1st Marine (Guadalcanal) Division, which had stormed the beaches of Guadalcanal, New Guinea, New Britain, Peleliu and Okinawa, and was led by reliable veterans of amphibious warfare, would run the affair until the beachheads were secure. The Marine regiments to beef O. P. Smith's forces into divisional size would be the 1st, which arrived at Kobe from San Diego on September 2, and the 7th, which arrived in battalion segments from September 9 into the operation itself. Timing was crucial and the distances were great, but MacArthur remained without anxiety. He was confident that Washington would have to furnish what he wanted, and when he wanted it.

In command of a weapons company at Camp Lejeune, in North Carolina, Major (later Brigadier General) Edwin Simmons had crossed the country by train with his unit to Camp Pendleton, where his regiment was augmented by grousing reservists recalled to duty. Only on the transport serving as Marine headquarters in port in Japan did field-grade Marine officers learn of Inchon, its tides, winding channel and seawall. "The whole thing looked like an invitation to disaster. . . . And after we'd listened with the gravest of reservations to the briefing, [Colonel] Chesty Puller got up and gave one of his famous inspirational speeches." He didn't give a damn about the likely conditions where they were to land, he said. "We'll find out what's on the beach when we get there. And as far as you people are concerned, I had to wait twenty years between wars, while you get one every five years. You've been willing to live by the sword, and you'd damn well better be willing to die by the sword."

The 7th Division, which was to land behind the Marines once the beachhead was secure, was a far less dependable outfit. As General Barr, who commanded it, knew, it was not even recognizable as an American entity. Not only were his troops mostly green replacements from the States, the division was also filling up with Koreans shipped over for side-by-side training in Japan. The KATUSA element was raised in the old-fashioned way, reminiscent of the Royal Navy's impressment of seamen in the eighteenth century. Syngman Rhee's lieutenants employed the police, who swept up seemingly able-bodied men off the streets. (One, returning home from buying medicine for his wife, found himself in a training camp in Japan with the pills in his pocket.) Further, all Army reinforcements from the States during the last week of August and the first week of September were allotted to the under-strength and multi-national 7th.

Despite GHQ releases that praised the KATUSA system, the Korean recruits were often hopeless components of a company otherwise composed of American draftees fresh from expedited basic training. With the motley 3rd Division to come—it was being trained with the Eighth Army—and the half-Korean 7th Division, Almond had to count heavily on the performance of the Marines.

Although reluctant to fight under an Army general, Marine headquarters recognized that it was vital for Marine Corps identity as a separate and elite force to be essential to any amphibious operation. Since the Marines were a Navy entity and the Navy provided the lift capacity for Chromite, a Marine division began from political as well as material strength, and had history on its side. No American force was viewed as better trained and equipped for waterborne operations. Realizing that X Corps would have to cross the broad Han, the Marine division's Engineer Battalion chief, Lieutenant Colonel John H. Partridge, arranged for the land dimension of the advance by loading portable Bailey bridges and fifty-ton floating bridge sections.

MacArthur's staff had produced two alternative landing options, but neither offered proximity to Seoul or the opportunity to sever North Korean communications. MacArthur's choice was to exploit these and other sites as feints, to be reconsidered only in an emergency. Air and naval strikes were scheduled against Chinnampo, Ongjin and Kunsan, as well as against Inchon, each intended to suggest the possibility of a landing, and to spread NKPA defensive operations, including mining, thin. Yet the tidal and weather hazards at Inchon furnished more anxiety than MacArthur's air of confidence evidenced, and his decision to flesh out American divisions with Koreans was only statistically successful. The half-formed 7th Infantry received 8,637 Korean recruits in its assembly area in Kyushu only three weeks before they were to land at Inchon. An exasperated lieutenant colonel in the 7th, Charles R. Scherer, described the draftees as on the remote side of raw, looking "as though they had been herded together to get them off the streets of Pusan. They spent their first week in Japan in quarantine, since they had to be deloused and cleaned. They could not speak English and we had few interpreters. Our instruction was given primarily in sign language. . . . They had no idea of sanitation, let alone the more complicated activities of military life. . . . They ate our rations, rode our trucks, used our supplies. But except for menial tasks, they were a performance cipher."

Unlike MacArthur, Almond actually visited the staging areas to inspect X Corps readiness. If he was appalled by some of what he saw, he seemed never to have intimated as much. MacArthur never materialized. He also stalled on communicating promised details of the operation to the Pentagon, where it must have been assumed that the integration of Koreans and American draftees was going efficiently. Washington knew little more a few days before the operation was to unfold than Collins and Sherman had learned from MacArthur's bravura performance in Tokyo.

While the Joint Chiefs of Staff recognized that they were being treated like little boys, the President had other reasons for being irritated. He had kept the clearly insubordinate MacArthur in charge because of the harm it would do his administration if the political right exploited a change at the Dai Ichi as a symbol of Truman's lack of commitment to anti-Communism. Yet MacArthur was not only high-handed with his overcautious military chiefs, but also intrusive in foreign affairs as if his shogunate in Japan made him an independent head of state. A month earlier, Truman would not forget, MacArthur had flown to Formosa without authorization to meet with Chiang, after which the Generalissimo, still a hero to ultra-conservatives, issued a communiqué that described their talks as covering the joint defense of what was left of Chiang's China. "In view of the many conflicting reports largely emanating from Formosa and the uncertainties engendered thereby," MacArthur had radioed the JCS icily on June 30, "I regard it as advisable to proceed there as planned."

"A picture had been taken of him kissing Madame Chiang Kai-Shek's hand," Averell Harriman (then special assistant to President Truman) charged. The wirephoto had appeared in American newspapers. More dangerous was MacArthur's promise to Chiang to send flights of F-80s for "familiarization" and for "morale build-up for the population of Formosa." Since the American jets would not be transferred from Japanese bases, MacArthur claimed that his gesture was "in consonance with existing directives." It clearly was not.

Harriman offered to fly to Tokyo to curb MacArthur's foreign policy adventures, and Truman advised, "I want you to tell him two things. I want you to tell him to leave Chiang Kai-Shek alone. [And] I do not want to have him get me into a war with mainland China."

Harriman met with MacArthur and stressed Truman's desire to have MacArthur "[not] interfere in any way with Chiang Kai-Shek or to encourage him [in mainland incursions]." MacArthur confessed, "I don't agree. I recognize the President is my Commander-in-Chief. [But] I don't agree with his point of view." Harriman restated Truman's position and MacArthur conceded with obvious insincerity, "I will obey any orders I receive from the President." With Harriman's party were Secretary of the Army Frank Pace and, from the military, Air Force Lieutenant General Lauris Norstad and Army Lieutenant General Matthew Ridgway, who returned from Korea with misgivings about the Eighth Army commander. Ridgway told Pace that he was concerned about Walker's "leadership, lack of force, acceptance of a mediocre staff, and an unsound base organization." None of that augured well for the projected breakout after Chromite was launched. Ridgway noted in a memorandum that Pace reacted by suggesting "that a change ought to be made as soon as possible," and Norstad suggested that Ridgway replace Walker, but nothing was done. The coordination of Chromite might be affected, and MacArthur had not been consulted. The Pentagon party, with Harriman, went home.

At a press conference in Washington, Truman fudged that he and Mac-Arthur had no disagreements over Formosa, or Korea, or over the need to fight Communism everywhere. The statement was ambiguous enough to further embolden MacArthur. In a message he sent to be read at the Veterans of Foreign Wars (VFW) annual convention in Chicago late in August, as the Inchon planning gathered momentum, he again nailed his worldwide anti-Communism banner to the Dai Ichi door. To make certain his views went public, the general's staff offered the message to editors known to promote the views of the China Lobby. *U.S. News & World Report* got a copy, and from its text the Associated Press released a story certain to embarrass the President.

"Nothing could be more fallacious," MacArthur declared—and officials in the State Department read—"than the threadbare argument by those who advocate appeasement and defeatism in the Pacific that if we defend Formosa we alienate continental Asia." Always seeing himself as a master of Oriental psychology, he claimed that it was typical of Asians to respect, from wherever it came, "aggressive, resolute and dynamic leadership" rather than "timidity and vacillation." To back away would inevitably "shift any future battle area five thousand miles eastward to the coasts of the American continents."

Dean Acheson, Dean Rusk and Averell Harriman met and determined to put the VFW matter before the President. Defense Secretary Johnson was asked to join them at the White House. Mad as hell, Truman ordered Johnson to demand that MacArthur "withdraw this letter."

An ambitious, exasperating former American Legion stalwart, and an admirer of both Chiang and MacArthur, Louis Johnson was politically useful as Truman's link to conservative Democrats. By the time he returned to his office in the Pentagon, Johnson knew he could not order MacArthur to do anything. By telephone to Acheson and Harriman he tried to water down Truman's directive, warning that it might lead to MacArthur's resignation. By mid-afternoon on Saturday, August 26, Truman had his fill of the bickering and dictated to Johnson over the telephone the precise language which the Defense Secretary was to employ to MacArthur:

The President of the United States directs that you withdraw your message for . . . [the] Veterans of Foreign Wars because various features with respect to Formosa are in conflict with policy of the U.S. and its position in the U.N.

Johnson continued to delay sending the rebuke, but MacArthur eventually got it and cabled that he would obey orders although the text was already public.

To explain further to MacArthur why "directing the withdrawal of your message . . . was necessary," Truman on the thirtieth sent him a copy of his message to UN Secretary-General Trygve Lie claiming American impartiality between the two Chinese factions, "without prejudice to the future political settlement of the status of the island [of Formosa/Taiwan]." The legal justification remains surprising still. "The actual status of the island is that it is territory taken from Japan by the victory of the Allied Forces in the Pacific. . . . The Chinese Government was asked by the Allies to take the surrender of the Japanese forces on the island. That is the reason the Chinese are there now."

The controversy marked the first time that MacArthur was asked to back down and to refrain from foreign policy intrusions. While it did not cost him his job, it cost the bumbling, bow-tied Secretary his. Rather than level with Johnson that he was being fired for disloyalty, Truman summoned him to the White House and explained awkwardly that the political heat on the presidency to get rid of him was too great to be withstood any longer. Johnson pleaded for time to think over the resignation—a useless gesture, as Truman had already called in General George C. Marshall, who had already served him with distinction as Secretary of State. On Tuesday, September 12, as MacArthur prepared to leave Tokyo for the Inchon operation, the obstinate yet beaten Johnson returned to the White House and wept as he signed a letter of resignation he refused to write. Chromite would begin with a new chief for the CINCFE at the Pentagon—a desk colonel in France in 1918 for whom the Armistice came too soon for him to match MacArthur's star.

To disguise the big push looming, MacArthur maintained his usual schedule, but preparations in Kobe, Yokohama and, especially, Sasebo could not be hidden, and Pusan was swarming with ships. Rumors of an amphibious operation were everywhere in Japan, labeled by reporters "Operation Common Knowledge." If the Russians, Chinese or North Koreans had any intelligence whatever from Honshu and Kyushu, it might have been disregarded as disinformation to mask some other operation. Still, a Soviet ship, hammer-and-sickle ensign flying, steamed boldly into Kobe, where American troops were loading for Inchon, and blacked-out convoys would be shadowed by submarines, presumably Russian. Even at that, Inchon might have seemed so hazardous a landing site as to create disbelief in Pyongyang about where the invasion force was going.

Since the primary thrust could come apart, MacArthur had to have contingency plans, and on August 30 had issued CINCFE Plan 100A, "to insert the X Corps by amphibious landing at Kunsan, [on the west coast, at the latitude of Taegu,] followed by a drive to Taejon." If the Inchon landing went on as scheduled, Kunsan would be downgraded to a feint. On September 8, Plan 100C provided for a divisional landing at Kunsan to assist a EUSAK breakout if necessary. On September 11, as the invasion fleet was assembling, Plan 100D authorized an amphibious landing at Koryo on the east coast to hasten the cutoff of North Korean troops to the south.

Given the vast, almost public extent of preparations, it is almost inexplicable that Rhee, on September 8, only a week before the landing that would utilize some of his own troops, would write to MacArthur to urge the opening of "a second front . . . by making an amphibious landing either in Inchon or somewhere north of Taegu." It was crucial to occupy the land before the rice harvest; otherwise the Communists would "reap the entire crop" and leave twenty million South Koreans to starve. Could he not have known? Rhee was a crafty old man, but he was also an old man.

Maggie Higgins wanted desperately to be in on the Inchon landing, but was put off (as a female) as inconvenient to the operation. Her appeals to high brass in Tokyo got her nowhere. As a last resort she broke whatever secrecy Chromite still had by telephoning from Tokyo to Mrs. Ogden Reid, majority stockholder in the *Herald Tribune,* to intervene with the Pentagon to permit her star correspondent to sail on what Maggie described as a secret Navy mission. When Mrs. Reid went to bat for her, Washington was horrified that the security of the operation had been blown.

"I am going," she wrote to Bill Hall in a note to be left for him in Tokyo (he was in the Far East briefly as an Air Force observer), "on a great adventure which, if successful, should bring this situation to a conclusion." Despite the vagueness, the message echoed MacArthur. Flying to Pusan to board an assault ship, she looked up at a transport, saw familiar faces of (male) correspondents and asked to join them. Turning her down, the troop embarkation officer used the excuse that the ship was already overcrowded. "I could sleep on the deck," she offered unsuccessfully. Reapplying at the *Henrico,* she repeated her offer to hole up in her sleeping bag anywhere. Marine Captain Francis "Ike" Fenton Jr. looked at her orders, which to her surprise, and his, read, "Miss Higgins may board any Navy ship." She was given a cabin for the four-day sailing; an irate junior officer was bumped into double-bunking. They all hoped the mission would survive Typhoons Jane and Kezia (reported on route) before they had to worry about surviving the Inchon tides.

With JCS conditional approval in hand, MacArthur had issued on August 30, along with his contingency CINCFE Plan 100A, his curiously numbered Operations Order No. 1, General Headquarters, United Nations Command—which had been functioning for nearly two months—covering the details of the Inchon landing. When by September 5 no copy had been received at the Pentagon despite an August 28 request, the JCS radioed again for final plans. Curtly, MacArthur replied that "the general outline of the plan remains as described to you," and that by courier he would deliver, by September 11, a detailed description of the operation. The intent was clear. The documents were to arrive when it was already too late to influence whatever MacArthur wanted to do.

Jumpy about Chromite, as late as September 7 the JCS again asked MacArthur to reconsider the operation and asked his estimate of its success. The Pentagon had committed troops in the tens of thousands, hundreds of aircraft and the most warships assembled anywhere since 1945, as well as the prestige of the U.S. and the UN, yet it appeared that Washington would learn about Inchon only from the newspapers and the radio.

Peeved by what he considered the Pentagon's lack of confidence in him, MacArthur replied that his concept was "the only hope of wresting the initiative from the enemy" and reversing a war of attrition. He saw "not the slightest possibility" of a Dunkirk at Pusan, but no victory by merely holding on there either. And he reminded Washington that he was not waiting for their approval. "The embarkation of the troops and the preliminary air and naval preparations are proceeding according to schedule."

The next day, only a week before the invasion date and three days after the first ships in Task Force 90 had left Yokohama, Collins conceded, "We approve your plan and [the] President has been so informed." Even so, the JCS had received no plan, for MacArthur had deliberately not furnished any. With everything in irreversible motion he now asked General Wright to send an officer "without too much rank"—a deliberate further snub—to brief the Pentagon. Wright supplied Lieutenant Colonel Lynn Smith, in operations. "Put him on an airplane," said MacArthur, "and send him back to Washington." But he cautioned Smith, who left Tokyo on September 10, not to arrive "too soon."

MacArthur's radio message, "personal for General Collins" and dated September 6, noted a "courier officer" was being dispatched "to arrive Washington approximately 11 September carrying GHQ Campaign Plan, copy of Operations Orders of GHQ, FEAF, COMNAVFE [Commander, Naval Forces, Far East], Eighth Army, Task Group and GHQ Reserve (X Corps), with accompanying annexes." There would hardly be time for anyone to read it all before troops jumped off.

"So we gave him a copy of all the plans," Wright remembered, "and padlocked it to his wrist [in the usual security fashion], and we sent word that he was coming. But we just said that a representative of this headquarters was en route and on such-and-such airplane. So he arrived, and it was all set up; the meeting was arranged, and somebody met him at the airport." When he was escorted to a meeting of the Joint Chiefs of Staff they recognized the intended insult, but listened to Lynn Smith's summary and waited for the results from Inchon. The presentation on the fourteenth, Washington time, was only hours before 6:30 a.m. the next day in Korean time, when the first Marine wave would go ashore. By that time the chiefs also had MacArthur's long and confident message that everything was proceeding on schedule and that chances of success were "excellent."

MacArthur and Almond left Tokyo with Marine General Lem Shepherd at about three o'clock in the afternoon on the day before the sailing from Sasebo. A typhoon was raging between Iwo Jima and southern Japan—one of the problems feared in the planning of Chromite—but as they reached Haneda Airport the clouds lifted briefly, revealing a rainbow. "Lem," said MacArthur, "there is my lucky rainbow. This operation is going to be a success. You know I commanded the Rainbow Division in France during World War I and I have always believed that a rainbow is my lucky omen." It did not seem to ruffle MacArthur that Admiral Burke had urged him to hurry the outloading "just as fast as you possibly can; all of those ships; get them out of there, get them on their way so you have time to kill if the typhoon doesn't go west . . . ; we can kill time, all right, but we can't make it up. . . . We've got to be in a position where we can slow down and . . . still land at the time we want to land."

MacArthur took off from Haneda in his sleek four-engine Lockheed Constellation christened *SCAP,* but the rainbow failed to hold out and typhoon winds forced Anthony Story to land at Itazuke air base near Fukuoka, short of their destination. There the generals secured a car and an MP convoy to travel the final eighty-six miles, over dusty, unpaved roads, to

Sasebo, arriving in the port area at ten in the evening. No one knew where the operations flagship, *Mount McKinley,* was docked, proving that at least some secrecy about Chromite remained. Fortunately, a Marine captain accompanying Shepherd spoke a smattering of Japanese. The Japanese dockworkers knew where it was.

Typhoons had created anxiety since September 3, when one hit the port of Kobe, where elements of the 1st Marine Division were to embark. Gusts of 110-mile-per-hour winds and lashes of forty-foot waves made a shambles of the harbor and nearly capsized troopships, but the tireless Japanese dockers made repairs and kept the operation on schedule. At Yokohama to the north, the weather was better but the efficiency far less. The 7th Infantry sailed late. Sasebo was buffeted by winds but escaped damage, and the flotilla of 261 transports, warships and supporting vessels, including some from Pusan, embarked between September 10 and 12, flying the flags of Australia, Britain, Canada, France, the Netherlands, New Zealand and the United States. Many American vessels were manned and piloted by Japanese—enemies five years earlier. Of the forty-seven LSTs carrying Marines, all but ten were crewed by Japanese seamen, and on the decks of the transports, issued one khaki GI blanket each, were hundreds of sturdy Japanese stevedores to do the unloading at Inchon. In Japanese ports they were a common presence at the unloading of each U.S. ship, performing all the heavy work and carrying cargo in dimensions that awed the Americans.

Japan was playing a major role in the war, although technically it was still an enemy nation under military occupation. While Washington objected to Manchuria and the westernmost finger of Siberia as a privileged sanctuary for Communist forces in North Korea, Japan was the West's oversized aircraft carrier, staging area and procurement zone, safe from attack and never pointed to by MacArthur as a parallel to the north-of-Yalu region. Other than the rebuilding of the war-shattered home islands, nothing contributed more to the resurgence of the Japanese economy than the war in Korea. Japanese factories boomed with American contracts; service industries and occupations from vehicle repair to prostitution thrived; everyone who wanted to work, and could, was employed. The chief spokesman for Communist ire was the Soviet representative on the deliberately toothless Allied council that was supposed to advise MacArthur on occupation matters, but all complaints were greeted by silence.

Major Simmons and his Marine weapons company boarded "this rusty travesty of a landing ship. The landing ships turned out to be old surplus

LSTs that had been used by the Japanese for inter-island trade and whatnot. They were not at all seaworthy. Ours kept breaking down. The crew had been patched together at the last minute."

At the wharf where MacArthur's flagship was moored, the *Mount McKinley*'s captain was nervous about departure. Typhoon winds and waves had delayed his docking and might prevent weighing anchor. "General," he appealed when MacArthur emerged, very late, from his MP sedan, "we're going to have to cast off very quickly. There's a storm coming up and I've got to clear the breakwater within fifteen minutes or the wind and the tide will be against me."

Unhurried, MacArthur returned to the car to shake hands with the driver, then led his party up the gangway. It was almost midnight, nearly September 13. Only hours remained before naval guns were to open against Inchon.

Inchon

MORE GLORIOUS for MacArthur than the Côte-de-Châtillon in 1918 or Leyte in 1944 was Inchon. Planned to the last degree and predicated upon the quality of Navy and Marine cooperation he had learned to count upon against the Japanese, the operation seemed bound to succeed if Chromite's timing could exploit the tides. The North Koreans could guess at landings elsewhere; Inchon still seemed impossible.

On the destroyer *Borland,* accompanying the escort carrier *Badoeng Strait* as the Inchon flotilla moved north, still well out to sea to avoid discovery, Marine and FEAF pilots could be picked up on ship's radio. Their first attack on Wolmi-do, the largest island off Inchon harbor, was scheduled for 3:30 p.m. on the tenth. "What we thought we heard," Ensign James Alexander scribbled down, "is not what they thought they said." A squadron approaching Wolmi-do from 120 miles away in Japan to make the first strikes was checking out its readiness. "Are you carrying napalm?" was a query the sailors strained to hear.

"Roger. We've got the napalm."

Aboard the *Borland,* seamen thought they heard "A-Bomb."

"Our hair stood on end. The rumor spread like wildfire throughout the ship." They recalled press reports that MacArthur wanted to "nuke" the Communists, and the misunderstood message took on a life of its own until they learned that 96,000 pounds of flaming napalm had been dumped on the western half of Wolmi-do.

Close to midnight on the cloudless evening of September 12, while the main force still sailed north, the British frigate *Whitesand Bay* approached Kunsan, and disgorged rubber dinghies with 120 officers and men from the U.S. Army and sixteen officers and men of the Royal Navy and Royal Marines. They paddled ashore, drew fire, then withdrew. All returned but nine, for whom they searched until the last dinghy made it back on its own with five aboard, one of them mortally wounded. Two more casualties were plucked from the water. Another commando was known to be dead, the last seriously wounded and unlocated ashore. It was five in the morning of the thirteenth and they could not remain any longer to give away the puny size of the decoy force. The *Whitesand Bay* retired to seaward.

Under Vice Admiral Arthur Struble, the Seventh Fleet commander, Chromite opened with surface attacks on D-Day minus one, September 14. Six destroyers exploited their shallow draft to fire more than 1,700 five-inch shells onto Wolmi-do. Return fire hit one, the *Collett,* and disabled it. Six- and eight-inch salvos rattled in from cruisers farther out.

Although the typhoons that had hit Japan had churned up the winds and the water, they had not slowed down the armada. The loading of supplies for the 1st Marine Division in Kobe had been suspended for a day and a half because of forty-foot waves at the waterfront. Fifty ships at anchor had been damaged, but MacArthur's luck held. Emergency repairs went on around the clock, and Struble's schedule was met.

The day before the landing, with the *Mount McKinley* pounding up the Yellow Sea with dozens of other ships, not an enemy was in sight. North Korea had few scouting aircraft, no submarines, little surface navy and apparently no radar tracking of Admiral Doyle's task forces. In an attempt to mislead NKPA intelligence with disinformation, officers of Lieutenant Colonel Raymond L. Murray's 5th Marines, withdrawn from the line in the Perimeter, had been assembled on the deck of a transport in Pusan harbor to listen to a lecture, over a loudspeaker system, on *In Min Gun* defenses at Kunsan. If any Communist informers were among the dockworkers, the phony briefing might have created defensive moves in the wrong direction. Leaflet drops intended further confusion. Stratemeyer's aircraft dropped warnings to civilians to flee inland at Ongjin, Chinnampo, Inchon and Kunsan. Inchon had to be included in the shell game because its omission might identify the actual landing site. In any case, the bulk of NKPA forces were preoccupied with the Pusan Perimeter, expecting General Walker's augmented forces to attempt a breakout somewhere along the line. And to add to *In Min Gun* problems, its best field commander, Lieutenant General Kang Kon, known as King Kong to Americans, both a veteran guerrilla fighter and a former Soviet officer, had just been killed by a land mine.

Aboard the command ship, a confident MacArthur enjoyed Doyle's lunch served by white-coated stewards—the Navy did things handsomely—and the top brass chatted over coffee and cigars. The long-expected replacement of Defense Secretary Johnson by George C. Marshall had occurred. MacArthur predicted that stuffy Dean Acheson would not last much longer at State and would be succeeded by Averell Harriman, who was a good troubleshooter but too patrician to be tough enough. Then, as if he were back in Tokyo, the general excused himself for an afternoon nap.

By midnight MacArthur had been up again for hours, and he remained on the bridge of the *Mount McKinley,* peering through the blackness and watching a flash of light clocked at forty-second intervals. It was the lighthouse at Palmi-do, outward from Wolmi-do, where the first landing off Inchon was to take place. In a joint CIA-military operation code-named Trudy Jackson, Eugene F. Clark, a rather elderly Navy lieutenant who had been a chief petty officer in the Far East before World War II, had scouted the islands offshore from Inchon to report on the seawalls, mudflats and defenses. On a sampan with a .50-caliber machine gun, Clark commanded three enlisted men and two ROK interpreters, and counted on the loyalty of local villagers. If all failed, he had a grenade for himself. One enemy patrol boat chanced upon them: Clark sank it.

At the mouth of Flying Fish Channel he had found a partly dismantled lighthouse and radioed that he could make it operative again if the Navy wanted it. Now wrapped in a blanket atop the lighthouse, he watched Doyle's ships move in.

MacArthur assumed it was evidence of his catching the North Koreans unawares. In his *Reminiscences* he wrote, "We were taking the enemy by surprise. The lights were not even turned off. I went to my cabin and turned in."

There was hardly time. Eighty-nine minutes later, at 6:29 a.m., the destroyer *DeHaven* logged, "Ceased all fire. Wave #1 nearing Green Beach." Four minutes after that, landing craft cruised into Flying Fish Channel and the first Marines went ashore on Wolmi-do. It was just after dawn on the fifteenth—early evening the night before in Washington. Fire was then followed by counterfire. Overhead, Marine Corsairs flew low over the island. "The roar of their engines," Pfc. Fred Davidson wrote, "hit us like a bomb . . . [as they flew] through the smoke toward the beach not more than thirty feet over our heads. Hot, empty machine-gun shells fell on us. Talk about close air support."

On board the *Mount McKinley*, according to Marine General Lem Shepherd, MacArthur, his staff clustered about him, surveyed operations from the admiral's chair on the bridge. He had donned "his old Bataan cap with its tarnished gold braid" and his leather Air Force jacket. While he watched the gunfire, press photographers aboard focused on him rather than on the action. On the ship's radio he heard reports of the landings, and as the dawn brightened enough for binoculars he picked out a flag raised atop the battered 335-foot hill on Wolmi-do. It looked out to the east over Inchon, linked to Wolmi by a narrow causeway.

The landings continued without any problems from mines, as few from a recent Soviet shipment, stored nearby, had been set. The rest never would be deployed. Reminding Marines of their field training exercises was the rattle of small-arms fire.

Descending from her transport into a shallow-bottomed landing craft via a cargo-net ladder, Maggie Higgins had been with the fifth wave to hit Red Beach, arriving early in the four-hour period when the tide was high. ("Dead high" was 6:00 p.m.) She rounded Wolmi-do, "which looked like a giant forest fire had swept over it," accompanying thirty-eight Marines from the 5th Regiment. With them were two other correspondents and a photographer. Jumping out of her assault craft, clutching her portable typewriter head high, she slogged ashore under the cover of tracer volleys that lit up the twilight under a Technicolor sunset. By seven o'clock there were sixty wounded on Red Beach, but the beach—"a rough vertical pile of stones"— was secure, and she found a beached LST on which she could type out a story. It made page one of the *Herald Tribune*.

To send it she had to flag a returning assault boat and find her way to the *Mount McKinley*, where a deck officer shouted down, "We don't want any more correspondents aboard!" She and her press companions climbed up anyway, discovering in the wardroom of MacArthur's flagship "the last word in warmth and luxury." The correspondents from GHQ in Tokyo were already aboard "putting the finishing touches on stories which they had obtained by going with MacArthur on a tour of Wolmi."

Admiral Doyle was awakened from a nap "to deal with this Higgins menace." Finally, at one in the morning, she was permitted to send her story and sleep on a stretcher in the dispensary. After that, despite her four mimeographed pages of clearance to board any ship, she was to be off by 9:00 p.m. nightly. She "slept on the docks or with the troops. This was no better or worse that what I had grown used to in the summer war."

By eight in the evening the initial fighting was over, and MacArthur asked for casualty data. Forty-five prisoners had been taken, he was told; someone guessed inaccurately at a half-dozen Marine dead, two or three times that many wounded. "More people than that get killed in traffic every day," he remarked lightly. Turning to Doyle, he asked that a message of congratulations go to Vice Admiral Struble on the cruiser *Rochester.* "The Navy and Marines had never shone more brightly than this morning," he dictated. Then he announced to Almond and Marine generals Smith and Shepherd, "That's it. Let's get a cup of coffee."

With coffee mug in his free hand, he drafted a message to the Joint Chiefs: "First phase landing successful with losses light. Surprise apparently complete. All goes well and on schedule."

The assault schedules had worked because enough professionals had been built into the operation to manage the newcomers and the inept. Major Edwin Simmons had been told that a "wave guide" would lead his landing craft to the line of departure, but discovered that the first boat he encountered was filled with press photographers and the second with interpreters who spoke Korean and Japanese but no English. He was feeling "faintly desperate" when he came alongside the control vessel and shouted to the bridge for instructions. A naval officer with a bullhorn directed him to Blue Two, but all Simmons could see was "mustard-colored haze and black smoke." He encountered another wave guide, who shouted that Simmons was headed for Blue One. Then he checked his map and asked his LVT (landing vehicle, tracked—amphibian tractor) driver, a recalled reservist, if he had a compass. "Search me," he said. "Six weeks ago I was driving a truck in San Francisco."

MacArthur's cables from the *Mount McKinley* emphasized the "clockwork coordination and cooperation between the services" and the "extraordinary conditions" that "demanded a complete mastery of the technique of amphibian warfare." As he put it, with some self-congratulation, "The command distinguished itself." The warmth would not last. He had arranged that once his troops were ashore and expanded their bridgehead, control of the operation would be transferred to the abrasive Ned Almond. Although spearheaded by Marine commanders, notably Colonel Lewis "Chesty" Puller, who had led the 1st Marines ashore, despite heavy fire, on Peleliu exactly six years to the day earlier, Chromite was Almond's show as commanding general of X Corps. Before dawn on the sixteenth, Almond's L-5 *Blue Goose* observation plane took off from the *Badoeng Strait* to search for the closest airfield, Kimpo, halfway between Inchon and Seoul. Kimpo was still in enemy hands. However, the plane could land on short strips, even roads, enabling Almond to revisit troops he had watched go ashore the day before. LSTs beached on mudflats in low tide were unloading equipment, ammunition and supplies, and MacArthur sent another reassuring cable to the Pentagon that "the landing of heavy equipment and supplies progressed throughout the night."

"You will be in Seoul in five days," he predicted to Almond.

"I can't do that," said Almond "—but I will have the city within two weeks."

On board the *Mount McKinley* for dinner with MacArthur and Doyle that night—the Marine generals were already ashore—Almond stood stiffly before his boss to have a Silver Star (actually an oak-leaf cluster representing his second such award) pinned to his field jacket for "conspicuous gallantry, aggressiveness and leadership as Commanding General of X Crops during the . . . invasion of Inchon. . . . General Almond was changed with the execution of Operation Chromite which involved the seizure initially of Inchon. He visited the front line units, and by personal example and fearless leadership encouraged them to seize assigned objectives with the minimum of delay." The premature citation went on to praise his "keen tactical judgment, initiative and unremitting devotion to duty in coordinating all tactical elements ashore during the initial phase of the operation. . . ."

Very likely the text had been prepared in Tokyo. Inchon had not yet been fully secured, but MacArthur often announced victories before they happened. (Another announcement, arranged through a leak to the Associated Press, was that "General Douglas MacArthur is so confident of victory in this bold amphibious thrust that one of the landing ships carries furniture to equip his office and living quarters—presumably in Seoul." No such office ever materialized.)

Curiously, Larry Zellers, in a prison camp in Manpo in the far north, heard about Inchon almost as soon as Washington did. As he and another civilian POW, Father Philip Crosbie, were drawing water from an outside well, a small boy watching them bowed low, whispered that he was a Christian of the Presbyterian faith and handed Zellers, a missionary before his capture, a crumpled piece of paper. Once indoors, Zellers looked at it and saw that it was a message in Korean. He passed it on to another prisoner, who recognized it as part of a communiqué broadcast by Radio Taegu, reporting the Marine landing on Inchon under the direction of General MacArthur. The date and 0800 time were only two hours after the event.

The next day the boy was back with an update, but soon a prisoner boasted to a guard that he had better information than the North Koreans, and Zellers had to tell the faithful little boy in fragmentary Korean, "Thank you for all you have done. . . . Coming here is now dangerous. Please go home and do not return. Now!" The boy disappeared.

By evening on the sixteenth, the Marines had pushed six miles inland, where General O. P. Smith took over command at a forward post. From a large map taped to a bulkhead on the *Mount McKinley,* Almond followed their progress.

Although outnumbered, early on the seventeenth an enemy infantry force of about two hundred escorted by six Soviet-made T-34 tanks moved from Ascom City, east of Inchon, to confront the Marines. The column was ambushed by American tanks and troops with rocket launchers. Few survived. One Marine was wounded.

That morning MacArthur happily paid his first visit to the field, going ashore with Admiral Struble and other brass in a motor launch commanded by Lieutenant Grant Sharp. They were feeling their way through the pre-dawn darkness just offshore, with the general and admiral watching the personnel carriers and tanks moving off, when someone on the seawall shouted, "Get the hell out of there. We're going to blow up the wall in a few minutes!" They scurried to open water, then found another place to land, en route to O. P. Smith's command post. MacArthur seemed unperturbed.

Eager to view the evidence of the reported firefight, he asked to see the burned enemy tanks, and jeeped with Almond and Shepherd to a small ridge where smoking wreckage lay. Although Marine officers warned of sniper fire, MacArthur went forward, remarking, Lem Shepherd remembered, that the North Koreans defending Inchon were second-rate. "You damned Marines!" said Almond, probably only half in jest. "You always seem to be in the right place at the right time. You could not have staged a more spectacular performance if you had planned and rehearsed it." (They had, in field training.)

This time, Willoughby's intelligence estimates for MacArthur were on the mark. Assuming no threat to Inchon, the NKPA had garrisoned the post complex with the newly conscripted 226th Marine Regiment of about two thousand trainees, backed by the 918th Coast Artillery Regiment with 76mm guns on the harbor approaches. The understrength 18th Division, with about ten thousand infantrymen, was the main force at Seoul, along with the 87th Infantry at Yongdungpo, adding another two thousand men. Other units, including armor, would have to be rushed toward Seoul—too late to keep the Marines out of Inchon.

Intraservice jealousy would corrode Almond's relations with the Marine division throughout the breakout from Inchon, but to MacArthur they were his troops. Whenever he went ashore, "as he did every day during the Inchon landing," Shepherd told an interviewer, "he would always go as close as his jeep would carry him to the front—too close in my opinion . . . as we were occasionally exposed to enemy fire." "General," Shepherd would ask, "don't you think we've gone far enough? I know you wish to talk to your front-line troops but I am sure they worry about your safety when you expose yourself unnecessarily."

"No," said MacArthur; "anywhere my men are I will go." And he would travel to command posts to talk to officers as low as lieutenant, actually speaking to an enlisted man if he learned of an act of conspicuous courage worthy of decorating the soldier on the spot. MacArthur's zeal to be seen up front would flag when things were going badly in November and December, but Inchon was different. Hazards now were to be savored. Yet as his party bumped back to the port area, a boy from a nearby village approached a Korean interpreter with them who then hurried off with an American lieutenant and shouted into a culvert where MacArthur's vehicle had been parked. Out emerged seven enemy soldiers, their hands over their heads. Watching the scene, Pfc. Doug Koch thought, "Just think how famous one of them would have been if he'd lobbed a hand grenade onto the road a few minutes before. . . ."

Almost as if proving MacArthur's contention that Marines instinctively knew the right places to be at the right time, Captain Ike Fenton walked to an apparently vacant foxhole on Wolmi-do occupied earlier by North Koreans, intending to relieve himself. As he began urinating, "All of a sudden out jumped a North Korean who began bowing and scraping and chin-chinning to me. Talk about getting scared out of your wits." But he had his first prisoner.

As troops moved forward on the mainland, they rapidly outran supplies offloaded with difficulty at Inchon, but an ammunition shortage was averted when Marines entered the abandoned depot at Ascom City and found more than two thousand tons of American ordnance, still packed in warehouse condition, which had been seized early in the advance south. Shortages created by tidal problems at the docks made it all the more essential that the airfield at Kimpo be secured, as it was—by Marines—on the eighteenth. Again Almond pressed to get his Army troops ashore, and Admiral Doyle landed the 32nd Regiment of the 7th Division the same day. Every third soldier, however, was a barely trained Korean draftee—1,873 South Koreans to 3,241 Americans. Like most soldiers new to combat, all the riflemen were reluctant to leave behind anything generously supplied by X Corps quartermasters. They staggered under cargo packs and duffel bags and weapons. A trail of abandoned gear would mark the regiment's forward progress.

"If those beaches had been defended by Germans or Japanese of World War II caliber," Ed Simmons thought later, "we would not have gotten ashore. . . . But they were defended by second-rate troops. And not many of them." If the NKPA had had aircraft to attack the invasion fleet, again the issue might have been very different, but they had already lost many of their better planes (and there was no kamikaze tradition), and Russian pilots flying air defense from Pyongyang up to the Yalu could not be risked where a downing might mean capture and exposure of Soviet involvement.

The only North Korean air attack on the invasion fleet would occur at 5:55 a.m. on the seventeenth. A Yak-3 and a Stormovik IL-10 went for Admiral Struble's flagship, *Rochester*. Caught unawares, its anti-aircraft failed to reply, but the bombs dropped were only near-misses. Three miles away the planes found a British cruiser, HMS *Jamaica,* and raked its bridge, killing one sailor and wounding two before the ship's gunners downed the IL-10. When Kimpo airfield was captured a Yak-3 was seized intact—possibly the partner in the raid.

The lack of interdiction, according to Rear Admiral Sir William G. Andrewes, the British commander of the covering force for the invasion, meant that warships on station, troop carriers, amphibious vehicles, store and supply ships, and specialist clearance vessels approaching or returning from Inchon could crowd offshore in such numbers that in the early morning hours "the sea in our vicinity bore a striking resemblance to Hampstead Heath on August Bank Holiday." With no appreciable opposition "the whole of the movement in and out of the port was conducted without further orders"—improvised from the original operations instructions. As a result, a plane from the British carrier *Triumph* encountered "an LST bound for the battle but far off her course, and [we] were able to direct her towards Inchon. Had she gone on [to the north] she might well have started a private invasion of her own in the Gulf of [the] Yalu."

On the twentieth MacArthur and his entourage jeeped along the Han River to watch the 5th Marine Regiment cross. The 7th Marines would follow behind them and the 1st would ford to the west, closer to Seoul. (The

32nd Infantry would cross to the east, to encircle the capital.) From Mac-Arthur's vantage point he could see Yongdungpo, on the south bank of the Han, burning—and not at his orders. The North Koreans were not about to relinquish Seoul easily.

The next morning, with Admiral Struble, MacArthur visited the battle-ship *Missouri*, which had participated in an east coast diversion before join-ing the fire support ships off Inchon. For the first time, he saw, on its quarter-deck, the plaque marking the site of the Japanese surrender ceremony at which he had officiated five years earlier. He studied it silently while his eyes welled with tears. Inchon seemed already a success, but September 2, 1945, when the world listened to his stage-managing the end of World War II, had been the most dramatic moment of his career. Turning to the ship's captain he confided, "You have given me the happiest moment of my life."

Rejuvenated by his immersion in the war, MacArthur at Inchon no longer needed the afternoon naps he took in Tokyo, but he was past seventy now and found other signs of aging difficult to hide. His waist had thickened and his stride had shortened; his eyesight had dimmed, but his cosmetic solu-tion was to wear corrective sunglasses at every opportunity—an evasion only practical outdoors. The Parkinson's tremor in his right hand was often hid-den in a pocket; and his thin hair, which he dyed black, grown long on the right side and trailed across the top of his head, was an artificiality rarely seen in photographs as he seldom removed his cap. In pictures taken on deck or in the field, a decade or two vanished.

Once ashore, Maggie Higgins intended to keep a promise to herself—to walk to Seoul. It proved easier to hitch rides in jeeps scrounged by other corre-spondents, few of whom appreciated the attention she received despite grungy, muddy GI fatigues. "Riding in a jeep with Maggie," Jimmy Cannon of the *New York Post* complained, "is like being a jockey on Lady Godiva's horse."

As she accompanied units of the 5th Marines toward Seoul, Maggie had no idea that MacArthur was even more determined than she was to get there. With the calendar in mind, he saw the twenty-fifth as the anniversary of the invasion which he was reversing. He wanted to replicate in Seoul the experi-ence of the *Missouri* quarterdeck and be seen and heard worldwide as the lib-erator who had begun the rout of Communism.

The North Koreans might have accomplished a more complete job of destruction had they known MacArthur's intentions, yet they succeeded any-way, with American assistance, in the wholesale obliteration of Seoul. For reasons of face as well as to prevent closure of the main escape route from the south, now that the Inchon landing had made their position investing the Pusan Perimeter untenable, the NKPA fought hard. Many were threatened with entrapment below Seoul. It was difficult to distinguish Korean friend from Korean enemy—or either, if concealed in civilian garb, from refugee. Thousands of POWs were penned in fields where they had surrendered, sprayed with DDT as a hasty form of delousing and enclosed by barbed-wire fences. Some captives were women; some were boys. Most were grateful to be out of the war, but the war would soon catch up to them.

MacArthur had taken pride that his island-hopping successes in the Pacific war had been accomplished with minimal loss of life (as opposed to the cross-Pacific carnage of Tarawa, Saipan, Iwo Jima and Okinawa, which were out of his jurisdiction), but taking Seoul became an exception. About twenty thousand North Koreans faced the 5th Marines, who began fighting their way to the Han behind sixteen-inch gunfire from the *Missouri,* twenty-eight miles away. Only eleven thunderous shots, each sounding like a freight train directly overhead, landed before the Marines outranged the battleship's guns. Further shelling was called off as too dangerous for the troops. Then natural obstacles slowed the Marines down. The NKPA had blown all the Han bridges.

Just after dawn, Marines began crossing at the Haengju ferry site, using amtracs—amphibious tractors—and laying down meshing on the opposite bank to prevent vehicles floated across on pontoon rafts from bogging down in the mud. Bridging sections—those not washed overboard by typhoon winds and waves near Kobe—were overlaid on pontoons, and heavier equipment brought across. By nightfall they were close to Seoul.

The 1st Marines, commanded by Chesty Puller, were to advance directly on Yongdungpo but had heavy going. Rows of towed 4.5-inch multiple-tube rocket launchers sent volleys toward enemy positions, then failed because the Marines ran out of working rocket fuses. Some assaults on hills ringing the city required hand-to-hand combat as the 9th NKPA Division came up to reinforce the weakening 18th Division. At about 10 a.m. on the seventeenth, MacArthur again left his headquarters ship for the mainland, accompanied by a contingent of general officers and reporters. Puller was commanding his men from up front and responded to a courier inviting him to meet the general, "If he wants to see me, have him come up to the front lines. I'll be waiting for him."

Responding to the challenge, MacArthur jeeped forward, then climbed still-unsafe Hill 186. There was nothing at the summit but Puller, who explained that his map case was his command post. Not eager to remain, the Supreme Commander abruptly announced, "Colonel, your regiment is performing splendidly, and I am gratified to present you with the Silver Star." But his aide, who took memoranda on such things and stocked MacArthur's pockets with medals for such occasions, had forgotten to resupply his chief. The general fished about and, coming up empty-handed, instructed his assistant, "Make a note of that." Since a Korean colonel and rear admiral were with Puller as observers, MacArthur awarded them paper Silver Stars as well. But the press preferred to show the general with lesser folk, as befit a democratic army, and newspapers printed a photo of MacArthur "exchanging greetings" with an "unidentified Marine" in rumpled fatigues. He was Corporal C. B. Stacy, who would later be killed in action. (General Almond would copy his chief's impulsive system of instant awards, but would make a point of disbursing them to enlisted men, especially the wounded.)

Below on the Yongdungpo road MacArthur's entourage saw more enemy tanks that had been disabled the day before. "Considering they are Russian," MacArthur remarked, attempting some humor, "these tanks are in the condition I desire them to be." (He had already cracked to a medical officer as they passed an enemy corpse, "There's a patient you'll never have to work on.") Some additional tanks had been knocked out that morning, and MacArthur was eager to see them, although the Marines did not want him exposed further. "General," an officer appealed, "you can't come up here!" He explained that the kill was fresh, but MacArthur strode to the crest of a rise for a look anyway. "[The tanks] were still burning," Lem Shepherd recalled, "and dead North Korean troops were all around them. The occupants lay half cooked on top of several of the tanks. . . . The turrets had been punctured by clean hits."

Beyond, MacArthur could see a firefight in the distance. He ordered his jeep ahead and stopped to watch. A Marine with a heavy battery-pack portable two-way radio always with the general rushed to catch up. Farther off, but visible, was Kimpo airfield. Trudging down again, MacArthur paused at the bottom of the hill to award Colonel Raymond L. Murray a promissory note for a Silver Star, then jeeped rearward to have a look at the bag of 671 prisoners now in the division's improvised stockade.

The 5th Marines were under MacArthur's injunction to "capture Kimpo as soon as you can." The airfield could open up quick new sources of supply from Japan and also speed the recapture of Seoul. The general also had a personal mission—more propagandistic than strategic—to reinstall Syngman Rhee as president in his own house of parliament on the anniversary of the invasion. MacArthur saw the symbolism as crucial. Only a week remained to meet that goal.

On the evening of the eighteenth, with Keyes Beech and Marguerite Higgins covering them, the 2nd Battalion, 5th Marines, took the first airstrip at Kimpo. In the fading light at 8:05 p.m. *Life* photographer Hank Walter snapped the scene. On board the *Mount McKinley*, MacArthur scrawled out a dispatch to be radioed to the Joint Chiefs. However premature, he announced that all of Kimpo was in American hands.

Officially, the first UN plane to land at Kimpo, even before bulldozers patched the cratered runways, was a Sikorsky helicopter from Marine Observation Squadron 6. The squadron's eight helicopters were the only such aircraft in Korea. On board was General Lem Shepherd, off a carrier. But preempting the chopper, a Marine Corsair, its oversized fifteen-foot propeller feathering, landed while a company of the 1st Engineer Battalion was still clearing the field. "The pilot climbed out . . . and he was hooting and hollering," Lieutenant David Peppin remembered. Marines on the ground signaled that the runways were still off limits, and the pilot prudently gunned his engine and left. MacArthur would soon use Kimpo to return to the Dai Ichi.

After dinner aboard the ship on the nineteenth, while troops were still pushing forward to reduce hotly contested Yongdungpo, MacArthur led a group of senior officers aboard the *Mount McKinley* down three decks to the operations room. A large map of Korea was tacked on the forward bulkhead. Impatient with the failure of Walker's Eighth Army to break out of the Perimeter despite the assistance from Inchon, MacArthur hinted darkly that EUSAK might never achieve juncture with the X Corps unless Almond's forces came to the rescue. Walker, he contended, was sluggishly defensive minded after more than two months of holding the line. (Yet MacArthur had stripped Walker's army of his most effective force, the 5th Marines, for Inchon.)

Another amphibious landing to the south, MacArthur thought, might be necessary—possibly at Kunsan, where he had been urged to land as an alternative to Inchon. Now he wanted the plans reexamined. Struble and Doyle promised the ships, but in the end no troops could be spared.

Walker was still 180 miles to the south. Even the river barrier he had counted upon to hold back the *In Min Gun*, the Naktong, had not yet been recrossed. In a light plane he flew along it above Waegwan and chose the ferry landing at Sonsan for the 1st Cav's jump-off. Shorthanded and without effective reserves, Walker had been cautious indeed, waiting for the NKPA to get word of Inchon and regroup in haste to the north. He still had problems with green troops and with units unweaned from occupation ways. As General Dean, now a POW, had put it painfully early in the war, "How am I to teach these boys that they all can't jeep to battle?" Four days passed before the North Korean command would inform its troops besieging the Perimeter of the landing behind them. As late as September 22, when troops from the Inchon bridgehead were nearing Seoul, the Eighth Army was still only a few miles beyond its Perimeter positions.

Impatient to take full command of X Corps, Ned Almond watched the first week of operations only as nominal commander. He had MacArthur looking over his shoulder, and the Marines, with their own officers, doing most of the fighting. On the twenty-first, when the 7th Division was finally ashore in large numbers and taking over a section of the front, Almond stepped in, and MacArthur left Kimpo for Japan. His parting reminder for Almond was to take Seoul as quickly as possible so that Rhee could be reinstated with ceremony.

After being moved south to the Mount Fuji maneuver area below Tokyo for combat training, the cannibalized 7th Division, which Walton Walker had dismissed as a "crust" and MacArthur deplored as "half-understrength," had been refitted with American draftees airlifted from the States and with green Korean levies. Some reservists who had been activated had even less training than draftees. Corporal Merwin Perkins, nineteen, a Marine but typical of troops rushed into action, had traveled westward by troop train to Camp Pendleton before embarking for Japan. It took five days. A sergeant questioned him about his experience, which consisted of three summer camps "where we mostly goofed off." His records were marked CR, for combat-ready. When he landed in Korea on September 21, it was one month to the day after he had left civilian life in Minnesota.* (Fortunately, some Marines had World War II amphibious experience.)

Recognizing themselves as the bottom of the barrel in replacement priorities, veteran cadre from Camp Crawford in Hokkaido had blamed their assignment to a "backwater camp" on Mrs. MacArthur, who allegedly referred to the 7th Division—a problem outfit in the Philippines—as "the future baby rapers of the world." On the other hand, she saw the historic 1st Cavalry, with its oversized yellow horse's head shoulder patch as the ideal palace guard. MacArthur had wanted to hoard the Cav for Chromite and

---

*The author went from civilian with no reservist training whatever to Army second lieutenant in Korea in little more than two months.

kept it at full strength, but the necessities of the Perimeter had meant relinquishing it to earlier action. Now he wanted it to strike north toward Suwon to link up with troops moving south from Seoul.

In the U.S. the Pentagon was relieved at the success of the operation, as was the White House. Newspapers headlined its strategic genius, attributed to MacArthur, and the futility of objections to Inchon, attributed to timid chair-warmers in Washington. Manipulating the press as usual, the Dai Ichi had initiated the congratulatory reports, and the JCS angrily quoted back the self-praise, in MacArthur's recognized style, to the SCAP himself:

> With invasion fleet off Korea—General MacArthur hopes that the invasion . . . at Inchon will save 100,000 American lives. . . . MacArthur sold the Joint Chiefs of Staff on the idea of an Inchon landing despite their unanimous objections to such an ambitious undertaking. He laid his plan before General J. Lawton Collins, Army Chief of Staff, and Admiral Forrest Sherman, Naval Chief of Operations, when they were in Tokyo on August 22. He promised that such an invasion would "end the war by winter and save 100,000 lives."
>
> Sources close to General MacArthur said both Collins and Sherman opposed the landing at Inchon. It would be too hard to put the troops ashore and supply them against counter-attacks, they maintained. They suggested landings further south.

General Collins and Admiral Sherman, the Pentagon continued, were releasing a statement correcting MacArthur's version of the facts:

> In reply to queries as to press reports that they had opposed the planned landing at Inchon and suggested landings farther south, Gen Collins and Adm Sherman stated that in accordance with the practice developed during World War II they, as rep[resentative]s of JCS, were sent by the JCS to consult with Gen MacArthur and to review plans for the Inchon landing, possible alternate landings, and subsequent operations. The JCS, after receiving the recommendations of Gen Collins and Adm Sherman, gave unanimous approval of the projected operations including the landing at Inchon. No further comment is planned here with respect to this report.

Many at the Pentagon felt that they were fighting two wars simultaneously, and that MacArthur was winning both. "REDS ON THE LAM," headlined the *Washington Daily News*. On seeing the banner, the new Dutch ambassador, J. Herman van Roijen, presenting his credentials to President

Truman, asked his State Department escort, John Simmons, "What does that mean—'ON THE LAM'?"

Unable to improvise a diplomatic definition, Simmons replied, "It is, I believe, the name of a river in Korea."

Diplomatic problems had meshed with military ones as MacArthur flew back to Tokyo in triumph and X Corps began to invest Seoul. He announced that when Seoul was retaken, which he expected to happen imminently, the war would be effectively over. In Korea, Syngman Rhee, meeting with Hugh Baillie, the head of United Press and a confidant of MacArthur, announced that he expected to preside over a unified Korea—north as well as south. And responding to Truman's comment to reporters than the United Nations would decide whether to cross the 38th parallel in force, Rhee challenged Baillie, "Show it to me. Where is it?"

Rushing both to effect a juncture with EUSAK and to take Seoul for MacArthur's political objectives, Almond moved among his scattered forces, some inexperienced, to urge them forward. He would leave his command post as early as 4:00 a.m., often driving his own jeep. His expected third star still to come, he was identifiable only by the two cloth white stars sewn on the shoulder loops of his fatigue jacket, his leather belt around it securing his .38-caliber sidearm, and his worn leather map case and little black notebook. (His posh command van was nowhere to be seen.) Turning up unexpectedly at advance locations, he might override an order about placement of supporting fire and arrange his own coordination of field units.

Pushing some ahead too close to the enemy for safe air cover, he ordered use of orange or red identification panels visible from above to prevent strafing the wrong side, but there were accidents. Jet fighters from carriers raked 7th Infantry tank columns with cannon fire, forcing an armor lieutenant to rip off a signal panel and wave it frantically to fend off a third pass. In another communications failure (of many), the commander of the 73rd Tank Battalion went to greet what he thought was his relief unit, flicking the headlights of his jeep and waving his arms. The four tanks were NKPA T-34s, which gunned him down, scattered his men and disappeared into the darkness. Almond mourned the loss of Lieutenant Colonel Henry Hampton, who, much like Stonewall Jackson in 1863, was accidentally killed by his own men. In another friendly fire episode, three Navy Corsairs shot up a 31st Infantry cargo truck disabled by flat tires, killing curious civilians crowded around it and seriously wounding the driver. Such blunders had also occurred in the first days of ground involvement in Korea, and were the price in every war of haste and inexperience. Yet on the outskirts of Seoul there was another factor—ego.

Almond's public relations–driven push toward Seoul created the conditions for further mistakes. Exactly three months after the date that South Korea was invaded, the recapture of the capital had to be announced. So MacArthur had ordered. But Marine General O. P. Smith warned Almond as NKPA opposition intensified "that I couldn't guarantee anything; that was up to the enemy. We'd do the best we could and go as fast as we could." Nevertheless, MacArthur's timetable drove Almond. Troops were in the outskirts of Seoul, eight miles to the west, by September 21. The next day, the 31st Infantry of the 7th under Colonel Richard P. Ovenshine occupied the airfield at Suwon, twenty-one miles below Seoul. With its mile-long runway, it could take C-54s. (One had brought MacArthur there in the early days of the war.)

Seoul would be contested street by street. It was as much of a political prize to the North Koreans as to MacArthur.

While the 7th Division augmented by two ROK regiments was to bypass the city from the south, the 1st Marines were to push into the center of the capital, the 5th to advance on Seoul from the northwest and the 7th to outflank the city above the 5th. The 7th Marines, under Colonel Homer L. Litzenberg Jr., had been landed last and assembled at Camp Pendleton only in mid-August from a core of a thousand regulars and two thousand reservists. Supplementing them were troops from the 2nd Marine Division at Fort Quantico in Virginia. An understrength battalion of 6th Marines, an artillery battalion of the 10th Marines and another battalion of the 6th Marines serving afloat in the eastern Mediterranean were combined into what would become the 7th Regiment. The shipboard battalion was transferred from Crete via Suez to Kobe, where it became the 7th's 3rd Battalion on arrival on September 17. On the twenty-first it disembarked at Inchon. General Smith hastily acclimated the men in two days of patrolling north of Inchon, after which the battalion became his left wing in the envelopment of Seoul.

Nothing was fast enough for Almond, who, according to Colonel Alpha L. Bowser, Smith's deputy, "had a habit of treating the Han River like it had five or six intact bridges across it, and of course it had none." Smith refused to cross without tank support, rigged ferries to get equipment across while Almond complained about delays and agreed reluctantly to a frontal assault of Seoul, although MacArthur had boasted in the past of limiting casualties by bypassing strong points. Early on September 24, Almond jeeped forward again to Smith's command post to threaten that if the Marines—in particular the 5th Regiment, which had been fighting unrelieved since the first land-ings—did not "make headway" in the next twenty-four hours, he would divert Major General David Barr's 7th Division to the center of the Seoul front.

Angrily, Smith noted in his diary that Almond "displayed a complete ignorance of the fighting qualities of Marines." But MacArthur's deadline loomed before Almond, who tore about the front without the amenities of his personal command vehicle, outfitted in Tokyo with refrigerator, fine china, hot running water, electricity, shower and flush toilet. Early on, Almond had nagged Admiral Doyle about unloading it from a transport, prompting Doyle to tell the ship's captain that if the general insisted on its being offloaded out of turn, the Navy should cut a hole in the bottom of the vessel to extract the vehicle. Offloaded in normal sequence on September 21, it was of little use to Almond.

Worldwide, the Communist press had been pondering how to confront the altered prospects facing the *In Min Gun*, which had seemed so close to its objectives. On September 18 a communiqué from Pyongyang suggested that something was happening off Inchon by announcing the fiction that two American carrier planes had been shot down there by coast artillery units. The next day, in Beijing, the *People's Daily* (*Jen Min Jih Pao*) acknowledged that the American imperialists had attempted a landing at Inchon, claiming that their "gamble" was "completely lost," as their troops were weakened by "low fighting spirit" and the realization that reinforcements were "distant." Should the fighting last "any length of time, they will surely be defeated." And NKPA forces occupying Seoul battled back as if that chance existed. The capital was a symbol, and the defenders had little desire to cooperate with MacArthur's schedule.

Ratcheting the Communist rhetoric a notch higher, *Pravda* on Sep-tember 23 compared Seoul with Stalingrad and added some cartoon-like propaganda:

> Cement, streetcar rails, beams and stones are being used to build barricades in the streets, and workers are joining soldiers in the defense. The situation is very serious. Pillboxes and tank traps dot the scene. Every home must be defended as a fortress. There is firing behind every rock. When a soldier is killed, his gun continues to fire. It is picked up by a worker, a tradesman, or office-worker. . . . General MacArthur landed the most arrant criminals at Inchon, gathered from the ends of the earth. . . . He sends British and New

Zealand adventure-seekers ahead of his own executioners, letting them drag Yankee chestnuts from the fire. American bandits are shooting every Seoul inhabitant taken prisoner.

Every aspect of the report was fiction except its sense of intense fighting. The North Korean roadblocks were exactly as described. Having fought through the gutted industrial sector of Yongdungpo to the Han, Marines crossed the river to face NKPA reserve regiments brought down from as far north as Pyongyang. In the streets of Seoul, London *Daily Telegraph* correspondent Reggie Thompson, who had covered France and Germany from D-Day to the surrender, was sickened by the destruction of the city, which would have fallen in time if isolated. In his notebook he wrote of the "inferno of din and destruction with the searing noise of Corsair dive-bombers blasting right ahead, and the livid flashes of the tank guns, the harsh, fierce crackle of blazing wooden buildings . . . [which] collapse in showers of sparks, puffing masses of smoke and rubble upon us in terrific heat." For several days every building and street was contested, but on schedule, although the NKPA was still counterattacking within the city on September 26, MacArthur had issued a communiqué the afternoon before, claiming:

> Three months to the day after the North Koreans launched their surprise attack . . . the combat troops of X Corps recaptured the capital city of Seoul. . . . The liberation of Seoul was accomplished by a coordinated attack of X Corps troops. . . . By 1400 hours 25 September the military defenses of Seoul were broken. . . . The enemy is fleeing the city to the northeast.

Keyes Beech of the *Chicago Daily News* reported a group from Dog Company of a Marine battalion near Seoul gathering around "a tattered copy of *Stars and Stripes*" flown to Kimpo from Japan. The headline contended, "YANKS ENTER SEOUL FROM TWO SIDES." "Hey, fellas, these gooks haven't got the word," said Pfc. Jimmie Frenchman, twenty, from Oklahoma. Ricocheting machine-gun bullets spattered into the dust and the Marines dived for cover. Three months later Beech got a letter from Frenchman's mother, who had read the dispatch back home. Her son, she wrote, was dead.

Flame-throwing tanks and air strikes demolished the last street obstacles put up by the NKPA, and the Marines pushed downtown despite continuing sniper fire. The blasted dome of the national Capitol still flew the North Korean flag, and random shelling echoed around the city, but jubilant crowds began surging around the advancing Americans, although Seoul dwellers had little to celebrate other than their precarious liberation. Ma-Po Boulevard had been a fashionable, tree-lined route to grocery, tea and wine shops, and boasted expensive homes. Double tracks for streetcars which had once plied through American cities had been ripped up, and the streetcars were gone. The shops still smoldered. In the central square of Seoul, the Capitol building, pocked by shell holes, appeared unready as a venue for the reinstallation ceremonies, but from Tokyo, MacArthur ordered that every possible laborer be rounded up to make the building habitable. All around the city, troops flushed out remnants of the *In Min Gun* to ensure security. MacArthur intended to return on September 28.

The cost of quick victory had been high—much higher, still, for the NKPA. One company of the 5th Marines suffered 176 casualties out of a strength of 206. Even tactical air losses were heavy. The North Koreans had effective anti-aircraft equipment from the Russians and knew how to use it.

As troops in the Perimeter had already discovered, even prisoners of war did not consider themselves out of action. The apparent dead were not necessarily so. POWs often concealed grenades in their clothes, requiring Marines to accept surrenders only from North Koreans who first stripped trousers and leggings, and soon everything else. From a cave at which a flame-throwing tank had flushed out 131 unwounded prisoners, all ordered to remove their clothes, two turned out to be female and were hastily furnished with long johns from an infantryman's pack. (By the end of the war nearly a thousand female POWs were in custody.) The enemy wounded were hoisted atop the tanks and the 129 "bare asses," Staff Sergeant Arthur Farringdon recalled, were lined up in ranks of three along a railroad track not far from a field of apparent corpses. "When about 40–50 Koreans jumped up to the left of the railroad tracks . . . [after] lying there doggo behind us all this time . . . we killed them with rifle, machine-gun and 90mm fire as they went across the paddies."

On the north bank of the Han, Maggie Higgins and Keyes Beech "passed a drove of North Korean prisoners who were being marched to the rear in the buff for security reasons. Higgins primly fixed her gaze on the road ahead. Out of the corners of their eyes the mortified prisoners spotted the passing American woman and hastily covered their loins with their hands." But, Beech recalled, their sense of delicacy was "entirely lost on the Marine guards, who promptly ordered the prisoners to raise their hands again."

To the south, where the EUSAK sweep of prisoners was almost too much to cope with, one surprise had been the capture of "four uniformed female prisoners" by F Company of the 7th Cav. Bill "Old Crowe" Collins remembered, "We started bypassing them after the breakout, first telling them, 'Strip to your skivvies, hands overhead, doubletime south.'" Not so with the females, they thought. To perform "a little front-line interrogation" his squad took them aside, and "just as the last one was entering the house we were going to use, the c.o. popped up from somewhere. Needless to say there was no interrogation on our part."

An even greater POW surprise was Senior Colonel Lee Hak Ku, who on the morning of September 21 shook two GIs of the 8th Cav awake to surrender to them. Although only thirty, he had the shoulderboard insignia of a senior officer—it was a young army. Chief of staff of the NKPA 13th Division, he was a catch so important that he was jeeped immediately to division headquarters for questioning, where he claimed that although the NKPA II Corps had been ordered to switch to the defensive on September 17, he had known nothing about the Inchon landing. From Taegu, Walker happily telephoned the news to Doyle Hickey, MacArthur's deputy, in Tokyo.

Seemingly cooperative, Lee reported confusion among NKPA divisions, and that vast personnel losses had been made up mostly by impressed South Koreans. NKPA trucks and tanks had been depleted and troops were allegedly on half-rations. In the circumstances his giving himself up seemed logical, yet the voluntary surrender of a ranking officer who could have employed a network of sympathizers to escape to the north raised no suspicions at EUSAK or the Dai Ichi. Lee might have been instructed to surrender so that North Korean prisoners of war would have a recognized leader and Kim Il Sung someone trustworthy to whom to send surreptitious communications through the captive network. Later, Lee would mastermind the POW mass riots on Koje-do that embarrassed the United States and had to be put down by force.

Ensuring that the Seoul area was cleared of the enemy—less than half the city had been taken—Almond ordered a night mission by the Marines on the basis of an air reconnaissance report of "enemy fleeing the city of Seoul. . . . You will attack *now* to the limit of your objectives in order to insure maximum destruction of enemy forces." Moving in darkness into the chaotic, unfamiliar and burning city—supposedly already seized—seemed to Colonel Bowser risky in the extreme. The fleeing masses were undoubtedly civilian refugees anyway. Bowser telephoned a protest to Lieutenant Colonel John H. Chiles at Almond's command post, only to be told that the order was to be carried out immediately. (The 32nd Infantry below the Marines received no attack order.) Bowser informed O. P. Smith, who protested to Almond's chief of staff, Clark Ruffner, and was again told to execute the order without delay. However uncomfortable with the idea of a risky and unnecessary night assault, Bowser arranged for Puller and Murray as commanders of the two regiments probing into the city to jump off at 0145 on the twenty-sixth. But it was not the *In Min Gun* that had been seen fleeing north toward Uijongbu. The Marines met tank-led defenses in the main avenues. Casualties were heavy on both sides. By dawn, some streets and wrecked buildings had changed hands several times. Ordered to take the Capitol in time for MacArthur's ceremonial restoration of Rhee, the 3rd Battalion of the 5th Marines stormed the National Assembly grounds, then routed the North Koreans room by room. Tearing down enemy flags, including those flying over the dome, they raised American flags and only as a cosmetic afterthought called for South Korean ones. Leading Company G, which took the most casualties, Lieutenant Charles Mize, a veteran of Okinawa, won a Navy Cross for valor.

Correspondents who followed in early daylight asked Puller about the reported enemy retreat the night before. "All I know about a fleeing enemy," he said, underestimating the cost, "is that there's two or three hundred out there that won't be fleeing anymore. They're dead."

Almond would claim to a *New York Times* correspondent, "Nothing could have been more fortunate than the tank-led enemy counter-attacks. It gave us a greater opportunity to kill more enemy soldiers and destroy his tanks more easily than if we had to take the city house by house." (Which is actually what had to be done.) "If the city had been liberated," an AP correspondent wrote, "the remaining North Koreans did not know it."

As early as September 22, once MacArthur had announced to the Pentagon his plans to ceremonially return the capital to Rhee, the State Department had objected to "any participation by the military commander in ROK government matters." MacArthur was asked to "submit without delay" plans for his involvement for the "approval of higher authority." He exploded, "Your message is not understood. I have no plans whatsoever except scrupulously to implement the directives which I have received." He explained that the ROK government had never ceased functioning and that all he intended was to restore it "to domicile in Seoul." That he wanted to do that personally and flamboyantly went unsaid. Helplessly, the JCS authorized him to "facilitate the restoration" but not to entangle himself in political issues respecting North Korea's future.

Korea's future and its import for the West had entered American politics just as had the future of Formosa. Korea was now seen in partisan terms as crucial to a non-Communist Japan. Richard Nixon, campaigning for a senatorial seat in California that September, charged that his Democratic opponent had declared herself against aid for Chiang, whom he equated with Rhee, conveniently forgetting that in the House of Representatives he had voted against aid for Korea. "All we have to do," he told a Republican rally on September 20, "is to take a look at the map and we can see that if Formosa falls, the next frontier is the coast of California." A senator from the neighboring state of Nevada, Pat McCarran, had already promoted a bill requiring Communist organizations and allegedly Communist front groups to register with the Attorney General within thirty days. Members of such associations clearly faced political and economic reprisals in the ongoing war against alleged Soviet encroachment (which troops did not notice) fought most visibly in Korea. On September 23, Congress overrode Truman's veto, turning the McCarran Act into law.

Returning in the *SCAP*, MacArthur landed at Kimpo at 10:00 a.m. on the twenty-ninth, a Friday, accompanied by his wife, Whitney, Stratemeyer and other GHQ officials. An hour later Rhee and his wife, with Muccio and other officials, arrived from Pusan in MacArthur's other personal plane, the *Bataan*. Almond intended to have them proceed into Seoul in elaborate style. But the bridges separating Kimpo from the city were still out, and the day before, X Corps had ordered an airlift of all the portable bridging sections that could be found in Japan. O.P. Smith's Marines shifted from mopping-up operations in Seoul to constructing a floating bridge for MacArthur and providing for him, the next morning, two honor guards, one at the airstrip and the other at the pitted and fire-blackened Capitol building. A cordon of Marines was to line the route while a Marine band played.

Since the Marines had left their instruments in Kobe, the Fifth Air Force was instructed to fly them to Kimpo by nightfall on the twenty-eighth. At that point MacArthur realized that the extravaganza would increase his troubles with Washington. He canceled the instrument airlift and the honor guards. He ordered troops to be out in force for security, but out of sight. And, he added, "I will personally conduct the proceedings."

Five Chevrolet staff cars shipped into Inchon by Almond led a convoy of forty jeeps filled with bigwigs and reporters eastward across the Han into thoroughly wrecked and still smoking Seoul. MacArthur's sedan displayed a five-star license plate. "It's just like old times," he said. As much wreckage as possible along the route had been hastily bulldozed for a neater appearance, but the effect was incongruous—much like General Almond's uniform for the occasion. While most military dignitaries were in dress khaki or naval white, Almond turned up in faded green fatigue uniform and cap, but with his field trousers sharply creased and his field jacket starched and open at the collar to reveal a black silken ascot.

In the streets, along the shattered buildings, women with small children and some old men—the only males except for soldiers and police—waved miniature South Korean flags distributed for the occasion, cheered and cried. MacArthur began the ceremonies in the shell of the Capitol promptly at noon, addressing an audience of military officers, Korean government officials and correspondents. The walls of the National Assembly chamber had been hurriedly hung with velvet drapes and temporary lighting had been installed. The honor guard permitted at the Capitol irked General Smith, as it consisted of spit-and-polish MPs flown in from Tokyo—"very nicely dressed and shined up" and "more or less out of place" in the blasted surroundings, he recalled. Attendees remembered the smell of charred wood and, from the uncollected corpses, the smell of death.

As MacArthur began, concussions from artillery and small-arms fire shook loose weakened panes of glass from overhead panels. The audience dodged them as they shattered loudly. Meanwhile, bare-headed and sonorous in voice, the general gravely restored to Rhee his seat of government on behalf, he said, of the United Nations. Then he intoned the Lord's Prayer, asking everyone to join him.* Tears coursed down his face. It was a consummate performance. "If there had been any chaplains around," Admiral Doyle remarked, "they would have had to have gone back to school again."

Rhee followed. Turning to MacArthur first, in advance of his prepared remarks, he said, "We admire you. We love you as the savior of our race. How can I ever explain to you my own undying gratitude and that of the Korean people?" Going on, Rhee declared the day one of "unity, understanding, and forgiveness" rather than one of "oppression and revenge." ("It was indeed a thrilling moment," Francesca Rhee, recognizing protocol, wrote later to Jean MacArthur.) But, a historian would write, "Despite the fine words, execution

---

*Rhee was a Christian, and missionaries of both Roman Catholic and Protestant persuasion were all over South Korea. Although MacArthur often identified the "Asian mind" with his own, it might have been a colonialist affront to most Koreans to invoke the Lord's Prayer during a purportedly national ceremony in a country where the traditional religions of shamanism, Buddhism and Confucianism still held sway. It suggested another Western imposition.

squads were [already] busily at work throughout Seoul. They were taking up where the Communists had left off. Thousands of 'class enemies' slain by the Communists during the North Korean occupation were being discovered in shallow graves all over South Korea. Now it was the turn of anyone accused of collaboration with the departed enemy. Old scores were paid off. Many an opponent of the Rhee dictatorship was conveniently liquidated. . . . The remaining populace tried to reconstruct their lives."

There were atrocity fabrications by both sides, as well as undeniable atrocities. Later on the twenty-ninth, when Taejon was recaptured by UN forces chasing the NKPA north, the bodies of several thousand South Korean civilians, forty American soldiers and seventeen ROKs were discovered. They had been murdered by North Korean security police in the last days of the occupation. The news would overshadow in the press, and even excuse, Rhee's brutality while undeniable *In Min Gun* excesses were discovered almost daily. There were other corpses reclaimed, too. Pfc. Leonard Korgie of the 34th Infantry recalled marching past a position in late September from which his regiment had retreated two months earlier. "Graves Registration people were collecting the bodies we'd left behind in July. What I could see made it look as if those bodies were made of coal. They were just pitch-black."

Crossing the Naktong with the 27th (Wolfhound) Regiment, and heading toward Kunsan on the west coast, Mike Michaelis got most of his vehicles to the opposite bank, although losing a few, by sandbagging the river until the water overflowed it. Then troops added more sandbags. It took four days, during which they had no resupply of rations, as everything was going north to Inchon. "We weren't getting ammunition, we weren't getting food, and we were rounding up prisoners by the thousands and tens of thousands." MacArthur's largesse was all going to X Corps.

After the Rhee reinstallation, in a separate exercise outside the Capitol, MacArthur awarded the Distinguished Service Cross to General Almond and to General Walker, who had flown up with Rhee for the ceremony. The nation's second-highest medal for battlefield valor, it was presented, in MacArthur's words, "for their fearless example." (Almond had already received the Silver Star, and for his L-5 flights, the Air Medal.)

Back in Johnny Walker's expanding Perimeter the once-dominant NKPA was finally withdrawing before it could be enveloped in the pincers which the operations east and north from Seoul threatened. Of the 71,339 men (including ROK troops) landed at Inchon, 536 had been killed, 2,550 wounded, and 65 remained missing and assumed dead or taken prisoner.

Most were Marines. (The U.S. had already suffered 20,756 casualties in the war.) X Corps estimated 14,000 enemy dead and 7,000 prisoners, a figure that would grow as EUSAK reached north to link up.

To assist the breakout from the Perimeter, the Air Force had dumped explosives and fire along Communist defensive positions almost as soon as the Inchon bridgehead was secured and no longer needed heavyweight interdiction. With low rain clouds often in the way, raids such as an eighty-two-plane B-29 sweep with 500-pound bombs over Waegwan proved useless, but the bombs had to be dropped somewhere, and the armada was sent far north to waste so-called secondary targets. Fifth Air Force Mustang fighter-bombers went out to blast areas above the Naktong River with 110-gallon tanks of napalm, and large numbers of casualties were claimed in the close-support sorties, but the dollar cost of ground-level horror (if troops were really there) was high—about $600 per tank.

Edwards Metcalf, a reserve lieutenant commander recalled ten days after the war began and assigned to aircraft supply, found that he could produce napalm in Japanese factories at $36.35 per tank. He set his own "Marshall Plan" going, and refused to concern himself with the inappropriateness of having a defeated and demilitarized nation produce explosives. After all, other Japanese were repairing American military equipment, unloading munitions at Inchon, manning troopships and operating minesweepers only leased to the U.S.

As resistance crumbled under the high-tech war, the North Koreans, knowing they were outflanked and had to retreat and reorganize, abandoned their offensive strategies of infiltration and surprise. They could no longer operate only at night, negotiating narrow mountain trails with guns and packs on their backs. Haste required continual movement and exposure to daylight harassment against which they had no air cover. Piloting a low-winged, two-seater AT-6 air control plane, Lieutenant George Nelson, spotting about two hundred enemy troops northeast of Kunsan on the west coast, swooped low and dropped a scribbled note ordering them to lay down their arms and gather at a nearby hill. He signed it "MacArthur." When they began to comply, he found UN patrols to scoop up his prisoners. Soon there would be more prisoners, cut off from return, than Walton Walker's forces were prepared to handle. The Wolfhounds in the west already had their fill of hungry POWs.

MacArthur and his party left Kimpo for Tokyo less than two hours after they had touched down in Korea. If the ceremony was regarded in the international press as MacArthur's most triumphant hour, it was less out of his feel for drama than the assumption that the UN war to reverse aggression was nearly over. Troops would soon be at the 38th parallel and the remnants of the *In Min Gun* would be gone.

Although the JCS should have been wary of MacArthur's open-ended ambitions, the acclaim for his *coup de théâtre* in Seoul led instead to a congratulatory message on the twenty-ninth. They were "proud of the successes you have achieved," which would have been "impossible without [your] brilliant and audacious leadership. . . . From the sudden initiation of hostilities you have exploited to the utmost all capabilities and opportunities. . . ." They expected a "successful conclusion" to the "great task entrusted to you by the United Nations."

With hardly less caution, Defense Secretary Marshall sent MacArthur a handwritten personal letter. "Please accept my personal tribute," it began with uncharacteristic effusiveness, "to the courageous campaign you directed . . . and the daring and perfect strategical operation." Almost certainly surprised, as relations between the two had never been friendly and MacArthur when chief of staff in the 1930s had nearly thwarted Marshall's career, MacArthur began his reply warmly with an unprecedented "Thanks, George, for your fine message." A MacArthuresque spin on their relationship followed, turning it into a fantasy which, perhaps, he may have believed at the moment. "It brings back vividly the memories of past wars and the complete coordination and perfect unity of cooperation which has always existed in our mutual relationships and martial endeavors. Again my deepest appreciation for your message and your unfailing support."

Marshall also radioed an eyes-only message: "We want you to feel unhampered tactically and strategically to proceed north of the 38th parallel." He wanted no public announcement, as it might precipitate an adverse vote in the UN. Rather, the move should be "found . . . militarily necessary." MacArthur was pleased. On September 26, before flying to Seoul, he had asked his staff for a plan to "destroy North Korean forces in another amphibious envelopment—coordinated with overland pursuit." Flushed with the Inchon success, he wanted to replicate it on the eastern coast of North Korea while Walker's forces pushed forward in the west. Although that made little logistical sense, there was no one at the Dai Ichi unwilling to follow MacArthur's orders. The victor at Inchon had the right to exploit his victory. Washington raised few questions because MacArthur offered the Pentagon little information.

With troops now coming up rapidly along the east coast from the Perimeter, the need for the operation was described as closing the trap on retreating North Koreans, but the cost in decelerating the offensive would go uncriticized, except privately. MacArthur had anticipated his freedom to do what he wanted. Yet, now in the background was a more restrictive National Security Council memorandum, 81/1, sent by Truman to Tokyo, Top Secret, on September 27. It reminded MacArthur that operations north of the 38th parallel were authorized only if "at the time of such operation there has been no entry into North Korea by major Soviet or Chinese Communist forces, no announcement of intended entry, nor a[ny] threat to counter our operations militarily. . . . Furthermore, support of your operations north or south of the 38th parallel will not include air or naval action against Manchuria or against USSR territory."

MacArthur had immediately responded that he had seen "no indication" of any such intervention, but a few days earlier, on the evening of the twenty-fifth in Beijing, Indian ambassador K. M. Panikkar had dinner with the Chinese Red Army chief of staff, General Nieh Yen-jung, an aging veteran of the Long March. Inevitably the Inchon success came up, and Nieh remarked that his government would not permit MacArthur's forces at its Manchurian border. "We know what we are in for," he conceded. "But at all costs American aggression has to be stopped. The Americans can bomb us; they can destroy our industries; but they cannot defeat us on land."

Panikkar cautioned that American military might had wings and could reach into the Chinese interior. Industrial progress could be set back for decades.

"We have calculated all that," said Nieh, seeing Americans on the Chinese border as a threat to the regime. "They may even drop atom bombs on us. What then? They may kill a few million people. After all, China lives on the farms. What can atom bombs do there? Yes, our economic development will be put back. We may have to wait for it [to recover]."

MacArthur's strategy of furnishing Washington with detailed plans "later"—and the new, optimistic climate at the Pentagon permitting that— foreshadowed the problems that apparent victory was bringing. Planners at the Dai Ichi had not figured out how to exploit success while taking into account its ramifications north of the 38th parallel. While claiming to understand the Asian mind better than the Europe-focused Departments of State and Defense, MacArthur's intelligence staff continued to see no problems looming beyond the North Korean border, or even below it. Large elements of the NKPA were escaping to the north along routes far to the east of Seoul, or melting into guerrilla bands which would create continuing instability. Most field officers would avoid entrapment although a few remained, under orders, often disguised as enlisted men, to take covert command in the prisoner-of-war camps. Anxious conferences were beginning about where to stop, even before Johnny Walker's forces achieved juncture south of Suwon, and it was already clear that Rhee might be unstoppable. "A more subtle result," General Ridgway would later put it, ". . . was the development of an almost superstitious regard for General MacArthur's infallibility. Even his superiors, it seemed, began to doubt if they should question *any* of MacArthur's decisions. . . ." Yet MacArthur continued to run his war, except for photo-opportunity flying visits, from seven hundred miles away in Japan.

9

Crossing the Parallel

ALTHOUGH DOUGLAS MACARTHUR had a large collection of books on military history and tactics in his library in Tokyo, he probably never heard of Sun Pin. According to the Chinese sage and military theorist there are five "postures" for an army commander: "The first is being strong and imposing; the second is being haughty and arrogant; the third is being unbending and obstinate; the fourth is being apprehensive and timid; and the fifth is being sluggish and weak." Nevertheless, in practicing the art of command, MacArthur rejected the fourth and fifth precepts in favor of the first three. Sun Pin also listed twenty-eight "fatal mistakes," among them:

> If he has a lot of favorites, and, as a result, his troops become indolent in their duties, this can lead to defeat.
> If he dislikes to hear about his own faults, this can lead to defeat.
> If he associates with incompetents, this can lead to defeat.

After the reinstallation of Syngman Rhee in Seoul in September, MacArthur was besieged by well-wishers in the battered parliament building. Although Marguerite Higgins had hung back, "the surge of those eager to congratulate him" after the ceremony pushed her in his path. Since she had been "busily burrowing in a dusty foxhole to escape a fire fight" only a few hours earlier, Maggie claimed that she looked bedraggled, but MacArthur, catching sight of her, called out, "Hello there, tall, blonde and ugly. Come up and see me sometime."

In October, on her way back, briefly, to the States to participate in a *Her-*

ald Tribune issues forum, she stopped in Tokyo and requested an interview. After six refusals from underlings she telephoned the Dai Ichi and instructed a puzzled switchboard operator, "Please tell the general that I consider that invitation to come up and see him sometime a military order."

Five minutes later an aide called back to say, "The general will be glad to see you as soon as you can get here."

She found MacArthur's usually clean desk "piled high with telegrams from President Truman and others congratulating him," and suggested that it must be satisfying to have such messages reversing the doubts before his Inchon gamble. "I'm afraid I can't take these messages too seriously," he said. "I learned long ago to be wary of praise, because it can turn into the opposite very quickly the moment that circumstances change."

He took several puffs at his corncob. "I learned that lesson at West Point," he explained. "I was a pretty good baseball player once, and I can remember my excitement at the approving roar of the crowds when I was a star of the team and we were running up a string of victories. In the middle of the game I ran for a fly, and as I reached, my knee gave way and I fell. No one would believe I had a bad knee. They thought it was just an excuse. The boos of the crowd were louder than the cheers had ever been. And so I have never forgotten how quickly cheers can turn into boos."

Also in Seoul covering the symbolic return of the keys to the city to Rhee had been Joseph Alsop, who had no difficulty arranging an interview in Tokyo with MacArthur. His syndicated column from Washington was influential. He wanted a "reading" of the Korean situation from "on high" as to whether the war was "for all intents over" and he should return home. The headquarters atmosphere suggested to him the court of Louis XIV. "Indeed," he recalled, "[the] Dai Ichi was proof of a basic rule for armies at war: the farther one gets from the front, the more laggards, toadies, and fools one encounters." The "Bataan gang," Alsop judged, "were insipid men, arrogant with the press, wary with each other, and generally incompetent. Their tone toward MacArthur was almost wholly simpering and reverential, and I have always held the view that this sycophancy was what tripped him up in the end."

Nevertheless, Alsop admired the "enormous guts" that inspired the Inchon operation when the Joint Chiefs were nervous, but he was concerned over MacArthur's apparent ignorance of China. Alsop had served there during World War II amid the pervasive corruption and incompetence of Chiang's regime, and recognized the irreversible political changes. "But anyone who encourages those around him to tell him over and over again that he can walk on water and has this judgment reinforced by a major success will have a tendency to believe that, indeed, he can walk on water. . . ."

Sitting opposite MacArthur's desk and squinting into the glare from the window, he found the general "in no mood to listen" to concerns about Maoist intervention. Rather, he "proceeded to give me a thumbnail analysis of the situation, not failing to point out that his landing at Inchon had changed everything. . . . He talked of the possible [Red] Chinese reaction, making very little of it."

"As a matter of fact, Alsop," he said, delicately flattering the writer by quoting the title of his widely read column, "if you stay on here, you will just be wasting your valuable time."

Alsop hitched a ride to Washington with a retinue of Air Force generals from the Pentagon, returning "in great comfort and very short order."

Among the reasons for MacArthur's confidence was the increasing haul of prisoners as the North Korean divisions, trapped below the 38th parallel, disintegrated. Over 110,000 POWs had already been picked up, most of them escorted to camps in the vicinity of Pusan. They were a vast problem to feed, clothe and guard, and the Pentagon was being asked to furnish surplus World War II uniforms of any sort, on which PW could be painted. Such manifest realities prompted the militants around MacArthur to urge him on. Even formerly cautious staffers were now eager to end the war with a quick victory.

Rhee had already declared that he would not be bound by any settlement that kept Korea divided anywhere in the peninsula. Still, Mao took the long view of the aging and erratic Rhee. Soundings from China were that loss of face would not be severe if South Koreans crossed the 38th parallel, but that Americans in hot pursuit would alter the outlook.

How far to pursue the fleeing *In Min Gun* became both a diplomatic matter and a military one. Paul Nitze of the Policy Planning Staff, responsible for the language of National Security Council directives, reflected the caution of George Kennan and Charles Bohlen, both Soviet experts, when they warned that neither Beijing nor Moscow would permit a hostile regime at their borders—the same rationalization used to justify the buffer of Russian satellites in Europe. The State Department, charged Hugh Scott Jr., the former chairman of the Republican Party and now a congressman from Pennsylvania, wanted to have MacArthur's forces "cringe behind the 38th parallel." Other Republicans, some previously known for objecting to all foreign commitments, called for broadly interpreting American (and UN) war aims so that the destruction of the North Korean army would imply going after it wherever it was, and unifying the country. "There is no stopping MacArthur now," Dean Acheson conceded to Averell Harriman. The mood was such, Harriman said later, that "psychologically, it was almost impossible not to go ahead and finish the job."

Success bred the obstinacy deplored by Sun Pin. MacArthur remained unwilling to incorporate X Corps with Walker's Eighth Army. Their lines had merged with Almond's forces into one confused front. Hickey and Wright, respectively MacArthur's acting chief of staff and his director of plans, both urged unification of command, something MacArthur denied after the war. He preferred unity of command to be exercised through his own person from Tokyo. Five years later Almond was candid about the matter. "Whether 'several principal advisors' advised Gen. MacArthur to place X Corps under Eighth Army after the Inchon landing, I do not know," he wrote. "It should be noted, however, that Gen. MacArthur was at all times fully capable of making up his own mind without benefit of advice." And after Inchon there was no dearth of willing subordinates. As General Ridgway later observed of that heady moment, had MacArthur "suggested that one battalion walk on water to reach the port, there might have been somebody ready to give it a try."

Walton Walker had suggested to MacArthur a simple overland movement across the peninsula to Wonsan by the Eighth Army, much of which was already in central or eastern Korea. X Corps, which Walker thought should now come under EUSAK, was best positioned to continue north toward Pyongyang. In insisting on their continued division, MacArthur may have prevented a quick ending to the war.

Walker's forces, now rapidly moving north, carried along with them more problems than MacArthur's divided armies. Although Walker had ROK troops under his command, Syngman Rhee was urging his commanders to pay no attention to American orders and move as quickly as they could to the 38th parallel, and across. Both U.S. and South Korean forces were outdistancing NKPA troops, which did not have the mobility of jeeps and trucks. While many North Koreans preferred to be fed, which required surrender, others remained to melt into the local population and pursue a guerrilla war. Outrunning his own supplies because logistical priority went to X Corps, Walker announced that he would halt near the 38th parallel for "regrouping." The outloading of X Corps was putting EUSAK into partial paralysis.

Regrouping was a vague term representing the vast confusion across Korea from Inchon and Seoul eastward to the Sea of Japan. Marshall had cautioned MacArthur to tone down his megaphone diplomacy, including in a draft directive to his command that their field of operations was "limited only by the military exigencies and the international boundaries of Korea"—which extended northward to the Yalu. "The so-called 38th parallel," MacArthur responded, "accordingly is not a factor in the military employment of our forces." To accomplish the defeat of the enemy—he was no longer referring only to expulsion of the aggressors from South Korea—his troops were directed "to cross this parallel at any time, either in exploratory probing or exploiting local tactical conditions." He intended to "seek out and destroy the enemy's armed forces in whatever part of Korea they may be located."

Since MacArthur was to feel, in Marshall's words, unhampered in proceeding north, it was easy in Tokyo to dismiss the diplomatic guidelines. MacArthur's confidence was reinforced by the agreement of State and Defense that he make a radio broadcast asking the North Koreans to lay down their arms rather than risk "early and total defeat." Although this was more to mollify MacArthur than in expectation of a response, when MacArthur made his unconditional surrender demands on October 2, he viewed it as his ticket into North Korea.

Marshall's instructions were to cross the parallel without fanfare, and to keep going as long as there was no evidence of "major" Chinese or Russian intervention. While such exchanges between the Pentagon and the Dai Ichi continued, with MacArthur making what he wanted of them, the UN debated a resolution of deliberate ambivalence introduced by Britain and jointly sponsored by seven other nations but not the U.S. (although Acheson had a hand in drafting it). It recommended that "all appropriate steps be taken to ensure conditions of stability throughout Korea"—another covert green light to MacArthur. And it recommended peaceful and representative elections throughout Korea "and the establishment of a unified government."

Prior to its incursion into the south, the North Korean government had called for an elected assembly in Seoul to unify the country. The UN resolution appeared to satisfy that desire, yet the Communists had refused to participate in national elections in 1948 and were unlikely to be a factor, willing or unwilling, in any election after they were driven from the seat of their own government. Still, on October 7 the UN resolution passed, forty-seven to five, with seven abstentions. MacArthur's interpretation would be: "My mission was to clear out all North Korea, to unify it and to liberalize it."

How he intended to accomplish that became almost irrelevant once the ROK Army began crossing the parallel on September 30. Consulting no one,

Rhee announced, "We will not allow ourselves to stop." Still, MacArthur had devised, also without consultation, his own end-the-war strategy—a solution that, Omar Bradley later said, if turned in as an answer to a problem posed by a major at the Command and General Staff School, "would have been laughed out of the classroom." Yet instead of registering dismay, Washington signed on. In the intoxicating post-Inchon atmosphere it was submitted to the JCS—of which Bradley was chair—and approved there as well as afterwards by the President.

In the aftermath of the retaking of Seoul, MacArthur had two large armies in Korea. Walton Walker wanted them combined to push north. Unified or not, one could have been ordered toward Pyongyang, in hot pursuit of the remnants of the NKPA. The other could have been directed overland to the northeast, to the port of Wonsan, trapping *In Min Gun* troops in central Korea just above the parallel in what later became known as the Iron Triangle. Instead, MacArthur withdrew his freshest force—X Corps had not fought for three months in the Perimeter and then slogged north—and ordered it off on a long, complicated, land-and-sea journey in more than two hundred ships down and up the Korean peninsula for an unnecessary amphibious landing at Wonsan.

While X Corps was reassembling to sail from Inchon and Pusan, taking the longest possible routes into North Korea, the Eighth Army, worn out and nearly out of supplies, was unable to maintain lines with Pusan or receive what it needed to advance from Inchon. Half of Almond's troops—largely the 7th Division segment—was returning by rail and road to Pusan to board ships there for Wonsan because Inchon, crowded with Marines, could not cope logistically, given the tides factor, with outloading all X Corps troops. Not only were experienced divisions eliminated for weeks from exploiting the rout of the demoralized North Koreans upward from Seoul; the Eighth Army was also handicapped in maintaining its offensive toward Pyongyang. Walker now had new M-46 .90mm tanks, but they were forty-five-ton gas guzzlers, and he was running low on fuel. Remote-controlled by MacArthur from Tokyo, Almond could get what he wanted direct from depots in Japan.

Although MacArthur and his palace guard at the Dai Ichi had doubts about Walker's fitness for high command, reservations reinforced by his apparent micromanagement of the Pusan Perimeter, they preferred to divide authority rather than risk replacing him just as his troops had turned ignominy into glory. In large part his hands-on running of every aspect of the Perimeter defense and then the breakout north was due to his lack of faith in the divisional leadership foisted on him by Tokyo and Washington.

MacArthur's ostensible reason for continuing the divided command, which appeared strategically unsound and a playing of favorites, was Korean geography: the mountainous spine known as the Taebaek Range that divides the peninsula through most of central and northern Korea. Still, there is a break in the terrain that would have permitted crossing to the Japan Sea—a fact he chose to ignore.

Urged on by Syngman Rhee, ROK troops continued to evade orders from MacArthur and from Walker, pushing rapidly north on wheels, treads and legs as if there were no topographical handicaps. On the central front, while diplomatic wrangling about crossing the parallel continued in Washington, London and Lake Success, the ROK 6th Division moved past it above Chunchon. The ROK 1st Division had crossed the 38th parallel near the west coast on September 30, and the ROK 3rd and Capital Divisions had moved beyond it on the east coast, in the direction of Wonsan.

Perplexed and enraged by the poor intelligence and poor planning that hobbled both the Inchon force and the Eighth Army while they exchanged positions, neither O. P. Smith nor Walton Walker could appeal the decisions from Tokyo being effected in early October. With roads and rails clogged with X Corps movement, Walker had to have ammunition and fuel flown in. Inchon had worked efficiently because the shore was lightly defended, and the Navy had run the operation until the troops had established and enlarged a beachhead. Now Almond, his strings pulled by MacArthur, was running things. Almond's *Blue Goose* L-5 liaison plane would set down at a convenient airstrip, and he would oversee outloading preparations or observe combat exercises he had ordered to keep waiting troops sharp—or merely busy.

With the 1st Cav relieving the 7th Division, Almond's aim on the morning of October 4, while he was still in the Seoul region, was to review Colonel Richard Ovenshine's 31st Infantry of the 7th Division and hope that the demonstration came off badly, as was likely. The 7th Division was, at the same time, frantically preparing for embarkation far to the south in Pusan, and at Suwon, en route, was stowing gear on trucks and railway cars. Almond wanted to sack Ovenshine because of a friendly-fire mixup after dark on September 26, when EUSAK and X Corps crossed into each other's lines near Osan. The cause was MacArthur's division of commands, but his headquarters in Tokyo had radioed messages to X Corps and to Far East Air Force units warning that elements of the Eighth Army could materialize from the Perimeter at any time, breaking out toward Seoul. Every precaution was to be taken to prevent bombing, strafing or firing on friendly forces.

A phosphorous grenade lit up the identifying white star on a 1st Cav tank that had penetrated 31st Infantry lines, which the official Army history calls "great good luck" in effecting the linkup as the recognition prevented a long casualty list. Still, Almond blamed Ovenshine and now found "administrative shortcomings in the exercise" to add to the Osan episode. The next day, October 5, the colonel was relieved.

That morning, still in the Suwon area, Almond put the division's 17th Infantry through its exercise. Colonel Herbert B. Powell's regiment had been the last ashore at Inchon and had the least combat experience—which showed when mortars fired live rounds into a cluster of his troops, killing five and badly injuring fifty-five others. Powell was not sacked.

On October 7, X Corps was formally relieved of responsibility for the Seoul-Inchon front to be taken over by EUSAK. The split in forces on the verge of the 38th parallel was about to occur. The 1st Marine Division was assembled in the port area to be loaded aboard ships for the 850-mile U-turn around the peninsula, while the 7th Infantry gathered by regiments for trains south to Taegu and Pusan. Some troops traveled by truck, although Communist guerrillas—NKPA troops left behind—were harassing convoys en route.

Almond left his former headquarters in Ascom City at 11:20 a.m., having arranged for quarters for his staff aboard the flagship *Mount McKinley.* One of his last acts before flying to Taegu en route to the port of Pusan was to write a sour letter to the commanding general of the 7th Infantry, Major General David Barr, with a copy to MacArthur, criticizing the performances of Barr's regiments. To do this prior to an operation in which the 7th Division was to be crucial was in character for Almond, and Barr warned his subordinates to obey every whim of Almond's because their careers—like that of the unlucky Ovenshine—could be in jeopardy.

In Pusan, Almond insisted that his corps be resupplied as if they possessed nothing—which meant duplication of materiel shipped from Japan, and even less made available for Walker's underprovisioned Eighth Army. Walker's forces would have a very low priority for winter gear, but MacArthur's command expected the war to be over before the first snows fell.

On October 9, with Almond back in Inchon to oversee the operation— he had Admiral Doyle to dinner the evening before—the Marines began debarking. Each vessel had to wait for peak tide to debark, and then move out to sea and wallow while waiting for others to join the convoy. Marathon card games began below decks. As the units loaded, Almond made inspection rounds, asking such routine questions as "How long have you been in the service?" He scolded a Marine who could not remember his rifle serial number. It was, Almond reminded him, his best friend.

On the same day that the Marines began their outloading at Inchon, the Eighth Army crossed the 38th parallel. Reports from the ROKs were that the North Koreans were withdrawing in disorder, and that the Marines could make a holiday jaunt across the waist of the peninsula. Nevertheless, by the next afternoon two battalions had boarded cramped LSTs, to remain until the entire convoy shipped out around Korea. It was a slow process. For an amphibious assault, troops and their equipment had to be loaded on the same ships, requiring specialized landing craft unnecessary for an unopposed landing. Marine supplies and equipment from Seoul had to be trucked to the port area and the loading accomplished quickly at high tide. Vehicles had to be waterproofed and securely deck-loaded rather than stowed below as bulk freight. Yet the outgoing vehicles first had to be used, often, as dock transport. MacArthur could not have been unaware of the absurdity of the operation, even from seven hundred miles away. "My corner in a bombed-out warehouse," Ed Simmons remembered, "looked like a stage set for *What Price Glory?*"

As the slow "combat loading" process continued on October 10, preparatory to storming Wonsan, on the opposite coast, from the sea, ROK foot soldiers were already entering the port almost unopposed, leaving—dangerously—what were called pockets of resistance to their rear, to be "cleaned up later." Many ROKs were shoeless, yet made fifteen miles a day on bleeding feet, and were often out of communication beyond the company level. Remnants of the NKPA 5th Division dropped mortar rounds on the narrow coastal roads, but the suddenly eager South Koreans pushed on. Units of the ROK Capital Division even moved beyond Wonsan toward Hamhung, fifty miles farther north, and its port, Hungnam.

Such was MacArthur's obsession with amphibious operations that despite reports to the Dai Ichi that Wonsan had been abandoned by the *In Min Gun*, he would not rescind his orders and permit the Marines to offload and cross overland. However, there was now no need for the 7th Division to sail to the beaches of Wonsan. Recognizing that, MacArthur's headquarters ordered the division delayed in transit from Pusan, its troops to be disembarked and, like the Marines, combat-loaded for another landing farther north. Since the 7th had been intended to follow the Marines ashore, it had not been outfitted to hit the beaches shooting. Now it was rescheduled for Hungnam, although it too was likely to fall to the ROKs before any GIs landed.

Admiral Doyle criticized Almond's strategy on further grounds. Hungnam's seaward approaches were mined, he warned; in addition, he reminded Almond of a Joint Chiefs of Staff directive of September 27 that "no non-Korean ground forces will be used in the northeast provinces bordering the Soviet Union or in the area along the Manchurian border." Almond replied that MacArthur had personally lifted Washington's restriction because North Korea had refused his invitation to surrender. It was MacArthur's war.

While the Eighth Army and the ROKs in the west moved rapidly northward, on the east coast other ROK divisions were poised to go beyond Wonsan and Hungnam, continuing to bypass demoralized North Korean remnants who would be trouble later. In Pusan, the disgusted men of the 7th Division were being moved off, then on, docks and ships until October 27, a month after they had participated in the liberation of Seoul. MacArthur had taken nearly half of his army out of the war.

Far off in Washington, Lawton Collins seethed over the seemingly capricious redeployments, but later conceded the old hero in Tokyo some small benefit of the doubt. "It is impossible to assess with any certainty the effect of the lull in the pursuit of the North Koreans. . . . It is an axiom of military tactics to press relentlessly on the heels of a defeated enemy. This was not done after the fall of Seoul." Nor had Collins's Joint Chiefs insisted on it.

On October 11 the X Corps command boarded the *Mount McKinley* at Inchon in time for a splendid dinner with Admiral Doyle and their staffs at 6:30 p.m. Yet the menu—Navy brass dined well—was overshadowed by news that barefoot ROK troops were already in Wonsan. The need to assault the port by sea was gone, and the Navy had not even raised anchor. Almond also learned of additional obstacles to the now unnecessary operation. The waters offshore at Wonsan were thick with perhaps several thousand chemical, pressure and electronic mines assembled and set under the supervision of since-departed Russian technicians. South Korean agents had verified their existence.

MacArthur insisted that the amphibious operation proceed, but with the 7th Division now to make an alternative assault at Iwon, 150 miles above Wonsan, in the arc of the Japan Sea coast, "to envelop the North Korean forces in that area." For Wonsan, Admiral Struble hastily assembled a twenty-one-minesweeper flotilla, including nine ships from the impounded Imperial Japanese Navy. Had Washington been asked for authorization it would have been denied, but MacArthur (and Admiral Joy) gambled that they could get away with it. Use of the vessels violated every rule in the diplomatic book.

Further, the Japanese contract crews were falsely promised extra hazard pay and falsely assured that they would not have to sail north of the 38th parallel. The crews were also promised that they would have to perform only relatively safe secondary sweeps, with American naval vessels doing the dangerous work. (When they discovered they had been lied to, they could not report to the Japanese Maritime Safety Agency because all ships' radios had been silenced according to combat directives.)

As the convoy of Marines loaded for Wonsan, Admiral Struble rushed his minesweepers there. No landing craft could approach the shore until the channel was safe, and ten miles of mines were intricately sown across the inner harbor. The sweep began on October 10 after the task force gathered at Sasebo and moved across the Japan Sea. It was a motley fleet, dependent upon three large Navy vessels not adapted to the shallow sweeping and three ROK sweepers lacking the necessary clearance gear. Captain Richard T. Spofford had to rely more on his seven small, wooden-hulled Navy sweepers. One of them, *Mocking Bird,* seemed a commentary on the operation.

After two days of tedious clearance, the remaining mines seemed to spawn additional ones. The cruiser *Rochester* with five destroyers first sighted sixty-one mines during a dangerous reconnaissance, then found more mines than could be charted. A 3,000-yard channel which first appeared cleared led to five additional lines of mines. Farther offshore four cruisers fired uselessly at bridges and rail tunnels onshore which landing forces would need, and the *Missouri* rifled 163 sixteen-inch rounds at nothing. To accelerate the clearing process by blowing up unseen mines, thirty-nine fighter-bombers from the carriers *Leyte Gulf* and *Philippine Sea*—their names recalling MacArthur successes in 1944—tried to blast a channel between Reito and Koto islands with thousand-pound bombs, proving only that concussion alone would not set off nearby mines.

Unfortunately, the sweepers located some mines only too well. On the twelfth, after the carrier plane attempts, the big Navy sweepers *Pledge* and *Pirate* blew up with a loss of 13 killed and 87 wounded. Rescue of the survivors was impeded by fire from enemy shore batteries bypassed by the ROKs and which the naval fire had not reduced. Spofford called for Mariner and Sunderland flying boats, which could cover the water from low altitudes, to drop depth charges to loosen moored mines and destroy any they located with .50-caliber machine-gun fire. But there seemed no end to the mines, even in apparently cleared lanes, for the magnetic devices were set to allow as many as twelve passes before exploding, leaving the area presumably safe for passage. Sweepers had to make at least thirteen passes, as the task force learned when the Japanese JMS-14 and ROK YMS 516 hit countermines and disintegrated, each with heavy losses.

While Almond's forces in the east were stalled offshore, Walker's Eighth Army, despite dangerously low supply reserves, pushed north. Since all GIs learned the survival skills of scrounging and pilfering, and few opted for walking when an alternative appeared, Ole John E. of the 21st Regiment (24th Division) was typical when he left Seoul for the parallel in a Willys Jeep station wagon. On patrol with his sergeant he had found a cave filled with South Korean civilians "massacred and burned" by the Communists, and also the jeep. Paralyzed by a dead battery, the vehicle was being pushed with futility by "the natives." John E. persuaded them to push it backwards down a hill; then he "popped the clutch while in reverse and it started with a roar." While they cheered, he shouted, "Adios, sayonara!" and left them behind.

At the Seoul police station he exchanged the wagon for a jeep with a canopy, and with a can of white paint identified it with L Company numbers. The jeep went north with him, where he "rounded up about 110" enemy chickens, only to find when he went through his chow line that he was given "the oldest and toughest damned rooster" in North Korea. Complaining, unsuccessfully, that he had "personally caught" most of the dinner, he went back to the source "and fried me a nice young pullet. Who in hell is going to skunk a hillbilly from Arkansas?"

So the Eighth Army, with the freebooting John E. along but still short in supplies, advanced incautiously into North Korea.

In Tokyo, MacArthur proceeded as usual to the Dai Ichi after a late breakfast, read and answered messages put before him, responded to no telephone calls, returned to his residence for lunch and a nap, listened to the three o'clock news on the Armed Forces Radio Network, went back to the Dai Ichi until the long summer afternoon waned into evening, then proceeded after a flurry of salutes at the entrance to the Dai Ichi back to the embassy for dinner and a movie.

In the hiatus before Walker's crossing of the frontier, the NKPA had time to reorganize its depleted divisions and was able to briefly mount stiff resistance, but the *In Min Gun* had nothing behind its front line, and two regiments of Hobart Gay's 1st Cav were able to get behind the North Koreans and capture Kumchon, on the road to Pyongyang. The remnants of the NKPA scrambled for safety, and the 1st Cav, the 24th Division and the ROK 1st Division raced toward Sariwon, the halfway point to the capital, where it was expected that the NKPA would mount its defense of Pyongyang.

A platoon of the Argyll 1st Battalion, mounted on American Sherman tanks, led the way for the 1st Cav, and found groups of exhausted and hungry North Koreans waiting to surrender. Their Russian-made trucks, gas tanks empty, had been abandoned. The Scots then cleared a mass of North Koreans from an orchard in which they were hiding, and were passed by the Australian 3rd Battalion, which continued on to the north. As night fell, the Argylls discovered more North Koreans trying to flee Sariwon, and in the confusion some UN soldiers associated NKPA troops trying to flee with South Koreans moving up with the 24th Division. The North Koreans thought that the British units were Russians rumored to be coming to their aid. In the darkness the enemies exchanged congratulations. North Koreans slapped Scots on their shoulders and offered cigarettes, even red stars from their caps. Lieutenant Robin D. Fairey, an Argylls mortar officer, stumbled into a group of North Koreans and, on realizing who they were, shouted for safety, referring to himself as "Russky, Russky!" He permitted a few pats on the back, then slipped away.

Inevitably there was some exchange of fire in the darkness at close quarters, the British losing one soldier, the North Koreans about 150. North of the town, where the Australians had set up a roadblock, 1,982 North Koreans surrendered after Major I. B. Ferguson climbed on a tank and shouted to them that they were surrounded. There would be more. Establishing radio contact with Lieutenant Colonel Charles H. Green, commander of the 3rd Australians, 7th Cav commander Lieutenant Colonel Peter Clainos warned that he would be entering Sariwon with his 1st Battalion's vehicle lights on, and a column of troops and many prisoners (who had been duped into believing, at first, that the Cavs were Russians). An hour before midnight on the seventeenth they reached the Australian perimeter, where Clainos overheard one Aussie remark to another, "Now what do you make of this? Here we are, all set for a coordinated attack in the morning, and the bloody Yanks come in at midnight with their lights burning, and bringing in the whole damned North Korean army as prisoners!"

The advances by ROK and EUSAK forces became so rapid that the Far East Air Force was almost put out of business. Once limited to five or six L-5s and AT-6 Texans, Pfc. William Hayward's 6147th Tactical Control Squadron, which he helped service, no longer needed to hoard its planes. "Our aircraft flew so low many times," he recalled, "that there would be tree limbs in the cowlings and once there was a rock imbedded in the leading edge of a wing." On October 6, FEAF sent its Bomber Command a list of thirty-three bridges north of Pyongyang and Wonsan. Disabling them would impede the retreat of the fleeing North Koreans. Within a week, ten of the targets had to be deleted because they were now in occupied areas. Since JCS directives mandated that aircraft were to "remain well clear" of the narrow border with Siberia and the lengthy one along the Tumen and the Yalu with Manchuria, targets within fifty miles of the frontiers could not be attacked without explicit FEAF permission, and then only visually. Running out of assignments, General Otto Weyland on October 10 ordered bomber sorties reduced to twenty-five daily. Nearly idle B-29 pilots looked for targets of opportunity. The Air Force official history reports, "Finding nothing better to bomb, one 92nd Group crew recorded that it chased an enemy soldier on a motorcycle down a road, dropping bombs until one hit the hapless fellow." Given the relative speeds of bomber and cycle, and the size of bombs carried, the alleged episode leaves little to admire and much to question. For Bomber Command, the war had become a bore.

Off the east coast, the frustrated Marines were still moving at slow convoy speed toward a target already taken, and where they would not be able to land, even as guests of the South Koreans who had preceded them.

From radio exchanges with Tokyo, the X Corps command knew that Soviet mines and countermines were stalling their operation. On October 19, nevertheless, the *Mount McKinley* arrived off Wonsan with Admiral Doyle, General Almond and six of his X Corps staff. Before them was a depleted fleet of minesweepers. The amphibious force, with dozens of transports loaded with men, munitions and vehicles, lay behind the flagship unable to negotiate the harbor. Almond raged in frustration, complaining of unskilled Navy crews and "incompetent" Japanese hirelings.

The Marines could not see the South Koreans onshore once the fleet reached Wonsan, but on one occasion the ROKs could be heard far out to sea. At the north end of the harbor they had stacked about a thousand 20-pound mines they had cleared from the beaches, which had also been sown. Finishing the job, one squad, a lieutenant and five enlisted men, remained on the beach to celebrate, apparently with strong drink. Moving off about two hundred yards from the stacked mines, the lieutenant happily fired his pistol at the inviting pile. Panes of glass in buildings two miles away were shattered, as were the six celebrants.

The Japanese minesweeper casualties were ringing alarm bells in Washington. International embarrassment loomed. Messages went to the Dai Ichi urging a cover-up. MacArthur assured State that use of the Japanese seamen was for "humanitarian purposes involved in neutralizing infractions of the accepted rules of warfare."

Unable to disembark, the Marines, having no idea why they were lingering offshore, discovered on the nineteenth that many of the two hundred ships in the armada were turning around and sailing south. "War's over!" one excited Marine shouted. "They're taking us back to Pusan for embarkation to the States." But the change in direction was only temporary. In conference with Struble aboard the *Missouri,* Almond discovered that wallowing in place would result only in mass seasickness. The troop transports were ordered to mark time by sailing up and down the Korean coast, reversing course every twelve hours. Soon the disgruntled Marines began using the phrase which GIs had applied during the long summer to their reversals of direction on land. They were stuck in Operation Yo-Yo—crossing, by sea, the 38th parallel every day.

10

Mohammed and the Mountain

On OCTOBER 10 the White House issued a statement by the President in which only the first and last sentences were accurate:

> General MacArthur and I are making a quick trip over the coming weekend to meet in the Pacific.
>
> When I see him I shall express to him the appreciation and gratitude of the people and Government of the United States for the great service he is rendering to World Peace. . . . He is carrying out his mission with the imagination, courage, and effectiveness which have marked his entire service as one of our nation's greatest military leaders.
>
> I shall discuss with him the final phase of United Nations action in Korea. . . .
>
> The task of reconstruction will be a heavy one. . . .
>
> Naturally, I shall take advantage of this opportunity to discuss with General MacArthur other matters within his responsibility.

Concerned about the threats from China, the JCS had met on October 7 to draft a directive to MacArthur about courses of action in the event of Chinese or Soviet moves to intervene in Korea. On the President's desk the next day was a draft which Truman would sign "Approved":

> Hereafter in the event of the open or covert employment anywhere in Korea of major Chinese Communist units, without prior announcement, you should continue the action as long as, in your judgment, action by forces

now under your control offers any reasonable chance of success. In any case you will obtain authorization from Washington prior to taking any military action against objectives in Chinese territory.

Ironically, although MacArthur's intelligence chief, Charles Willoughby, had downplayed the likelihood of Chinese intervention, on the day that the President signed off on the directive, Chinese forces were already moving across the Yalu into Korea. No codes had to be broken to interpret Mao's policy. On September 25 in Beijing, Ambassador K. M. Panikkar had been told by Nieh Yen-jung, acting chief of the People's Liberation Army, that the Chinese would not "sit back with folded hands and let the Americans come up to the border." Panikkar had also reported a meeting with Zhou Enlai on October 3 during which Zhou took an unequivocal stand on U.S. presence north of the 38th parallel. "The South Koreans did not matter," he said, assuming that the *In Min Gun*, somehow augmented, could take care of them, "but American intervention into North Korea would encounter Chinese resistance." Acheson considered the Chinese warnings "a bluff." Willoughby in Tokyo, to whom MacArthur paid more attention than he did to the Secretary of State, took it no more seriously.

In London, *The Times* published a piece from its Washington correspondent expressing concern that Truman would return a convert to his viceroy's Asia-first ideas: "So many men have left Washington to explain the Administration's policy to General MacArthur in the past—and have been converted to his point of view." *The Times* hoped that MacArthur would not "devour" the President.

As the White House announcement of the imminent meeting with MacArthur was making headlines, a more ominous meeting was secretly taking place at Sochi in the Crimea. Stalin's heart trouble required a long rest in a mild climate away from the pressure of Moscow, but he could not escape the problems beyond Soviet borders created by his uneasy satellites. On October 1, after midnight, he was brought a cable from Pyongyang signed by Kim Il Sung and his second-in-command, Pak Hong-yong. The Americans had not only retaken Seoul but were poised to pour into North Korea almost unopposed. The *In Min Gun* could no longer offer serious resistance. "The moment enemy troops cross the 38th parallel," they appealed, "we will desperately need immediate military assistance from the Soviet Union. If, for some [political] reason, this help is not possible, then [would you] assist us in organizing international volunteer units in China and other people's democracies to provide military assistance in our struggle?"

Unwilling to be drawn into a war with the U.S. despite his belligerent rhetoric, Stalin nevertheless wanted to keep the Americans tied down in the Far East. He knew how slowly the Soviets were recovering from the catastrophe of World War II, and he knew, as the West did not, how dysfunctional the Soviet economy was, how corrupt its system remained, and how useless and untrustworthy were his European client states. While Cold Warriors in the West saw his every move as leading to the anticipated hot war, Stalin knew that he could not afford one. He dictated a message to Mao Zedong and Zhou Enlai requesting China to "move immediately at least five or six divisions" not merely to their Yalu River border with North Korea but "to the 38th parallel." Claiming that he could offer little advice, he explained that he was "far from Moscow and somewhat cut off from the events in Korea." Nevertheless, he suggested that they could send troops posing as volunteers but "of course, with the Chinese command at the helm" (the Chinese had already thought of it). He signed his cable with the Chinese alias Pheng Xi.

Mao answered with pseudo-loyalty on October 2 that a few divisions would not be enough for the task. He warned that if China intervened, the U.S. might declare war, thus involving the Soviets through their mutual assistance treaty with the People's Republic. Not waiting for decisions by Stalin, whom he distrusted, Mao called Lin Biao (Piao), a general since he was twenty-three, in 1930, and the commander of the elite Fourth Field Army, to ask him to lead the "volunteers." Lin declined, blaming debilitation from old wounds and the need for medical treatment in Moscow.

Mao then offered the task by telephone to Peng Dehuai, fifty-two, the peasant-born commander of the Northwest Field Army. He was to fly immediately to the Politburo meeting already called for. Peng took it as an order, and arrived on October 4, an hour late for the opening, but in time to hear Mao urge intervention. The next morning Mao called him in. "Old Peng," he said, "you didn't have time to speak out [in the Politburo] yesterday. We do indeed face enormous difficulties, but what favorable conditions do you think we have?" Peng had no idea what to say, having been sleepless the night before pondering the problem. Cautiously, he declared that he supported the decision, but needed an army.

While the Korean situation deteriorated further, Stalin cabled Mao again, reassuring him that the U.S. "was not prepared at the present time for a big war," and if faced with such a prospect would "have to give in to China, backed by its Soviet ally, in [any settlement of] the Korean question." Such an accommodation, he enticed Mao, could include American abandonment of Formosa and any "separate peace with Japanese reactionaries." These "concessions," he suggested, required the Chinese to give an "impressive display of its strength."

If, despite American "unpreparedness," it decided to "pull itself into a big war, out of prestige," Stalin professed to be unconcerned, "since together we will be stronger than the United States and Great Britain." The other "capitalist states," Stalin cajoled, had no "serious military power." He was not, he lied, afraid of World War III. "If war is inevitable, let it happen now, and not in a few years, when Japanese militarism will be restored as a U.S. ally, and when the United States and Japan will have a beachhead on the continent ready, in the form of Syngman Rhee's Korea." The picture he drew was remarkable for its similarity to MacArthur's worldview.

Meeting with General Matthew Ridgway (as Bradley's deputy) in Tokyo in August, MacArthur had discounted Chinese intervention in Korea while adding, "I pray nightly that they will—[I would] get down on my knees." In his last years he would deny that, writing in his *Reminiscences,* "I will always believe that if the United States had issued a warning to the effect that any entry of the Chinese Communists in force into Korea would be considered an act of international war against the United States, then the Korean War would have terminated with our advance north. I feel that the Reds would have stayed on their side of the Yalu." But rather than ask for such a sweeping warning, he wanted the retaliatory air strikes vetoed by Washington.

Without intimating to Stalin that the decision for intervention had already been made, Mao accepted Stalin's offer to fly Zhou across Asia to confer about logistical assistance for the proposed nine Chinese divisions. Having won the civil war against Chiang using weapons scrounged from Russia during World War II, captured from the Japanese or surrendered by fleeing Kuomintang troops, Mao now wanted up-to-date equipment to counter MacArthur's hardware. Stalin was expected to demonstrate his gratitude. Zhou assumed commensurate transfer of weapons and ammunition from Soviet Far East stockpiles, and air support for the Chinese army.

On October 8, the day after a UN resolution empowering its forces in Korea to unify the country, Mao formally but secretly declared that "the Northeast Border Defense Force"—in effect the armies in Manchuria—"is renamed the Chinese People's Volunteers and it should get ready to move into Korean territory immediately." Peng was appointed commander and ordered to deploy troops. He left immediately for Shenyang, in Manchuria, taking with him only one aide.

Even as Mao's forces were arranging to slip into Korea, intending to drive

The UN flag joins the American flag atop the Dai Ichi Building, July 14, 1950. Across the moat behind the viewer is the Imperial Palace area. On the top floor of the Dai Ichi is MacArthur's office, overlooking the palace grounds. (Army photo)

Joint Chiefs of Staff Chairman General Omar Bradley with MacArthur in Tokyo on June 17, 1950, on an inspection trip only a week before the war. (Army photo)

John Foster Dulles at the 38th Parallel. (National Archives)

Brigadier General John H. Church (foreground) and MacArthur watch American aircraft overhead in South Korea, June 28, 1950. (Army photo)

MacArthur returning from Haneda airport after his first flying trip to Korea, June 28, 1950. Jean had come to the airport to accompany him "home" to their Embassy residence. (Army photo)

Marguerite Higgins of the *New York Herald-Tribune* with MacArthur at Suwon, June 28, 1950. She would hitch a ride to Tokyo on his plane, then return to cover more of the war. (Army photo)

MacArthur in Korea in July 1950 talking to correspondents Don Whitehead and Frank Coniff. (Army photo)

Taipei, July 31, 1950, MacArthur with Generalissimo and Madame
Chiang Kaishek. (Army photo)

MacArthur examines a disabled North Korean tank on September 17, 1950, on his first land inspection after the Inchon landing. Behind him is the ever-present Major General Courtney Whitney. (Army photo)

MacArthur holding a press conference at the K-2 (Taegu) airbase on July 26, 1950, before returning to Japan. Wearing a pained (or resigned) expression is Eighth Army commander Lieutenant General Walton H. Walker. (Army photo)

Two members of the Joint Chiefs of Staff, General J. Lawton Collins and Admiral Forrest Sherman, arrive in Tokyo on August 21, 1950, to confer with MacArthur. To the right is Pacific Fleet commander, Admiral Arthur W. Radford. (Army photo)

MacArthur on September 15, 1950, observing the Inchon landing from the bridge of the command ship Mount McKinley. Behind him left to right are Vice Admiral Arthur D. Struble, General Edwin K. Wright and General Edward M. Almond. (Navy photo)

MacArthur at the port of Inchon following the landing, September 16, 1950. At his side is 7th Fleet commander, Vice Admiral Arthur D. Struble; to his left is Major General Oliver P. Smith. (Army photo)

A prisoner of war holding area at Inchon being inspected by MacArthur, September 17, 1950. Behind him to his right is Major General Oliver P. Smith. (Army photo)

Crossing the Han River into Seoul on a temporary bridge just completed, MacArthur on September 29, 1950, prepares to conduct a ceremony at the shattered capitol building, restoring Seoul to the Korean government. (Army photo)

MacArthur with Major General Edward M. Almond in front of the capital building in Seoul, September 29, 1950, after the arrival of their motorcade from Kimpo airbase. Almond has turned his combat fatigues into a conspicuous dress uniform, with scarf, belt, and brilliantly shined boots.

MacArthur ceremoniously restoring the retaken Korean capital of Seoul to President Syngman Rhee, September 19, 1950. (Army photo)

Truman and MacArthur at Wake Island, October 15, 1950, as seen through the rear of the old Chevrolet that met them at the airport. (Army photo)

President Truman pinning
yet another Distinguished
Service Medal on General
MacArthur, Wake Island,
October 15, 1950. Looking
on is Ambassador to South
Korea John J. Muccio.
(Army photo)

MacArthur peering down from his Constellation at the Yalu boundary
between Manchuria and North Korea, November 24, 1950. Forward of
him is FEAF commander Lieutenant General George Stratemeyer;
behind are Major General Edwin K. Wright and Major General
Courtney Whitney. (Army photo)

A medic fills out casualty tags while a GI who has just become acquainted with blood and death is comforted by another, Korea 1950. (Army photo)

American troops interrogating captured Chinese soldiers in North Korea, November 1950. (Army photo)

A Communist Chinese offer to accept the surrender of UN soldiers, November 1950. (Army photo)

Burials of 117 dead in a common grave at Koto-ri on December 8, 1950, before the Hungnam evacuation. (Army photo)

A Korean patriarch now a refugee carries all his possessions on an A-frame. (Army photo)

"Lieutenant Colonel Ralph Monclar" of the French Battalion leads MacArthur on an inspection, in Wonju, February 20, 1951. Behind the Frenchman's right shoulder is Major General Edward M. Almond wearing his new 3rd star. (Army photo)

MacArthur visiting the Marines, March 17, 1951, and talking from his jeep to Brigadier General Lewis (Chesty) Puller, standing to his right. (Army photo)

On what he did not know would be his last flying trip to Korea, MacArthur, on April 3, 1951, is greeted by Lieutenant General Matthew Ridgway at Kangnung, prior to a symbolic jeep trip across the 38th parallel to Yang Yang, which was just captured. (Army photo)

MacArthur's party leaving the Embassy compound on April 16, 1951, for Haneda Airport, and the United States. The Tokyo Metropolitan Police Band plays on their way out. (Army photo)

Japanese line the streets on the morning of April 16, 1951, to watch MacArthur's motorcade proceed to Haneda airport on his final days in Tokyo. The flags above are obviously handmade. (Army photo)

MacArthur's emptied desk at his Dai Ichi office, his calendar at April 12, 1951.
(Army photo)

the Americans south before winter, Stalin was backtracking on his promises. On October 8, Zhou flew from Beijing to see Stalin at Sochi. With Zhou was an interpreter, Shi Zhe, and Zhou's confidential assistant, Kang Yimin. In Moscow they were met by Lin Biao, who had duly gone to Russia for medical treatment. All four flew to the Black Sea resort where Stalin was resting, arriving on October 11. That afternoon Stalin offered the delegation a litany of excuses. He could only lend some munitions and supplies, and would have no aircraft, with pilots, available for two-and-and-half months. The Soviets, he explained, were overcommitted in Europe. There were shaky satellites to prop up. He was not prepared to fight another war so soon after 1945 and so distant from Soviet supply sources. The terrain between North Korea and Russian Siberia was too difficult to permit overland supply from Vladivostok—only a narrow corridor of seafront—and shipments by sea were vulnerable to American subs and aircraft. Nevertheless, he expected China to do its regional duty, or "Socialism in Korea would collapse within a very short time." If China would not, Stalin was ready to cooperate with Mao in offering sanctuary to their Korean comrades forced to evacuate the North. The Soviets, he maintained to the surprised Zhou, could do little in Asia. They had to be ready for the ultimate confrontation with the forces of imperialism, which would doubtless take place in Europe.

Although outraged by Stalin's excuses, Zhou was too sophisticated a diplomat to let that show. Instead, he asked what bottom line in assistance China could count upon. Would his forces have Soviet air cover? Would the divisions already committed be supplied?

Intending to furnish very little, Stalin agreed to help, but Zhou left with no guarantees. He was to submit a specific shopping list of arms and equipment, clearly a stall for time. With the Soviet bloc in Europe, and Russia itself, in persistent economic difficulties, Stalin wanted no war with the West despite the provocations emanating from Moscow. The nuclear catch-up competition with the Americans was itself absorbing more resources than the Soviets could spare, and Stalin wanted to adventure only on the cheap.

Western realization of Soviet limitations was blinded by Russian bluster. "So what?" Stalin allegedly told Nikita Khrushchev. "If Kim Il Sung fails, we are not going to intervene with our troops. Let the Americans be our neighbors in the Far East." He meant it. On October 8 two errant Air Force jets had strafed a Soviet airfield near Vladivostok, sixty-two miles beyond the North Korean border. The State Department, concerned about the violation of Russian territory—the FEAF had been warned in August even about flying as close as seventeen miles from the frontier—offered compensation for damages. Stalin opted to ignore the incident, preferring no perception of being bought off by the U.S., yet wanting no excuse for war.

Truman was so concerned about the incident that he told aides he had to have a private talk with MacArthur about such provocations; yet the subject would never come up at Wake. (Four days after the blunder, MacArthur would relieve the commander of the 49th Fighter-Bomber Group at K-2 in Taegu, and order the two pilots court-martialed.)

On the same day, Truman sent a memo drafted by the Defense Department for the President's signature, warning MacArthur of "the possible intervention of Chinese Communist forces" and the need to be prudent in his advances about "a reasonable chance of success" against them. Otherwise, confrontation with the Chinese should be avoided. Also, given the mistaken attack on Soviet soil, Truman added a warning to "obtain authorization from Washington prior to any military action against objectives in Chinese territory." The President did not want to draw in either Russia or China, and had no idea how little appetite Stalin had for war. Bugging the Soviet embassy in Washington and the UN Mission in New York had elicited no such clues.

On October 12, as Truman was leaving Washington for the MacArthur meeting, Stalin cabled a message to Kim, who was in deep trouble and about to evacuate Pyongyang, advising him to rescue what was left of his army by crossing into Manchuria or Siberia, and returning to fight another day. This was, he lied, "the recommendations [of the] conference of Chinese and Soviet leading comrades." Zhou had nothing to do with it.

Had Kim accepted what seemed inevitable, MacArthur's war would have been over—as he anticipated. While MacArthur prepared for the unwanted conference with Truman, Mao stubbornly responded to Stalin on the thirteenth that China would intervene whatever Stalin's assistance. That day, with the beginnings of a Chinese presence across the Yalu unperceived abroad, the Politburo Standing Committee in Beijing confirmed its willingness to bail out the North Koreans. Mao had explained to his rubber-stamp Politburo on October 2 that failing to assist an ideological partner and neighbor would be a disgrace. If a clash with the U.S. were inevitable at some point in China's development it would be best in Korea rather than at home.

As Zhou later described Mao's argument, made prior to Stalin's rebuff, Korea offered "the most favorable terrain, the closest communications to China, the most convenient material and manpower backup, and the most convenient way for us to get indirect Soviet support." Advance units began testing covert crossing tactics. Full deployment across the Yalu was ordered, then withdrawn, then ordered again. On the thirteenth Mao stubbornly warned, despite Zhou's cool treatment at Sochi, "If we don't send troops to Korea"—they would begin crossing in force the next day—"the reactionary forces in the world will become bolder and that will be disadvantageous. . . ." Mao cabled Zhou, who was about to fly home, that the Chinese would intervene, but as "volunteers" in order to reduce the likelihood that the U.S. would respond with a formal declaration of war. That afternoon Zhou was back to see Stalin, who said in surprise, according to Khrushchev, "Didn't we say goodbye this morning?"

"I have just received a telegram from Mao Zedong and the Political Bureau," Zhou explained to Stalin. "Our Political Committee has taken the decision to march troops into Korea at once."

Pleased to be free of responsibility, Stalin remarked, "The Chinese comrades are good after all, are good after all."

Without explicit war Stalin would not have to put his mutual assistance agreement with China to the test, while China would do the sacrificing for the cause. Immediately, he cabled to Kim Il Sung in Pyongyang, reversing his earlier insistence on evacuation and ordering him "to postpone temporarily" any flight into sanctuary. "Detailed reports from Mao Zedong" were forthcoming. On the fourteenth, the next day, he announced—as if he had arranged the rescue—that "after hesitation and a series of provisional decisions, the Chinese comrades at last [have] made a final decision to render assistance to Korea with troops." He offered Kim nothing but "luck."

The Chinese were already confirming their decision with their feet. Willoughby and MacArthur had known of the beginnings of a Chinese presence when broadcast warnings from Beijing hinted that troops might be sent across the border to protect the huge Suiho hydroelectric plant on the Korean side of the Yalu, which generated much of the electric power used in Manchuria. In Tokyo, Admiral Arleigh Burke, concerned that such intervention would be only the beginning, had approached retired Admiral Kichisaburo Nomura, who had been Japanese ambassador in Washington before Pearl Harbor and who remained knowledgeable about Chinese affairs. Would the Chinese, Burke asked, really intervene in force, or were such threats merely rhetoric? Nomura's opinion was that if the 38th parallel were crossed, Chinese troops would enter Korea. Burke took the estimate to Willoughby, who dismissed it as guesswork.

In Washington, only low-level officials—experts who actually knew

China—warned of intervention, but the ambiguous language from the President and the Pentagon failed to rein in MacArthur, who was anticipating imminent victory after Inchon. Rarely had anyone challenged the broad interpretations which MacArthur applied to directives he received. Their grounds, logical although dangerous in dealing with MacArthur, were that commanders in the field needed operational flexibility. Further, Truman and the Pentagon would not risk offending the victor at Inchon or his backers in the political opposition.

The meeting of Mohammed and the Mountain had been considered by Truman for several weeks. "For a short time," he claimed in his memoirs, "I thought of flying to Korea to pay our troops there a brief visit. I realized that MacArthur would feel his place in those perilous days was near his forces and that he would hesitate to make the long trip across the ocean for what might only be a few hours' talk." Had Truman forgotten which one was President?

Unmentioned was the blatant public relations motive—press coverage and photo opportunities just prior to the November elections, when all the seats in the House and one-third of those in the Senate were at stake. The White House needed the political boost, as allegations of "softness on Communism" and the "selling out" of Chiang Kaishek became major Republican campaign themes. Senator Joseph McCarthy had declared earlier in the year, offering no evidence, that 205 members of the Communist Party were "still working and shaping policy in the State Department," and Senator Kenneth Wherry of Nebraska called Secretary Acheson "a bad security risk."

Security risks were alleged everywhere. In California, the university Board of Regents had already struggled over one of the earliest of loyalty oaths, voting that faculty who did not sign a Communist disclaimer were to be dismissed by June 30. Following the North Korean invasion on June 25, Governor Earl Warren's battle over the oath was lost.

In mid-September a far-Right organization funded by a millionaire businessman and lobbyist for Chiang Kaishek and calling itself Counterattack—in actuality three ex-FBI agents—published out of an office on 42nd Street in New York a 213-page paperback offered at one dollar that would almost paralyze the electronic media. Titled *Red Channels: The Report of Communist Influence in Radio and Television,* it displayed on its cover a red hand seizing a microphone. Much the opposite had occurred. The purported "Newsletter of Facts to Combat Communism" would become the bible of blacklisting in radio and film and television, often ending the employment of professionals reported to have attended a fund-raiser for Spanish refugees or who belonged to an alleged

Communist front group. Actors, singers, composers, writers, broadcasters—even William L. Shirer and Howard K. Smith—were on the list.

Some of those charged undoubtedly had Communist leanings, then or in times past, but the publication led to a wave of arbitrary and protected slander that had begun with Senator McCarthy's Wheeling, West Virginia, allegations about Reds in government on February 9. Amateur anti-Communist sleuths, targeting almost anyone who had ever belonged to a Left-leaning organization as far back as the Depression years as disloyal, mailed accusatory letters by the thousands to the FBI, receiving in return a copy of J. Edgar Hoover's pamphlet, *What You Can Do to Fight Communism and Preserve America.*

MacArthur would write later to General Bradley, darkly suggesting domestic treason or foreign espionage: "Indeed it is self-evident that the Red Chinese . . . would not have risked the entry of major forces into the Korean Peninsula without the knowledge previously gained, through indiscretion or leakage, or the extraordinary and unprecedented protection our military policy restrictions would afford his supply lines and bases north of his point of entry which otherwise would have been at the complete mercy of our then largely unopposed air power." Yet all the Communist Chinese actually had to do was to read the newspapers in the U.S. or abroad.

Truman would always claim higher motives than public relations for the Wake Island meeting, writing in his memoirs that the "first and the simplest reason" for seeing MacArthur "was that we had never had any personal contacts at all, and I thought he ought to know his Commander in Chief and that I ought to know the senior field commander in the Far East." The 1944 precedent (on the eve of a presidential election) when Franklin Roosevelt met MacArthur in Hawaii was Truman's preference, but the JCS, timid as usual in coping with the general, suggested offering an alternative site. "If the situation in Korea is such that you should not absent yourself for the time involved in such a long trip," Truman cajoled, Wake would be a reasonable substitute. MacArthur was satisfied that every literate person would notice that the President would have to fly more than seven thousand miles to an isolated Pacific atoll while the Supreme Commander had to travel a mere 1,900 miles. Public perception of their relative importance was a foregone conclusion.

It seemed a political mistake on Truman's part not to go all the way to Korea—perhaps to a photo opportunity on the 38th parallel. The President could have grandstanded his anti-Communism for the American press, pinned medals on draftee privates and shaken hands with UN soldiers from

Britain or Greece or Turkey who had given a politically significant international coloring to the intervention.

"I would be delighted [to] meet the President on the morning of the 15th, at Wake Island," MacArthur cabled. But he was far from delighted. Since MacArthur had only Truman's public advance statement and was never supplied with an agenda, he had reason to believe that he was being exploited, telling diplomatic adviser William Sebald that the trip seemed a "political junket" for the President. MacArthur's suspicions appeared confirmed when he asked that the chief correspondents covering his headquarters be permitted to accompany him. He was turned down with excuses of security. The White House knew that his band of devoted pressmen would put a MacArthur spin on whatever took place. They were certain to get a MacArthuresque briefing from the general on the plane returning to Tokyo. MacArthur would nurse his anger over the snub all the way to Wake and back.

Responding to MacArthur, Marshall, who declined to make the trip with the excuse that someone had to be in charge at the Pentagon, asked the general to bring Ambassador Muccio with him. "[The] President will discuss with you rehabilitation of Korea," Marshall explained to justify the ambassador's presence, "for which the Army will be designated the executive agent, as well as other matters." To ensure that Muccio learned of his invitation, the State Department sent him a cryptic message: "If invited, take the trip." Two hours later he was cabled almost as cryptically by MacArthur: "I have been instructed to invite you, and if [you are] at Haneda before 11:00 in the morning, should be glad to have your company." Muccio secured a courier flight, packed a bag and left Korea for Tokyo without any idea of where he was going next. He found out when MacArthur boarded, ascending a ramp labeled "Northwest Airlines" and looking "mad as hell."

Among the "other matters" left unspecified, Averell Harriman recalled, was "the possibility of the Chinese [intervening]." Events created their own agendas as the momentum for the meeting accelerated. ROK troops were already across the 38th parallel and other forces would follow. Emboldened by the rout of North Korean forces in the south, the UN—with the U.S. hardly holding back—approved a resolution calling for Korean unification, although the original reason for UN involvement had been only to throw back the Communist invasion. Truman had much more to talk about with MacArthur than he had first expected, yet would raise little of it.

Although rehabilitation of postwar Korea was the optimistic focus—publicly—of Truman's agenda, the Panikkar signals from Beijing were, more quietly, up-front in the CIA briefing book prepared for the President and delivered to the White House on October 11. Yet the Indian ambassador to Beijing was largely discounted in Washington. He was a conduit for messages from a regime unrecognized by the United States and with no official channels of its own. The Chinese, American intelligence equivocated, "are capable of intervening effectively" on the ground, "but not necessarily decisively." Despite threats from Chinese officials, "there are no convincing indications of an actual Chinese Communist intention to resort to full-scale intervention in Korea." While China might achieve a "major gain in prestige" by defeating the U.S. in Korea, the CIA weaseled for Truman's briefing book, "The Chinese Communists undoubtedly fear the consequences of war with the United States. Their domestic programs are of such magnitude that the regime's entire domestic program and economy would be jeopardized by the strains." In its confidence the agency failed to credit the cohesion war brings to a nation and the economic stimulus of war industry—and the powerful illogic of ideology. The CIA also failed to evaluate its suspect sources of intelligence and the ingenuity of the Chinese in masking preparations by moving large forces only at night and concealing their presence by day.

MacArthur's intelligence from Tokyo was no better. Although Willoughby's summaries at the Dai Ichi conceded the presence of large Chinese armies in Manchuria and their "capacity for crossing the Yalu," he advised MacArthur that the Chinese would intervene only if Stalin insisted upon it. Behind their doubts that Stalin or Mao would widen the war was preponderant American airpower and the American ability to deliver the bomb. Among the skeptics was Rear Admiral Arleigh A. Burke, deputy chief of staff to Admiral Joy in Tokyo, whose own intelligence people thought otherwise. One of them even told Burke, "It looks to us like the Chinese *are* in North Korea."

Burke showed his staff's data to Willoughby, who called in his own experts. They saw no reason to question their own estimates to MacArthur. "I don't think they're in there either," Willoughby insisted, "and I don't think they will come in." Willoughby thought Panikkar was biased toward Beijing, and that Beijing was bluffing. But Willoughby sent Eugene Clark, the Navy lieutenant who had scouted the approaches to Inchon, on a new mission, with 150 South Korean agents and guerrilla fighters in five powerboats, up the Yellow Sea coast to the northernmost outer islands of the Korean peninsula to look for evidence of the Chinese. They would leave Inchon on the day that Truman planned to arrive at Wake.

As what Acheson called "the Mikado of Japan," MacArthur was accustomed to traveling with a legion of aides and reporters, but it was Truman who flew to the pinpoint of Wake Island, just west of the International Date Line, in executive style. With MacArthur on the *SCAP* were only Muccio, Whitney, Bunker and Colonel Charles C. Canada, a physician on the general's personal staff. Truman had his entourage on three aircraft led by the presidential DC-6, the *Independence*. His absurdly oversized twenty-four-person party included Harriman, Rusk, Philip Jessup (ambassador-at-large), Pace, Bradley, Charles Ross (press secretary), Wallace Graham (presidential physician), Harry Vaughan (crony and military aide), Jack Ramagna (White House staff) and six Secret Service agents. An Air Force Stratocruiser (transport version of the B-29) carried representatives of the press, and a C-121 Constellation brought additional support staff from Washington. Because of the distance and the time zone changes, Truman planned stopovers in California and Hawaii. MacArthur could fly nonstop from Tokyo.

On Sunday the fifteenth—the fourteenth in Hawaii—the President arrived at Wake at 6:30 a.m. MacArthur had landed at about six the previous evening—it was three hours earlier than Japan time—and would not set his watch back while at Wake. He was billeted overnight with his party in a Quonset hut that was the residence of a Civil Aeronautics Board official on the island. Persistent myth has it that the planes from east and west arrived over Wake at the same time, and that at MacArthur's orders, the *SCAP* continued to circle, impelling Truman to radio MacArthur to land first. Even so, the story goes, MacArthur delayed meeting the President until nearly an hour after the *Independence* had touched down, causing Truman to reprimand the general for his discourtesy. The petty drama never happened. MacArthur was up early and, ferried to the runway in an old black Chevrolet, was at the ramp of the presidential plane when Truman disembarked. Instead of saluting his commander in chief, he reached out to shake hands, exclaiming, "Mr. President!"

"How are you, General? I'm glad you are here," said Truman, but noticing, he recalled rather nastily in his memoirs, that the general appeared "with his shirt unbuttoned, wearing a greasy ham-and-eggs cap that evidently had been in use for twenty years." Truman would later allege to Merle Miller, "A man I know who was on MacArthur's staff insists that the general had an enlisted man, I believe a corporal, who did nothing but fray battle caps that had come straight from the Post Exchange, fray them so they would look as if the general had just stepped out of some firing line or other."

Truman had waited "a long time" for the meeting, he said, and MacArthur responded, "I hope it won't be so long next time, Mr. President."

They posed for photographers, Truman dapper despite the tropical heat in his business suit and hat. Chatting privately as the cameramen clicked away, MacArthur expressed regret that his VFW statement on Formosa had created any misunderstanding, and Truman responded, "Oh, think nothing more about that." The pair climbed into the rear of the Chevrolet and headed for the small, coral-faced, pinkish concrete-and-frame building where their conversations would be held. According to their accompanying Secret Service agent, Truman asked as they went whether it appeared that the Chinese would intervene in Korea. MacArthur said confidently that his intelligence people didn't think so, but that if the Communists did, his forces could handle them.

Although Truman came prepared, he said, to discuss the rehabilitation of postwar Korea, what was more on his mind was the reality of neighboring China. In the post-Inchon euphoria, the Panikkar warnings were being dismissed as those of a Mao sympathizer rather than from an indirect representative of Beijing. National Security Council recommendations for restraint were going unheeded as each was reinterpreted in Tokyo to afford MacArthur more latitude. Even the alarm over MacArthur's belligerent VFW convention remarks had been forgotten after Inchon. At the time MacArthur had been challenged largely on the issue of Taiwan. Acheson believed MacArthur's aim was "to increase the nature of U.S. military commitments concerning Formosa," while "greatly strengthen[ing] the hand of the Soviet Union in putting pressure upon the Chinese Communists to attack Formosa at a time when it is believed that the Chinese Communists are resisting such pressure."

The ease of the Inchon success and the flight of the *In Min Gun* to the north had seemingly changed the strategic equation in Korea. Still, even prior to Chromite, the National Security Council had warned (on September 1) that it was "unlikely that the Soviet Union will passively accept the emergence of a situation in which all or most of Korea would pass from its control, provided it . . . would not involve a substantial risk of general war." Although the NSC saw North Korea as a Soviet puppet, it would not exclude the possibility "that Chinese Communist forces would be used" short of general war. Almost reading Stalin's mind the NSC observed shrewdly, "It is possible that the Soviet Union may endeavor to persuade the Chinese Communists to enter the Korean campaign with the purpose of avoiding the defeat of the North Korean forces and also of fomenting war between the United States and the Chinese Communists should we react strongly." All this was lost in the mood of mutual congratulation that pervaded Wake on October 15.

The China matter came up again when Truman and MacArthur spent their first hour privately, Truman in a wicker chair, MacArthur on a rattan settee. Again MacArthur brushed off the possibility of Chinese intervention, and the President turned to small talk. "This is no weather for coats," Truman remarked as he removed his jacket. MacArthur pulled out his long corncob and asked if he could smoke, and Truman joked about having spent his political life having smoke blown at him. For the general meeting, five folding tables were pushed together. On the other side of a swinging louvered door, Philip Jessup's secretary, Vernice Anderson, took notes, assuming that her boss had brought her to record what was said. In the meeting room itself, Colonel Bunker, MacArthur's aide, also began to take notes, but Charlie Ross undiplomatically objected, saying that no formal minutes should be taken on either side. Yet Anderson was visibly in the anteroom already doing so. Bunker, accustomed to taking notes, had a good memory for talk and would jot down his version afterwards.

The interchange continued about ninety minutes, beginning with MacArthur's views, which Truman asked for, on the postwar rehabilitation of Korea. The general prefaced his response by reviewing the military situation, which he said had to be resolved first. The discussion ranged, often in disorganized fashion, from the future of Korea to the failures of the French in Indochina, with MacArthur responding to about thirty questions by the presidential party. Although it was obvious that a stenographer was taking notes as trade winds swayed the lightweight louvered door back and forth, MacArthur's staff would later deny their accuracy. Whether columnist Stewart Alsop got his text soon after from Tokyo or Washington made little difference, for Larry Bunker's notes closely parallel those of General Bradley and Miss Anderson. Yet when Alsop published a *New York Herald Tribune* story on November 13, 1950, less than a month later, and quoted MacArthur's scoffing at the possibility of effective Chinese intervention, the general himself cabled the *Freeman,* a conservative journal which asked him to confirm or deny Alsop's account, that statements attributed to him were "entirely without foundation."

The evidence of the loyal Bunker's own notes contradicts MacArthur. The transcript was stamped TOP SECRET, filed and forgotten. Bunker kept it. "Organized resistance," MacArthur predicted, not for the first time, "will be terminated by Thanksgiving. . . . They are thoroughly whipped. The winter will destroy those we don't. . . . In North Korea, unfortunately, the government is pursuing a forlorn hope. It has no possibility of success."

The North Koreans, "poorly trained, led and organized" in newly slapped together divisions and depleted of veterans, were likely to fight on, although further resistance was futile. "It just goes against my grain to destroy them," MacArthur deplored, "but they are obstinate. The Oriental values 'face' over life." He described the rapid northward advances of his divisions on both flanks and predicted that X Corps would be in Pyongyang shortly. "That closes the gap. The North Korean command . . . has made the same mistake as . . . in South Korea. . . . It will be over by Thanksgiving. I hope we will be able to withdraw the Eighth Army almost immediately into Japan, probably by Christmas." He expected to return EUSAK to Japan by Christmas, leaving X Corps, reconstituted with infantry divisions and UN detachments, as a security force until order was restored in a unified Korea.

General Bradley raised the subject of getting some troops made surplus by victory to NATO in Europe. "Could the Second or the Third Division be made available to be sent over to Europe by January?"

"Yes," MacArthur assured. "I will make one available by January."

With that easy optimism as a basis, the questions turned to Korean national elections and, said Muccio, "matters of money, land laws and tax laws." MacArthur proposed to keep North Korean currency circulating above the 38th parallel, but noted that although the UN resolution stipulated that the North Korean government "should be retained," he saw that as impossible. "They will either flee or the South Koreans will kill them."

Harriman wondered about "psychological rehabilitation" in the North —decommunizing the people—and Muccio suggested employing only South Koreans. "They know their own people better than we do. We should provide them with radios and text books and also scientific guidance. We could set up a very effective system with a radio or loudspeaker in every school and village center. I had sound trucks which were very, very effective. With no newspapers and radio service we sent them out to rural districts and village centers."

"I believe in sound trucks," said Truman. "I won two elections with them." (Vernice Anderson's minutes note "Laughter.")

Bradley then wondered about depoliticizing prisoners of war. (MacArthur had noted that he already had sixty thousand, a number that was already doubling.) "They are the happiest Koreans in all Korea," MacArthur responded, having seen exactly one temporary POW enclosure near Inchon.

"For the first time they are well fed and clean. They have been deloused and have good jobs for which they are being paid under the Geneva Convention." (The only accurate part of the sentence dealt with the delousing.) "I believe there is no [political] split, but their attitude is due only to the banner that flies over them. There is no difference in ideology and there are no North and South Korean blocs [among POWs]."

If the general believed that, he was grossly misinformed—or naive. He had seen enough war to understand how POWs behaved behind the barbed wire. Unlike the South Koreans impressed into service as the Communists moved across the 38th parallel, and offered some rations but seldom a rifle or a uniform except for those plucked from dead or captured enemy, the North Koreans were trained with ideological rigidity. In prison compounds they remained at war, often formed into covert regiments, furnished with orders by guerrillas or fifth columnists beyond the fences, sometimes led by officers pretending to be ordinary privates. The prisoner situation would eventually explode in bloody mutinies, but MacArthur's rapt audience at Wake assumed that he knew everything. What he had told them was exactly how they hoped and believed the situation would turn out.

Bradley asked what MacArthur would do with additional offers of troops from UN members, especially with the war likely to wind down. "Are not some of them more trouble than they are worth militarily? (Politically they are fine.)"

"They are useless [now] from the military point of view and," MacArthur predicted, "probably would never see action. From the political point of view, they give a United Nations flavor. I think that the balance between these two considerations should be struck in Washington. I cannot do it." (JSC would cable MacArthur on October 24: "Have this date recommended to Sec Def that he inform Sec State that services of French Bn schedule[d] to sail for Korea 25 Oct are no longer needed." Since it was too late to cancel the offer and impolitic anyway, both the French and Netherlands battalions arrived in Korea and by December were attached to the 2nd Division. They proved to be needed and fought well.)

"I have one more question," said Truman, according to Bunker's own transcript. "What will be the attitude of Commie China and the Russians to this . . . ? Is there any danger of interference?"

"There is very little in my opinion," MacArthur insisted confidently. "Had either one intervened in the first two months of the war, their intervention would have been decisive. . . . But not at this time. We are no longer fearful of their intervention.* In the case of the Chinese Communist armies, they have in Manchuria probably 300,000 troops. Of those probably not more than 100–125 thousand are along the Yalu. . . . They would have the greatest difficulty of getting more than 50 thousand across the river and would face great logistical difficulties. The Chinese Commies have no air umbrella. There would be the greatest slaughter if China tried to put ground troops across. They would be destroyed."

Even as MacArthur spoke, tens of thousands of Chinese were swarming across the Yalu by night, remaining invisible from the air by day. Neither his intelligence nor the CIA thought that any more than a trickle of Chinese could be across the border. But, warming to his theme, MacArthur continued that any Chinese who intervened would be pounded into "a rabble." On the other hand, although he did not see any Soviet intervention likely, they had a good, well-maintained air force in Siberia. Still, "they would not be a match for our air." Besides, the Russians had, in the region, "practically no ground forces. They would have difficulty in massing 50 thousand troops. It would take [Stalin] at least six weeks before he could get his first division into action. Their winter is so bitter they could do little." Russia, he was convinced, had no interest in a land war in Asia.

Listening with more awe than understanding, Army Secretary Frank Pace concluded that MacArthur "was indeed a military genius." "He was the most persuasive fellow I ever heard," Charles Murphy, Truman's special counsel, recalled. "I believed every word of it." MacArthur had figures of every sort—enemy troops, artillery, aircraft—in his head. He knew where every force of his own was and where it would be in hours or days. He knew distances, temperatures and terrain.

Turning to the forthcoming disaster of the French in Indochina he predicted, MacArthur wondered ominously why "the best France has" couldn't win, and saw no purpose in propping them up with American support. "If the French won't fight, we are up against it. Here . . . was the flower of the French Army . . . and not an ounce of aggressiveness."

"It has baffled me, too," Truman agreed, and Admiral Radford added, "Troops cannot make headway without [the] simple cooperation of the people."

---

*This sentence is from the Washington transcript. Bunker wrote, more awkwardly than MacArthur very likely spoke, "We are no longer in a local position of fearfulness of such intervention." Otherwise the texts remain very close.

The first ten American military advisers had already arrived in Vietnam. Soon, propelled by domestic anti-Communism, the American military aid program in behalf of the French would be second in dollars only to the effort in Korea.

"You can't do anything with the damned French," said the President, closing the subject. "Is there anything else?"

After the general session, which took up such issues as the difficulties of dealing with Syngman Rhee, Bradley and Pace adjourned with MacArthur for some private talk. Truman relaxed in the Quonset hut while Ross worked on a conference communiqué, written as a first-person summary by the President. (MacArthur would sign it, although he very likely didn't read it.) "On all these matters [discussed], I have found our talks most helpful," Truman declared in Ross's handout for the newsmen waiting for their final photo opportunity, "and I am very glad to have had this chance to talk them over with one of America's great soldier-statesmen who is now serving in the unique position of the first commander-in-chief of United Nations peace forces. We are fully aware of the dangers which lie ahead but we are confident that we can surmount these dangers. . . ."

MacArthur would write from Tokyo on October 30, in response to a warm message from Truman, "Operations in Korea are proceeding according to plan and while, as we draw close to the Manchurian border, enemy resistance has stiffened, I do not think this . . . would materially retard the achievement of our border objective." (He had carefully made the Manchurian border a collective goal rather than his own.) "It is my current estimate that the next week or so should see us fairly well established in the border area, after which it shall be my purpose, as I outlined during the Wake Island conference, to withdraw American troops as rapidly as possible—this to the end that we may save our men from the rigors of [the] winter climate at that northern altitude. . . ." He had left Wake, he closed, "with a distinct sense of satisfaction that the country's interests had been well served. . . ."

MacArthur had not been speaking only his own mind when he announced the Yalu and a united Korea as his objective. He had every reason later to feel that he had been sold out, although events were more to blame than Washington. As far back as July 1, John Allison, who had just returned from Korea and Japan with Dulles, ignored what he saw as only temporary bad news, and advised Dean Rusk at State that "we should continue right on up to the Manchurian and Siberian border, and having done so, call for a UN-supervised election for all of Korea." Warren Austin, the American UN ambassador, and Secretary of State Acheson had both delivered similar speeches. Even Truman himself, in a nationwide radio broadcast on September 1, as troops were still seemingly in a hopeless position in the Pusan Perimeter, had called for a "free, independent and united" Korea.

As Truman's boilerplate departure language was being drafted, MacArthur returned from his discussions with Bradley and Pace for small talk with Truman, who expected the general to remain for lunch. According to Courtney Whitney, who had his report of the private meeting from MacArthur, the general asked Truman if he intended to run for reelection in 1952. Truman countered by asking if MacArthur had any political ambitions. "None whatsoever," said MacArthur. "If you have any general running against you, his name will be Eisenhower, not MacArthur." Truman laughed.

Consulting his watch, MacArthur announced, "There are many pressing matters awaiting my return to Tokyo"—as if his responsibilities a few time zones away were far more demanding than any awaiting the President in Washington. Their aircraft were ordered to be readied, and lunch was canceled. On their way in the Chevrolet to the airstrip they continued their political talk, pausing by the *Independence* for the cameras. Harriman asked MacArthur if he would ever consider returning to the United States, and the general said that he would come home for good "after the Japanese peace treaty was concluded." He would remain in Tokyo until then, but hoped his work would be over in a year.

Truman was still thinking of generals in politics, venturing that Eisenhower "doesn't know the first thing about politics. Why, if he should become President, his administration would make Grant's look like a model of perfection." Pausing near the ramp of his plane for a brief ceremony, Truman, his light fedora gleaming in the intense noonday sun, smilingly proffered a Distinguished Service Medal (the recipient's fifth) to MacArthur, and the general, shaking hands for the cameras, replied, "Goodbye, sir, and happy landings. It's been a real honor to talk to you." He remained courteously at the *SCAP,* not boarding until Truman entered the *Independence* and took off at 11:35 a.m. Only five hours after his arrival, Truman was heading back to Hawaii, and then to Washington.

Somehow, despite the final pleasantries, the views of the General and the President had failed to connect. "The conference at Wake Island," MacArthur would later write in his *Reminiscences,*

made me realize that a curious, and sinister, change was taking place in Washington. . . . The original courageous decision of Harry Truman to boldly meet and defeat Communism in Asia was apparently being chipped away by the constant . . . whispers of timidity and cynicism. The President seemed to be swayed by the blandishments of some of the more selfish politicians of the United Nations. He seemed to be in the anomalous position of openly expressing fears of over-calculated risks that he had fearlessly taken only a few months before.

This put me as a field commander in an especially difficult situation. Up to now I had been engaged in warfare as it had been conducted through the ages—to fight to win. But I could see now that the Korean War was developing into something quite different. There seemed to be a deliberate underestimating of the importance of the conflict to which the government had committed—and was expending—the lives of United States fighting men.

The word *sinister* suggested MacArthur's state of mind after he no longer had a role in shaping events. While Truman had tried to make it clear that the United States wanted no war, even by accident, with China or Russia, MacArthur's response was only to assure the President that neither antagonist could gain any military advantage by intervening.

Much the same message was picked up by the CIA, which intercepted a report from Brazilian diplomat Rio Branco to his Foreign Office after talking to a MacArthur intimate. MacArthur, the source reported, told the President at Wake that there had to be "an integral occupation of the two Koreas" before he could "regard his mission as ended." According to the CIA intercept the general also promoted the Formosan cause, declaring to Truman that if Taiwan fell to the Communists "there will be nothing left for the United States to do but abandon Asia." MacArthur insisted, however, that "certain defeatists" in Russia and China would not "have the courage to declare war," and had "told the President that it would be better to face a war now than two or three years hence, for he was certain that there was not the least possibility of an understanding with the men in the Kremlin, as the experience of the last five years has proved. . . . In order to attain peace it is necessary to destroy the focus of international bolshevism in Moscow."

Rio Branco's message, transmitted to Brazil on October 21, five days after the conference on Wake ended, was translated, transcribed and sent by General Collins to MacArthur for his comments on November 11. MacArthur responded the same day, describing "your WST 268" as "so completely at variance with the actual facts as to demonstrate that they could not have come from any responsible or reliable source." He referred to General

Bradley's notes, calling the Brazilian intercept "false, slanted and biased," for there was no "leakage of consequence" from his headquarters. "Please," he closed, "give my personal reassurances to the President."

Although he was JCS chairman, Bradley remained intimidated by MacArthur. In his own perception, despite his own five stars, Bradley remained the very junior officer he once had been when MacArthur was Army chief of staff. It was, Bradley had written on October 19, before the Brazilian flap, "refreshing to see and to talk to you again. . . . The conference, I feel, was most satisfactory and profitable—all of us from here got a great deal out of it. I am enclosing five copies of the substance of statements compiled from notes made by those of us who made the trip from Washington."

Very likely MacArthur did not read Bradley's remarks until he received the Brazilian intercept, which either included private comments to the President or, opportunistically, how he wanted them to appear. It sounded like MacArthur's political agenda, but Bradley brushed off any sense of disquiet in his closing. "We all think that you are doing a grand job—as exemplified in this morning's reports on the good news from Pyongyang."

The enemy capital reportedly had just been captured, and North Korean troops were fleeing toward the Yalu. MacArthur's forecasts at Wake looked good indeed.

To the Yalu

MACARTHUR RETURNED to Tokyo at 4:00 p.m. on October 15, confident that his Wake meeting had left him with a free hand in Korea. As was often the case, the news he had arranged for at his departure from Wake earlier in the day—the capture of Pyongyang—was premature. The North Korean capital was, in fact, entered on the seventeenth and secured the next day.

Seven divisions had converged on the city, four of them American (with British forces attached), three ROK. The NKPA could assemble only about eight thousand effectives (about half a division) from its 32nd and 17th Divisions to mount a defense while other divisions got away across the Taedong River running through the city. The Americans were especially eager to take Pyongyang because rumors were rife that it was the final U.S. objective in the war, after which Korea would be left to the South Koreans to clean up.

Many American soldiers expected to enjoy Thanksgiving dinner in Japan or on troopships en route home. Charles Willoughby's sweepingly satisfying intelligence summary released at the Dai Ichi on October 20 appeared to confirm GI hopes. "Organized resistance on any large scale has ceased to be an enemy capability," he declared for MacArthur. "Indications are that the North Korean military and political headquarters [staffs] may have fled into Manchuria." (Actually, Kim Il Sung had fled to the far northwest of Korea, just below the Yalu, where he was attempting to keep together the four divisions he had left.) "Communications with, and consequent control of, the enemy's field units have dissipated to a point of ineffectiveness. In spite of these indications of disorganization, there are no signs, at the moment, that the enemy intends to surrender. He continues to retain the capability of fighting small-scale delaying actions. . . ."

General Peng was at Andong (Antung), just above the Yalu in Manchuria, where Kim sent an emissary to urge that the Chinese cross in force without delay, before all of Korea was lost. Peng slipped across just after dusk on October 18 with one of his units, reaching the town of Pakchon, above Unsan, on the morning of the nineteenth. By dawn his men had concealed themselves in a gully northwest of the town.

Peng had left his deputy, Deng Hua, to order the mass movement of troops to begin. Every soldier, Deng specified, should be disguised as a refugee over his uniform; vehicles should move without using headlights; units should avoid all radio, telegraph and telephone communications. On the rainy evening of the nineteenth, four infantry armies, three artillery divisions and an anti-aircraft regiment—260,000 men in all—began crossing the Yalu, concealed by darkness. A concrete road atop the dam at the Suiho power plant was safe to use; MacArthur had been ordered to leave it unbombed. Only when B-29s dropped flares over the Korean side did Chinese troops lie low. According to Xue Li of the 4th Engineering Corps, his commanding officer, Du Ping, had the task of constructing bridges over rivers to the south which could not be bombed because they could not be seen. Du's specialty was wooden bridges painted "the color of the water" and submerged below the surface. Trucks could cross at night at wheeltop depth with their cargoes, and troops could wade on the platforms through the icy water.

With the temperature at subzero levels, soldiers and officers, fortified by strong wine, worked in the darkness nearly naked, shouting to each other, "It isn't cold! It isn't cold!" When they emerged for rests, Xue and others rushed to them with dry padded coats and "when we poured wine into their mouths, the teeth of these heroes clattered and they could not hold on to the flasks." By order of General Peng the locations of the submerged bridges were kept secret. After the rivers had frozen, the hidden crossings were no longer needed, but when in use they forded tens of thousands silently southward.

Another assignment of Xue's group was to prepare politicized entertainments for troops out of action, and in "two days and nights" with several assistants improvised three operettas, including the music for them, one titled "Changjin Bridge." At one dawn the house in which they rehearsed was bombed, but the performances went on and were even filmed by a unit from Beijing as part of a documentary for home consumption, "Resist the U.S. and Assist Korea."

Having enlisted for a year, Tang Bao Yi was caught up in the mobilization for Korea. MacArthur, Communist Party exhortations went, was a Capitalist bandit. His "invading army has thrown bombs to the front door of our home. This seriously threatens the peaceful reconstruction of our mother country. . . . The Koreans are in a sea of fire. Considering the mutual interests of China and Korea, we have to join the Chinese People's Volunteers and go to the Korean front." Male volunteers were formed into transportation and prisoner-overseer teams, and female volunteers staffed an amateur medical corps divided into subteams on crossing into Korea. Little more than girls, they were sent to makeshift hospitals converted from schoolhouses where wounded already lay on wheat sheaves.

Medicines were in short supply and within weeks amputations were common. Chen Hoi Li, a "nurse" of fifteen with no training, fetched water, helped the wounded to crude toilets—basins and tins—and sang to them, including "The White-Haired Woman" and a "Song of the Volunteers." Her primary assignment was to the "Waist Drum Team," a euphemism for the purveying of political propaganda. The sick and wounded beat out the rhythm on pots and pans.

Like the others, Tang Bao Yi crossed the Yalu from Antung wearing his padded coat inside out to match the snow-covered ground and be hidden in "a white world." Each "volunteer" carried a gun or several grenades, and two bags of rice. "We ate cold fried rice and fried noodles every day, and drank balls of ice in our mouths," he said. At first, he related, their duties involved "burying the gloriously dead, conveying prisoners of war, repairing damage, and receiving the [sick and wounded] comrades who had left their armies." They arrived on the third day after the first battles, "hitting the outrageous enemy on the head, making the U.S. Army leave many cars, weapons and explosives, and retreat awkwardly."

After napalm raids "it was very difficult to identify the bodies." They had to examine the residue—padded but charred shoes, brown buttons and remains of wooden-handled Chinese hand grenades. Short in supplies and equipment, they borrowed from the ruins of villages emptied of inhabitants. At one hut Tang found a "debtor's note" scratched on a mud wall: "Volunteers Group 8 has borrowed two small grindstones."

As they began moving into staging areas in the hills below the Yalu, the Chinese were only eighty miles to the south of the ROK 2nd Corps. Early that morning, unaware of the Chinese presence in the north, MacArthur flew to Korea for his fourth wartime visit. With Stratemeyer, Wright and

Whitney, he arrived in time to watch the 4,000-man 187th Airborne Regimental Combat Team parachute from C-119 twin-boomed transports into Sukchon and Sunchon, each about twenty-six miles beyond Pyongyang. Sucking on his corncob pipe from a seat far in the rear of the Constellation, his tin of Prince Albert tobacco tucked into a pocket of the seat, MacArthur leaned into the window to observe the operation while photographers snapped away at the general watching his war.

The paratroop drop was intended to cut off North Korean officials reportedly fleeing by train with their families and belongings, and to rescue American prisoners of war reportedly being moved northward on a train that was concealed in tunnels by day and ran only after dark. The 187th found neither, but did touch down in front of the 239th NKPA Regiment, an isolated 2,500-man force that found itself attacked from the north. Cut off behind by units of the 27th British Commonwealth Brigade moving with the U.S. 89th Tank Battalion, the North Koreans fought hard but lost nearly their entire complement. What happened to POWs held by the *In Min Gun* became clear when units of the 1st Cav, moving toward Sunchon, found the bodies of sixty-six murdered Americans in a railway tunnel. Seven others appeared to have died of starvation or disease. Twenty-three were found barely alive nearby. Feigning death, they had been abandoned. (Two expired the night they were rescued.)

They were all that were left of about 370 Americans who had been marched north from Seoul after Inchon. From Pyongyang they had been put on two trains, in open coal gondolas and in boxcars. As men died en route their bodies were removed. The survivors had been ordered off for an evening meal. Once off, they were shot. The trains continued north.

Walking down the ramp of the *SCAP* at the Pyongyang airfield, MacArthur was jubilant. Taking the Communist capital—the only one ever to be captured in combat by the West—seemed almost the end of the war. "Any celebrities to greet me?" he joked. "Where's Kim Buck Tooth?" The racial slur, a throwback to 1941 and earlier, was a reference to the elusive Kim Il Sung. MacArthur's intelligence chief apparently never told him, if he knew himself, that Kim Il Sung was a name adopted by earlier Korean leaders in the anti-Japanese resistance. It was their equivalent of Robin Hood.

Intelligence was wanting in Washington as well as Tokyo. Although Mao's writings on war circulated widely in many translations in the Communist world, they were disregarded in the West for lack of interest and shied away from even by the interested few, for fear that reading Mao would suggest a suspicious attraction to Communism. His ideas on strategy and tactics were literally an open book but not obtainable until a radical publishing house in New York published English translations in 1954, just after another in London—too late for Korea.

Clad as usual in Air Force leather jacket, open shirt and faded suntans, with his scrambled eggs cap tilted jauntily, MacArthur claimed to reporters that the "expert" airdrop "was a complete surprise. It looks like we closed the trap. Closing that trap should be the end of all organized resistance. The war is very definitely coming to an end shortly."

Conferring with Rhee, Walker and EUSAK staff officers, MacArthur exuded optimism. Demonstrating that was his motorcade, a procession of open jeeps through Pyongyang, so new to occupation that North Korean flags still flew, and posters of Stalin and Kim Il Sung remained displayed on buildings and light standards. Afterwards, at a brief ceremony that surprised even reporters and veteran airmen inured to the Supreme Commander's vanity, MacArthur received the Distinguished Flying Cross from General Stratemeyer for "outstanding heroism and extraordinary achievement while participating in aerial flights" (the term itself was extraordinary) to Korea under "precarious" conditions four times since the beginning of the war.

Although Pyongyang had fallen almost unopposed to General Paik Sun Yup's 1st ROK Division, bolstered by American armor, MacArthur arranged for a ceremony to recognize the achievement as that of the 5th Regiment of the 1st Cav. Its F Company had been the first American unit to enter Pyongyang. He asked all men who had been with F Company since it landed in Korea in July to step forward. Nearly two hundred were in the company when it first went into action; only five were left, and three of those had been wounded.

Shortly after 3:00 p.m. MacArthur and his party reboarded the *SCAP* for the return flight to Tokyo and civilized dinners to follow. Walker moved into his new headquarters, the vast former offices of Kim Il Sung, where above Kim's broad desk hung a portrait of a vigorous, idealized Stalin.

Later, in the stark, mountainous territory above Wonsan, where the Marines from Inchon would debark to trek into a frozen waste, Captain William B. Hopkins told Colonel Lewis Puller that he couldn't understand why the division, after taking Seoul, wasn't just sent north to occupy the enemy capital.

"Who's in charge of the whole deal?" asked Puller.

"Why, General MacArthur."

"An Army officer. The Marines captured Seoul, didn't they?" If you were MacArthur, would you let the Marines capture Seoul *and* Pyongyang?"

Back at the Dai Ichi the next working day, MacArthur prepared a new directive, which he issued on October 17 without consulting Washington. Ostensibly it restricted (but actually expanded) troop movements in a line above Sonchon, forty-five miles below the Yalu on the west coast, eastward across Korea to Songjin, which was fifty miles north of Iwon on the Japan Sea. Strategically the line was longer and less defensible than a Chongju-Hungnam line across the peninsula just before it flared out toward Manchuria and Siberia. Politically, MacArthur was challenging a JCS message of September 28 instructing him to permit only South Korean forces in the provinces bordering the Chinese-Soviet frontier. Later—but only later— Collins called the eased restraint zone "the first, but not the last, stretching of MacArthur's orders beyond JCS instructions." It was far from the first, and the failures to rein in MacArthur because of timidity and irresolution in Washington left him calamitously free to conduct his personal war.

Even so, his Sonchon-Songjin line, which reached northeast almost to the 41st parallel, was a model of MacArthuresque moderation compared to the willfulness of Syngman Rhee, who had ostensibly put his troops under the general yet urged them on beyond their orders. Rhee's aim was to create new facts on the ground, and MacArthur might not have been entirely unhappy about the president's militancy. Despite UN objections, Rhee announced ambitiously on the twenty-third that he was taking civil control of North Korea—as much as had already been occupied. In a telephone interview with *U.S. News & World Report,* a weekly MacArthur often used for pronouncements that exasperated the White House, Rhee asserted that he was sending five provincial governors into North Korea. "The war is to unify Korea," he declared. "When the war is over, the country will automatically be reunited." Although the UN had resolved to conduct elections in the liberated areas, Rhee reinterpreted that his own way, realizing that he could control the occupation. "If the people say the north and south could have a general election, it will be carried out." But he called on the United Nations to act only as an "observer." Otherwise, he contended, the Communists would denounce the new government as a "UN puppet."

It was an opportune time for MacArthur to stretch his limitations, as State and Defense seemed too busy with Rhee to recognize what the directives from the Dai Ichi foreshadowed. Since the operations maps in Tokyo showed the Eighth Army pressing quickly beyond Pyongyang, MacArthur abolished the Sonchon-Songjin line for non-ROK troops as obsolete, and exhorted commanders in the field "to drive forward with all speed and utilization of their forces." They were to employ "any and all ground forces . . . to secure all of North Korea," although as a sop to State he ordered all non-ROK elements to be "withdrawn from border areas as quickly as feasible and replaced by ROK units." Washington notwithstanding, Walker and Almond were ordered to drive to the Yalu.

On October 24, Almond's abilities to push his X Corps forces that far were very limited. Operation Yo-Yo had gone on for a week. In code the convoy to Wonsan was Operation Tailboard, but, even more than Chromite, it had been "common knowledge" and now open embarrassment. Rear Admiral Allan E. Hoke radioed Chief of Naval Operations Forrest Sherman, "The U.S. Navy has lost command of the sea in Korean waters." Reading that in Washington, Sherman observed, "Hoke's right; when you can't go where you want to, when you want to, you haven't command of the sea." Within the "invasion" fleet itself, the questionable tactics that brought it to frustration created bitter if cautious comment. Admiral Doyle later fulminated, "Almond pushed for a sea lift to Wonsan, in my opinion, [only] because he knew he had no possibility of retaining his independent command if X Corps moved on shank's mare to Wonsan."

Two more days of minesweeping still appeared to be necessary, although the *Mount McKinley* had made it into the inner harbor. Doyle directed the amphibious fleet to prepare for an "administrative" (noncombat) landing, but on the Kalma Peninsula to the north, away from the still-dangerous inner harbor. The long northeastern extent of coastal Korea seemed almost undefended.

Expecting to do a USO show for the Marines, whom he had entertained on obscure Pacific islands in 1944 and 1945, Bob Hope and his troupe left Seoul for Wonsan, to perform for the Leathernecks on the evening of the twenty-fourth. (His journeys to entertain servicemen, past, present and future, were performed at government expense, and would result in recorded and filmed material for his commercially sponsored broadcasts back home.) Out in the harbor was the *Mount McKinley,* and unseen beyond it was the amphibious force which Hope had come to amuse. The high brass from the flagship had no difficulty in helicoptering in for the show. Also present were the Marine air maintenance crews, who had been in Wonsan for twelve days. From the air, Hope's party had seen the armada and smaller ships close to shore—the minesweepers, rather than landing craft.

"*That's nice,* I thought," he wrote in a memoir. "*They're coming in to see our show.* But when we arrived in the Wonsan airport, there wasn't a soul in sight. We wondered where everybody was. We just went over to the hangar and stood there. Finally the brass—Major General Edward M. Almond, Vice Admiral Arthur D. Struble and the rest showed up." Politely, one of them asked how long Hope had been waiting.

"We've been here for twenty minutes," I told them.

"Twenty minutes!" they said. "You beat us to the beach."

"How do you mean, we beat you to the beach?" I asked.

"We've just landed," they said.

Lacking his intended audience, Hope, with singer Marilyn Maxwell and their company, entertained the Marine aircraft maintenance crews, the ranking officers from the flagship, the ROKs who cared and such curious *In Min Gun* remnants as had slipped within listening range. "There were guerrillas all around us," Hope was told, "but we didn't know it, and the fact that we beat the Marines to the beach made the A.P. wire. But I didn't believe it until I talked to the newspapermen who were there."

Bob Hope landing ahead of the landing force off Wonsan. October 1950.
Illustration from his Have Tux, Will Travel.

The scene recalled the "I shall return" photograph at Leyte in 1944 of MacArthur wading bravely through the low surf to the beach with his official party into the lenses of an army of waiting news cameramen.

Walking onto the improvised stage in the Wonsan airfield hangar, backed by a C-54 complement of bandsmen led by Les Brown, Hope addressed such Marines as were there, "It's wonderful seeing you. We'll invite you to all our landings." Inevitably he spiced the show with quips about the leathernecks absent offshore, then adjourned to a tent set up for the company and "a lot of brass. . . . The party was complete with K-rations and beer and such items."

Struble invited Hope to spend the night on his own ship "the *Big Mo*," and the pair took a helicopter to the battleship, where Hope indulged in a bath and a bottle of Scotch, did an impromptu show for the crew of two thousand, then watched a shipboard movie with the sailors—Randolph Scott in *Colt Forty-Five*. Firearms went off constantly in the film, and at the end Hope stood up and joked, "I want to go home. This is too rough for me. It's rougher than the war."

The next morning the *Big Mo* radioed to the shore to have Marilyn Maxwell and her singing group fly out, "and we did another show. Then we took a helicopter to the *Valley Forge* and did a show on her flight deck for [Rear] Admiral [J. M.] Hoskin[s] and two thousand more guys. We helicoptered back to Wonsan, got into our C-54, whipped over to Pyongyang, [and] did a show in the yard of the former Communist headquarters for a lot of troops who'd just been pulled out of the front lines."

Only after Hope had left did the Marine division, long marooned on their transports, go ashore—thirty-nine waves of troops plus service groups, artillery and armor. Sourly, General Almond called it "Doyle Day." Already ashore—he had been in Bob Hope's audience at the airfield—O. P. Smith delivered to Chesty Puller a message that he had been selected for promotion to brigadier general.

It took until October 31 for the Marine division to be completely offloaded. Once supporting ships were outloaded of their cargo and a count was made, the total number of vessels involved reached 128, excluding twenty-one minesweepers and an armada of outlying warships. None would have been needed for an overland operation. But MacArthur later contended that his plan "followed standard military practice in the handling and control of widely separated forces where lateral communications were difficult or impossible." A senior officer on the scene commented, "Almond got what he wanted, though it didn't make good military sense to the rest of us."

Although much that was emanating from the Dai Ichi failed to make military or diplomatic sense in Washington, the echoes of the Inchon success kept the Pentagon supine, while anti-Communist and China Lobby zealotry kept Truman's minority government (including the State Department) cautious about how it was viewed by an anxious electorate. Mid-term balloting for House and Senate seats and many governorships was only two weeks away when MacArthur's orders to drive to the Yalu finally prompted the Pentagon to react. Weakly, after noting the violation of their directive, the JCS cabled MacArthur: "While the Joint Chiefs of Staff realize that you undoubtedly had sound reasons for issuing these instructions they would like to be informed of them, as your action is a matter of some concern here."

Recognizing the timidity of the language, MacArthur responded in his usual manner, alleging (as always) that any other action than his own was fraught with danger and likely to magnify American casualties:

> The instructions contained in my [message to commanders] were a matter of military necessity. Not only are the ROK forces not of sufficient strength to initially accomplish the security of North Korea, but the reactions of their commanders are at times so emotional that it was deemed essential that initial use be made of more seasoned and stabilized commanders. There is no conflict that I can see with the directive . . . dated 27 September, which merely enunciated the provision as a matter of policy and clearly stated: "These instructions, however, cannot be considered to be final since they may require modification in accordance with developments." The necessary latitude for modification was contained also in . . . [the message] dated 30 September from the Secretary of Defense which stated: "We want you to feel unhampered tactically and strategically to proceed north of the 38th Parallel."
>
> I am fully cognizant of the basic purpose and intent of your directive and every possible precaution is being taken on the premises. The very reverse, however, would be fostered and tactical hazards might even result from other action than that which I have directed.

Paul Nitze of the State Department Policy Planning Staff thought that the directives of Marshall and the JCS were sufficiently clear. "Although MacArthur could go above the 38th parallel to clean up pockets of resistance, he was not authorized to engage in large operations that might provoke the Chinese or Soviets and thus jeopardize chances for an early negotiated settlement. MacArthur, as I suspected, would interpret this order differently. . . . Meanwhile I learned, from cable traffic coming across my desk, that MacArthur's real aim was to expand the war to China, overthrow Mao, and restore Chiang to power."

Nitze was certain, however unreliable his sources of information, that Truman would soon have to relieve MacArthur for overreaching. Nitze advised his chief, Dean Acheson, that to prepare for the eventuality, the President would have to put his own house in order. To deflect criticism he would have to remove the much despised General Vaughan, "who was now improperly exploiting his White House connections," and also replace Ambassador to Mexico William O'Dwyer, "another crony with a doubtful reputation." Acheson duly and cautiously brought up the matter with Truman, and was verbally booted out of the Oval Office.

To the east, in the X Corps area, by the end of October over sixty thousand troops were being redeployed, including the latecoming 7th Division still en route. On the beaches at Wonsan containers of cargo were piling up, and Almond's adjutant general, expecting to be in North Korea for a long time, ordered enlisted men to poke through the crates for desks and file cabinets. After three days of fruitless searching they came up with little of administrative use but two cases of Purple Heart medals. They would prove to be essential.

Almond was less than pleased with inheriting Major General Robert Soule's 3rd Division, which had been brought to strength by improvisation. Its 7th Infantry was historic; it had fought in the Battle of New Orleans in 1815. The 15th, which had served over twenty years on China station, had a black battalion. The supporting 999th Field Artillery, 58th Field Artillery and 64th Tank Battalion were also black units. Almond also considered the predominantly Puerto Rican 65th Infantry as black, and therefore an unreliable regiment. At his orders, the 3rd Division would be scattered about the desolate landing area to guard rail junctions and bridges, maintain construction site security, make (abortive) contact through the Taebaek Range with EUSAK, probe into suspected guerrilla territory, mop up behind Marine advances and act as corps reserve. Effectively, the division would cease to exist, and its racial disharmony was exacerbated when South Korean KATUSA soldiers augmenting it (as Shelby L. Stanton writes in *America's Tenth Legion*) "displayed their usual reluctance to participate in any action and expressed even more reluctance in black units (in Japan, the KATUSA recruits had revolted when paired with black soldiers)."

Press reports were that UN forces on the Eighth Army's front were driving north with little opposition, with the South Korean 6th Division leading the race to the Yalu. Yet hints of Chinese intervention multiplied. On October 24 two American planes flying over Korea about three miles south of the

Yalu were fired upon by anti-aircraft guns across the river in Manchuria—
"too accurate[ly] to be comfortable." The Far East Air Force set a line twelve
miles from the border, past which became a no-fly zone except for targets
specifically approved before takeoff. MacArthur's faith in airpower was such
that the failure of daytime reconnaissance in the vicinity of the Yalu to discover mass crossings continued to convince him that there were none. He
had already claimed confidently to Truman at Wake that Chinese divisions
would expose themselves to "the greatest slaughter" if they chanced across,
and the few Chinese captured identified themselves as volunteers.

When MacArthur would finally charge that the Chinese had entered in
force, the Ministry of Foreign Affairs in Beijing coyly described its Chinese
People's Volunteers as in the tradition of the Abraham Lincoln Brigade in the
Spanish Civil War and even Lafayette and his French recruits in the American Revolution. The labels suggested idealism rather than cynicism.

To maintain concealment, Communist forces accelerated the conversion
of abandoned horizontal mine shafts in the mountains near Kanggye into
roughly partitioned headquarters spaces. Foul in air, poorly lit and with rust-
ing rails under foot, they were nothing like the Dai Ichi, but NKPA and Chinese officialdom were safe below ground unless the mines were overrun. (In
Beijing, Mao austerely made his own war headquarters in a small building
where he lived and worked, meeting with few leaders other than Zhou Enlai
and communicating through runners.)

In Tokyo, despite the new reality of a Chinese presence in Korea, the
planned parallel corridors for EUSAK and X Corps were refined to keep
Almond's forces on the eastern side of the Taebaek ridges. (They no longer
had any need to cross toward Pyongyang.) The northward push was going so
well in the west that on the same day that American planes had been shot at
near the Yalu, MacArthur had authorized commanders nevertheless "to use
any and all ground forces . . . as necessary to secure all of North Korea." It
remained a tall order. North of Wonsan in the east and Pyongyang in the
west, the peninsula flares out broadly to the Yalu and the Tumen. Still,
MacArthur was so positive of a quick end to the war that he left unchanged
his October 21 message to the Pentagon reminding the JCS that he had proposed at Wake "that the Eighth Army complete should be withdrawn from
Korea and returned to its position of readiness in Japan at the close of hostility. It was envisioned that this movement would start before Thanksgiving
and be completed by Christmas." (Later he would deny having mentioned
Christmas in any context.) He proposed also for JCS approval that the 2nd

Division then be returned to the U.S. and the 3rd kept in Korea for six more months, then also returned to the U.S.

Throughout October the British 29th Infantry Brigade Group had been moving toward Korea. Brigadier Thomas Brodie, its commander, arriving by air in Japan, reported to MacArthur on the twenty-sixth. Once desperate for such troops, MacArthur's staff now wondered how Brodie's surplus brigade could be employed. Leaving the Dai Ichi, Brodie wondered to the War Office, "It is difficult to be sure what we are getting into: some Americans here seem to think the war will be over before we arrive." He discussed his role with Air Vice Marshal Bouchier, British liaison with the Far East Command, who suggested an occupation assignment. Puzzled, Sir Alvary Gascoigne, informal ambassador to Japan pending the peace treaty, and Lieutenant General Sir Horace Robertson, the Australian who commanded Commonwealth occupation troops in Japan, would not hazard a guess as to what MacArthur would do with the 29th Brigade. Brodie went on to Korea to meet in the field with his counterpart in the 27th, Brigadier Coad, and with General Walker, both of whom predicted that operations against bypassed NKPA troops reduced to becoming guerrillas would continue for weeks after the war.

MacArthur's positive forecasts also prompted the Pentagon on October 25 to cancel scheduled shipments of troops to the Far East for November and December except for seventeen thousand noncommissioned officers needed to fill gaps in existing divisions. Even Walker felt surfeited and asked that ammunition ships sailing directly from the U.S. to Korea be diverted to Japan. Plans in X Corps were to reduce the American component to a single division. Yet the concern over massive Chinese intervention, so easily dismissed at the Dai Ichi, was not a small matter at the Pentagon. Concerned about being drawn into a massive land war in Asia, the British and American chiefs of staff had met in Washington on October 23—something neither Brodie nor Coad knew—to develop a contingency plan that MacArthur claimed was unnecessary. "We all agree," Bradley concluded wryly, "that if the Communist Chinese come into Korea [in force], we get out."

The same day, General Paik Sun Yup's 15th Regiment (1st Division) captured a Communist Chinese soldier near Unsan, halfway between Pyongyang and the Yalu. He wore a thick, quilted uniform that was khaki on the outside but could be reversed to its white side for snow camouflage. His cap had attached earmuffs, and only his rubber sneakers were not winter gear. Paik was summoned to attend the interrogation in the presence of the concerned I

Corps commander, General Frank "Shrimp" Milburn. In a flat, matter-of-fact tone the POW from Kwangtung Province, as he identified himself, asserted that he was from the Thirty-ninth Army and was only one of tens of thousands of Chinese swarming in the gray hills north of Unsan. "Are you a Korean resident of China?" Paik asked. "No," the prisoner insisted, "I'm Chinese."

Milburn radioed Willoughby's office in Tokyo through Eighth Army channels. To Paik it was "the most shocking news I had heard since the war began."

On October 26, the same day that the Marines finally disembarked at Wonsan, the ROK 6th Division, pressing far ahead of EUSAK units on its flanks, reached the Yalu at Chosan, halfway between Kanggye, where it was first assumed that Kim Il Sung had set up temporary headquarters, and Sinuiju, far to the west (below Antung in Manchuria), where he really was. It was foolhardy to be so exposed, but Rhee and the South Koreans wanted pride of place in reaching the frontier. No other division under Walker would reach the Yalu.

The next day, the intelligence summary for the Far East Command in Tokyo duly reported the capture and interrogation of the first Chinese. Willoughby's office skeptically described the identification as "based on PW reports and . . . unconfirmed and thereby unaccepted." The next day the Dai Ichi intelligence summary was sweepingly and blindly MacArthuresque. "From a tactical standpoint, with victorious U.S. divisions in full deployment, it would appear that the auspicious time for such [Chinese] intervention has long since passed; it is difficult to believe that such a move, if planned, would have been postponed to a time when remnant North Korean forces have been reduced to a few effectives." In actuality, the bypassed NKPA elements were capable of a lot of trouble, both in the north and in the narrower waist of Korea above the 38th parallel, where, in the highlands the roadbound Americans failed to probe, the *In Min Gun* was quietly awaiting its opportunity.

Even much farther south, Colonel Mike Michaelis discovered that his regiment was "overrunning . . . ammunition dumps that contained ammunition that was not common to the North Korean Army." Local people explained that these were stockpiled for the Chinese "in spite of the fact that GHQ was saying that there were no Chinese." More than mere North Korean "remnants" lay ahead.

Many NKPA soldiers who had slipped above the 38th parallel now had months of contacts with American troops, often as close as listening distance. In the areas above and below Wonsan in the east they tested their English by infiltrating at night within grenade-throwing distance and shouting, "Don't shoot! We're friends!" Marines died before they could extricate themselves from their sleeping bags; others fled in the darkness and lost contact with their units.

The first Chinese prisoners wore North Korean cotton uniforms, seemingly unprepared for winter weather. Many more of Marshal Peng Dehuai's men were already in Korea, yet those wearing quilted Chinese mustard-brown winter uniforms remained undetected. Underneath they wore their summer gear, and all had laceless cloth shoes with rubber soles—but no gloves. Officers wore no badges of rank but had vertical red piping on their trousers. Footpower gave the Chinese the mobility that MacArthur's troops, dependent on wheels, lacked. Informers in occupied areas of North Korea, who could not be told apart from ROK soldiers or refugees, radioed intelligence about UN movements. "Neither the US nor the puppet forces"—as Mao called the South Koreans—"have by far expected the entry of our volunteers," he informed Peng; "that is the reason why they dare to advance in two separated (east and west) lines."

Mao had no idea why MacArthur had divided his armies, but his was as good a guess as any. A steady radio traffic informed Peng, who lacked air support, what was happening on the ground to his south and enabled the Chinese command to take advantage of any weakness. It was quickly clear that the primary problems in Walker's large area of operations were the fault lines between ROK and American forces rather than the separation from X Corps. Mao saw the opportunities "to wipe out three or even four puppet divisions with a surprise attack," outflanking the Americans, who would then have to reconsider their positions. The Chinese could "march and fight at night," he advised Peng, "so that the enemy, even with a large number of planes, could not inflict heavy casualties or make our movement difficult." The Americans, Mao realized, were reluctant to fight at night and, robbed of sleep, would be worn down by physical exhaustion and emotional stress.

Walker's headquarters in Pyongyang didn't know it until the twenty-sixth, but the day before, rear elements of the ROK 6th Division at Onjong, fifty miles below the Yalu, were attacked in the early morning fog and forced to retreat. At first the Chinese did not know whether the army was American or Korean because scouts failed to identify the "foreign language" used. The ROK 2nd Regiment was also under fire, and hundreds of prisoners were taken, including an American adviser. The Chinese shouted *"jiaoqiang busha!"*—"lay down your weapons and we will spare your life!" Many who did not understand paid the price, and the warning would soon become familiar.

Mao was not ready to have the enemy know he was in Korea in force, and paradoxically telegraphed Peng that the victory was premature and unwelcome. "It becomes very difficult for us [now] to surround and attack two or three entire [ROK] divisions, and it is unlikely that we can disguise our entry any more." Mao was directing his troops from Beijing in a much more hands-on manner than was MacArthur from Tokyo, and through good intelligence and the instincts of an old guerrilla captain, succeeding at it. The ROKs began reeling, exposing the flanks of unprepared U.S. divisions.

X Corps in the east, then just widening its beachhead, seemed less susceptible to the massing of hidden Chinese forces, but the intruders were gathering, slipping stealthily southward via roadless tracks. Peng's legions remained of little concern to MacArthur's headquarters, where General Willoughby's daily intelligence summary for October 28 explained smugly, "It is to be recognized that most of the CCF troops have no significant experience in combat operations against a major power. In addition, their training, like that of the original North Korean forces, has been greatly handicapped by the lack of uniform equipment and assured stocks of munitions." Lieutenant Colonel John H. Chiles would observe from the X Corps G-3 position, "Anything MacArthur wanted, Willoughby produced intelligence for." As for MacArthur's statistics placing few Chinese in Korea, Chiles charged, "Willoughby falsified the intelligence reports. . . . He should have gone to jail." He had years of experience at that, having invented an invasion of Luzon for the press just after Pearl Harbor, which MacArthur allegedly threw back; having buried intelligence data that might have brought Emperor Hirohito to a postwar trial; and having kept a wanted war criminal under wraps and unpunished because he was a militant anti-Communist. Even more insignificant staff understood what MacArthur wanted, and when he once declared that Christianity had been gaining in Japan since the occupation, and asked for corroborating figures, the numbers proved the opposite, making it necessary to add a zero—for, said the underling to Major Faubion Bowers, "MacArthur won't like this."

On the same day, the 26th ROK Regiment, which had moved forward while the Marines waited offshore, had encountered only scattered NKPA resistance. The 7th U.S. Division was headed even farther north for another unopposed landing. To their surprise the ROKs had captured, near the

Chosin (Changjin) Reservoir, what General Almond would confirm to be "sixteen fully equipped and well uniformed Chinese soldiers." To see for himself, Almond left his command post at Wonsan, flew in an L-5 to the last possible strip and jeeped to Hamhung with an interpreter.

Separately and out of hearing of the others, Almond asked each of the prisoners what their organizations were, and they gave "large Chinese division numbers." "Whose forces do you belong to?" he asked, but they had no idea of higher commands and named Lin Biao, who was the nominal chief in northeast China and Manchuria.

"What is your mission?" Almond asked, and they uniformly agreed that it was to drive southward. "How far?" he continued, and they responded, "To Pusan."

When Almond asked why, they answered, in the general's words, "To kill the enemy, the Americans and any South Koreans"—and to obtain food and supplies "from the defeat of the enemy."

Eight of the sixteen turned out to compose a full mortar squad, complete to its disassembled mortar. Almond assumed that they were an advance unit heading to the reservoir area, with others of an "organized CCF force" certain to follow. None of them were individual "volunteers." That seemed significant enough to him to radio urgently to MacArthur in Tokyo on October 29, but it did not alter MacArthur's optimistic post-Wake assessment to Truman the next day.

Pfc. Robert Harper of the 24th Division's 19th Regiment on the EUSAK front did not need to see the Chinese to know they were close. Two or three days prior to Halloween his battalion's radio operators began listening to "a lot of enemy talk. They said it sounded like Chinese." Although American units were reputed to shy away from night patrols, after more talk was picked up one went downhill with Harper trailing a telephone wire to avoid radio communication. "We waited while a small recon[naissance] patrol disappeared into the night. It was Halloween and colder than a witch. No one had been issued winter gear yet. . . . We waited and froze." When the patrol reappeared it reported "a large enemy force in front of us." They returned "faster than we'd gone down."

Only on October 31—Halloween—did the FEC daily intelligence summary belatedly, and still ignoring Almond's POW interrogation, acknowledge that the Eighth Army had taken ten Chinese prisoners well below the Yalu, and that the ROK II Corps to which the South Korean 6th Division was attached had suffered severe reverses and was withdrawing southward. Its survivors nevertheless brought back with them a bottle of muddy Yalu water for Syngman Rhee.

The adverse turn, Willoughby's report conceded, "may signify the commitment of Chinese Communist Forces in the Korean conflict." What Tokyo now suspected but kept to itself was the possibility that it might not be a cakewalk to the frontier. Thirty miles below the Yalu, Captain Norman Allen of the cocky 5th Cav had just written home that he had told his men "that by tomorrow afternoon we'd be lined up pissing in it." Other than the battered South Koreans, however, the only Eighth Army personnel who would get that close to the Yalu would be prisoners of war.

On November 1 the 21st Regiment of the 24th Division, from which Task Force Smith had been spun off to confront the North Koreans in the first days of the war, had reached the village of Chonggo-dong, near Namsidong. They were only eighteen miles from Sinuiju, on the Yalu, and still unaware of the Chinese. Behind them were the Argylls and the Australians of the Commonwealth Brigade, and in the Kuryong valley forty miles south of the border was the Middlesex Battalion. Brigadier Basil Coad thought, echoing MacArthur, that they "had cracked the nut" and that the show was nearly over.

Soon after, MacArthur received yet another request from the nervous JCS asking for an "interim" evaluation of the "overt intervention" by the Chinese, and again he downplayed the involvement, suggesting several tolerable scenarios. One was that the Chinese were "permitting and abetting a flow of more or less voluntary personnel across the border to strengthen and assist the North Korean remnants in their struggle to retain a nominal foothold in Korea." Another was that "such intervention as exists has been in the belief that no UN forces would be committed in the extreme northern reaches of Korea except those of South Korea. A realization that such [ROK] forces were insufficient for the purpose may well have furnished the [CCF] concept of salvaging something from the wreckage."

What MacArthur called "full" intervention and still refused to acknowledge would be, he conceded, "a momentous decision of the gravest international importance." It was a "possibility," although he found "many fundamental logical reasons against it" and contended that "sufficient evidence has not yet come to hand to warrant its immediate acceptance." He recommended "against hasty conclusions," deploring unnecessary foreboding in Washington.

Both the Dai Ichi and the Pentagon had just learned of a declaration issued in Beijing that should have reinforced anxieties. "Aid Korea, Protect Our Homes" proclaimed that the defense of North Korea was the "moral duty" of the Chinese people, and that the security of the two nations was intertwined. "To save our neighbor is to save ourselves." The manifesto described "the American imperialists and their accomplices" as "not only unwilling to withdraw their aggressive forces," but as having "frenziedly pushed the aggressive war northward across the 38th parallel. . . . Thus we have been forced to realize that if the lovers of peace in the world desire to have peace, they must use positive action to resist atrocities and halt aggression."

In effect it was an informal declaration of war, but intelligence officials who hoped it was only rhetoric could take their chances and read the action below the Yalu MacArthur's way.

The first days of November were building toward a catastrophe for the Eighth Army in the west. Mao saw events as the beginning of the end for MacArthur's grand design. Based on early reports from commanders in the field, he sent Peng a summary evaluation of what to expect from the enemy as the Communist response grew. Combat effectiveness was "low," he judged. The South Koreans fought incompetently and the Americans were "overly dependent on firepower support" because of fears of "close combat" with bayonets and grenades—Chinese "pocket artillery." American gunnery was intense but inaccurate, and rifle fire was ineffective, according to Mao, for their soldiers were "poor at making shots." They needed "fierce cover fire" for advances and withdrawals, and "lived in their trucks," attacking by daylight and pulling back at night. They failed to dig in their artillery, locating their guns "out in the open field or in the road," for their equipment was "too heavy to be mobilized in the mountains." It was "certain," he concluded confidently, "that we could eliminate all enemy units."

The first encounters with the Americans had suggested as much. The Chinese Thirty-ninth Army, roughly equivalent to an American corps, was then sending its 116th and 117th Divisions against UN troops in the Unsan region, below Onjong. The 8th Regiment of the 1st Cav was in the process of relieving the 12th Regiment of the surprised and beleaguered ROK 1st Division. Effective at infiltrating enemy positions, the Chinese quickly created panic. Organized resistance evaporated. Rushed forward to help, the 5th Regiment (1st Cav) lost whole units to encirclement. Suddenly it was a new war.

Attacking in darkness, eerily summoning their forces with technological simplicity by bugle calls, cymbals and whistles, stalling tanks at roadblocks with satchel charges and grenades, and firing flares and tracers into the night, Peng's "volunteers" turned the American withdrawal into a jumble of disabled vehicles. Troops fled. At dawn on November 6, General Walker ordered an overall retreat, covered by air strikes and artillery fire to pin down the pursuers. When heavy rain also assisted the backtracking, chilled and sodden UN troops were able to cross to the comparative safety of the south bank of the Chongchon River, nearly half the distance south to Pyongyang. They outdistanced an enemy that never followed.

Most of Walker's units had been able to evade being outflanked, but only at a heavy price in lost ground, abandoned vehicles and guns, and the heaviest casualties thus far in the war. What appeared to be imminent victory had vanished overnight. So did more than a thousand men from the 1st Cav, although some managed to slip back to their shrunken lines. Assembling hundreds of prisoners, a Chinese captain identifying himself as Lao tried out his long-unused mission school English, and a POW, discovering that he was a captive of the Chinese rather than the *In Min Gun*, exclaimed, "For God's sake! This isn't your war!"

"It is now," said Lao.

Anticipating the rout on the afternoon of November 4, Peng had declared to Mao by radio, "The counteroffensive in North Korea is over." He wanted to regroup. Explaining why he wasn't following up the headlong withdrawal, Peng confided that because his command was "very fearful of the air raids" his armies had only devastated six to seven regiments of the enemy forces. . . . Our troops are very tired, and it has been very difficult to transport food and munitions due to the fact that the vehicular roads are too narrow and our trucks cannot move in daytime but drive without headlights at night." It had also begun to snow, and it was "increasingly difficult to preserve the strength of our troops who have to sleep outside and in the snow."

What Peng did not know was that the Far East Air Force, having run out of "strategic" targets in North Korea and concluding that the war was winding down, had ordered two B-29 groups back to the United States. And nature was beginning to assist the Chinese supply situation. The Yalu was freezing over.

While EUSAK was beginning its disintegration, Colonel Litzenberg's 11th Marines on the other side of the Taebaek spine of North Korea were confronting the reserve regiment of the Chinese 124th Division. Five days and nights of artillery barrages, ending after dark on the sixth, had driven the enemy from the hills south of the Funchilin Pass, on the winding dirt road to Koto-ri and the Chosin Reservoir. About 1,500 Chinese in their quilted uniforms and canvas shoes with crepe soles lay dead. The others had fallen back. Each man, a search of bodies discovered, carried a five-day supply of cooked food, mostly rice and beans, to eliminate the need for identifying fires. The Marines counted about fifty of their own dead, and two hundred wounded. Almond arrived in a liaison plane to inspect the scene and saw the barrels of the eighteen Marine howitzers pointing up at high angles to direct fire over the forward slopes, and remarked lightly to the puzzled Litzenberg, "I didn't know you had antiaircraft guns up here." Yet the fighting above Sudong got no notice in his command diary for November 6, where he entered only, "Inspected the Pullman and coach car which are to be prepared for the use of the X Corps staff." (Almond had already moved from Inchon his personal van equipped with shower, flush toilet, refrigerator, fine linen, china and napkin rings. He also had a daily staff airlift from Tokyo of fresh fruit, vegetables and meat. His style did not endear him to the troops.)

Alarmed only about the EUSAK sector, and understanding that he had overreacted in sending back his heavy bombers, MacArthur ordered his remaining B-29s to destroy "the Korean end" of the bridge over the Yalu connecting Sinuiju with Manchuria.

In a rare act of disloyalty, Air Force commander Stratemeyer, sensitive about being forced by MacArthur to exceed his authority, radioed Hoyt Vandenberg, Air Force chief of staff, in Washington. Vandenberg immediately had the JCS contravene the order, pointing to an agreement to consult the British before taking any action affecting Manchuria. (The British were protecting their interests in Hong Kong.) In hurried discussions in Washington, General Collins described MacArthur's reversal in mood to the JCS as "a touch of panic," but the facts on the ground were grim. It was election day in the U.S., and Truman was in Kansas City casting his congressional ballot. Largely on grounds of their more militant anti-Communism, the Republicans would gain seats.

On the telephone to Acheson, the President, citing the agreement with London, said no to bombing as much as an inch of China. MacArthur had encouraged the Chinese response by violating JCS mandates and now wanted to be bailed out. In Tokyo, MacArthur received the denial only an hour and twenty minutes before seventy-nine of Stratemeyer's B-29s were to take off for the Yalu. Turning to his deputy chief of staff, Doyle Hickey, a livid MacArthur growled that he would resign rather than compromise his troops. Hickey calmed him down by observing that abandoning his command would accomplish just that. MacArthur cabled the JCS in flash 062235Z—it was already November 7 in Japan—in the most alarmist language he had yet sent to Washington. He wanted the President to know that JCS limitations on him "may well result in a calamity of major proportion for which I cannot accept the responsibility without his personal and dir[ect] understanding of the sit[uation]." He wanted immediate reconsideration of the veto on his action because

> Men and materiel in large force are pouring across all bridges over the Yalu from Manchuria. This m[o]v[e]m[en]t not only jeopardizes but threatens the ultimate destruction of the forces under my command. The actual mvmt across the river can be accomplished under cover of darkness. . . . The only way to stop this reinf[orcement] of the enemy is the destruction of these bridges and the subjection of all installations in the north area supporting the enemy adv[ance]. . . . Every hour that this is postponed will be paid for dearly in American and other United Nations blood.

Bradley telephoned the President and read the alarmist message to him. Truman agreed reluctantly to authorize bombing of the Korean sides of the Yalu bridges, realizing that any military catastrophe resulting from a denial of MacArthur's plea might lead to a further political calamity.

Stratemeyer's FEAF staff prepared new instructions to assure that only Korean territory would be hit. However, the bridges were of no strategic consequence to the Chinese, who had the icing Yalu and their secret below-surface crossings. The border bridges had only political value.

When the 7th Marines began the new day's operations below the Chosin Reservoir on November 7, they found that the Chinese troops facing them the day before had vanished, just as they had done above the Chongchon River in the west. No one in the Dai Ichi, which coordinated the two commands, perceived anything significant in what had to have been planned simultaneous pullbacks. For several days there were brief exchanges of fire on both fronts, then silence.

On November 8, B-29s plus three hundred fighter-bombers duly bombed the Yalu bridges. Spans on the Korean side were damaged and the town of Sinuiju largely destroyed. The Yalu would soon freeze completely, but until then Peng had his other alternatives. It was clear in Washington that MacArthur would be urging escalation again, and soon. He saw the enemy as Communist China and wanted a collision that would bring in all of America's power without UN restraints.

MacArthur's continuing exasperation surfaced in a top-secret cable of November 9 requesting a reexamination of his mission in Korea. He still wanted to drive the Chinese back across the Yalu rather than merely lick his embarrassing wounds and stabilize the front somewhere else. "I plan to launch my attack for this purpose," he announced, "on or about November fifteenth.... Any program short of this would completely destroy the morale of my forces and its psychological consequence would be inestimable. It would condemn us to an indefinite defense line in North Korea and would unquestionably arouse such resentment among the South Koreans that their forces would collapse or might even turn against us." He went on with further fantasies, recalling Munich and the sellout of Czechoslovakia and pointing to such "lessons of history." Washington was being lectured on the necessity for pressing on "to complete victory which I believe can be achieved if our determination and indomitable will do not desert us."

As his only peer in the command structure, George Marshall tried to ease the tension with a "very personal and informal" letter on November 7. "We all realize your difficulty," he soothed, "in trying to direct a multinational army in a war fought in difficult terrain" and while being bound by "necessarily limiting" diplomatic factors. "Everyone here, Defense, State, the President, is intensely desirous of supporting you," but the delicate international balance had to be maintained to avoid a "world disaster." MacArthur thanked Marshall and claimed that he understood the need to localize the war. He thought, though, that the power plant issue—the unbombed Yalu dams powered Manchurian industry—was now trivial, for China was really thrusting toward Asian domination. Korea was only a symptom. Chinese seizure of Tibet and its aid to rebels in Indochina evidenced the larger purpose.

Like the Secretary of Defense, the JCS attempted to be conciliatory. Misunderstanding the precarious situation south of the Yalu, Truman, Acheson and Marshall also ignored the risks underlying MacArthur's ambitions which their mutual intelligence failures might nourish. MacArthur would continue to evade as many restrictions as he could get away with. Violating Pentagon strictures, pilots crossed into Manchuria to achieve appropriate angles to bomb North Korean targets, and troops probed north—but not far enough—to search out suddenly silent Chinese troops. Things seemed not to look so bad after all. At the Waldorf-Astoria in New York, to receive a citation from the New York Newspaper Women's Club as outstanding woman reporter of the year at its annual Front Page dinner, Maggie Higgins, back from Korea, wondered whether it was useful after all to rejoin the Marines at tranquil Wonsan.

As part of the new conciliatory mood in Tokyo and Washington, encouraged by the quieting front due only to Peng, MacArthur's G-3, Edwin K. Wright, on November 10 sent a personal letter to General Almond meant more to mollify General Walker in EUSAK and critics at the Pentagon, claiming that MacArthur wanted X Corps to do everything it could to assist the Eighth Army in the west. Almond replied that he could help best by continuing north beyond the reservoir highlands, after which he could turn west toward EUSAK. Wright then asked that a plan be drafted for MacArthur to examine.

Almond emphasized the tough terrain—some mountains were nearly a mile high—and the bitter winter weather as inhibiting factors, but MacArthur still anticipated a quick close to the war. Lieutenant Colonel John H. Chiles, Almond's G-3, flew the X Corps plan to Tokyo, where, to assist Walker, MacArthur moved the proposed boundary between commands farther west and south in the Marine division zone. Despite the brief Chinese scare he was again ready for his end-the-war offensives, each of which was to push to the Yalu and preempt the Chinese.

Mao had cultivated MacArthur's complacency. Dai Ichi intelligence had no idea what forces the Chinese had put across, and assumed that they had no armor or artillery, little motorized transport and no air cover. (Tokyo never even knew that Peng, rather than Lin Biao, was running the Chinese Communist Forces.) MacArthur was counting on blowing the Chinese away. Mao, however, was planning new traps for both EUSAK in the west and the Marines in the east, and telegraphed Peng on November 9 that he expected to fight "one or two battles on the eastern and western fronts between late this month and early December to destroy another seven or eight regiments of the enemy forces." He predicted that the likely retreat southward of MacArthur's forces would shift the front to the Pyongyang-Wonsan line.

Summoning a meeting of commanders of Chinese troops in Korea for the thirteenth in Beijing, Mao asked Peng for an evaluation of the results to date. In proper Communist fashion Peng confessed his mistakes. "We routed the enemy forces more than annihilated them," he conceded. And he warned commanders not to overestimate the enemy. "We will employ a strategy of luring the enemy forces into our internal line and wiping them out one by one." Annihilating "two or three U.S. and ROK divisions," he predicted, would "fundamentally turn" the war around.

MacArthur's forces remained baffled by the sudden lull after the chaotic days of early November, but X Corps began moving forward again up the hilly reservoir country to the northwest. The Marines were not eager to change from an amphibious force to slogging infantry, but had to take their orders from the Army. O. P. Smith was anxious, and exploited the respite to begin construction of an airstrip in the rugged hills at Hagaru, sixty-four miles inland from the port at Hungnam. The crushed stone runway would bring in equipment and supplies, and evacuate casualties, he explained.

"What casualties?" Almond asked on an inspection. (He was interested only in small airstrips to accommodate his L-5.) Like Smith, Marine regimental commanders were skeptical of anyone who accepted the intelligence estimates from the Dai Ichi.

"As I indicated to you when you were here," Smith wrote with concern to the Marine commandant, General Clifton Cates, who had recently visited Korea, "I have little confidence in the tactical judgment of the [X] Corps or in the realism of their planning. . . . Manifestly, we should not push on without regard to the Eighth Army. We would simply get farther out on a limb. . . . I believe a winter campaign in the mountains of North Korea is too much to ask of the American soldier or Marine. . . ."

To their north, the Chinese Twentieth, Twenty-sixth, and Twenty-seventh Armies, with 150,000 men, continued crossing the iced-over Yalu at night. Under cover of darkness they deployed in the Chosin Reservoir area while 60,000 Chinese service personnel moved supplies on foot southward and, also by night, repaired roads, highways and bridges. They operated with excellent intelligence data furnished by guerrillas and by villagers, supplemented by press reports of American correspondents, often complete to the identification of units and their officers. The folks at home needed to know how their boys were doing. (After the lessons of November, the Eighth Army would insist in December that newsmen not pinpoint its positions.)

Fresh from the meeting of commanders at Mao's faceless headquarters, General Peng on November 16 ordered each army in Korea to deceive the enemy in its area that "we are being intimidated into retreat." Meanwhile to Mao, according to Nikita Khrushchev, Peng "composed lengthy telegrams expounding elaborate battle plans against the Americans. . . . The enemy would be surrounded and finished off by decisive flanking strikes. The American troops were crushed and the war ended many times in these battle reports which Peng sent to Mao, who then sent them along to Stalin." To further spread disinformation, Peng directed the release of about thirty American and seventy ROK prisoners on Walker's front, expecting them to report that they had heard that the Chinese were withdrawing toward the Yalu because of air interdiction and the superior firepower of UN forces. In order to "hook a big fish," he explained, "you must let the fish taste your bait. MacArthur boasts that he has never been defeated. We'll see who is going to wipe out whom!"

12

A Turkey for Thanksgiving

"HEARTIEST CONGRATULATIONS, NED," MacArthur radioed to Almond on November 21, "and tell Dave Barr that the 7th Division hit the jackpot." Thanksgiving Day was only two days away, and MacArthur had been predicting since Wake that victory would be assured by then. Most troops would be Stateside by Christmas. Now elements of Barr's 7th Division had reached the Yalu in the east at the battered village of Hyesanjin.

Few enemy troops had been encountered by the 17th Regiment, but the cold seemed enough of an enemy. Division HQ urgently requested airdrops of 250 squad tents and delivery of five hundred oil-burning potbelly stoves. Ignoring the thermometer, Korean troops broke through the ice and filled a bottle from the Yalu to send symbolically to Syngman Rhee. (He already had one from the west.) Some jubilant Americans expressed themselves in a manner that press photographers forbore recording for the folks back home. Standing at the snow-covered riverbank within sight of the Chinese side 150 yards beyond, they urinated into the frozen Yalu.

NKPA resistance from log-covered trenches had not prevented the easy seizure of the village of Kapsan on the nineteenth, leaving only twenty-three miles between the Americans and the frontier. Without opposition they advanced on foot over the hills the next day, and by ten in the morning of the twenty-first were in Hyesanjin, nearly destroyed the week before by carrier planes. Almond and Barr flew in for the occasion, and followed the lead company two miles down the road from the crest to the river. With field glasses they could see Chinese sentries in the village on the other side impassively walking their rounds. The generals scanned a wide arc for possible raiding parties. The frozen Yalu "was very little of an obstacle," Almond recalled, "but otherwise there was no serious concern."

Returning to his headquarters at Hungnam, Almond formally congratulated Barr the next day. The message was almost certainly meant more for MacArthur, who also received a copy. "The fact that only twenty days ago," Almond began, "this division landed amphibiously over the beaches at Iwon and advanced 200 miles over tortuous mountain terrain and fought successfully against a determined foe in subzero weather will be recorded in history as an outstanding military achievement."

Private Bob Hammond of the 57th Field Artillery Battalion turned eighteen at the Yalu. "This is it!" he was told, as if their mission was accomplished. "The top of Korea! You can't go any further than this, or you wind up in China."

Although the 7th's other regiments, the 31st and 32nd, were moving up behind the 17th, surviving North Korean units stubbornly impeded them, blowing up bridges and cratering roads before slipping back toward the reservoir highlands. Yet the real foe remained the arctic temperature. Frostbite caused more casualties than gunfire and grenades. Almost nothing, however, kept the logistical services from furnishing Thanksgiving dinner sometime from Thursday through that weekend for all troops in Korea, even if the dinners, complete to the holiday trimmings, had to be air-dropped. Soldiers from New Zealand and Turkey, where the deep-breasted bird was unknown, received identical menus.

From Pusan to the Yalu, the occasion was a triumph of American ingenuity. Divisions lacked spare parts for vehicles, but trestle tables up and down the peninsula were heaped with aluminum containers of roast turkey with gravy, cranberry sauce, shrimp cocktail, asparagus, tomatoes, stuffed olives, sliced pineapple, fruitcake and pumpkin pie.

In a few sectors the festive fowl had to be thawed for consumption the next day. At Hagaru, at the base of the Chosin Reservoir, Lieutenant Colonel Raymond Davis's battalion of the 7th Marines found their turkeys as "frozen hard" as the weather, but the night before Thanksgiving an officer at HQ "came up with an idea. He made a mountain of the frozen birds around two field kitchen stoves that had been fired up. Next he covered the whole thing with two pyramidal tents that he sealed tight with snow and brush. By morning the birds were thawed enough for them to be cut up and cooked." The 7th Marines could not dine on their turkeys until the day after Thanksgiving, but, medic William Davis recalled, "no one minded." The cooks worked by truck headlights and troops ate in their glare from tin trays "just like aboard ship. . . . You had to eat fast because everything was turning cold. The gravy and then the mashed potatoes froze first. The inside of the turkey was still warm."

A chaplain in the division, Navy Lieutenant Cornelius J. Griffin (who would be wounded two weeks later), recalled asking the mess sergeant "to save the red cellophane the frozen turkeys came wrapped in from the packer and, once dinner was over, to wrap all the bones he could find in it." He wondered what Griffin wanted to do with the "junk," and the chaplain explained, with no theology intended, "When we get up farther north, if we have to, we can boil the hell out of those bones in melted snow and make some damned good turkey broth." (Within the week the soup was necessary.) "Then we took the red cellophane and reused it a second time to cover all the holes and loose corners in the sick bays during blackouts."

Morale was high, and troops up and down the length of Korea talked between mouthfuls, in less than festive circumstances, of the chances of enjoying Christmas dinner back home. That vision was vivid to Lieutenant James H. Dill of B Battery, 31st Field Artillery Battalion, 7th Division, which employed 155mm howitzers pulled by tractors. Arriving on the coast at Iwon, Dill had made it with his guns, climbing switchbacked one-lane mountain roads as far as the village of Kapsan on November 22, but he would never reach the Yalu thirty miles farther north. The next day, Thanksgiving, he wrote was "an unbelieveable joyous break" from corn beef hash rations. The battery was told at a festive dinner "that the war was almost over, and that we should prepare for a return to Japan. The advisory [bulletin] also included an example of how forms should be made up for returning our ROK's to their own army. We were to tell them that most would soon be discharged and sent home. An unofficial note was added to brush up on close order drill since the 7th Division would be expected to take part in a Grand Victory Parade as soon as we reached Japan."

The next night Dill was awakened with orders from division G-3 to move his guns south as quickly as he could or blow them up before leaving. "We had a message brought in to our forward outpost by relays of Korean runners. It was written in Korean and it was from the headman of a village downriver from Hyesanjin. In it he says that thousands and thousands of Chinese are crossing the Yalu near his village and heading due south." It was 4:30 a.m. and −36°F. From division commander Barr, who had served in China in World War II, the operations officer had learned "that there was no terrain that Chinese troops could not cross, regardless of the weather." Dill got going. Almond's X Corps offensive had not even begun.

Before Thanksgiving the 31st Infantry of Barr's 7th Division had begun moving into barren highlands on the eastern shore of the Pujon (Fusen) Reservoir, which seemed to have no military use to anyone and housed only a few remote villages of mud huts. To its south, the mostly Puerto Rican 65th Infantry had been the first regiment of the 3rd Division to join X Corps ashore. After it came the 15th and the 7th, their tasks in part to relieve the Marines moving northward and inland. Accustomed to balmy weather, the Puerto Ricans had debarked in shock, but their 1st Battalion had orders to probe westward to link up with EUSAK patrols. At best they made some radio contact. Although the Taebaek Range was steep and treacherous, Almond complained to Colonel William Harris that his 65th "had not been energetic in its movement west from Yonghung." Harris sent another column into the Taebaek, but it would never make physical contact with the Eighth Army. The gap, some fifty miles by cratered excuses for roads and boulder-strewn trails, was penetrated only by North Korean guerrilla bands which kept trails impassable.

Seemingly even less energetic than the 65th Infantry were O. P. Smith's Marines, who to Almond hogged newsprint in the U.S. but were not making the headlong rush to the Yalu which MacArthur had expected. Almond hinted at obstructionism—that while Smith "never refused to obey an order in the final analysis," he "delayed the execution of some orders." Almond had complained about the Marine command since Inchon; now Smith refused to disperse his troops and insisted on stockpiling ammunition and supplies at each stage of his advance. "I was told to occupy a blocking position at Yudam-ni with the 7th Marines after Thanksgiving," Smith conceded, "and to have the 5th Marines go up the east side of the Chosin Reservoir until it hit the Yalu. I told Litzenberg not to go too fast." Yudam-ni was beyond the high Toktong Pass, exposing a "tremendous open flank in the west" above reservoir country. Smith's men moved out, Lieutenant Joseph Owen wrote thirty years later, in a "colorless dawn, and the men in the subzero darkness beat their [numb] hands against their sides. . . . They were helmeted, shapeless figures in their long, hooded parkas, showing only a small patch of face to the north wind." A rifleman walking backward for shelter from the wind muttered to Owen, "Nothing but Chinamen from here to Mongolia."

Both Almond and MacArthur were convinced that some symbolic presence along the Yalu would intimidate the Chinese into inaction, and the mid-November lull initiated by Peng had seemed a validation of Dai Ichi thinking. Mao's strategy, however, was to draw UN forces forward into positions in which they could be outflanked and trapped, yet MacArthur and Willoughby interpreted the Chinese withdrawals as signs of unwillingness to confront American firepower. What Chinese there were, according to American intelligence, were light infantry armed with only the company weapons they could carry. MacArthur's orders of October 24 to EUSAK and to X Corps to advance to the Manchurian frontier, while modified somewhat, still stood. Tokyo's obtuse operatives failed to discern the movement or dispersal of nearly 200,000 Chinese troops. Somehow also invisible were tens of thousands of supply porters with shoulder poles or A-frames, as well as the camouflaged weapons and rations dumps to support seven full armies. Two legs were better than four wheels, went a Maoist saying.

On the EUSAK front, Walker planned to jump off for the border on the fifteenth, if resupplied in time up to the Hongchon River line. On November 14 he was still below appropriate levels in food, fuel and ammo—ten times more than it took to sustain the hardy and unmotorized Chinese. Without the wherewithal to support offensive operations, Walker postponed his offensive. Half his needs were coming up by slow train on the long diagonal from Pusan, while some were being offloaded from ships at Chinnampo, the port for Pyongyang. The harbor had just been cleared of 242 mines as well as many large jellyfish mistaken for mines and duly blown up. (The busy sweepers had to shuttle around the coast from Iwon and Wonsan, where they had opened ports for X Corps.)

Seventeen planes from Japan rushed 33,000 winter field jackets, and six more conveyed 40,000 pairs of mittens and 33,000 mufflers. Airlift, however, could not outfit all forward troops, even badly. Many winter shoepacs were too large and all were poorly designed. Their airtightness caused them to retain body moisture, encouraging frostbite.

On the seventeenth Walker told Tokyo that he would be ready to attack on November 24, although his 2nd Division listed half its vehicles as inoperative because of parts shortages. MacArthur reported the new date to the JCS, claiming also on the basis of Tokyo's fanciful intelligence that Far East Air Force attacks had prevented reinforcements from supplementing enemy strength. Operating at night without radios and lights, and concealing themselves by day, the Chinese had performed miracles of mobilization and discipline. Even what food they cooked was prepared under tarpaulins before five in the morning, to eliminate the possibility of visible smoke. Nothing moved after dawn.

The Eighth Army notified each of its three corps that their attacks would be timed for 10:00 a.m. on the day after Thanksgiving. Everyone could first feast on roast turkey. The Chinese in the west remained ten to twelve miles distant from UN forces, to forestall discovery. Two days later soldiers of the 25th Division would capture a prisoner from the Chinese 66th Army who carried a document dated November 20 explaining why there was little to fear from American troops:

> Their infantry men are weak, afraid to die and haven't the courage to attack or defend. They depend on their planes, tanks, and artillery. . . . They must have proper terrain and good weather to transport their great amount of equipment. . . . They specialize in day fighting. They are not familiar with night fighting or hand-to-hand combat. They are afraid of our big knives and grenades; also of our courageous attack, regular combat, and infiltration.
>
> If defeated, they have no orderly formation. . . . They become dazed and completely demoralized. . . . They are afraid when the[ir] rear is cut off. When transportation comes to a standstill, the infantry loses the will to fight. . . .

As usual, Chinese prisoners and their documents were not taken very seriously, but the Communists since Long March days had done away with the caste system of officers and ranks. Ranks below the highest command levels had been replaced by job titles, such as squad leader and company commander. The rank and file had pre-combat briefings and contributed to tactics. And since the Chinese had few weapons larger than mortars, each soldier felt that he contributed equally. Poor in communications equipment, each squad had to know more about what was expected of it. Soldiers also learned the identity of units supporting them. American intelligence suspected that the more they seemed to know, the more likely they had been planted to furnish disinformation. Even after some prisoners carefully explained that battalion designations concealed entire divisions, Tokyo smelled a hoax. By November 23, Willoughby skeptically estimated twelve Chinese divisions across the Yalu rather than nine armies with thirty infantry divisions.

Another paper issued on the twentieth, to working-level staff at the Pentagon, was concerned about the will to fight of America's UN partners in Korea. On November 10 the State Department had asked for opinions from London, Paris, Canberra, Ottawa, and even Delhi and Moscow about authorizing "hot pursuit" of Chinese aircraft into Manchuria. Responses were uniformly negative. Separately, London had argued, and other nations had agreed, that occupation of all Korea was not worth a third world war. MacArthur's forces, the British maintained, should consider stopping far enough south of the Yalu to create a demilitarized buffer zone leaving shorter lines to defend.

The British embassy in Washington had reported to London that American thinking remained stubbornly impractical. "State Department officials are turning over in their minds a proposal for a nonbelligerent band north and south of [the] Yalu," a concept clearly anathema to the Chinese, who would have to submit to UN inspection of their sovereign territory. MacArthur had already derided a zone which the Chinese could dominate south of the Yalu as appeasement on the lines of "the historic precedent . . . taken at Munich on 29 September 1938." Ignoring that implicit slap at the British, Field Marshal Sir William Slim, speaking for the military at a cabinet session in London on the thirteenth, backed a zone south of the Yalu and warned against a resumption of the offensive. Only a shorter line, he explained, could be held.

In response, the Pentagon under the signature of the Army's influential G-3, General Charles Bolté, objected to a de facto rump North Korean state. A backer of MacArthur, he had recently returned from Tokyo and was "unalterably opposed" to any compromise which awarded the Communists advantages. A hard-liner, Bolté argued that "a show of strength will discourage further aggression while weakness will encourage it." Echoing MacArthur, he proposed that standing pat "would be wholly unacceptable to the American public and not in consonance with the principles for which we have fought."

As the home-by-Christmas offensive was to open, MacArthur, in his Dai Ichi sanctuary remote from the "neck" of Korea, exuded confidence. Despite Bolté's helpful intransigence in Washington, doubts persisted at the JCS, but no senior officer was senior to MacArthur or had his clout. On the afternoon of November 21 the National Security Council met with only Truman absent. Present were the Joint Chiefs of Staff, the Secretaries of State and Defense, and their key subordinates. They reviewed MacArthur's messages and the Bolté memo. The minutes of the meeting record that "General Marshall expressed satisfaction that Mr. Acheson had stated his belief that General MacArthur should push forward with the planned offensive."

Whatever their private anxieties, and it is difficult to believe that Acheson and Marshall had any enthusiasm for the push, most participants hoped it would end the war. As JCS liaison with MacArthur, Collins radioed to Tokyo that the consensus of political and military opinion was "that there should be no change in your mission." Yet he did alert MacArthur that UN opinion was still strongly for a demilitarized zone short of the Yalu.

London remained most vocal in misgivings about what was going on above the Yalu. Foreign Secretary Ernest Bevin—the most powerful minister in Attlee's cabinet—opposed hot pursuit and almost any other possible provocation of the Russians and the Chinese. "No ultimatums to China," he warned Washington, "would be supported by me." Further, Bevin cabled to his ambassador, Sir Oliver Franks, he wanted Acheson to realize that Mac-Arthur was likely to exceed his authority. Once his offensive was launched, "We don't know what is going on, or [whether] MacArthur is acting outside of the UN scope." He wanted the ambassador to "speak to Acheson urgently about it." Bevin's messages were immediately accessible to Guy Burgess and Donald Maclean, longtime Soviet spies now in the American department of the Foreign Office and the embassy in Washington. In effect, Bevin was inadvertently talking to Moscow and perhaps Beijing.

After listening sympathetically, Acheson promised Franks that he would warn MacArthur. But the lull in Korea continued, and since the next day was Thanksgiving, the Secretary of State hoped that the matter could be put off to Friday.

Unimpresssed by what he considered as cowardly international anxieties, MacArthur had already told British diplomat Sir Alvary Gascoigne—Bevin's informant—on November 13 that UN forces would pursue the remnants of the North Koreans (MacArthur still ignored the Chinese) to the banks of the Yalu, where they would be crushed. Puffing intermittently on his corncob, MacArthur explained on November 14 to William Sebald, to whom agitated messages came from State, that it was crucial to hasten to the Yalu before the river froze over and permitted masses of Chinese to cross. Walter Bedell Smith of the CIA had warned Tokyo that the Chinese had moved three armies from South China to Manchuria; he had no idea that many more than that were already camouflaged in Korea. If their movement across the Yalu appeared imminent, MacArthur responded (after the fact, although he didn't know that), he would have to bomb the Manchurian side, which could bring Russia by treaty into the war. The Chinese, MacArthur contended, were demonstrating only a token solidarity with the North Koreans and their readiness to confront a "first-class" foe. Once these propaganda points were made, they had nothing further to gain from increasing their investment and much to lose.

On the seventeenth, with the beginning of Walker's offensive delayed on logistical grounds, MacArthur had invited in John Muccio, visiting from

Seoul. The ambassador was concerned about whether the Chinese were bluffing. MacArthur was satisfied, according to Muccio's notes, that "our Air Forces and our Intelligence" would have detected the movement of large forces across the Yalu. Covertly, the Chinese might have managed to get "25,000, and certainly no more than 30,000, soldiers across the border." If they tried to put more men across, he predicted, Stratemeyer's planes would bomb hell out of them and "this area will be left a desert." MacArthur expected to clear the way to the Yalu in about ten days.

Patrols had gone out only as far as a thousand yards from American lines—not much more than half a mile—and found no signs of the enemy. Walker and his division commanders had not ordered deeper or more aggressive probes, nor had MacArthur, who relied on Willoughby's sources. Intelligence on the ground, often via defectors and prisoners, was distrusted in Tokyo. MacArthur's Far East Command communiqué of November 6, whch had spun an embarrassment into self-congratulation, had reinterpreted the Eighth Army's headlong retreat into an escape from "a possible trap . . . surreptitiously laid [and] calculated to encompass the destruction of the United Nations forces." MacArthur saw no signs for worry in the mysterious quiet along the front. He and his planners were apparently ignorant of Mao's study *On Protracted War,* in which he advised, "To achieve quick decisions we should generally attack, not an enemy force holding a position, but one on the move. We should have concentrated, beforehand under cover, a big force along the route through which the enemy is sure to pass, suddenly descend on him while he is moving, encircle and attack him before he knows what is happening, and conclude the fighting with all speed."

Planning to divulge his intentions by a dramatic flying visit to the front on the morning of an offensive—his standard self-promotional strategy—MacArthur took off for the airstrip at Sinanju, about fifty miles north of Pyongyang, early on November 24. The location abutted General Frank Milburn's I Corps headquarters, and MacArthur was using his sleek new Constellation, Lockheed's newest four-engine transport. Even so, he could not wait to arrive before releasing a blindly smug communiqué. From Tokyo as he left, the Dai Ichi issued what appeared to be his next-to-last declaration about the course of the conflict. The next one would confirm the end of his war:

> The United Nations massive compression envelopment in North Korea against the new Red Armies cooperating there is now approaching its decisive effort. The isolating component of the pincer, our Air Forces of all

types, have for the last three weeks, in a sustained attack of model coordination and effectiveness, successfully interdicted enemy lines of support from the North so that further reinforcement therefrom has been sharply curtailed and essential supplies markedly limited. The [X Corps] eastern sector of the pincer, with noteworthy and effective Naval support, has steadily advanced in a brilliant tactical movement and has now reached a commanding enveloping position, cutting in two the northern reaches of the enemy's geographical potential. This morning the western sector of the pincer moves forward in general assault in an effort to complete the compression and close the vise. If successful this should for all practical purposes end the war, restore peace and unity to Korea, enable the prompt withdrawal of United Nations military forces, and permit the complete assumption by the Korean people and nation of full sovereignty and international equality. It is that for which we fight.

Those aware of the potential for catastrophe in MacArthur's confident misjudgments were alarmed, but few could say anything. Undoubtedly he had already heard, directly or indirectly, from General Barr in the far north, but had discounted the village headman's report as from an unreliable source. A correspondent with the British 27th Brigade wrote of MacArthur's premature victory communiqué that "this document filled us with alarm and despondency." In his command diary O. P. Smith referred to MacArthur's "usual flowery communique." Smith's operations chief, Alpha Bowser, called it a "goofy order." Only in 1979 did Major General Clark Ruffner, MacArthur's hand-picked chief of staff for Almond, concede that it was "an insane plan."

Flying from Haneda on the Friday after Thanksgiving to announce in person, before it had even begun, the final push of his war, MacArthur included aboard the *SCAP* his familiar courtiers and the usual chiefs of news bureaus in Tokyo. With a fleet of jeeps to tour rear-area headquarters for ritual briefings, Walker and Milburn ceremonially met the party at the rough airstrip just south of the Chongchon River. In the fifteen-degree frost MacArthur pulled on a parka and fastened a checked scarf around his neck. He reached down to pet Milburn's dachshund, who always rode with the general. Most commanders were gone, as troops were already moving north, and Milburn prudently predicted tough going for both IX Corps and I Corps. General John Church, however, was at his 24th Division HQ, where he claimed that his troops were facing little opposition.

As Church, Major General John Coulter and other ranking officers clustered around MacArthur's jeep, and reporters listened in to the ritual briefing, Church added that if enemy resistance did not pick up, he thought his division could go all the way to the Yalu. "Well, if they go fast enough," said MacArthur lightly, "maybe some of them could be home by Christmas." Recalling that he had already made such promises, he added, "Don't make me a liar." The UP quoted MacArthur as telling Coulter buoyantly, "You tell them that when we get up to the Yalu River they can all go home," and the AP reported his saying, "I hope to keep my promise to the GIs to have them home for Christmas."

Courtney Whitney, as usual at MacArthur's side, recalled the words as "half in jest but with a certain firmness of meaning and purpose." MacArthur would later call all references to Christmas misquotes. Promising Christmas dinner at home, a skeptical Pentagon official cracked, was a confusion of domiciles. "General MacArthur has been in the Far East so long he's come to think of Japan as home."

At home, Lowell Thomas reported on radio that when he saw the story that had come over the wire, "I shook my head and told my associates I was positive that MacArthur had never made any such statement. Today the correction came. The General says he was misquoted." Yet it was no misquotation, for he had been saying the same thing at least since Wake Island. Afterwards he would allege to have displayed far less optimism. "What I had seen at the front worried me greatly," he claimed once foreboding seemed more appropriate than self-congratulation. "The ROK troops were not yet in good shape, and the entire line was deplorably weak in numbers." He also claimed, years later, that the home-by-Christmas embarrassment, "twisted by the press into a prediction . . . with which to bludgeon me," was really intended to assure the Chinese "that we would get out of Korea the moment the Manchurian border was reached."

At his command post in the northwest reaches of Korea, Peng was told of radio reports about MacArthur's statement. "Liar!" he was quoted as saying. "So you plan to drive up to the Yalu by December 25th? That's a groundless tale. I think that MacArthur is too optimistic."

At his headquarters that morning, Peng experienced an unforeseen calamity very likely related to MacArthur's flight to Korea. To enhance security during MacArthur's presence, the Far East Air Force intensified its activity below the Yalu, following up carrier aircraft from the *Leyte*, which had just bombed the southern spans of the Sinuiju bridges. (The strikes were a deliberate distraction as well as part of the pre-offensive buildup.) Bombs also hit the Chinese People's Volunteers headquarters area—hardly a triumph of intelligence, as Stratemeyer's pilots had no idea where it was. The Chairman's eldest son, Mao Anying, twenty-eight, had volunteered, with his father's permission, to join the CPV. He wanted to command an infantry regiment, but Peng, realizing that young Mao's experience was only as party secretary of the Beijing Machinery Factory, named him instead his Russian-language translator at headquarters. It seemed also more safe.

Early on the twenty-fourth, as bombs fell below the Yalu, Peng and some of his staff rushed to shelter in a nearby mine shaft. Mao Anying and another officer, Gao Ruixin, were in a wooden farm cabin in a nearby field—Peng's office. It was hit before they could flee, and both were killed. Despite the likely embarrassment to his command, Peng realized that he could not withhold the news from Mao. He radioed Zhou Enlai that Anying's body should not be treated any differently than other casualties, but buried in North Korea. "I, on behalf of the CPV command, will inscribe a tombstone tablet indicating that he joined the CPV on his own free will and died on the battlefield, and [that] he has proven himself as a fine son of Mao Zedong."

Zhou agreed after consulting with leaders like Deng Xiaoping (who would be the Chairman's successor), but Mao was not informed. Months later when Peng apologized for not better safeguarding young Mao, the Chairman was shocked and grieved, but agreed, "Anying has just done his duty." He accepted the decision to inter his son in North Korea as it was "characteristic of our revolutionary spirit to share weal and woe." Anying remained under his wooden red star.

Five hours into the pre-offensive tour brought MacArthur's party back to Sinanju, where Walker and his staff saluted goodbyes at the ramp to the *SCAP.* As the doors closed, Walker murmured, while heading for his jeep, "Bullshit!" His pilot, Mike Lynch, had never before heard him say a derogatory word about his chief. Walker did not share MacArthur's grandstanding optimism, yet was too cowed to confess it. Like O. P. Smith on the X Corps front, he had stalled the opening of the offensive as long as he dared. All Walker could now do was to offer an anxious message to General Church for Colonel Richard W. Stephens, whose 21st Infantry would lead the 24th Division's advance: "You tell Stephens that the first time he smells Chinese chow, [he should] pull back immediately." But that afternoon when Walker's deputy, General Leven Allen, returned from Sinanju to EUSAK headquarters, he remarked privately to staff officers, "I think the attack will go. General MacArthur would not have come over if he did not think so."

Nothing remotely pessimistic was evident as the Constellation took off. MacArthur even surprised his pilot, Tony Story, by ordering him, as they began the three-hour flight to Tokyo, "Head for the west coast and fly up the Yalu." He wanted to go to the mouth of the river and then swing along it, just below the border, eastward. "I don't think we should do it, General," said Story.

"I don't care," said MacArthur. ". . . I don't want to go right back to Japan. I want to follow the Yalu River all the way to the other side [of Korea]." From about five thousand feet—it was cold and clear—he wanted personal confirmation that there was no buildup of enemy forces on the Korean side.

The others in the unarmed transport lacked his fatalism. "Sid," an anxious correspondent appealed to one of MacArthur's Manila-vintage aides, Colonel Huff, "is this trip really necessary?" MacArthur would not put on a parachute, although others did. "You gentlemen wear them if you care to do so," he said. "I'll stick with the plane."

Story urgently radioed for a fighter escort, and jets from Kimpo quickly caught up to the Constellation as it lingered back to wait for them. "At this height," MacArthur claimed extravagantly, "we could observe in detail the entire area of international No-Man's Land"—except to MacArthur it was sovereign territory—"all the way to the Siberian border. All that spread before our eyes was an endless expanse of utterly barren countryside, jagged hills, yawning crevices, and the black waters of the Yalu locked in the silent death grip of snow and ice. It was a merciless wasteland. If a large force or massive supply train had passed over the border, the imprints had already been well covered by the intermittent snowstorms of the Yalu Valley."

It was not all that dramatically stark. Kanggye, believed to be Kim Il Sung's emergency headquarters, was still smoldering after FEAF raids. The Yalu dams and power plants seemed quiet and untouched. Where spans of the big steel bridges were down on the Korean side of the river, it appeared as if nothing moved. Yet after dark, trucks and coolies bearing supplies and equipment crisscrossed the ice unseen; and before the first light of dawn, a small army of villagers and farmers emerged with brooms and swept away the telltale tracks. Hyesanjin, newly reached by U.S. troops, looked no different in friendly hands and MacArthur joked, "Flap the wings, or something."

From a height much greater than the Constellation flew, northern Korea resembles an upside-down boot with its heel in the west and foot in the east. The heel end is at Sinuiju; on the other side of the arch the foot continues from Hyesanjin to the Tumen River toe in Siberia. As the plane approached Soviet airspace, Story prudently turned south toward Japan. The jet escorts pulled away, and MacArthur radioed to them, via Story, "Thanks for the grand ride." It had been a heady experience, but MacArthur saw less than was there.

On the flight to Tokyo, despite concerns even from the toadying Willoughby that the unseen Chinese were capable of infiltrating large numbers of troops under cover of darkness "in preparation for a counteroffensive," MacArthur drafted a message to the Joint Chiefs that would go out on November 25, the next day, justifying his advance to the Yalu. "My personal rcn [reconnaissance] of the Yalu River line yesterday demonstrated conclusively that it would be utterly impossible for us to stop upon commanding terrain south of the river as suggested . . . ," he maintained. There wasn't any alternative, he claimed, to "the natural features of the river line itself." He also had a political case to make. Failing to unify all of Korea would be "a betrayal" of its people "and the solemn undertaking entered into on their behalf."

Chinese intervention, MacArthur continued, "was a risk we knowingly took at the time we committed our forces. Had they entered at the time we were beleaguered behind our Pusan perimeter beachhead, the hazard would have been far more grave than it is now that we hold the initiative and have a much smaller area within which to interdict their hostile moves. Our forces are committed to seize the entire border area, and indeed in the east [we] have already occupied a sector of the Yalu River with no noticeable political or mi[litary] Soviet or Chinese reaction." Once he consolidated positions along the length of the Yalu, he expected to withdraw American forces "as far as possible" and replace them with ROK troops. After complete victory he would return American units to Japan and the States, parole POWs to their homes and leave Korean unification to "the people, with the advice and assistance of the UN authorities."

His message was for the Joint Chiefs only. He assumed that Walker's troops had already jumped off for the Yalu and might make political concessions moot before "certain other countries" could substitute negotiation for "the desired result." Leaving enemy forces south of the border was military foolishness, he felt. And, he pointed out, one of the chief concerns of other nations, the Yalu power installations on which Manchuria appeared to be dependent, was based upon a misconception. When the ROKs had reached the Yalu at Chosan in October, it appeared to them that the big Suiho power plant, the source of most of the controversy, had been shut down. (As late as December 27, MacArthur continued to report the plants there to the Department of the Army as "inactive. . . . Their preservation or their destruction is predominantly a political rather than a military matter.") "One is brought to the conclusion," he charged, "that the issue of hydro-electric power rests upon the most tenuous of grounds."

For the press in Tokyo, MacArthur issued a communiqué ostensibly addressed to the United Nations, announcing, as if true, "The giant UN pincer moved according to schedule today. The air forces, in full strength, completely interdicted the rear areas and air reconnaissance behind the enemy line, and along the entire length of the Yalu River border, showed little sign of hostile military activity." The Yalu reconnaissance had been his own, a tourist flight by amateurs. "Our losses were extraordinarily light," he imagined, having no such information. "The logistics situation is fully geared to sustain offensive operations." (Walker would hardly have agreed with him.) "The justice of our course and promise of early completion of our mission is reflected in the morale of troops and commanders alike."

While things were quiet in Hagaru, Captain Benjamin Read's 105mm How Battery was holed up in the north end of the village awaiting orders to move up. At 1:45 a.m. on the twenty-sixth, a Sunday, Sergeant Elmer Walling awakened Read and suggested that he listen in on the field telephone link between gun crews. As Read adjusted his headset Pfc. Stanley Lockowitz was announcing, "This is broadcasting station H-O-W, deep in the wilds of cold Korea. The *Mystery Voice* program is now on the air, sponsored by Lieutenant Wilbur Herndon's Tennessee Twist Chewing Tobacco. . . . But before we hear the Mystery Voice, Pfc. Bergman is going to favor us with a Christmas carol." Then Siert Bergman, a Swede from Michigan, duly sang "Silent Night." Lockowitz, perhaps then masking the mouthpiece of his crank-up phone, introduced the solemn "Mystery Voice," challenging the men in the gun pits to call in a solution. When the first guesses were wrong, he tried a new identity, intoning solemnly, "You shall return, as *I shall return*, by Christmas."

"You have just won the grand prize," he told the first of the Marines who called in MacArthur's name, "which is a 105mm howitzer with two rounds of white phosphorus and the opportunity to fire both rounds at a target of your choice. Good-bye and good luck." Their morale, Read realized, was very high. But after a brief snowfall the thermometer began to plunge, and the next day, Monday, November 27, it bottomed out at twenty-five below.

On MacArthur's orders, X Corps was planning its attack to commence that following Monday, November 27. O. P. Smith made no secret of his dismay, but Almond insisted that the Marines were his most "battle-worthy" troops, able to negotiate the nearly impassable reservoir country. Almond's personal prisoner interrogations had already convinced him of a disconcertingly massive Chinese presence above the reservoirs, at least equal to X Corps strength. His orders from MacArthur, however, were to draw the Chinese away from Walker's right flank while occupying Korean territory up to the Yalu.

Although Smith preferred to have the Marines defend the long Hungnam-Wonsan beachhead over the frigid winter, leaving the frostbite casualties to the Chinese, the instructions from the Dai Ichi were to coordinate offensives with EUSAK and win the war by Christmas. Marine pilots returning from sorties to the north reported few visible soldiers, but southbound traffic from China that was "heavy, very heavy, tremendous, and gigantic." They were supplying someone. Up at the Chosin Reservoir briefly to hand out medals, Almond assured the Marines, "We are still attacking and we're going all the way to the Yalu. Don't let a bunch of Chinese laundrymen stop you."

Smith kept his men moving warily north up the western slopes of the reservoir—cautiously enough to exasperate Almond. The Marine command did not want to be overrun or put itself out of reach of a support system. It was already so cold in the higher elevations, where the passes are at 3,500 feet and the peaks at 6,500 feet, that men gasped in the first shock of exposure. Still, Smith realized that Colonel Homer Litzenberg's 7th Marines were expected to bypass Chosin and move northeast, beyond the Fusen Reservoir, to more open country and the upper Yalu.

Prompted by his misgivings, Smith had prepared a long message to Marine commandant Clifton Cates in Washington twelve days before the Marines were to jump off. They were dangerously strung out, he warned. No EUSAK unit was closer than eighty miles to the southwest; the only mountain track from Hamhung (inland from Hungnam on the coast) to the Yalu was nearly two hundred road miles long. Smith had no confidence in Almond and expected to "simply get further out on a limb." He contended "that a winter campaign in the mountains of North Korea is too much to ask of the American soldier or Marine, and I doubt the feasability"—in his haste Smith misspelled the word—"of supplying troops in this area during the winter or providing for the evacuation of sick or wounded."

In dealing directly with Cates, Smith was trying to reach and influence the JCS, but the dominating presence of MacArthur and his confidence that he could end the war between Thanksgiving and Christmas left the Marine commandant without influence. Cates did not know at the time that one of Litzenberg's counterparts, Chesty Puller of the 5th Regiment, marked the anniversary of the founding of the Marines by hacking at a hundred-pound birthday cake with a captured North Korean sword. Despite a closing tribute to Marine traditions, Puller found it necessary to add that "raggedy-tailed North Koreans have been shipping"—dispatching—"a lot of so-called good American troops, and may do it again." His warning did not even mention the looming Chinese. A week later another contact with Washington came when Truman's friend Major General Frank Lowe, who had been commissioned by the President to report on the performance of National Guard and reserve units, appeared in Hungnam. With him were map overlays of pre-offensive EUSAK troop dispositions—the first knowledge which the Marines had of the whereabouts of half or more of the Korean command. Liaison was conducted largely through MacArthur in Tokyo.

From the Pentagon, Matthew Ridgway observed with disquiet the preparations for MacArthur's two-pronged plunge to the border. He recognized it, he wrote later, as "an advance to contact" rather than an attack: "It is not possible to attack an enemy whose positions are not known, whose very existence has not been confirmed, and whose forces are completely out of contact with your own." As Eighth Army units jumped off on the morning of the twenty-fourth they were indeed, as MacArthur's communiqué from Tokyo had declared, nearly unopposed. But in the Unsan area above the Chongchon River, where disaster had struck earlier in the month, I Corps headquarters reported to correspondents covering the push that the area was heavily defended. The only progress was along Walker's right flank, where the Chinese drew him in. At risk were the reconstituted ROK II Corps, which had been smashed earlier, and the American IX Corps.

Everywhere the Eighth Army moved forward, enemy soldiers let them pass, following strictly Mao's dicta in his *Protracted War,* "The first stage is one of the enemy's strategic offensive. . . . The second stage may be termed the stage of strategic stalemate. . . . We say that it is easy to attack an enemy on the move precisely because he is not then on the alert. . . . We have always advocated the policy of 'luring the enemy to penetrate deep' precisely because this is the most effective military policy for a weak army in strategic defence against a strong army."

The third Maoist stage would be a surprise counteroffensive. The home front, through a "Hate America" propaganda campaign, was prepared for heavy losses. Troops disciplined by two decades of cheaply held life had accepted the Maoist contention that the outcome of war "is decided by the people, not by one or two new weapons." To the Chinese, the United States was "the paradise of gangsters, swindlers, rascals, special agents, fascist germs, speculators, debauchers, and all the dregs of mankind." American soldiers, led by "the Wall Street house-dog General MacArthur," could not be any better than the "depraved" civilization that had spawned them.

By the second morning of the offensive, virtually unopposed advances of up to eight miles were made all along the EUSAK front. Then, surprisingly, the Chinese emerged in daylight, heaving grenades and showering troops with rifle fire from their flanks and even from the rear. The trackless hills, ridges and valleys made movement on wheels and treads difficult. Troops dependent on radios and field telephones sometimes panicked when their frozen equipment failed. When night came, to the sounds of signal bugles and whistles, more Chinese exploded out of hiding, their newly unleashed six armies equivalent to eighteen American divisions. They appeared to the flanks and the rear as well as forward of the 2nd, 24th and 25th Divisions, shouting as they heaved their wooden-handled grenades, "Come on back, GI! Afraid, GI?"

To the right of the Americans, the three divisions of the ROK II Corps collapsed and fled, entangling miles once behind them with inoperable tanks, trucks and jeeps. On arriving at their forward positions, the ROKs had built bonfires on frozen hilltops to keep warm. Had the Chinese not known where II Corps was, the Koreans had identified themselves. Refugees clogged roads; artillery was abandoned; panicky units out of contact imagined Chinese advances which took on lives of their own.

The Turkish Brigade, on its way to help the floundering South Koreans, met a Chinese roadblock and was ambushed. Turning toward the right flank of the 2nd Division, they encountered ROK troops fleeing south, and mistakenly killed or captured about two hundred. Knowing neither Korean nor Chinese, and receiving confused orders in minimally understood English, the Turks lost all of their vehicles and nearly a thousand of their men. The first 300-man Turkish unit to see action took 255 casualties. In all, 770 Turks would remain buried in Korea. After years of self-imposed isolation it was Turkey's inglorious debut on the modern world stage. By 1952 the nation was in NATO.

At Lake Success the Soviet bloc, with neutral support, had managed to invite a delegation from Beijing to address the Security Council about its claims to Taiwan and its legitimacy as claimant for the UN China seat. Warren Austin, the American delegate, had condemned China for "blatant, criminal aggression" in Korea, but on the morning of November 24, as MacArthur's end-the-war offensive had begun, nine Chinese diplomats, led by Soviet-trained Wu Xiuquan, checked into the Waldorf-Astoria. Wu, who would sit behind a guest placard reading "People's Republic of China," had prepared a two-hour tirade accusing the United States of "unlawful and criminal act[s] of armed aggression against the territory of China. . . ."

The Security Council convened under its chairman for the month, Yugoslav delegate Ales Bebler. Wu found himself seated at a U-shaped table opposite the representative of "China"—Taiwan. "Who has shattered security in the Pacific?" Wu charged, raising an accusing finger. "Have Chinese armed forces invaded Hawaii? Or have U.S. armed forces invaded . . . Korea and Taiwan? The real intention of the U.S., as MacArthur has confessed, is . . . to dominate every Asiatic port from Vladivostok to Singapore." Those UN members who have joined to assist the puppet government of South Korea, he warned, "must bear the consequences of your actions."

On November 29, IX Corps received a message from Pyongyang that ten truckloads of Turks had arrived there with an American KMAG officer. "What shall I do with them?" the switchboard operator asked. There was no need to send them back, for the rapidly dissolving front was moving in their direction. In the post-Thanksgiving panic that did not even require contact with the Chinese, the offensive to end the war was becoming a disorderly 120-mile withdrawal. Hard-pressed by the collapse of troops on their flanks, the 24th Regiment began a staggered retreat while the 35th Regiment moved up to block, and Lieutenant Colonel Welborn G. Dolvin used all of his administrative personnel but his switchboard operator to defend his command post. Nearby he saw three men he didn't recognize apparently loafing, but armed with carbines. "What are you doing?" he asked. "Nothing," one admitted. "Get up to Easy Company's hill," Dolvin ordered, "and join the fight."

They took off, and only the next morning did Dolvin discover that one was a pilot without a plane, and two were enlisted men on some official business about which he never learned. It had been a hell of a night. Easy would win a Distinguished Unit citation, and its captain, Reginald B. Desiderio, who died holding off the Chinese, a posthumous Medal of Honor. As the remnants of Easy passed Dolvin's command post the fighter pilot remarked, "I got my Chinaman. Now I will return to being an air pilot. I've done my share of ground combat."

Although the advance of the Eighth Army was imploding on the second day of its push, Almond, unaware of the debacle as he got his news from Tokyo, brought O. P. Smith the final X Corps offensive plan, approved in Tokyo by MacArthur. (Even when Almond learned of the disaster to EUSAK, he and his staff delayed informing the Marines.) The Marines were to advance beyond the reservoirs to the Yalu. Barr's 7th Division was to advance to the Yalu on the eastern side of the Chosin Reservoir. Major General Robert Soule's 3rd Division on the far left flank was to move northwest to establish contact with the Eighth Army, expected to be forty miles away on a parallel course, while also protecting the Marine advance. General Kim Baik Kil's ROK I Corps was to move northeast toward the Yalu and Tumen Rivers. Ridgway would call it later "like a pure map exercise put on by amateurs, appealing in theory but utterly ignoring the reality of a huge mountainous terrain largely devoid of lateral communications, and ordered for execution in the face of a fast-approaching sub-arctic winter." Years later Almond defended the plan as "orders from General MacArthur to determine whether the enemy on our front . . . would threaten either the front of the X Corps or the front and right flank of the Eighth Army. . . . What General Smith was really complaining about was . . . that his division happened to be the division that would determine the strength of that [unknown] force."·

Just after noon on the morning of the X Corps push, Eighth Army deputy chief of staff Colonel Eugene M. Landrum telephoned Doyle Hickey at the Dai Ichi with an urgent message from Walker. He was not requesting orders to withdraw, but announcing that his troops were in retreat. As Landrum quoted Walker, "Indications are that en[emy] is no longer on def[ensive] but is taking action in str[ength]. Main effort at the moment is against IX Corps (center) and II ROK Corps on our right. . . . We are consolidating positions of I Corps until situation clarifies. . . ." The terse report went on in the cautious language of a commander reporting that his troops were buckling under pressure and that their intended offensive had collapsed. What he did not confide was that despite the bitter cold, many men were discarding their helmets, bayonets, grenades, guns and even boots in order to unburden themselves for flight. The lightly armed, sneaker-clad Chinese would be the beneficiaries.

Under darkening winter skies, X Corps had jumped off as scheduled just after eight on the frigid morning of November 27. It was even more wintry in the reservoir highlands than in the west. Unfortunately, the units of Walker's army that were supposed to link up to the north with Almond's corps were in retreat in the opposite direction, often without exchanging any fire with the enemy. Almost everywhere in the X Corps area the Chinese had also infiltrated in large numbers almost unseen. They were lying in wait in force near Yudam-ni, halfway up the Chosin Reservoir, when the Marines reached the miserable village late in the afternoon. It was seventeen below, and frigid winds made it seem colder. Litzenberg's 7th Regiment was to move northwest to Mupyong-ni, fifty-five miles to the west, but in a night briefing in a drafty tent he noted that three Chinese POWs had revealed that their 58th, 59th and 60th Divisions were lying in wait until the 5th and 7th Marine Regiments had passed, and would then cut them off. The 27th People's Liberation Army, with four experienced divisions, was east of the reservoir and would isolate the U.S. 7th Division.

As the night wore on into the next day, and the temperature dropped below minus twenty, the Chinese attacked from seemingly every direction with mortar fire and grenades. Preceded by bugle calls and whistles, the Chinese infiltrated through gaps they had made, even though waves of their infantry were cut down by machine gun fire. As dawn came, the 5th and 7th Marines were surrounded.

MacArthur did not know how precarious the situation in Korea would become when, poised for his end-the-war offensives, he agreed to an interview with the Tokyo correspondent for Henry Luce's flagship magazine, *Life*. The focus was the proposal for a militarized buffer zone offered by Britain with other UN participants in Korea. *Life* was a mass-circulation platform for MacArthur's contrary views. Luce, the China-born son of a Presbyterian missionary and Waldorf Towers friend and neighbor of Herbert Hoover, was an inflexible anti-Communist and supporter of Chiang. Luce's newsmen were welcome at the Dai Ichi, but it appears that the Supreme Commander was suddenly cautious about saying anything for direct attribution. Instead, an indirect pseudo-interview would appear, probably prepared by Courtney Whitney, who often assumed MacArthur's voice.

The result appeared in the guise of a Luce editorial, "Yardstick from Tokyo," in the next issue (December 4, 1950), on newsstands and in the mail on the last day of November, by which time events had turned for the worse. It had been "a week of grave decision," the unsigned piece began. "General MacArthur is not infallible—far from it. But his estimate of the actual situation in Korea, and his attitude toward the Communist aggressors, are in healthy contrast to the sick and fearful atmosphere of London, Washington and Lake Success." What followed, in question-and-answer form, seemed the Dai Ichi spin on the situation south of the Yalu, a posture already obsolete when *Life* reached its readers.

Q. How bad is our situation in Korea? Is it as "impossible" as Washington thinks?

A. General MacArthur would not agree with the view . . . that we are even in a bad situation in North Korea. . . .

Q. If General MacArthur were completely free to dictate his own course, how would he try to resolve the military situation on the Korea-Manchuria border?

A. He would do exactly what he is doing—that is, seek a military decision through the destruction of the opposing forces, whether North Korean, Chinese, or mixed. . . .

Q. Is some concession indicated in order to avoid a major war?

A. History demonstrates unmistakably that yielding to unjustified international pressure leads inevitably to war. . . .

Q. Must the United Nations forces go all the way to the Yalu border? Is there anything good in the idea of offering the Chinese Communists a "buffer zone"?

A. General MacArthur believes that to give up any portion of North Korea to the Chinese Communists would be the greatest defeat of the free world in modern times. To yield to so immoral a proposal would bankrupt our leadership and influence in Asia. . . .

Q. If the Chinese Communists were calling on General MacArthur in Tokyo . . . , how would he receive them and deal with them?

A. His reply would be characteristically terse: "Get out of Korea and stay out. Those who persist in practicing international banditry . . . will be destroyed."

MacArthur would have to employ more of his public relations resources as the military situation made the buffer zone debate an anachronism. Messages deluging the Dai Ichi on the afternoon of the twenty-eighth established that his offensives on both fronts had failed. EUSAK was in retreat and now Almond was ordered to withdraw from his reservoir positions. MacArthur then urgently radioed the Pentagon, which learned of the shocking turnabout in the war at 4:00 a.m. Washington time. As always, the bad news was described as someone else's miscalculation, discovered only because the general shrewdly planned a reconnaissance in force to expose enemy intentions:

The developments resulting from our assault movements have now assumed a clear definition. All hope of localization of the Korean conflict to . . . NK troops with alien token elements can now be completely abandoned. The Chinese military forces are committed . . . in great and ever-increasing strength. No pretext of minor support under the guise of volunteerism or other subterfuge now has the slightest validity. We face an entirely new war. Interrogation of prisoners of war and other intelligence information establish the following enemy order of battle . . . comprising an aggregate strength approaching 200,000. The NK fragments, approximately 50,000 troops, are to be added to this strength. . . .

It is quite evident that our present strength of force is not sufficient to meet this undeclared war by the Chinese with the inherent advantages which accrue thereby to them. The resulting situation presents an entirely new picture which broadens the potentialities to world embracing considerations beyond the sphere of decision by the theater commander. This command has done everything possible within its capabilities but is now faced with conditions beyond its control and strength.

MacArthur was describing an unanticipated attack on the order of Pearl Harbor, yet the intelligence indicators had been out there for him to see for more than a month. Even the loyal Almond had interrogated Chinese POWs and warned of the hidden potential for trouble. MacArthur's "immediate plan," he radioed the Pentagon ambiguously although in panic, was "to pass from the offensive to the defensive with such local adjustments as may be required by a constantly fluid situation."

The duty officer at the Pentagon just before dawn on November 28 was Colonel John R. Beishline. He awakened General Ridgway, deputy chief of staff for operations, at 4:15 a.m. Ridgway asked that MacArthur's frantic message be brought to his quarters, and while he waited for it he telephoned General Collins. An hour later, after studying MacArthur's long appeal, Ridgway suggested in another call to Collins that he thought the JCS would want the President to have the bad news right away. Truman would learn of the disaster in the making through Omar Bradley, who described the cable from Tokyo as "rather hysterical." He doubted, he told the President, that it was "as much of a catastrophe as our [morning] newspapers were leading us to believe," but confirmed that the Chinese had "come in with both feet."

Despite Bradley's downplaying the disaster, Red China, without heavy artillery, tanks or an air force, had emerged suddenly and surprisingly as a major world power, threatening the entire UN position in Korea. At the Pentagon, Ridgway urged Lieutenant General Wade H. Haislip, the Army vice chief of staff, to begin immediate planning for a possible evacuation and to issue contingency instructions to MacArthur. Anticipating the worst, Admiral Turner Joy in Tokyo quietly began to assemble ships for withdrawing X Corps from Hungnam and Wonsan.

At the Dai Ichi, MacArthur put his panic aside long enough to compose a communiqué for the world press, which was already headlining his reverses. From the first sentence he pushed aside personal responsibility for the situation. At 5:25 p.m., little more than two hours after his message shocked Washington, MacArthur issued a statement charging that a major portion of Chinese ground forces were now committed against the United Nations without a declaration of war. According to Communiqué No. 14,

> Consequently we face an entirely new war. This has shattered the high hopes we entertained that the intervention of the Chinese was only of a token nature on a volunteer and individual basis as publicly announced. . . .

Finally, MacArthur had come to a belated understanding of Maoist strategy:

> It now appears to have been the enemy's intent in breaking off contact with our forces some two weeks ago, to secure the time necessary surreptitiously to build up for a later surprise assault upon our lines in overwhelming force, taking advantage of the freezing of all rivers and roadbeds which would have materially reduced the effectiveness of our air interdiction and permitted a greatly accelerated forward movement of enemy reinforcements and supplies.

Evasively, he then twisted the catastrophe into a cunning strategic initiative of his own making, contending that the Chinese attack "has been disrupted by our own offensive action which forced upon the enemy a premature engagement." Yet, since he knew otherwise, he summoned Walker and Almond to an emergency conference in Tokyo—an arrangement that looked better, should the news leak, than his rushing to the front in panic. (He had been in Korea only six times since the war began, five of these flying visits of only a few hours.) Almond found out about the summons after a day of conferences with Marine commanders near the Chosin Reservoir, and the regimental commanders of the 31st and 32nd Infantry, on the reservoir's east slope. He held hurried meetings with 7th Division commanding general David Barr, and Australian general Sir Horace Robertson, who was inspecting Commonwealth troops, then flew out of Yonpo air base on the coast with a handful of staff. When Almond's plane arrived at Haneda at about nine that evening, an FEC colonel was there to escort the X Corps group to the embassy. A late-night meeting at the Dai Ichi would have attracted notice.

Walker was already there. It was his sector that seemed in the most immediate trouble, and he had wasted no time in rushing to Tokyo. His troops were not only already on the defense, but in a headlong retreat that would be described later as a breaking off of contact. It would take all of MacArthur's verbal magic to explain the reversal without embarrassment, and he would get to that right away. In a cable to the influential Arthur Krock of the *The New York Times*, MacArthur claimed that "every major step" in his offensive plans had been "previously reported and fully approved" in Washington, and "every strategic and tactical movement" had been "in compliance with directives." To his friend Hugh Baillie of United Press he cabled, "It is historically inaccurate to attribute any degree of responsibility for the onslaught of the Chinese communist armies to the strategic course of the campaign itself." To the supportive *U.S. News & World Report* he claimed in an interview, "The tactical course taken was the only one which the situation permitted."

When the Tokyo conference began at 9:30 p.m. Admiral Joy and Generals Stratemeyer, Hickey, Willoughby, Whitney and Wright were with MacArthur, Walker and Almond. No official record was kept during the four anxious hours they discussed their options. Both commanders remained stubborn in face of the known facts. Walker claimed that he could hold a defensive line across the narrow neck of Korea above Pyongyang, yet after three demoralizing days and nights his troops were rapidly backtracking toward the city. Almond contended that X Corps could advance toward Kanggye and the Yalu, cutting off the Chinese. MacArthur did not have to be able to read minds to realize that their postures of defiance were more to impress him with their resolve than with their sense of reality. Walker was instructed to hold the Pyongyang line if he could, but under no conditions to permit his forces to remain anywhere only to be outflanked. Almond was told to withdraw his troops from the reservoir highlands and try to hold the Hamhung-Hungnam area on the eastern coast, taking action against the enemy "wherever possible within good judgment." In the morning Walker and Almond flew back to their beleaguered commands.

The Dai Ichi's next orders went to the FEAF Combat Cargo Command in Tokyo, run by Major General William H. Tunner, who had commanded the India–China Hump operations in World War II and the Berlin airlift in 1948–49. He sent quartermaster packers and C-119s to Yonpo, to prepare drops of supplies to cut-off troops in the Chosin area. Quickly he added C-

46s and C-47s, to increase the tonnage. Not easy to work with, Tunner was characterized as "a great guy if you were a cold infantryman on the main battle position."

Almond and Walker were back at their command posts by late afternoon on the twenty-ninth. Walker immediately ordered a withdrawal behind the Chongchon, an action already anticipated by many of his units. It was, he added, "imperative to prevent movement of refugees over bridges," to assure access for military traffic, but nothing would dissuade civilians fleeing south. Almond's X Corps order No. 8, drafted with his staff at Yonpo air base on returning, called for discontinuing offensive action and withdrawing to the Hamhung-Hungnam area.

In Washington, the Joint Chiefs convened that morning. Only Admiral Sherman, responsible for the Marines, was willing to give MacArthur tactical orders. He wanted X Corps withdrawn to the narrow waist of Korea, to link up with EUSAK and hold the line there. Bradley felt that the theater commander needed his own options, which left the JCS only able to radio MacArthur weakly, "What are your plans regarding the coordination of the Eighth Army and X Corps and the positioning of X Corps, the units of which to us appear to be exposed?"

By afternoon on the twenty-eighth, the IX Corps and I Corps units of the Eighth Army had broken contact with the Chinese everywhere they could, and were on the run. Walker would call it deep withdrawal. X Corps had the problem of withdrawing from the reservoir highlands, at least to the tiny airstrip—just becoming operational—at Hagaru, below the southern end of half-frozen Chosin. When MacArthur asked Almond what he could do to help the Eighth Army, which was already in disarray, the X Corps commander pointed out that his first priority was to rescue increasingly isolated Marine and Army troops along the reservoirs. Pinky Wright, MacArthur's operations chief, working from his map in Tokyo, proposed that Almond send men from the 3rd Division over the road through the Taebaek Mountains toward Tokchon to attack the Chinese on Walker's eastern flank. On the map, Almond said, the road existed, but in reality it was a dirt path unable to handle military traffic and now frozen over. The only way the two MacArthur armies could link up was in deep retreat, which itself would not be easy for X Corps.

The air reconnaissance about which MacArthur had boasted had seemed on the money when the Eighth Army, innocent of Maoist deception, had made unopposed advances of up to eight miles. But then, Air Force General

Stratemeyer told a Senate subcommittee four years later, "Lo and behold, the whole mountainside turned out to be Chinese." As Private First Class Jack Wright remembered, "the guy on watch" woke up his platoon with "Man, the hills all around on both sides are lit up like Christmas trees."

Across northern Korea the experience was the same. On the flanks of the frozen reservoirs, the jagged black skyline stark under a full moon, the Chinese fired from bunkers only visible when their guns flashed. Below, their probing parties grenaded Marine outposts, which, firing back, became targets for machine guns. Wave attacks by assault troops followed, accompanied by blaring bugles and signal whistles, and infiltrators streamed into the gaps as the Marines gave ground.

At Yudam-ni, at the northern end of the reservoir, two spearhead battalions were trapped, Lt. Col. Robert D. Taplett's 3rd Battalion, 5th Marines and Lt. Col. Raymond G. Davis's 1st Battalion, 7th Marines. It was fifteen below when Keyes Beech and Maggie Higgins listened to the tall, lean 5th Marines Commander Raymond L. Murray brief a cluster of his officers. Above them transports released via gaily colored parachutes color-coded supplies in red, green, blue and yellow toward a drop zone two hundred yards away. Murray's slow Texas delivery and the bright sunlit parachutes belied the urgency of his message. "Gentlemen," he said, "we are going out of here. And we are going out like Marines. We are sticking together and we are taking our dead and wounded and our equipment. Are there any questions?"

There were no questions. Although they fought their way through, with heavy casualties, the ice remained as much of a foe as the Chinese. On occasion, Davis recalled, "we had to climb on our hands and knees holding on to roots and twigs to keep from sliding back down the icy trail." He worried about snipers as well as frontal attacks; about his men falling asleep, which would have meant death; about men dragging or carrying back the wounded and even the dead; about men cracking under the strain (two had to be forced into improvised straitjackets and died en route back). On a rescue mission in snow and ice Ray Davis had his head grazed by a spent round but survived to win a Medal of Honor and become commandant of the Marine Corps.

The cold—twenty below and more—affected the performance of weapons as well as vehicles. For a time GIs thought that ROK troops could not fire their rifles because oil had congealed in them or because they had run out of ammunition. Many Koreans, it turned out, carried their weapons but never fired them, yet they remained integrated into Army units where they were of little use and a logistical burden. Coming south from the Yalu into the reservoir highlands, Bob Hammond remembered, in the fading darkness just before dawn, the Chinese coming "out of nowhere, hundreds of them, all lined up, screaming, yelling, bugles blowing, shouting and rushing at us. . . . I am scared out of my mind. I get off a couple of rounds at the mob rushing me, and I scream at the guys, 'Here they come!! Get out of there!!'"

GIs had tried to shelter in mountain caves for the night, but the Chinese flushed out each cave as they advanced, and Hammond ran for his life. "I stumble and fall in the snow, regain my feet and as I start running again, see 3 or 4 little spurts of snow jumping up from the ground just a few feet away from me. For a moment I don't recognize it for what it is, and then realize it was bullets!! They are shooting at me!!"

In his "side vision" he saw bodies everywhere and did not slow down to determine who they were, but, reaching a road, joined "about 20 or 30" others, one of whom called, "I don't have a weapon!"

"Grab his!" Hammond shouted as they passed the body of a GI; and in minutes that seemed like months, they were at Baker Battery's relocated position, where they sensed a false security. Baker had lost its guns, but that was better luck than at Able Battery, which had been overrun. Regrouping in the dawn, they managed to take back Able's position, and the guns, but their "wounded shack" overflowed. "Many guys are laying outside on stretchers, including a buddy . . . who's been hit several times in the chest and is delirious. He wants water. Can't do that. I moisten his lips with snow, and for the first time, I cry."

The JCS had no idea how chaotic the EUSAK front had become. Remote from the action, MacArthur knew little more, and was the recipient of unintended consequences. There was no front. The 2nd Division, for example, trapped by the Chinese between Kunu-ri and Sunchon, had nowhere to go but backwards in a hail of mortar and machine-gun fire. Regimental commanders received useless "How Able" (Haul Ass) orders from Major General Laurence Keiser, as their troops were already in a disorderly withdrawal that would cost the division four thousand of its men on the morning of the thirtieth. It was a confusion repeated across Eighth Army positions, for even troops not under attack retreated hurriedly to avoid being outflanked, abandoning weapons and equipment never used against the enemy. The 2nd Division alone abandoned sixty-two artillery pieces. Keiser left his jeep despondently to survey the mess and stepped across GI corpses in the road, inadvertently clipping one with his boot. "You damned son-of-a-bitch," said the body, not quite dead.

"My friend," said the general, "I'm sorry." And he walked on.

Late in the afternoon of the twenty-ninth in Washington—already the thirtieth in Korea—the JCS convened for the fourth time in four days, this time to consider MacArthur's already twice-rejected appeal to import Chiang's troops from Taiwan. The old excuse that exploiting them might draw the Chinese Communists into the war was no longer sufficient. Truman approved a draft reply written by Marshall and Acheson to which the Joint Chiefs agreed. Rather than acknowledge that the defeated Nationalists were an unwise military bet, Washington stalled by claiming that MacArthur's proposal was "being considered," but that it involved worldwide political and diplomatic consequences. And they warned him indirectly that his failures in Korea were having broader repercussions. "Incidentally," the message read, "our position of leadership is being most seriously compromised in the United Nations. The utmost care will be necessary to avoid the disruption of the essential allied lineup in that organization." Considering MacArthur discredited, the British were calling for a multi-national committee to direct the war, and General Bradley retorted in a now-famous top-secret memorandum that a war could not be run by a committee.

"I should have relieved General MacArthur then and there," Truman confessed in his memoirs. "The reason I did not was that I did not wish to have it appear as if he were being relieved because the offensive failed. I have never believed in going back on people when luck is against them, and I did not intend to do it now." Instead, the Army chief of staff, J. Lawton Collins, was again sent back to size up the situation for Washington, which would have a horrendous week in the press. Satisfied to see the situation through from the Dai Ichi, MacArthur did not fly back to Korea to size up his "entirely new war."

13

The Nuclear Option

As the continuing catastrophe in Korea prompted banner headlines, speculation began about whether the crisis called for atomic weapons. Such talk was not new. On the first Sunday evening of the war, dinner conversation at Blair House had ranged far wider than Korea. The President had a lot of questions on his mind. Was the invasion by a Communist surrogate a Moscow feint to draw the U.S. away from the real action to occur elsewhere? Would the Soviets intervene directly? Would Mao's Chinese? Was Korea even worth saving? Was a preemptive strike against Soviet air bases on the edge of North Korea even possible?

"This might take some time," said Hoyt Vandenberg, speaking for the Air Force, "but it could be done if we used A-bombs."

Mention of the ultimate weapon was guaranteed to engender an uneasy silence. Truman and his service chiefs knew that nearly three hundred bombs were in the burgeoning American stockpile. Only the President could order them deployed and delivered.

The Soviets now possessed fission bomb capability—and possibly two dozen bombs—and were pressing ahead on a thermonuclear weapon. In two signed statements to the FBI, on May 22, before the war began, and again on July 10, atomic spy Harry Gold detailed what he knew of Soviet nuclear espionage in the U.S. beginning well before Hiroshima and continuing into the Cold War. On the basis of Gold's confession, German prewar refugee physicist Klaus Fuchs had been arrested in Britain and interviewed at length on his spying for Moscow at American atomic establishments. In the U.S., Gold's testimony had identified David Greenglass and Julius and Ethel Rosenberg as contributors to atomic espionage. The interrogations of Gold would lead to seven additional arrests and encouraged belief in the sweeping accusations by Senator Joseph McCarthy. He charged that a "pattern of infamy" pervaded American institutions. Anyone who had ever supported ideas or organizations characterized by the Right as pro-Soviet was under suspicion of disloyalty.

The nakedly Communist invasion of Korea had supported the rumors of vast networks of Soviet agents inspired by the arrest of Gold. Imagining Communist conspiracies became a domestic pastime that would cost some careers and reputations while propelling others. However illegal, J. Edgar Hoover's FBI bugged both the Soviet Embassy and its mission to the United Nations in New York. The Russians conducted equivalent and even more thorough surveillance of Americans in Moscow and elsewhere. In that atmosphere, Truman had found himself often forced to overreact, both in public and private, about alleged security risks in government. Diplomats were charged with having sold out Chiang's China to the Communists, and other Americans were suspected of working covertly for Russia, conveying more secrets than nuclear ones.

Although Stalin had long derided the atomic bomb as "a paper tiger which the reactionaries use to scare people," the President ordered preparation of plans for launching an atomic onslaught on the Soviet Union if it intervened to assist North Korea. No one at the table voiced an objection. After all, plans were not the same as actual Strategic Air Command (SAC) missions.

In the first weeks of the war, before being hobbled by a new UN level of policymaking, JCS Operations considered the Bomb as more than a paper tiger. General Curtis LeMay's SAC had nearly three hundred of its 868 aircraft configured to drop atomic bombs, and on June 6 from SAC headquarters in Nebraska he had directed a simulated first strike on the Soviet Union. Code-named Sunday Punch, the operation sent more than one hundred planes over remote areas of domestic Air Force bases to drop "pumpkins"—unarmed A-bombs. An internal and perhaps self-congratulatory survey declared this "first realistic test" a success.

Convening the Cabinet on July 7, Truman sought some way to "let the world know we mean business," and had two studies in hand to try out. A document from Roscoe Hillenkoetter of the CIA, "Memorandum on Psychological Use of the Atomic Bomb in Korea Conflict," dated July 6, recommended asking for UN sanction to use the Bomb as a means of deterring Stalin. A G-3 memo dated the day of the Cabinet meeting was headed, "Utilization of

Atomic Bombardment to Assist in Accomplishment of the US Objectives in South Korea." MacArthur knew of it, as did Ridgway in Washington. A memo the next day from Admiral Arthur Radford, commander of the Pacific Fleet, to his boss in Washington, Admiral Forrest Sherman, predicted that if the situation in Korea became desperate for American troops already involved, Congress and the public would demand the use of atomic weapons.

Major General Charles Bolté, once an aide to Eisenhower in Europe and now operations chief, first opposed sending MacArthur more divisions. He teleconferenced him on July 13 proposing using atomic weapons "in direct support [of] ground combat," thinking in terms of ten to twenty bombs. Conventional low-yield bombs as tactical weapons were still in the experimental stages. Teased by the possibility Bolté raised, MacArthur envisioned a way to keep the Chinese and the Russians from intervening. "I would cut them off in North Korea," he projected. "In Korea I visualize a cul-de-sac. The only passages leading from Manchuria and Vladivostok have many tunnels and bridges. I see here a unique use for the atomic bomb—to strike a blocking blow—which would require a six months repair job. Sweeten up my B-29 force." Bolté had to advise him that conventional air-burst A-Bombs, all that existed at the time, couldn't do the job.

Although the JCS on July 14 recommended that "if the USSR precipitates a general war, United Nations forces should be withdrawn from Korea as rapidly as possible and be deployed for service elsewhere," Hoyt Vandenberg felt that the Soviets would not enter Korea overtly if their territory was not attacked. (No one was thinking of China because North Korea was a Russian client state.) Assuming that atomic bombing could be kept south of the Chinese and Russian frontiers, he promised MacArthur that nuclear-capable FEAF B-29s would be available. On July 31, Top Secret JCS 87570 was cabled to Tokyo authorizing planeloads of the promised goods "in accordance with previously approved long-range plans formulated prior to the Korean incident. . . ." That the bombs were coming confirmed a Korean link, whatever the language employed. "Non-Nuclear components for [10] Atomic Bombs," it went on, "will be placed in storage on Guam. The expected date of completion of the movement is 12 August 1950. Shipment of Nuclear components, requiring seventy-two hours, plus Presidential decision authorizing use[,] would be necessary before Atomic Bombs could be employed." Ten planes from the 9th Bomb Group were readied. Other nuclear-configured aircraft were sent to England to pre-position them for possible war with Russia. The deployment, agreed to with great reluctance by

Britain, was to remind Moscow, without undue provocation, of America's nuclear capability.

When Army Chief of Staff Collins flew to Tokyo late in July he took with him a G-3 study, "Employment of Atomic Bombs Against Military Targets," which suggested possible uses of the Bomb to soften up ports in preparation for amphibious assaults, or against enemy air bases. At the same time a JCS memo to MacArthur recommended "mass air operations against North Korean targets" to "assist future operations" but did not mention nuclear bombs. The memo specified two munitions plants in Pyongyang, three chemical plants in Konan, an oil refinery and railroad yards in Wonsan, and a petroleum storage facility in Najindong. These were trivial objectives for an atomic strike. At that point, MacArthur was well aware that the option to ask for atomic authorization was his. He might have armed bombs in seventy-two hours. Still, the nuclear capability evaporated, for Washington could identify no appropriate targets that were purely North Korean without spillover into Chinese or Soviet territory. The prime sites were the Yalu power plants which MacArthur wanted to bomb, at least conventionally, but they risked the intervention of the Chinese. Besides, international revulsion was anticipated if the Bomb were to be employed under less than desperate circumstances.

On assessing advice from military and civilian staff, Truman had already determined to keep the war limited, if possible, to Korea. Since the JCS and State both still considered Korea only a likely Stalinist diversion for the overrunning of Europe, overextending the U.S. in Asia might permit the Soviets to do what they pleased elsewhere, and the Russians saw all the theatrical gestures and impassioned talk about the Bomb as for domestic U.S. political consumption. In England, old Bernard Shaw, a professed Communist at ninety-four, although no longer sure what that meant, declared during a birthday interview late in July that the Bomb would be "a boomerang, fatal alike to the bomber and his victim." It would be "disused in the next war just as poisoned gas was disused in the last."

Despite second thoughts about using the Bomb in Korea or China, nuclear-configured aircraft left what is now Travis Air Force Base in California for the Pacific on August 3. One of them, with the commander of the strike force aboard, crashed in flames on takeoff. The explosion was huge and widely covered in the American press, but contrary to rumor it was not atomic. The accident cast a pall over the deployment, yet made it all the more obvious to Russian and Chinese intelligence that a nuclear capability was intended for the Far East. Still, Chinese preparation for entry into the war continued without pause.

Before Inchon, while MacArthur's forces were holed up in the Perimeter, the Bomb continued to come up as a solution. Blaming the Soviets for miring the U.S. in Asia, Navy Secretary Francis P. Matthews, a Nebraskan known as the "rowboat secretary" because that accurately delineated his sailing experience, recommended the Bomb. Sufficiently lightweight to be entrusted with little of the Korean War planning, he nevertheless presided over the rapid naval expansion which war appropriations made possible. In Boston on August 25 for the Navy Yard's 150th anniversary, he spoke at the commemoration, recommending that the U.S. pay any price to "compel" world peace, even a preventive nuclear war against Russia. The notion fit in with the domestic mood of aggressive anti-Communism, and Hanson Baldwin in *The New York Times* labeled the idea a "trial balloon," observing that Matthews' boss, Defense Secretary Johnson, had been privately suggesting the same thing.

The State Department criticized the speech, and Truman called Matthews in to give him a firm lecture, stopping short of asking for his resignation. (Looking for something less controversial for the prominent Roman Catholic layman to do, the President eventually named him ambassador to Ireland.)

Less fortunate was Major General Orville A. Anderson, commandant of the Air [Force] War College, who was suspended on September 1 for offering a course on preventive—which meant nuclear—war. Anderson had boasted to an interviewer, "Give me the order to do it and I can break up Russia's five A-bomb nests in a week. . . . And when I went up to Christ—I think I could explain to Him that I had saved Civilization."

With imprudently aggressive talk proliferating, Truman was forced to issue a general public disavowal, declaring, "We do not believe in aggressive or preventive war." In August, nevertheless, prodded by public opinion polls and by Congress, both registering the heating up of anti-Communism as prospects in Korea worsened, Truman asked the Atomic Energy Commission (AEC) and the JCS to consider increasing American nuclear capabilities. On September 6 the President was offered a $14 billion plan to double the existing nuclear potential, from research to production to the acquisition of "essentially all of the foreseeable world supply of uranium ore" outside the Soviet bloc. On September 11 the JCS set "production objectives" anticipating "new types of atomic weapons" from hydrogen bombs to atomic warheads for guided missiles.

The assumption was that having succeeded in breaking the atomic monopoly, the Soviets were moving beyond, to hydrogen. Ironically, the scientist most associated with H-bomb development, Edward Teller, was then in the middle of the anti-Communist frenzy as it was developing in California, where the university Board of Regents had just ordered the dismissal of thirty-one professors who had refused to sign a loyalty oath—the fashionable new test for anti-Communism. Other faculty had resigned in protest, and the chairman of physics at Berkeley deplored publicly that "we cannot now induce a single first-class theoretical physicist to accept a position." Teller had just agreed to go to UCLA but now threatened to renege. Governor Earl Warren thought he found a politically safe solution by applying the loyalty oath to all public employees in California, rather than singling out the professoriat. "So long as we are in conflict with Soviet Russia," he rationalized, "we are in imminent danger of sabotage."

The hostile domestic climate only worsened as Mao's forces after Inchon stealthily began their intervention in Korea. Atomic threats from American sources gave the Chinese additional cause for anxiety. The Bomb was overkill against an air base, but might be employed against major cities in China, sprawling port facilities or massed troops in the field. To reassure local Chinese officials in possible target areas, Mao's government issued a memorandum on October 26, 1950, which argued that a fission bomb was unsuitable for use in Korea. Further, it contended, the U.S. had too few bombs to expend on non-Soviet targets, and China had too many people and too many large cities for atomic bombs to make a difference. And the Americans were unlikely to endanger their own troops by use of the Bomb in combat areas. Officially, the Chinese were not to worry.

With China in the war, State Department planner Paul Nitze brought up the Bomb again. He had been largely responsible for the post-Korea NSC-68 policy document on building American global strength to oppose further Soviet expansion. Truman had approved that pillar of Cold War doctrine in September, and the bomb had a place in it. Both publicly and secretly, it would not go away. To Brigadier General Herbert B. Loper, the Army's atomic energy specialist, Nitze on November 4 raised the question of dropping atomic bombs on Chinese troops that had entered Korea. He was less interested in creating massive casualties than the deterrent effect which the unleashing of nuclear energy would have. Loper persuaded him that the Chinese presented no targets for which current fission weapons would be feasible. Nitze then argued for the Policy Planning Staff that tactical atomic bombardment, impractical with present weaponry, might work against troop concentrations and massed artillery, but "such targets would probably not come about normally" and that "few targets could be created" through action on the ground. "It does not appear that in present circumstances the atomic bomb would be militarily decisive in Korea."

The key words were *in Korea*. With intervention in Korea now public knowledge in China, and propaganda campaigns underway to make it popular, the controlled press was forced to allay the nuclear concerns of the civil population. With proper precautions, the government advised, one could survive an atomic bomb. Besides, newspapers predicted, if the United States launched such an attack, Soviet retaliation in kind would occur. What form that might take was left for the imagination, for the Russians had exploded their first nuclear devices only a year before. They could strike the U.S. only by concealing a nuclear weapon aboard a merchant ship in an American harbor or by sending one airborne, if the device could be made to fit, in a one-way bomber.

Despite the dearth of purely military targets, General Bolté began preparing a new set of contingency plans, each more extreme than any envisaged by MacArthur in Tokyo. In a paper on November 20, Bolté was skeptical that the Chinese could drive "presently committed UN forces from Korea, unless materially assisted by Soviet ground and air power." MacArthur's command, he noted cautiously, "has sufficient forces to successfully hold any line in Korea in the light of circumstances now prevailing."

The same day, having seen Bolté's overconfident assessment, Lawton Collins informed the Joint Chiefs that it was "conceivable that the JCS would be required to present their views [to the President] concerning the use of the atomic bomb in Korea on short notice. It is also conceivable that, in the event of an all-out effort by the Chinese Communists, the use of atomic bombs against troop and materiel concentrations might be the decisive factor in enabling the UN forces to hold a defensive position or to effect [an] early drive to the Manchurian border." He recommended that the possibilities be studied.

Eight days later, on November 28, with the situation on the ground rapidly worsening, the Army plans division suggested an "or else" ultimatum to the Chinese to leave Korea. "The United States should take all necessary steps to assure the capability of prompt use of the atomic bomb against the Chinese Communists as, if, and when directed by the President." It was the day that MacArthur had declared the massive intervention across the Yalu "an entirely new war."

Also on the twenty-eighth, Rear Admiral W. G. Lalor, the JCS secretary, rushed a "priority" request to the Joint Strategic Survey Committee in the

Pentagon. He was worried now about even further Communist pressure. Should the Russians also enter the war, Lalor wanted recommendations on "the possible use of the atomic bomb as a factor to discourage such continued intervention and/or to assist in the evacuation of UN forces from Korea." He asked for specifics on the number of bombs necessary, targets and recommendations about "use, timing, transportation, etc." Lalor also sought comments on the "use of conventional and atomic bombs against China, with or without previous ultimatum." And he wanted the request and the information "very closely guarded."

Two days later, in what was either a press conference fiasco or a deliberately planted question, the President was drawn into a discussion on nuclear weaponry. After a rather dry statement that the United States would remain firm in the face of the new danger from China, Truman opened the floor to questions.

ANTHONY LEVIERO, *The New York Times:* Mr President, will the attacks in Manchuria depend upon action in the United Nations?

TRUMAN: Yes, entirely.

LEVIERO (following up): In other words, if the UN should authorize General MacArthur to go further than he has, he will?

TRUMAN: We will take whatever steps are necessary to meet the military situation, just as we always have.

JACK DOUGHERTY, *New York Daily News:* Will that include the atomic bomb?

TRUMAN: That includes every weapon that we have.

PAUL R. LEACH, *Chicago Daily News:* Mr. President, you said, "every weapon that we have." Does that mean that there is active consideration of the use of the atomic bomb?

TRUMAN: There has always been active consideration of its use. I don't want to see it used. It is a terrible weapon, and it should not be used on innocent men, women and children who have nothing to do with this military aggression [from China]—that happens when it's used.

The questions and responses shifted elsewhere briefly, but Merriman Smith, the veteran reporter for United Press, returned for a clarification of the Bomb matter.

MERRIMAN SMITH: I wonder if we could retrace that reference to the atomic bomb. Did we understand you clearly that the use of the atomic bomb is under active consideration?

TRUMAN: Always has been, Smitty. It's one of our weapons.

ROBERT DIXON, International News Service: Does that mean, Mr. President, use against military objectives or civilians . . . ?

TRUMAN: It is a matter that the military people will have to decide. I am not a military authority that passes on these things.

By this time several pressmen had slipped out to file stories on the Bomb, but the President was not yet out of harm's way. Frank Bourgholtzer of NBC News asked, "Mr. President, you said this depends on United Nations action. Does that mean that we would not use the atomic bomb except on a United Nations authorization?"

Rattled by the insistence on Bomb matters, with the deterioration of MacArthur's front in progress, the worried President made one misstep after another. "No, it does not mean that at all," he explained lamely. "The action against Communist China depends on the action of the United Nations. The military commander in the field will have charge of the use of the weapons, as he always has." MacArthur, it suddenly seemed, had been handed the Bomb by Truman.

Under the Atomic Energy Act, he had forgotten momentarily, only the President could authorize the use of an atomic bomb—not General MacArthur. As a result, only fourteen minutes after the press conference had begun, United Press had a bulletin on its wire:

WASHINGTON NOV. 30 (UP)—PRESIDENT TRUMAN SAID TODAY THAT THE UNITED STATES HAS UNDER CONSIDERATION USE OF THE ATOMIC BOMB IN CONNECTION WITH THE WAR IN KOREA.

A minute later came AP's similar bulletin, and then others. As press secretary Charles Ross ripped off each dispatch from the wire service tickers in his office, he grew more and more alarmed. Once the press conference was over, he quickly met with the President and issued a statement in Truman's name intended to prevent any "misinterpretation":

Consideration of the use of any weapon is always implicit in the very possession of that weapon. However, it should be emphasized that, by law, only the President can authorize the use of the atom bomb, and no such authorization has been given. If and when such authorization should be given, the military commander in the field would have charge of the tactical delivery of the weapon.

It was too late. By then *The New York Times* had reported, "The Truman press statement said the United Nations will fight . . . for justice and world peace, and we will if necessary use the atom bomb."

In the White House preparing a series on the President and his staff for *The New Yorker* was John Hersey, the author, ironically, of *Hiroshima*. He was following the worldwide media frenzy:

> There were glaring headlines in Paris. . . . Big headlines in Finland gave the impression that MacArthur had already received the go-ahead. In Vienna, the story had the lead spot in all the morning papers except the Soviet army sheet. . . . *Volkstimme,* the Communist paper in Vienna, threw in an ingenious invention of its own, declaring that Truman's statement proved that the United States planned to intensify pressure for a Western European army. All the papers in Rome carried sensational headlines. *Il Momento* reported that the Tokyo bomber command was ready to take off with the bomb one hour after Washington gave the order. The Socialist *Avanti* had this headline: "WASHINGTON WILL DISREGARD UNITED NATIONS." The sensible Swedes featured the second, clarifying statement; their newspaper stories made it clear that Truman's statement had been in reply to questions and had been taken out of context. In Poland, the *Kurier Codzienny* headed its story "ATOMIC BOMB PLANS OF TRUMAN, ACHESON & CO." In Moscow, *Tass* put out its own version of the first bulletin: "President Truman has given it to be understood that the ruling circles of the United States are considering the possibility of using the atomic bomb against the Chinese People's Republic if necessary." The *Times of India* ran an editorial under the heading "NO! NO! NO!" The *Indian News Chronicle* spoke of "the immense risk of earning the passionate hatred of the Asian peoples."

From New Delhi, Nehru echoed his press, describing the "wide-spread feeling in Asia that the atomic bomb is a weapon [to be] used only against Asiatics." And even Arab representatives at the United Nations registered similar feelings. The Saudi delegate, particularly wooed by the United States, observed that using the bomb anywhere in Asia would be regarded "as an action of the white race against the colored races"—a rare instance of such self-description from the snobbish Saudis.

If the presidential misstep had really been choreographed, it was without the knowledge of the cautious Charles Ross, who was appalled by Truman's hasty miscalculation and the journalistic irresponsibility and international crisis that followed. Five days later Ross collapsed and died of a heart attack.

Immediately after the news conference, speculation had arisen about MacArthur's atomic intentions in Korea. From Washington, David Lawrence, editor of the conservative-leaning *U.S. News & World Report*, fired off fifteen questions to the general. Number twelve was, "Nine out of ten persons on the street here and throughout the country are asking why [the] atom bomb is not being used. Can anything be said as to the effectiveness or ineffectiveness of [the] bomb in the type of operations in which you are now engaged?"

Warily, MacArthur responded on December 1, "My comment inappropriate at this time."

By coincidence, on the very day of the press conference but before Truman had spoken, General Stratemeyer in Tokyo had sent a cable to Hoyt Vandenberg requesting that the Strategic Air Command be "prepared to dispatch without delay medium bomb groups to the Far East. . . . This augmentation should include atomic capabilities." MacArthur's staff was confronting yet again the possibility of hastily evacuating Korea or of facing a humiliating armistice.

At 8:30 a.m. the next day in Washington, a high-level meeting that included just about every policymaker but the President convened in the JCS conference room in the Pentagon. Bradley worried whether MacArthur could hold at any point in North Korea, and whether Chinese airpower would have to be interdicted so that troops could withdraw safely. "To do so might draw in the Soviet air [force]. If this is true, we might have to defer striking."

Collins supported Bradley. "If we hit back, it is a strong provocation of the Chinese and may possibly bring in Soviet air and even submarines." (Subs could raise hell with resupply or evacuation.) "The only chance then left to save us is the use or the threat of use of the A-Bomb. We should therefore hold back from bombing in China even if that means that our ground forces must take some punishment from the air." He was beginning to think that Korea "was not worth a nickel."

"If we do hit back," Acheson agreed, "it may bring in Russian air support of the Chinese and we would go from the frying pan into the fire."

If that situation developed, Bedell Smith and Bradley predicted, "We would have to evacuate [Korea] and probably would be engaged in war [with Russia]." At that, Collins repeated his contention that the U.S. would have to "consider the threat or the use of the A-bomb. It would [otherwise] be very difficult to get our troops out. . . ."

Later in the day, Bernard Baruch, long a White House adviser on military and atomic matters, visited Defense Secretary Marshall to press on him the feeling "in the country, in view of what is regarded as a very desperate situation, for the use of the atom bomb." Marshall replied diplomatically that he didn't think it would "do any good in the circumstances," and questioned what it could "be dropped on." Baruch agreed that the Bomb should be used only where it could be employed effectively.

Baruch had known when he saw Marshall that Prime Minister Attlee would panic as soon as the nuclear option had resurfaced, even if inadvertently. The veteran adviser of governments, who had counseled Wilson in World War I and Roosevelt in World War II, understood that Attlee, who had praised MacArthur's Inchon operation as brilliant, claimed to speak for all UN members supporting the war, yet he also had a private agenda. Britain was bent upon protecting its international trade, its colonial anachronisms. Attlee and others had proposed recognizing facts by awarding China's UN seat to Mao and condoning a future takeover of Formosa. To Britain that was a far more reasonable solution than having the untrustworthy MacArthur on the rim of Asia with his finger on the nuclear trigger.

Across the world, K. M. Panikkar, Indian ambassador to China and Mao's prime conduit to the West (Dean Acheson referred to him archly as "Pannicker"), interpreted the Truman gaffe as a sly announcement "that he was thinking of using the atom bomb in Korea. The Chinese," he reported, "were totally unmoved by this threat. . . . The propaganda against American aggression was stepped up." Marshall scoffed at the Nehru-Panikkar claims of neutrality as an "Indian rope trick."

While atomic talk was swirling about Washington, and Attlee was flying to the U.S., Curtis LeMay, SAC chief and former commander of the 20th Air Force, which had flown the Bomb over Hiroshima and Nagasaki, responded to Stratemeyer. Strategic Air Command understanding, said LeMay, had been that nuclear weapons would not be used except during "an overall atomic campaign against China." If the situation had changed, he wanted to be in on the deployment. He and his men, he boasted, were the only ones with "intimate knowledge" of the delivery of atomic bombs.

Preparing on December 3 for Attlee's hurried visit, State Department officials reminded the Joint Chiefs of Staff of "the rather widespread British distrust of General MacArthur and the fear of political decisions he may make based on military necessity. Bearing on this is the British belief in the [establishment of a] buffer area and their stand against attacks across the

Yalu. Also involved is the fear of the effect on Asiatics of use of the Atomic Bomb or even open consideration of its use." British concerns, Acheson went on, were "very sincere." MacArthur had already established a history of flouting orders.

In the agonized preparatory State-Defense conference in the JCS War Room in the Pentagon, General Ridgway sat impatiently during the review of the situation, seeing "no one apparently willing to issue a flat order to the Far East Commander to correct a state of affairs that was rapidly going from bad to disastrous. Yet the responsibility and the authority clearly resided right there in the room." He spoke up, but Vandenberg dismissed the idea of sending MacArthur further orders. "What good would that do? He wouldn't obey the orders."

Ridgway exploded. "You can relieve any commander who won't obey orders, can't you?" The meeting ended with no decision about MacArthur except for sending Collins back to Tokyo to consult with him. Yet the conferees did agree that Truman should make no commitment to Attlee restricting American freedom of action on deployment of the Bomb.

Attlee arrived in Washington on December 4 in the midst of what would have been a hectic week even without his visit. To his suggestion that Formosa be abandoned to Mao—a political impossibility in the United States—Truman and Marshall observed cautiously that while the island was of no military importance, it would become a serious liability in the possession of an enemy. In Korea, Truman reminded Attlee, Mao's Chinese had become exactly that. As for the nuclear threat, the President issued a statement to mollify Attlee and his constituency that he hoped "world conditions would never call for use of the atomic bomb." He also proposed "to keep the Prime Minister at all times informed of developments which might bring about a change in the situation." He was not giving in to entreaties that the Bomb be declared off-limits. In extreme circumstances, it might have to be used. But Truman realized that if under inauspicious conditions for its employment in Korea it failed to produce decisive results, it would lose credibility as a Cold War deterrent.

Concern about diminishing the American atomic stockpile was never in the strategic equation. The 292 bombs that the U.S. possessed when the Korean War began in June were being supplemented weekly, while the Soviets had at best ten to twenty bombs by the end of 1950. Nevertheless, that was enough to cause widespread anxiety.

General Collins was then back in Tokyo, this time with Air Force intelligence chief General Charles Cabell, a vigorous proponent of atomic weapons. They found MacArthur confident that he could stabilize what he admitted was a poor situation. He even advised postponing any decisions on nuclear deployment until he knew whether the atomic option would be needed to cover a total withdrawal from Korea. Still, the combination of Cabell's being brought along to Japan and Truman's stonewalling Attlee about the Bomb emboldened MacArthur to ask for the weapon. As a matter of prudence, since the atomic-configured aircraft from California had already returned home, he requested on December 9 that the Pentagon grant him a field commander's discretion to employ nuclear weapons as necessary. He wanted them stockpiled in Okinawa, within his Japanese jurisdiction.

Despite that, when queried by the Joint Chiefs later in the month about how he would respond to Soviet intervention, or even more massive Chinese intervention, intended to drive reeling UN troops completely from Korea, MacArthur again refused to consider using the Bomb. It would be practical, he thought, *only* to prevent or protect the ultimate fallback. The war might have to be widened, he suggested, to forestall termination of his mission.

Even Harry Truman agreed about the risk of loss of face in Asia, especially in Japan. With the repercussions on the Japanese of defeat in Korea in mind, MacArthur on December 24 proposed to "blockade the coast of China, destroy through naval gunfire and air bombardment China's industrial capacity to wage war," and "release existing restrictions upon the Formosan garrison . . . possibly leading to counter-invasion against vulnerable areas of the Chinese mainland." He also sent the Pentagon a list of what he described as "retardation targets" for which he wanted thirty-four atomic bombs. Four were (in Paul Nitze fashion) to drop on Chinese troop masses and four were for "critical concentrations of enemy air power." Since no such airfields existed in Korea, the bombs had to be meant for Manchuria.* Much later, in talking to Eisenhower (on December 17, 1952) about ending the war, MacArthur explained where he thought nuclear bombs would have done the most good. "I would have dropped between 30 and 50 atomic

---

*A secret study commissioned by the Army at the Johns Hopkins University Operations Research Office concluded that thirty-four Bombs would be inadequate to impede the estimated 120 Chinese divisions the Communists could put in the field, and that 360 would be needed to inflict 30 percent casualties. Since only twenty-six Chinese divisions were estimated to have crossed into Korea by then, it was possible, according to the study, to stabilize a defensive line of seventy-five miles with radiation effect using only fifteen bombs, but no mention was made of the consequences upon friendly troops.

bombs . . . strung across the neck of Manchuria" and "spread behind us—from the Sea of Japan to the Yellow Sea—a belt of radioactive cobalt. . . . For at least 60 years there could have been no land invasion of Korea from the north." The Russians, he claimed, would have been intimidated by the boldness of the act into doing nothing.

Cobalt 60, from the reprocessing of plutonium, would have possessed such powerful radioactivity as to endanger populations remote from the drop zone. But MacArthur's suggestion was not science fiction. The Joint Chiefs of Staff had already discussed a radioactive *cordon sanitaire* sown north of the Manchurian border. It had even been proposed in Congress by Representative (later Senator) Albert Gore Sr., of Tennessee, a member of the Joint Committee on Atomic Energy who had probably received the details from a physicist at the Oak Ridge atomic facility in his home state. Since Korea had become "a meat grinder of American manhood," Gore felt that it would be "morally justifiable under the circumstances" to make any Communist soldier who crossed the radioactive "neutral zone" risk "certain death or slow deformity." Ignored were the potential ill effects on the soldiers or airmen who would have to deliver the "hot" waste, or what means might be employed by the enemy to fly over the radioactivity, or even to bridge it. The proposal, nevertheless, remains linked to MacArthur, who had merely borrowed it in frustration. While recognizing its impossibility, he would keep probing for "field" authority, in an emergency, to deploy the Bomb. Yet the threat of nuclear thunderbolts thereafter would emanate less from MacArthur than from Washington.

14

Korea for Christmas

By December 3, Walton Walker had succeeded in withdrawing most of his troops to an unstable front north of Pyongyang. Contact with the Chinese was minimal, but that did not diminish the haste of the pullback. Lieutenant Carl Bernard's rifleman Ole John E. recalled the time as "a lot of C rations from bent cans, bent from air drops because we were cut off from conventional means of supply. Sure we killed an ox now and then; we had to have a bite to eat, even if it meant wrapping up the meat in a couple of ponchos and transporting them in a jeep trailer. After all, the weather kept the meat frozen and in a good state of preservation."

The trestle bridge over the Imjin River at Pyongyang was guarded during the retreat by a company led by Lieutenant Sam Walker. Taking a little time off, he jeeped to General Walker's command van and knocked on the door. "Happy birthday, Dad," he greeted his father, who had made it to sixty-one. But it was a melancholy day. Backtracking continued. American supply and ammunition dumps in the area were being put to the torch. Whatever couldn't be moved south had to be denied to the Chinese. Neither Walker nor MacArthur felt that they could hold at the neck of Korea, and might not even be able to hold at Seoul. MacArthur, who wasn't there, radioed to a shocked Pentagon that they were "facing the entire Chinese nation in an undeclared war and unless some positive and immediate action is taken, hope for success cannot be justified and speedy attrition leading to final destruction can reasonably be contemplated." At the Paris embassy, veteran diplomat and Soviet expert Charles (Chip) Bohlen commented to Cy

Sulzberger, making his journalistic rounds, that MacArthur was "caught with his pants down and disregards the basic military assumption that the enemy will always do what he appears capable of doing; and it was evident from the last bloody nose we received in Korea from the Chinese a few weeks ago that they were capable of plenty."

MacArthur's frantic December 3 message to the JCS rejected a defense line at the waist of Korea. It was already too late for that "because of the numerical weakness of our forces as considered in connection with the distances involved." Each of his seven American divisions, he argued, implicitly discounting the unreliable ROKs, would have a front of twenty miles to defend "against greatly superior numbers of an enemy whose greatest strength is a potential for night infiltration through rugged terrain." It would "invite penetration with resultant envelopment and piecemeal destruction." Well below the waist by then, the Eighth Army was rushing to positions which Walker hoped to hold on the line of the Imjin River barely twenty miles above Seoul.

The day before, MacArthur had sent his chief subordinates, Doyle Hickey and Edwin Wright, to confer with Walker, and learned of the decision to evacuate Pyongyang. Without a veto from MacArthur and the fallback already in progress, Walker ordered evacuation to begin on December 4. Lieutenant Colonel Paul Freeman of the 23rd Infantry recalled raging to his executive officer bitterly, "Look around here. This is a sight that hasn't been seen for hundreds of years—the men of a whole United States army fleeing from a battlefield, abandoning their wounded, running for their lives."

A dispatch in the *New York Herald Tribune* on December 2 reported embarrassingly, "Reporters have been wandering like lost souls for the last few days looking for front lines." Eighth Army command posts seemed the most mobile locations in Korea, with commanders of every rank fleeing not from contacts with the enemy or warnings based on ground reconnaissance but from G-2 red-marked maps imagining where the enemy was or would be. British Brigadier Basil A. Coad would write scornfully of "a 132-mile withdrawal from a position 35 miles north of Pyongyang, for, as far as we could see, no apparent reason other than some ominous red arrows marked on the operational maps, showing that the whole of the UN forces were about to be encircled."

Visiting Korea at the time, British General Leslie Mansergh sent a secret evaluation of the situation to his chiefs of staff in London about the American "lack of determination and their inability . . . to stand and fight. . . .

British troops, although sympathetic to the South Koreans in their adversity, despise them and are not interested in this civil war. . . . I would judge the American morale as low, and in some units thoroughly bad." He reminded his chiefs that many of the Americans in uniform had joined in peacetime "for the purpose of getting a cheap [GI Bill] education after their service and . . . never expected to fight. Their training is quite unsuited . . . and, in spite of lessons learnt, they will not get clear of their vehicles. . . . Their rations, supplies, and welfare stores are on such a scale as to be comic if they were not such a serious handicap to battle."

Mansergh lauded the gunners in American artillery units, but found the infantry untrained for defense, especially against infiltration, quick to overestimate the enemy and "feel[ing] very naked when anybody threatens their flank or rear." He excoriated their leadership. "At night, main headquarters blazed like gin palaces. . . . Roadblocks, car parks, [supply] dumps etc. were as crowded as Hampstead Heath on a bank holiday."

Fortunately for the Eighth Army, Chinese forces were rapidly approaching exhaustion, their supplies of food and ammunition now little more than what Walker's troops had abandoned. Had MacArthur ordered Walker to make a stand above Pyongyang, the outcome of the war might have been far different. Even from the distance of the Dai Ichi, however, it was obvious that Walker had lost control of his army. Still, MacArthur hung on to Walker, although without any confidence. When Mansergh met the shaken Supreme Commander in Tokyo at the time the reasons seemed clear. "He appeared to be much older than his seventy years. . . . Signs of nerves and strain were apparent. . . . When he emphasized the combined efforts and successes of all front-line troops in standing shoulder to shoulder, it occurred to me that he could not have been fully in the picture."

A week earlier MacArthur had been pondering which units to send home by Christmas. His misplaced confidence was gone. On the telephone from Seoul to a rewrite man in New York, *Herald Tribune* correspondent Homer Bigart was scathing. On November 28 he had written acidly that the decision to launch an offensive "north of the peninsula's narrow neck" had immediately proved catastrophic. Now he renewed his charges:

Already some thoughtful officers are beginning to question the sanity of recent military decisions which may not have caused, but which certainly accelerated, this crisis. The most questionable decision of the last few weeks was MacArthur's abortive offensive. Before the offensive was launched, it was noted by some observers that any attempt to push beyond the neck of the peninsula was unsound—even if the Communists withdrew. To fan out on a 700 mile frontier made no sense. It was an invitation to disaster.

While EUSAK, in much more disorder than acknowledged, fled the cold and the unknown, troops in X Corps were in direct contact with the enemy in temperatures that almost made withdrawal too numbing to attempt. "Everything was frozen," Navy Lieutenant Commander Chester M. Lessenden, with the 5th Marines, told Keyes Beech. Lessenden ran the Marine hospital tent at Yudam-ni, where rifle fire had punched holes in the canvas and the overflow wounded were placed outside under tarpaulins. "Plasma froze and the bottles broke. We couldn't use plasma because it wouldn't go into solution and the tubes would clog up with particles. We couldn't change dressings because we had to work with gloves on to keep our hands from freezing. We couldn't cut a man's clothes off to get to a wound because he would freeze to death. Actually, a man was often better off if we left him alone. Did you ever try to stuff a wounded man into a sleeping bag?"

Pfc. Win Scott remembered the Marine order, "When you come off the hill, carry your dead with you." Once wounded, he "could feel liquid," and thought he'd be one of them. "Corpsman!" he yelled, and yelled again. Finally a Marine came over the ridge and promised to find a medic. "Doc," said Scott, "give me a shot." The corpsman carried the morphine Syrettes in his mouth to keep them from freezing. Cutting a slit in Scott's clothes, he punched in the morphine, placed Scott on his poncho and dragged him down the hill. In the hospital tent later, "I thought I was in heaven. My God, they even had a stove in there."

Many wounded died, but in the intense cold they died quickly. "We were grateful for what the cold had done to these bodies," recalled Robert Tyack, a British Marine, unsentimentally. "You were looking at a chunk of frozen meat, rather than a messy, stinking corpse." American Pfc. John Bishop remembered seeing "a six-by truck full of frozen bodies waiting to move out. It looked like a load of meat going to market. I saw a Marine strapped over the barrel of a howitzer. He was covered by a poncho, all but his stiff legs. It reminded me of a deer carcass tied to the top of a car." Major General Clark Ruffner, Almond's deputy commander, was not pleased by the priority given the dead, when transport space should be held for the wounded. O. P. Smith reminded him that Marines revered their dead and, if at all possible, would not leave them "in a desolate village in northeastern

Korea which we were about to evacuate." Smith merely "slipped the bodies in, and it was very simple—they were frozen stiff. . . ."

On a flying visit himself, Almond tried to sympathize with Marines huddled in frost-covered parkas, in which they slept with their M1s to keep them from freezing. He confided that he wore a dental plate, and "When I got up this morning, there was a film of ice on the glass by my bed."

"That's too fucking bad, General," said a bedless Marine from under his muffler.

When severe frostbite cases were being evacuated to gleaming state-of-the-art hospitals in Japan, MacArthur's office blamed the glut of casualties on "lack of leadership." The slap at the Marines made the bony, white-haired Smith "mad as a hatter." He had his fill, he griped, of 2nd Division malingerers who had thrown away their weapons and feigned injuries to get out. "Even Genghis Khan," he would say, "wouldn't have tried Korea in the winter." Smith sent a bitter message to Marine commandant Clifton Cates:

> Here I have just given a Silver Star to a sergeant who pulled off his mitten in order to heave a grenade, and he got frostbitten fingers. Are you going to court-martial that man for not taking proper precautions against frostbite? Are you going to court-martial his battalion commander, his regimental commander, his division commander?

After the war Smith recalled MacArthur's surrogate, Ned Almond, flying in to Hagaru "a couple of times. The first time he came he was full of beans—wanted our schedule for rescuing T[ask] F[orce] Faith." Earlier—before it had been overrun by white-clad Chinese—Almond had been at Lieutenant Colonel Don Faith's command post and given him a Silver Star for heroism. Faith had been polite about it, but once Almond was airborne, Staff Sergeant Chester Barr "saw Colonel Faith rip the medal off his parka and throw it on the ground." As commander of the 3rd Battalion, 31st Infantry, moving up the east shore of Chosin, Faith explained that his advance units had been battered and that he had lost the high ground, as had the 5th and 7th Marines farther north. Almond pulled a map from his leather case and unfolded it on the hood of a jeep. The enemy, he claimed, was "nothing more than remnants of Chinese divisions fleeing north. We're still attacking and we're going all the way to the Yalu." The next day, Faith's regimental commander, Colonel Allan MacLean, directed the 31st to withdraw to the south. It was near dawn and snowing heavily. Faith ordered all vital parts removed from abandoned vehicles and trucks loaded with wounded. A queue of sixty trucks and jeeps was crawling downhill when MacLean jumped off his jeep to check a reported roadblock and ran into an ambush. The Chinese held the lower end of a bridge over a reservoir inlet. In a firefight MacLean fell several times on the icy bridge, but picked himself up each time and went forward. None of his men knew whether he had been wounded—only that several Chinese pulled him out of sight.

After an exchange of sick and wounded POWs in 1953, a former prisoner reported that MacLean had died of his wounds on the fourth day of a march of captives north toward a prison camp. Task Force MacLean became Task Force Faith until Don Faith, too, was killed running a roadblock toward Hagaru, four miles too far. His unit held out for eighty hours in subzero weather, disintegrating under relentless grenade attacks. Faith would get another medal, posthumously—a Medal of Honor. Only 1,050 survivors of the original MacLean-Faith force of 2,500 would be found alive. Among them was a platoon led by Private Glenn J. Finrock, who had tried to get the shot-up truck in which Faith was found started again. After failing, and trudging away, they were captured on the ice by Chinese soldiers who bandaged their wounds, gave them shots of morphine, held them a few days until they were mobile, then freed them to walk toward Hagaru. It was a rare act of chivalry in a mean climate and a mean war.

Three hundred of the dead, including Faith, had been found in abandoned task force vehicles. The Chinese considered truck drivers special targets, as they knew that GIs moved on wheels. Foot soldiers considered volunteering to drive a "six-by" as a form of suicide. In the snow and ice, many vehicles became coffins.

Emboldened that they had the Americans on the run, the Chinese now materialized by day as well as night, partly camouflaged by their quilted white uniforms. Their discipline, whether under fire from the ground or the air, was complete and awed Americans. A tactical air controller on the ground was heard asking a Marine pilot by radio, when it was difficult to see anything, "What'n hell [are] you guys shooting at?"

"You won't believe this," the pilot reported. "We've got Chinese walking five abreast. We're throwing everything we got in the cockpit at them and they won't break. They will not break ranks. Almost out of fuel, but we'll be back." The gull-winged Corsairs were almost the only source of heat in the icy reservoir area. "One of the craziest sights," Pfc. Francis Killeen remembered, "was to stand on a mountaintop and look down at Corsairs making strikes against the enemy. The place looked like one gigantic Christmas card, except most of it was on fire. You could watch this speck move down, then the orange glow of a napalm bomb. . . . Often we led them in with tracers."

Once Killeen's unit passed "all these dead Chinese—I mean hundreds—and their quilted uniforms were still smoldering." But sometimes the canisters of jellied gasoline fell too close. Bob Hammond "could tell immediately" that a Corsair attempting to blast a path for trapped Americans was "coming down short" as the Marine pilot dropped his napalm tanks, which were "going to hit our guys up front. Many others saw it too, and we all started yelling, 'Watch out! Watch out! Napalm!' but there were only seconds to react, and when the stuff hit, there was a tremendous ball of fire that rolled up into the air, and then I saw about 8 guys running away, their whole bodies engulfed in flames that must have been 15 feet high. I think some of them were shot by their buddies, for there was no saving any of them." Pfc. James Ransone Jr. of Task Force Faith just missed incineration. "Men all around me were burned. They lay rolling in the snow. Men I knew, marched and fought with, begged me to shoot them. It was terrible. Where the napalm had burned the skin to a crisp, it would be peeled back from the face, arms, legs. It looked as though the skin was curled like fried potato chips. Men begged to be shot. I couldn't. The medics arrived and did what they could. It wasn't much." In military euphemism they were casualties of friendly fire.

Unfriendly napalm was no less a horror. Two Chinese who survived an attack and were taken prisoner were known as No Face and Half-Face. They somehow lived through captivity and were repatriated back to their villages.

Few small-scale episodes in the useless Chosin venture symbolized the waste of wrongheaded war more than the unlucky downing of a Corsair late on December 4. Scouting potential targets in the mountainous terrain about ten miles behind enemy lines, Lieutenant Jesse Brown was hit by Chinese fire at too low an altitude for him to bail out. He was the Navy's first black pilot. Looking down from his accompanying Corsair, which required real flying skill, Lieutenant Thomas Hudner could see that Brown was still alive, his leg caught in the twisted fuselage.

Hudner radioed for a rescue helicopter, but, concerned that Brown's smoking aircraft might explode, he crash-landed his own plane nearby into the snow. Brown's leg was mangled; he was drifting in and out of consciousness. Wedged in the wreckage, he could not be extricated by a single pair of frostbitten hands. Darkness loomed; the temperature dropped well below zero as Hudner worked frantically to peel away what he could of the plane from Brown's legs, yet he could get no footing in the deep snow. The Marine helicopter finally arrived and clattered down. Lifting off would not be easy. The pilot, Lieutenant Charles Ward, struggled to help Hudner for nearly an hour, but Brown was near death and removing him seemed hopeless. Finally Hudner conceded to Ward that whether or not the Chinese nearby materialized, if they didn't get airborne soon, the chopper's primitive night navigational equipment would be worthless and there would be three bodies on the mountain instead of one. "I'm sure," Hudner recalled of Brown forty-seven years later, "that he died within a few moments of the time we left." They would not make it back to their carrier for three days. The futile reconnaissance had cost a pilot and two planes.

In the first days of December, Chinese attacks slowed, and the airlifting of wounded and dead began. Overloaded C-47s struggled to get airborne from too-short runways. The lone strip bulldozed by Marine engineers at Hagaru was 2,900 feet long and fifty feet wide, less than half the length the rule book decreed was permissible at that elevation. But there was neither more space nor more time. Casualties had to be evacuated, and troops fighting their way south from Yudam-ni would bring more wounded and frostbitten men. Loaded with twenty-four wounded, the first C-47 strained to get enough lift to clear the mountains. Three more followed. One, overloaded, had to be dragged off and abandoned when its landing gear collapsed. Yet regular runs to Yonpo air base brought medical supplies and even 537 Marines recovered from wounds and returning to duty. When the last workhorse C-47 lifted off by nightfall on December 5, 4,312 men had been flown out—3,150 Marines, 1,137 soldiers and 25 British marines.

Despite his initial skepticism about the Hagaru airstrip, Almond had planned to shift X Corps headquarters there for the move farther north. Now his engineer company and signal platoon trucked there for the work had to become infantrymen in order to get out.

The Chinese divisions, now almost quiescent, had suffered crippling losses. They needed to regroup and to be reprovisioned. Many were weak from hunger and exposure. Attacking largely at night to evade American aircraft and artillery, they had suffered massive losses when fighting into daylight. Their quilted uniforms retained moisture as well as heat, and froze. "Dazed" also by the cold, Ray Davis encountered an enemy example when a big Marine sergeant called to him one night on a snowy ridge, "Come with me, Colonel, I wanna show you something." The sergeant pulled out of a depression in the snow "a solid chunk of ice that was a Chinese soldier." Davis asked, "Is he dead?"

"No, sir," the sergeant said, " his eyes are moving." In the area, dug into holes, were a half-dozen more bodies, frozen solid and very dead. It had been an enemy outpost. Pfc. Ransone had found a much more live Chinese soldier in an icy foxhole. "He dropped his gun and raised his hands. Then he put one of his hands inside his quilted jacket. I watched close, afraid he'd have a pistol there. He slowly took out a small wallet and handed it to me. Inside I found a picture of a woman and child. I guess it was his family. I thought I would have done the same thing to keep from being killed."

Bob Hammond called the cold "unbearable," but survivors bore the unbearable and improvised. Staying alive was a full-time occupation. "My feet are numb, and I took my boots off to massage them and try to get some circulation going, but I cannot get the left boot back on. The foot is too swollen, so Clyde McElroy and Doyle Smith, of my squad, take me to where we've got all the bodies lined up in the snow. We pick out the bodies with the biggest pairs of feet and the three of us spend twenty minutes trying to get them boots off." Since their frozen fingers failed them, and more exposure could lead to frostbite, "We finally tie a C-ration box around the 3 socks I've got on, and let it go at that. It lasts a couple of days." (One alternative for the immobile was to wrap a sandbag, or part of one, around the feet and lower legs.) A twenty-year-old Marine from Rhode Island, Conrad Johnson, remembered of his frostbitten buddies, "They had elephant feet."

C-119 Flying Boxcars parachuted in 372 tons of ammunition, gasoline and rations, "the margin necessary," said O. P. Smith, to keep going, but some chutes drifted toward the Chinese and provided the enemy with a pre-Christmas bonus. Overhead, whenever the weather lifted, fighters from carriers and southern air bases appeared overhead to help shepherd the exhausted Marines, many of them walking wounded, from Yudam-ni down the reservoir tracks toward isolated Hagaru. On December 5, Maggie Higgins hitched there on a plane from Hungnam, where a flotilla was gathering to evacuate X Corps. She had just heard on Chinese radio the prediction that "The annihilation of the . . . First Marine Division is only a matter of time," and in Hagaru, where the snow lashed hard at the troops, it seemed that the Chinese might not even be needed for the task. At daylight Lieutenant Colonel Ray Murray of the 5th Regiment was briefing his officers, "We advance to the rear. Those are division orders."

Maggie had not seen Murray since the heady days of Inchon. He was briefing the haggard officers who had already withdrawn with difficulty from Yudam-ni, to the north. It was not a retreat, he explained, because when one is surrounded, there is no rear. "This is an assault in another direction [for] there are . . . Chinese blocking our path to the sea. . . . But we're going to get out of here." He offered any who wanted air evacuation to apply by going "lame"—and expected no "takers." Maggie found that they "had the dazed air of men who have accepted death and then found themselves alive after all."

Not all, however, were dazed. Some openly gawked at the only comely correspondent in Korea, who—despite layers of winter gear—was clearly a young woman. "My god!" thought Corporal Roy Pearl. "I hadn't seen one of those in months." Aggressively interviewing those she could, she took out her notepad and approached a stretcher case in pain from shrapnel wounds in the stomach. What was the toughest thing, Maggie asked, that he had to contend with in the fighting so far? Since the answer was obvious, the Marine thought it over, then answered gamely, "The toughest thing is getting three inches of dick out of six inches of clothing when I have to take a leak." Without any visible reaction, Higgins moved over to the next stretcher.

Although she wanted to cover the operation as it played out, O. P. Smith ruled that it was too hazardous and reminded her that he had let her come on condition she left the perimeter by nightfall. Lewis Puller escorted her to a C-47 where visiting Marine general Lem Shepherd was waiting to board. "This is the biggest story of the war," she pleaded vainly to Shepherd. "I don't want to miss it, General."

It was a matter of pride to Maggie that she make the march with the troops. "I had been asked by a company of the 5th Marines, with whom I had made the landing at Inchon, to walk out with them." After the burial of the last dead, wrapped in their ponchos, because there was no space for their bodies on the last planes out, she began the trek down the snow-swept slopes, although General Smith, in "a strong seizure of chivalry," insisted that it was too dangerous.

"I walked down the mountain anyway," she wrote, "at least a good half the way," before Smith insisted that he had let her come on the condition that she leave the perimeter by nightfall. She flew out from the Koto-ri strip with General Lem Shepherd and would send her story from Hungnam. As their plane took off at twilight, it came under Chinese fire. "My God, Maggie," said Shepherd as they watched tracer bullets reach out toward them, "won't it be awful if the two of us are found crashed together?"

"It is now an open secret," Maggie Higgins would write in a book published the following spring, "that the Marines believe that faulty generalship was partly responsible for the extent of their entrapment. The Marines were a part of the 10th Corps and so were subject to . . . army orders." Without naming names, it was obvious that she was targeting Almond. "Personally," she had already confessed in the book, "I have the highest respect and a deep sense of loyalty toward General MacArthur," and she pointed to his "selflessness" which went "beyond personal ambition." Writing while he was still in command, she ascribed his "miscalculations" to the legend of infallibility "built up assiduously by his aides." Even so, she defended him on the premise that "No amount of military genius could have prevented the Chinese from hurling us back a considerable distance . . . once they chose to strike." Why the Marines were there at all, to be hurled back, had to be some underling's bad advice to the chief.

The anxious march south to Koto-ri and, eventually, Hungnam, would begin at daybreak on December 6 in a frozen fog. A night of saturation shelling by 155s had softened the Chinese while disposing of surplus ordnance. Captain Robert E. Drake's 31st Tank Company was among the last units out of Hagaru, after what was left of the town was set ablaze. Through the smoke they watched hungry Chinese soldiers far less interested in the Marine rear guard and the miles-long column stretching toward Koto-ri than in burrowing into the burning debris for food.

Only forty Marines remained in Company G, which had taken the Capitol dome in Seoul two months before. They were exhausted, hungry and suffering from the subzero cold. "We are in a hell of a mess," Lieutenant Charles Mize recalled telling his men. "But you and I together have gone through many battles. We've always done the job, I know we can do it again." Marine artillery was to proceed about five miles forward to protect the line of march. Marine Carl Youngdale remembered "this one kid," a clerk in better times, who was ordered to report to a sergeant in "that hole." He found "this great big guy who had a great big beard," a machine gunner, who instructed him, "Son, all you have to do is, when the shit hits the fan, start opening up those ammunition boxes. Now, I'm going to take a nap, and when you see something out there that needs to be taken care of, you wake me. But don't you wake me unless there is something out there."

The cold weather, recalled Youngdale, was "our ally," because the Chinese wore tennis shoes. When they walked, "it sounded like somebody walking with ice cubes. Their feet were just simply frozen." Most "were not interested in following us as much as they were in getting warm, and getting food," but at first the withdrawal stalled when the Chinese opened fire from high ground. A tank and two trucks carrying wounded were hit before the hills on either side of the narrow road were cleared. The two columns were attacked again in mid-afternoon, and Corsair fighters were called in, leading to a rare surrender. Used to infiltrating in darkness, a Chinese unit of more than two hundred gave themselves up in the waning daylight to a Marine platoon which had no way to hold them. Disarmed and expecting to be shot, the Chinese were turned loose, and very likely joined a much larger force moving down to attack again after nightfall. It was a long eleven miles to Koto-ri, itself only a way station to the coast.

At Hamhung, Maggie rode aboard a weapons carrier to the base of the mountain, to await the Marines. "The frost and wind, howling through the narrow pass, were almost as deadly as the enemy. Bumper to bumper, trucks, half-tracks, and bulldozers slipped and scraped down the mountain. Half a dozen vehicles skidded and careened off the road. Mortars lobbed in, and sometimes the convoy had to stop for hours while engineers filled in the holes. It was a struggle to keep from freezing. . . ."

By then Lawton Collins, who had met with MacArthur in Tokyo, had flown to Seoul. Walker was evacuating Pyongyang. When Walker seemed uncertain that he could hold any line above the 38th parallel Collins suggested planning a perimeter around the symbolically crucial Seoul-Inchon area. Leven C. Allen, the EUSAK chief of staff, remembered Walker insisting that he would do it only under a direct order. Obviously shaken, he was more interested in having "specific places in Japan set aside for the Eighth Army if it evacuated Korea." He had just received from MacArthur CINCFE Plan No. 203 (December 6, 1950), thirty-eight sheets detailing "the orderly withdrawal" of all UN forces and equipment from Korea to Japan, including ROK troops and even enemy prisoners of war, "due to pressure from superior forces."

After visiting the I Corps and the 25th Division command posts for briefings, Collins met with reporters at Kimpo and announced, with far more confidence than he felt, "I think the Eighth Army can take care of itself." MacArthur had assured Collins (all the while preparing his evacuation plan) that EUSAK could hold a front well above the 38th parallel, but Walker seemed uncertain that anything other than distant disengagement could save his forces. He had more wheels than the Chinese, and hoped to outrun them until their supply lines were stretched and vulnerable. That meant denying the Communists abandoned American equipment and supplies. Yet both Walker and Almond operated as if everything destroyed was replaceable from MacArthur's endless stockpile in Japan and line of credit in the U.S. Almond and Smith always had something to argue about. When Almond advised abandoning vehicles and guns once rendered unusable, Smith saw the practice as dishonorable and contrary to good order. "Don't worry about your equipment," said Almond impatiently on his final flying visit to Hagaru; "once you get back we'll replace it all." (Dai Ichi policy assumed that MacArthur could get what he wanted from the bottomless resources east of San Francisco.)

"I'm not going to do that," Smith snapped. "This is the equipment we fight with."

"OK," said Almond. "I just wanted you to know that we would replace it."

Once Almond was airborne for another briefing, Smith explained to Colonel Alpha Bowser, his operations officer, "This guy is a maniac. He's nuts. I can't believe he is saying these things."

Almond's flight from Koto-ri in his familiar L-5 was to meet General Collins in Hamhung. Exasperated by the confusion and anxiety in the west, Collins was more confident after seeing the disciplined organization in the east, even though it was organized for withdrawal. With Almond, he visited the headquarters of the 3rd and 7th Divisions, and then flew up the Marines' hazardous withdrawal route only as far as Sudong, a village halfway between Koto-ri and Hamhung. Reboarding his transport at Yonpo after his briefings, and realizing that no troops should have been in the forbidding Chosin area in the first place, Collins asked why they were there. Almond said frankly that MacArthur had ordered the movement to assist the Eighth Army in the west.

While Walker had worried that he might not be able to retain any presence in Korea, even in distant Pusan, unless merged far southward with X Corps, Almond told Collins that X Corps could, if ordered, hold a substantial perimeter through the winter in the Hungnam-Hamhung area far above the 38th parallel. But Almond expected Tokyo to order his withdrawal by sea.

Returning to Tokyo from the Yonpo air base late on December 5, Collins again conferred with MacArthur, who put the worst possible interpretation on events. Without reinforcements from the U.S. or Taiwan, and permission to bomb Manchuria and blockade China, he would have to withdraw from all of Korea. MacArthur continued to go public with his complaints in the face of a White House directive to clear communications with the press on military and foreign policy. When Erle Cocke Jr., national commander of the American Legion, cabled that four veterans organizations had demanded that Truman authorize the bombing of Manchuria, MacArthur wired back his "profound thanks," knowing that the papers would pick it up.

Grossly overestimating enemy strength, MacArthur told Collins that the Chinese had a half-million men facing him, and that the North Korean army was already rebuilt to 100,000 men. The Dai Ichi figures were no more accurate than was MacArthur's catastrophic underestimation of November 24, when his failed offensive had opened—and closed. Thousands of American prisoners had already been taken in the first encirclements of units in the north, and the Chinese were circulating "safe conduct passes" that included a drawing of a dead soldier on one side and a bloated cigar-smoking, wine-swilling capitalist on the other with the caption,

Korea's where the GIs die,
Home's where the politicians lie . . .

The leaflets offered false assurances that those surrendering would find "peace and safety," be able to write to their families and receive medical treatment. "We have already set free many American and British prisoners," one "pass" promised. "You will certainly be freed and get home in the end." Most who surrendered were marched to the Yalu; their numbers were fewer each day as frozen bodies were stacked along the road.

One of MacArthur's junior intelligence officers, Lieutenant Colonel James H. Polk, wrote to his wife from Tokyo as Collins was being briefed, "The whole of GHQ . . . has a bad case of the blues. . . . The old man, MacA I mean, is really one hell of a gambler. . . . Well, this time he gambled it a little too hard and really pressed his luck a bit too far and the whole house fell in on him." He had chanced "staking it all on one big throw, and for once the great MacA's luck ran out on him. He just didn't believe that the whole CCF would be thrown against him. I really admire him in defeat but it sorta looks like the end of an era."

A die-hard admirer, Polk blamed the mess on old (but unnamed) loyalists. In a follow-up letter he added, while Collins was making things "rugged" at the Dai Ichi, "Why oh why oh why does MacA put up with some of the people that he does? Why does he keep people around him that will lead him into pitfalls?" At a press conference, MacArthur's G-2, General Willoughby, had told correspondents with more than usual frankness that his chief's tactics had been based on the premise that large-scale Chinese intervention was only a "potential," and admitted that MacArthur had been "gambling" that most Chinese would remain on their own side of the border. The Bataan clique left Polk feeling helpless.

On returning to Tokyo from a mission to Walker, MacArthur's G-3,

Pinky Wright, recommended reinforcements of a sort for EUSAK. He proposed that the 3rd Division be transferred to the Eighth Army, and that the remainder of X Corps be kept under Almond when it rejoined other troops in South Korea but placed under Walker's overall command. MacArthur was reluctant to place Almond under Walker. A message to Almond offered him the alternative of returning to Tokyo as FEC chief of staff, still his paper title, or remaining as chief of X Corps. Almond stayed.

The Eighth Army's less than systematic withdrawal included the mostly systematic destruction of trackage, rail rolling stock, locomotives, bridges, signal equipment, communications lines, vehicles, artillery, and thousands of tons of supplies and ammunition moved up earlier at great effort and cost. Air strikes burned thousands of winter parkas that were already badly needed, but not where they were. Even before the newly arrived British 29th Brigade, the rear guard for the evacuation of Pyongyang, had departed, its path had been impeded by the hurried, premature firing of millions of gallons of gasoline and tons of supplies. When an Indian field ambulance unit with the 27th Brigade received orders to burn a six months' supply of medical stores, its commanding officer managed not to comply. Instead, he found a working locomotive, had the boiler filled by using a human chain of water carriers, cut wood to fire the engines and got his supplies over the last working bridge before it was blown.

Much of the wreckage was quickly exploited by the Chinese and North Koreans. In their haste and hysteria, retreating troops often abandoned weapons and bungled or bypassed the demolitions ordered, and the enemy proved adept at improvising. Prisoner interrogations of Chinese in December found that they preferred to fight Americans "because they abandoned so much usable equipment during retreats, including personal clothing, weapons and many luxury items." A rifleman with the 5th Cav, James Cardinal, remembered having nothing to discard in the minus-twenty cold because his outfit hadn't yet been issued proper garb and was short in everything: "MacArthur's strategy . . . envisioned a quick victory in North Korea before winter set in. . . . At night we had to sleep with our rifles, grenades, and canteens of water inside our sleeping bags. . . . It was extremely dangerous to touch anything made of metal unless you wore gloves. Bare skin would instantly adhere to the metal, causing painful and bloody injuries before you could pull away, as I learned to my dismay."

Dismay became panic when troops found that the ground was too frozen to dig a foxhole, weapons would not fire, and vehicles would not start.

Food became so scarce in front-line units, Cardinal remembered more than forty years later,

> that we were reduced to eating a slice of Spam and half a canteen cup of juice each day. The bleak countryside was scoured for anything edible, and we even ate dogs. . . . When the retreat began, the winter clothing that had not been issued and food, ammunition, gasoline, and other equipment and supplies were still stored in vast supply dumps awaiting distribution. . . . As is probably true of every war, we saw rear echelon personnel wearing winter equipment of the sort that had not been distributed to us. We passed those supply dumps riding on the outside of tanks and occasionally came to a stop in front of them. Appeals for cases of C rations or bundles of clothing fell on deaf ears. The Army guards . . . told us that they had strict orders not to give anything away and to shoot anyone, American or otherwise, who attempted to remove anything.

Immense supply depots were destroyed by EUSAK engineers "to deny them to the enemy." Cardinal recalled seeing the northern horizon lit up, as the Cav retreated south, by the firing of the fenced-in supply enclosures around Pyongyang. It was "one of the reasons for the poor morale that beset Eighth Army in the weeks that were to come."

While EUSAK withdrew in bumper-to-bumper bitterness and confusion, it was further impeded as it backtracked to the 38th parallel by hundreds of thousands of refugees carrying everything they could on their backs and atop their heads. As Lieutenant Colonel Roy Appleman, himself a Korean veteran, would describe it in *Disaster in Korea*, "The evacuation of the city [of Pyongyang] was not an example of superb planning and execution; it was done in great haste. In its last days in American control, the situation was chaotic and characterized by too much haste and fear in Eighth Army that the Chinese would appear, although intelligence was adequate to indicate that there was still time to save and evacuate military supplies and equipment." Many soldiers hoped they were leaving Korea and everything there for good, and would indeed be home for Christmas. As the 25th Division G-4 (Logistics) report for December 1950 described in unbureaucratic terms, "The apparent careless abandon and indifference with which some troops were observed to burn and destroy equipment with the slightest excuse is almost criminal. . . . It is almost impossible to name [cases of willful destruction] . . . since they range from abandoning individual clothing and equipment to burning [needed] vehicles and trailers, but it is clearly indicated that positive command action is called for in this matter." Yet the willful abandonment and destruction was a command order. The buck stopped nowhere.

Despite the easy pickings, Peng reported to Mao, "If we go too far south it will increase the difficulties of further advances." His armies were exhausted, and low in food and ammunition, pilfering what they could from enemy leavings and incomplete destruction of supply dumps. Advancing on foot-power, they could not outrun the Eighth Army, and Peng was content to let Walker concede ground without a struggle. "Therefore," he proposed, "we intend to stop several dozen kilometers north of the 38th parallel and let the enemy hold that line." He would "destroy the enemy's main forces" early in the new year when the weather was better. When Mao learned that Walker had ordered more hasty withdrawals, he instructed Peng, "If the enemy in Pyongyang has already retreated, then advance to the 38th parallel."

By late afternoon on December 6, having made little contact with EUSAK, Peng's troops were reoccupying the North Korean capital. The fears in Pyongyang and in Tokyo, based on abysmally bad intelligence and sheer panic, furnished the enemy with an unexpected pre-Christmas gift.

Back in Tokyo late on December 6, Collins conferred again with MacArthur, who had seen for himself none of what was happening in Korea. He very likely knew from Almond that Marines moving along the west bank of the Changjin River were blocked at the Funchilin Pass, where a steel Treadway bridge built by Army engineers had been blown during the night by Chinese infiltrators. Water from the Chosin Reservoir was discharged into the mountain chasm 3,500 feet below the pass. Vehicles and tanks could not descend and cross the twisting one-way road, and thousands of very cold troops, supplied only by airdrops, were trapped in the snow until something could be done.

Crews from Japan, including parachute riggers, test-dropped a 2,500-pound bridge section from a C-119 at Yonpo. Four sections would be needed to fill the twenty-four-foot gap. With larger parachutes prepared during the night by a hundred-man work detail, eight C-119s each dropped a steel sec-tion on the morning of the seventh. One hit the frozen surface and was dam-aged; another drifted into Chinese hands; the others were hauled the three and a half miles to the bridge site. Had the Chinese been up to keeping the jaws of their trap closed, it was the ideal moment. They had seen the colorful parachutes descend, and had even acquired one Treadway unit for which they had no use. But the Chinese 60th and 76th Divisions were worn out from forced marches and freezing weather, and were close to starvation. They were taking enormous casualties from American artillery and—when the skies were clear—air strikes of explosives and napalm. They could still make trouble, but not much of it.

Withdrawing columns could not move until the high ground above the next village, Chinhung-ni, was taken. At first light on December 8, in a swirling snowstorm that reduced visibility to fifty feet, men from the 1st Battalion, 7th Marines broke through a roadblock and routed Chinese from the 60th Division with such surprise that they found a kettle of prized rice still cooking in the largest bunker. Troops moved out of Koto-ri, with refugees, including two newborn the night before with the aid of Navy medics, following the Marine rear guard. The narrow bridge designed for treads required skillful handling of wheeled vehicles, which had barely half an inch play. They were guided across in darkness by engineers with flashlights while Major Webb D. Sawyer's 1st Battalion, 7th Marines kept the Chinese at a safe distance.

"White is the color of mourning in Korea," Lynn Montross and Nicholas Canzona (who was then a lieutenant in the division) wrote in the third volume of the Marine official history of the war, "and snowflakes drifted down gently over the common grave in which 117 Marines, soldiers, and Royal Marine Commandos were buried on the 8th at Koto-ri. Lack of time had prevented the digging of individual graves in the frozen soil. . . . All available space in planes and vehicles was needed for the evacuation of casualties." (Even C-47s of the Royal Hellenic Air Force were pressed into service from Yonpo to Koto-ri.) Three mass gravesites were dynamited. The dead were wrapped in ponchos while a Graves Registration officer paced over the area and drew a map in case the bodies could someday be extricated. A chaplain recited "The Lord Is My Shepherd" to an audience of two privates, several officers and a few reporters. Everyone else was hastening toward the repaired bridge.

The logistical heroics made it possible for 14,000 men to negotiate the snowswept Funchilin Pass by December 10, when O. P. Smith, satisfied that all was going well, boarded a helicopter for Hungnam to open a new command post from which to oversee the evacuation by sea. On the road, David Duncan, a photographer for *Life*, snapped a Marine hacking his breakfast out of a frozen can of beans. There were ice crystals on the beans and on the Marine's scraggly beard. "If I were God, and I could give you anything you wanted," Duncan asked, thinking of the likely reproduction of the scene in the Christmas issue, "what would you ask for?"

"Gimme tomorrow," said the Marine.

It was a melancholy flight back to the U.S. for General Collins. While he had been in Korea and Japan a meeting of top officials at State had discussed the crisis. Questioning the command's "capacity to resist," the top-secret minutes note, Dean Rusk "mentioned the possibility of using General Collins as a Field Commander with General MacArthur spending full time on the Japanese Peace Treaty." It was the first overt suggestion about replacing the heretofore untouchable MacArthur.

The capital was still reeling from the retreats in Korea and the ruckus over Truman's atomic gaffe. Collins would return convinced that despite MacArthur's defeatism a forced exit from Korea remained remote. But MacArthur was trying to influence policy, if not in the Pentagon, at least in the media, and—through its influence—Congress. One success was in *Time*, where Henry Luce's editors imagined, "The policy of [Communist] containment was dead. There remained only the policy of retaliation and positive action by the U.S. and its allies to damage Communist power at the sources from which aggression flowed."

With the press reflecting MacArthur's anxieties and anti-Communism, and deflecting any blame from him, such right-wing stalwarts as Republican senator William Jenner of Indiana put the onus on the President. "Our only recourse," Jenner declared, "is to impeach President Truman and find out who is the secret invisible government which has so cleverly led our country down the road to destruction." Truman himself would be forced to the airwaves to declare extravagantly in a radio address to the American people that "our homes, our nation, all the things we believe in, are in great danger."

Almond returned to his command post late on the afternoon of December 7 from a visit with General Soule at 3rd Division headquarters in Hungnam, where they discussed using the division as a covering force for the evacuation of the Marines. There he found a confirming radio message from MacArthur. X Corps would ship out "in successive positions" to the Pusan area for redeployment. The Eighth Army would hold the Seoul area "for the maximum time possible." It was not MacArthur's most optimistic language.

As the withdrawal down the line from Chosin continued, the units leapfrogged each other until relieved from the rear by another. All went well but for the pressure of refugees, some of whom inevitably were infiltrators. Marines were ambushed just after midnight on the eleventh. A stalled American tank was set afire short of the Treadway bridge. A Marine demolition team waited for the last tanks to pass, then blew the span. Stragglers did not make it. Twenty-four other vehicles had to be abandoned en route and destroyed because malfunctions in the subzero cold or accidents on the ice made them inoperable. By eight on the evening of the eleventh, the 14,000 survivors, bent under packs, parkas, weapons, sleeping bags and fatigue, had entered the 65th Infantry perimeter, mission accomplished. In the near distance the lights of Hagaru had looked, to Marine captain Edward Stamford, "like New York City." An anticipated assault of the bivouac area never materialized. The enemy, too, was exhausted.

The withdrawal was compared (first by *Time* on December 18, 1950) to the classic march of the ten thousand in Xenophon's *Anabasis,* or *The March Up Country,* the account of the epic retreat of a Greek mercenary army which fought for the Persian king Cyrus in 401 B.C. General Smith's much abbreviated if far more frigid fighting retreat, Roy Appleman wrote in *Escaping the Trap,* "is a textbook application of Xenophon. . . . The prime lesson, if there was a single most important one, was that enemy-held high ground along the route of march must be seized before a column attempts to pass below it. The Marines and the attached X Corps troops did this. It is a pity that the Eighth Army, fighting in the west at the same time, did not do it. . . ."

Mao understood the analogy. In a message to Peng he reported "from a secret source" that General Collins, "who was authorized [by Washington] to inspect the Korean front, commented after a meeting with MacArthur and Walker that the situation concerning the US/UN forces in Korea is becoming hopeless." Mao knew as quickly as did Almond and Walker that MacArthur, after long reluctance to return to Korea, was flying in to meet with Collins and the field generals. He landed at still-safe Yonpo air base just before noon on the eleventh—not for a firsthand look at the evacuation, but only to be there. He would not leave the Yonpo area.

With MacArthur were Hickey, Wright, and the inevitable and militarily insignificant Whitney. In the pilots' briefing room at the airfield, itself reaching the end of its usefulness, Almond reviewed for MacArthur the outloading of X Corps, predicting that every man would be available for duty in South Korea by December 27. The major problem remaining, Almond reported, was that thousands of refugees, their numbers increasing daily, were straining at the edges of the corps perimeter. He hoped to evacuate those civilians who wanted to leave, but he stressed that the military came first.

After forty-five minutes on the ground, MacArthur was back in the air en route to Kimpo airfield, near Seoul, for a painful meeting with Walker. The exchanges were unrecorded but almost certainly dealt with holding

Seoul, and where the Eighth Army was going to regroup to hold a line across Korea. A series of code-lettered contingency positions across the peninsula had been drawn up by Walker's staff. The most optimistic of them, line C, followed the lower bank of the Han River just below Seoul, and stretched northeast to Hongchon and then on to the Sea of Japan. Other lines gave up even more ground.

Humiliated by the retreat of his regiment, Staff Sergeant W. B. Woodruff Jr. of the 35th Infantry (of Kean's 25th Division) wrote, "By my reckoning we had yielded up to the enemy some eighty miles during the runaway, 100 miles altogether since I joined the [L] company on December 8. I had seen no enemy, fired no round, and the company had sustained no casualty. I felt disgusted, ashamed, and frustrated."

Francesca Rhee was dismayed, writing in her diary on December 16, "Kaesong"—where the war began—"has been evacuated by the Americans and the bridges burned. Why nobody knows. The reports are always *everything is quiet* on the front. . . ." She accepted the "inside story" of the American 2nd Division, that "Gen. Kean who was in command was sent back to the States to be court-martialled as he abandoned position without saving the heavy armament. . . . Whatever it is, he is replaced by someone else." Kean would be replaced, but not that way, and not yet.

Although disgusted by the Eighth Army's performance, before returning to Tokyo that afternoon MacArthur paused to make one of his least persuasive public relations exhortations to the press. It had the rhetorical earmarks of having been drafted in Tokyo by Whitney before the flight. His command, MacArthur claimed, "in spite of recent heavy fighting"—there had been little contact with the Communists on the EUSAK front—"is in excellent shape, with high morale and conspicuous self-confidence. . . . The enemy plan has failed. All our units are intact and the losses inflicted on the enemy have been . . . as high as ten to one compared with our own. . . . Notwithstanding the enormous danger inherent in the drastic change I consider that the [Korean] command for the time being is relatively secure."

Mao did not see the situation MacArthur's way. In a message to Kim Il Sung he predicted that the Chinese would defeat the Americans and their allies because events had shown that the Americans "have a lot of steel but little fighting spirit. . . . Our forces are absolutely capable of defeating the U.S. forces no matter how superior their equipment and air power are." Less sanguine was Peng, who at a conference of Chinese commanding officers on December 15 conceded frankly that "because of political considerations, the central leadership requires us to cross the 38th parallel. Therefore we are obliged to do so." He was not eager to penetrate far below the parallel to "claim a victory," for in doing so they were outrunning their primitive resupply system. Afterwards Peng sent a long message to Mao predicting a long war. He saw no way that the U.S. could afford, politically, to abandon Korea and expected bridgehead positions to be maintained, perhaps at Inchon as well as Pusan. "In my opinion, the Korean War will remain protracted and arduous."

What the Chinese would do next remained beyond the reach of American intelligence. According to retired Marine General Pedro A. del Valle, General Walter Bedell Smith, the new CIA director, called him in and suggested that he set up an operation in Tokyo "to pull the rug out from under MacArthur." Del Valle's suspicions reflect Willoughby's long-standing refusal to let the CIA into MacArthur's territory or to cooperate with the agency in any way, rather than a Pentagon or White House plot. MacArthur, del Valle argued, was "the greatest soldier-statesman this country had," and, storming out, he wrote to MacArthur on December 14 of new enemies gathering against him. The Supreme Commander's paranoia about Washington hardly needed the additional stimulus. MacArthur would write to Roy Howard of UP that the order from Truman to require that he clear his public pronouncements with Washington was only "the most open drive . . . against me but with little effort to conceal the individuals responsible at [the] source. It reminds me that I was warned back in August from various sources—all reliable—that just such a campaign was to be initiated, based upon the pretense of my inability to break out of the Pusan perimeter. That plan was abandoned when the Inchon landing took place."

At Hungnam, the Marines who bore the brunt of the fighting in the east were the first to board ship. Press photographers covering the outloading shouted, "Wave and look happy!" Marines obliged, but Lieutenant Charlie Mize, who had been in Korea since Inchon, wrote to his wife from shipboard that he would never forget "the misery and the bravery" or the many buddies who had died. "We know nothing of the big picture, just that we're going aboard . . . to Pusan to reorganize. One thing I know is that only an outstanding Division would have gotten out of the mess the great Mac put us in. . . ."

The huge tent city at Hungnam shrank daily. While Marines dined on B rations awaiting departure, on the twelfth a dinner was held at X Corps headquarters remote from the bivouac area to mark General Almond's fifty-eighth birthday. Delicacies were flown in from Japan. The next day, O. P. Smith attended memorial services at the cemetery at Hungnam for Marines who would not be returning. It took dynamite to blast a final mass grave in the frozen ground. In another excavation Chinese POWs were permitted to inter the bodies of their dead brought down from Chinhung-ni.

Stowage diagrams for troops and equipment were ignored daily as troops filled whatever ships arrived, and the inevitable closing operations began. Marine fighters left Yonpo on the fourteenth, and on the morning of the fifteenth the USS *Bayfield* sailed with General Smith aboard. In twenty-nine ships, thirteen of them LSTs and seven commercial cargo vessels, 22,215 Marines had embarked.

In the days that remained before the two Army divisions and the ROKs sailed, the press of refugees threatened to disrupt further sailings. The command set aside LSTs and cargo ships for the refugees. One LST hauled five thousand in sardine-tin fashion, and a commercial freighter outloaded twelve thousand. All beaches were cleared by the afternoon of the twenty-fourth, with no serious attempts by the enemy to interfere—as if a gentleman's agreement were in force. The 3rd Division completed boarding at 2:36 that afternoon, leaving only two Marine amphibian tractor companies to cover the flanks of the operation before outloading themselves. In all, 17,500 vehicles, 550,000 estimated tons of bulk cargo, 105,000 troops and 91,000 refugees were outloaded. As the last LSTs weighed anchor, 400 tons of dynamite too frozen to ship back and 500 abandoned thousand-pound bombs were set off, blowing apart the Hungnam waterfront. It was an unquiet Christmas Eve.

In the days before Christmas on the EUSAK front there was an eerie calm, although troops continued to fall back as if being chased. Morale at Eighth Army headquarters, British Brigadier Coad wrote in his war diary, "was . . . appalling. The axis [south] was universally called the escape route and complete evacuation by sea openly talked about." On December 15, in Seoul, a hundred tons of South Korean paper currency was destroyed to keep it from enemy hands. The Chinese were still moving south, largely unopposed, but the bulk of their forces remained along the Taedong River in the Pyongyang area. Unsure where the enemy was, the Eighth Army began probing north. Also frustrated that the Chinese seemed invisible, FEAF commander General Stratemeyer on December 20 sent out Fifth Air Force reconnaissance planes "to find out where these Communists are." EUSAK had apparently retreated from ghosts.

For ten days thereafter, Fifth Air Force planes photographed areas across Korea forty miles deep and north of Eighth Army positions. At headquarters in Taegu, 27,643 aerial prints were examined but the Chinese armies failed to surface. In the days before Christmas, however, line-crossers and a few prisoners taken established that the enemy was approaching the Imjin River just above the 38th parallel. To General Peng's disappointment, FEAF aircraft were effective across Korea in destroying what they *could* see. For days, bombers and fighter-bombers searched out equipment left to the enemy— six thousand vehicles and a thousand tanks and weapons carriers had been abandoned—and withered them into scrap metal with napalm.

The Chinese were more conspicuous in New York, where on December 11 an Arab-Asian group of thirteen UN states began an effort to arrange a cease-fire, and asked Mao's government to permit its ambassador, General Wu, to remain for negotiations. Since the Chinese had already succeeded in reestablishing a buffer Korean Communist state between the Americans and the Yalu, Mao had an opportunity which many UN combatant nations would have welcomed. But his government rejected all proposals on grounds that all UN actions taken while Beijing was denied a seat were illegal. On December 23, Foreign Minister Zhou Enlai sent the thirteen-nation group a message, also broadcast on Chinese radio, rejecting any settlement as long as "American aggression forces" remained in Korea. The 38th parallel, Zhou asserted, had been obliterated forever by the UN invasion of North Korea, and decisions on Korean affairs had to be made "by the Korean people themselves." His policy on the parallel and on Korean self-government could have been made by Douglas MacArthur.

In Korea on December 23, General Walker got into his personal jeep at about 10:30 a.m. to go from his Seoul headquarters to I Corps at Uijongbu, about twenty miles to the north. He was to present Syngman Rhee's Republic of Korea presidential unit citations to the 24th Division and the British 27th Brigade. As usual his driver was Master Sergeant George Belton, who had driven him through France and Germany. Walker's jeep had flashing red lights and sirens mounted on each front fender to speed him along, and a steel handrail welded on so that the general on occasion could stand while holding onto the bar. Wearing a pile-lined hat with earflaps, Walker sat with a rug around his knees to keep out some of the cold.

In the opposite direction came a solid line of ROK trucks and jeeps from its 6th Division. South Korean vehicles seemed always headed south. After Rhee's proclamation the next day moving the capital to Pusan set off a mass exodus that would overwhelm roads and railways, the congestion would get far worse. An ROK weapons carrier clipped the left rear of the speeding jeep, which hurtled off the icy road and turned over. Walker and his driver were killed instantly.

MacArthur was immediately informed by the nearby 8055th MASH. Hickey in Tokyo radioed Washington. Talking to correspondents at the Dai Ichi, MacArthur lavished more praise on the unfortunate Walker in death than he had ever offered in life, and declared that he had "recently" recommended a promotion for Walker to the four-star rank of full general. That was news to the Department of Defense, but members of Congress came forward to push for the posthumous additional star that would make good on MacArthur's flight of fancy for a general he would have preferred to relieve in some less violent way. In Korea, Syngman Rhee felt disgrace for his country as well as shock over the news. He would order the driver of the weapons carrier executed, but American protests caused a reduction in the sentence to three years' imprisonment.

The flag-draped coffin was flown to Tokyo in MacArthur's Constellation, with General Partridge at the controls. The body was then flown to Washington for burial in Arlington National Cemetery. But wars do not pause to mark a single death, and on the day that Walker died, the Eighth Army was expecting, imminently, a resumption of the Chinese offensive. Mao knew that opportune times for attacks were the enemy's holidays, and Christmas Eve was only hours away as Walker's body began its trip home. In some divisions, as in the 25th, Christmas dinner was served a day early in anticipation of trouble. It did come, as anticipated, against ROK divisions. American troops had been reflecting on their enthusiasm for the war by such headquarters-mimeographed Christmas messages to fortunate friends elsewhere as

Xmas greetings from Korea
Land of lice and diarrhea.
From mucky shores we've half-mastered,
Merry Xmas, you lucky bastard!

Lieutenant General Matthew Bunker Ridgway, fifty-five that December, would miss his Christmas dinner at home. In conversations between Collins and MacArthur early in August, Ridgway had been picked to replace Walker if something happened to him. The contingencies had included Walker's firing. At Fort Myer in the Virginia suburbs of Washington, Ridgway was dining with old Army friends—it was still the night of the twenty-second in their time zone—when the telephone call came from Collins that "turned my evening upside down." Ridgway was to depart without delay for Korea.

Truman, Marshall and Pace had all agreed on it, and MacArthur had sent a message to Collins, "Thanks and deepest appreciation, Joe, to you and the Secretary for letting me have Ridgway." To Ridgway himself, MacArthur teleconned with warm hyperbole that he looked forward to "the resumption of a comradeship which I have cherished through long years of military service."

In the 1920s, when MacArthur was briefly commandant at West Point, young Ridgway had served under him as an instructor. Their paths then diverged. In 1944, Ridgway had led the 82nd Airborne Division into Normandy on D-Day. Their most recent meeting had been in August when Ridgway accompanied Harriman, Collins and Norstad to Tokyo, and the Air Force chief mentioned afterwards that MacArthur wanted to see Ridgway succeed Walker if anything happened to him. Shortly afterwards, in Washington on August 16, Ridgway and Collins discussed the troubled EUSAK command and Collins confided that James A. Van Fleet, who had brought the Communist insurgency in Greece to an end, was "the natural selection." Then he added, "You could do it too," and asked Ridgway about his own preferences. "If we are going to war," said Ridgway candidly, "I would prefer to fight in Europe."

"I am planning to put you in Haislip's place when he retires within a year," said Collins. "and if I send you to Korea, you might be so involved I couldn't get you out." Wade H. Haislip was Army vice chief of staff.

When Ridgway left Washington, he knew that EUSAK would not be his last top posting unless he went the way of Walker. With Ridgway was a letter from Collins, "Unfortunately, one of the penalties of great ability is that it inexorably draws to itself great responsibilities. It was almost inevitable that General MacArthur should turn to you to assume command of the Eighth Army. . . . The Secretary [of Defense] and I have unbounded confidence in your capacity to meet this challenge." With her boundless faith in MacArthur, Francesca Rhee saw the appointment differently, writing in her diary on December 29, "It seems that the Pentagon or the State Department put this man in purposely to have their man here so as to counteract MacArthur's highhanded way of running this war."

Tough, and with a reputation for humorlessness, Ridgway was what the dispirited Eighth Army needed. His appointment, however, must have disappointed Ned Almond. At the time of Walker's death, Almond was on the amphibious force flagship *Mount McKinley*, nearing Ulsan, a port about thirty miles north of Pusan. "I went into a dead sleep after dinner [on Christmas Eve]," he remembered, "and woke up mid-morning. . . ." Two days later he would report to Ridgway in Seoul.

On December 26, Ridgway was to report to MacArthur, who was then issuing a communiqué ostensibly marking the completion of the Hungnam evacuation. It was, he claimed, a "redeployment" that had "served a very significant purpose—possibly in general result the most . . . fortunate of any conducted during the course of the Korean campaign." And, he added with portentous ambiguity, "We exposed before too late secret [Communist] political and military decisions of enormous scope and threw off balance enemy preparations aimed at surreptitiously massing the power capable of destroying our forces with one mighty extended blow."

Ridgway expected to encounter such Olympian rhetoric as well as the irresistible MacArthur manner. He realized that he had to exorcise the spell of the legendary chief, who had been asleep when Ridgway arrived at the guest house of the American embassy in the early hours of December 26.

Early that Tuesday, Ridgway was driven to the Dai Ichi, to the sixth floor for a nine-thirty appointment with MacArthur, who had arrived unusually early. MacArthur was now realistic, even hopeful, although Ridgway worried about a New Year's offensive, timed for the holiday. Ridgway was to maintain a line of defense as far north as he could, and attempt to hold Seoul. MacArthur recognized that "supply discipline" in the Eighth Army was poor, and that airpower would not stop the Chinese from crossing the parallel where and when they wanted. The Chinese no longer resorted only to flanking tactics and infiltration, and they made better use of their infantry than did the Eighth Army. "They attack in depth. Their firepower in the hands of their infantry is used more extensively than our own. The enemy moves and fights at night. The entire Chinese military is in the fight." MacArthur credited Mao's favorite general, Lin Biao, as architect of the intervention. American intelligence was so ineffective, still, as to fail to identify Peng Dehuai.

A "mission vacuum" which MacArthur claimed existed was blamed on Washington, and he hoped that the U.S. government would permit Chiang's Nationalists to take the heat off the 38th parallel by letting them attack southern China as a diversion. MacArthur no longer expected to unite Korea under Syngman Rhee, but hoped to hold on to South Korea. "Form your own opinions and use your own judgment," he told Ridgway. "I will support you. I will assume responsibility. You have my complete confidence."

Having arrived prepared to discount MacArthur, Ridgway was "deeply impressed by the force of his personality. . . . He was a great actor too, with an actor's instinct for the dramatic—in tone and gesture. Yet so lucid and pene-trating were his explanations and his analyses that it was his mind rather than his manner or his bodily presence that dominated. . . ."

Emboldened by MacArthur's resolve, which concealed more than a little desperation, Ridgway, without having seen the plethora of problems on the ground, asked, "If I find the situation to my liking, would you have any objections to my attacking?"

"The Eighth Army is yours, Matt," said MacArthur. "Do what you think best."

After meetings with the FEC staff, Ridgway, with Eighth Army red-and-white shoulder patches already sewn on his uniforms, was driven back to Haneda Airport, where he boarded a B-17 for K-2. Via Leven Allen, his inherited chief of staff, in Taegu, he had already sent a terse message which became his first general order:

> I have with little notice assumed heavy responsibilities before in battle, but never with greater opportunities for service to our loved ones and our Nation in beating back a world menace which free men cannot tolerate. It is an honored privilege to share this service with you and our comrades of the Navy and Air Force. You will have my utmost. I shall expect yours.

At Eighth Army headquarters in Taegu, which he felt was too remote from the war, he unpacked his combat uniforms from World War II. He had left Washington in a hurry and had only civilian gloves and a cotton cap. "I nearly froze there the first few days," he recalled, "until some major saw me one day holding my ears, and he . . . got me one of those pile-lined caps with the flaps and a pair of GI gloves." Flying to Seoul he wore his trademark grenade fastened to the right shoulder strap of his airborne trooper's gear and a first-aid kit attached to the left shoulder strap. At his web belt was a .45 pistol. GIs would begin calling him "Old Iron Tits," but they recognized, too, that he expected to go up front, where they belonged. That led sourly to another name from those who would have preferred to go home, "Wrong Way Ridgway." Overdoing his tough-guy act, he told groups of officers, "I am not here to get real estate—don't give a damn for that. I am here to defeat the enemy." Then, pointing a finger at his audiences, he would add, "And you are going to do it, now!" It was first seen as a piece of theater. Dispirited, defeatist troops were unimpressed until he began shoring up the vulnerable front by moving men about.

Dispirited himself by the openly poor morale he saw everywhere, Ridgway became gloomier as he began shifting units to better prepare for a Chinese New Year's offensive he saw brewing. A message from the Dai Ichi left him feeling undercut by Washington as well as by MacArthur. On December 29 a JCS directive on Korea approved by the President went to Tokyo. Described by Undersecretary of Defense Robert Lovett as "the jig is up" message, it ironically accepted much of MacArthur's gloom-and-doom estimates since the Chinese intervention. It agreed that the Chinese possessed the capability of driving UN forces out of Korea "if they choose to exercise it." Ruling out any role for Chiang, the policy statement conceded that it was "not practicable to obtain significant additional forces for Korea from other members of the United Nations. And it declared that Korea was "not the place to wage a major war"—reminding MacArthur not to expand the conflict into a war against Communism in Asia.

Finally, it directed MacArthur, and in effect Ridgway, "to defend in successive [fall-back] positions . . . , inflicting such damage to hostile forces in Korea as is possible," recognizing that "developments may force our withdrawal from Korea." It was, then, crucial, "particularly in view of the continued threat to Japan, to determine, in advance, our last reasonable opportunity for an orderly evacuation." MacArthur was paying the price for his persistent post-Yalu defeatism. Disconcertingly for Ridgway, the message, which he had no hand in preparing before leaving Washington, also left the JCS's new commander in Korea with what seemed only a negative and impossible mission—to resist without endangering his army.

When MacArthur read the Joint Chiefs' message only days after having his hopes raised by the arrival of Ridgway, Courtney Whitney, his aide since Manila, gushed, "I cannot recall when I have seen heartache etched so vividly on his countenance." It seemed confirmation of the "loss of the will to win" in turbulent Asia while resources were being diverted to Eisenhower and NATO in a peaceful if divided Europe. The Republican Right saw political opportunity and voiced outrage at the imposing of possibly fatal restrictions on MacArthur. Acheson and Marshall were again charged with appeasement and even subversion. Republicans in the Senate and the House passed resolutions to the effect that the Secretary of State had lost the confidence of the country and should be removed from office. To the JCS, MacArthur argued hawkishly but unconvincingly, given his paper record, that "the thought of defeat in Korea had never been entertained by me." Yet he had suggested with regularity that the choices were escalation or evacuation.

On the same day, to Collins's surprise, he received a message at the Pentagon from Ridgway asking that Chiang's forces be permitted to operate on the Chinese mainland without limitation, to relieve the pressure on the Eighth Army. MacArthur's logic "is convincing to me and I feel it would be negligent not to state my full concurrence at once." MacArthur, Ridgway added, "has no repeat no knowledge of this message nor of my intention of sending it. I shall however repeat it to him promptly after dispatch." It was a sign of Ridgway's desperation about what he had already found in Korea in less than three days on the job. Then he waited for the Chinese offensive.

"The so-called 38th parallel," Mao had already telegraphed Peng, "is an old impression in the people's minds, and will no longer exist after this [new] campaign. . . . Should we gain another victory in early January as you have planned by annihilating a few more ROK divisions or American units, . . . we would greatly impress the democratic front and the peoples of the capitalist countries, thereby to strike a new blow at the imperialists and enhance pessimism among them." It was New Year's Eve.

15

Ridgway's War

ON NEW YEAR'S MORNING Ridgway jeeped north from Seoul "into a dismaying spectacle," as he wrote in his memoirs. "ROK soldiers by [the] truckloads were streaming south, without order, without arms, without leaders, in full retreat. Some came on foot or in commandeered vehicles of every sort. They had just one aim—to get as far away from the Chinese as possible. They had thrown their rifles and pistols away and had abandoned all artillery, mortars, machine guns, even crew-served weapons." Although he could not speak Korean, Ridgway jumped from his open jeep and stood in the road waving his arms over his head. The first trucks careened around him, "but I did soon succeed in stopping . . . trucks all carrying ROK officers. The group in the advance truck listened without comprehension and would not obey my gestures. The only effective move now was to set up straggler posts far to the rear, manned by our own MPs under officer command, to regain control." Buoyed by the no-nonsense leadership, MacArthur wrote a personal message to Ridgway about how "delighted" he was "at the energy and effectiveness with which you have taken hold."

Ridgway would not blame "untried" troops who were badly led, but would never have any confidence in ROK officers despite writing supportively to Rhee and to Chief of Staff Chung Il Kwon about fighting together. Truman's on-the-scene observer, General Frank Lowe, would write two eyes-only messages to the President later in the month about "these ROK units." He had been with them since early August, and it was "a risky business; they are cowardly and in no way to be depended on. . . . We know that ROK military units have lost, stolen and black marketed tremendous amounts of U.S. property and that they are now calling for, and expecting, much more. It should not be supplied to them." It was his second exasperated message in two days recommending that "no more time, energy or money should be spent on the ROK Army."

If the U.S. was ever to leave Korea or reduce its presence, something had to be made of the inefficient ROKs, who had none of the discipline or drive of the *In Min Gun*. Even MacArthur advised the JCS, as what he called the "retrograde movement" continued, that arming more South Koreans was a bad investment. (Rhee had just urged him to arm "our 500,000 youths.") Ridgway agreed with MacArthur that the ROKs were hopeless. "In view of the past accomplishments of ROK armed forces," MacArthur advised the JCS in a rare use of irony, "the probable restricted size of the battle field in which we may operate in the near future, . . . the value of attempting to organize train and arm additional ROK forces in the immediate future appears questionable."

In an evaluation that might have been generous, Ridgway blamed some American indiscipline on ROK failures. "A battalion of the U.S. 19th Infantry," he recalled, "had also been caught up in an untidy retreat when the ROKs next to them had broken." He went to a casualty clearing station to question the wounded that New Year's morning and found them "thoroughly dispirited, without the eagerness to rejoin the unit that American fighting men, when not too severely wounded, usually show." He was appalled by their leadership. "I remember asking one [division commander] the names of very prominent peaks in his own sector. He did not know them. He did not even know the name of the river that ran through his sector." Ridgway asked him whether "the ground over there" could handle tanks. "Well, he didn't know that either."

Realizing that he had no hope of holding Seoul, Ridgway tried to secure the bridges over the Han River. Choked with floating ice and unfordable, they were held open by the 1st Cav for the remaining UN troops still above Seoul. The disintegration and flight of troops by the time of Ridgway's arrival had become so notorious that one joke he must have overheard, in which the numerical designation of the unit was interchangeable, was, "Have you heard that the 24th Division has been relieved?"

"By whom?"

"By the Chinese."

Peng's "Third Phase" offensive seemed unhampered by the FEAF airpower which MacArthur once assumed would win the war. (An exception had been a raid on the morning of December 30, when two Chinese artillery regiments were hit before their guns could be hidden in the snow, and nineteen pieces were destroyed.) Even when the first five days of the new year were as clear as they were cold, and fighter-bombers averaged five hundred sorties daily, the Chinese stepped over their dead and continued south. Flares dropped by night fighters restricted enemy movements in darkness to about a quarter of a usual night's advance, but the Chinese moved nevertheless. Bad weather in January would keep aircraft on the ground and assist them.

At General Peng's new command post on a hill above Seoul, which was burning again from bombings and demolitions, the Chinese ambassador to North Korea and the new Soviet ambassador watched the retaking of the "puppet" capital. From them Peng learned of Soviet information that the Americans "were prepared to completely withdraw" from Korea. "I don't believe it. It's unreliable," said Peng, although the Russians had apparently intercepted American exchanges in which the evacuation of Korea was being considered by both MacArthur and the Joint Chiefs. MacArthur's sixteen-page "general emergency" plan of January 7 proposed redeployments of troops from Korea "to the Ryukyus, to the Philippines, as well as to Japan, [with] UN POWs to Saipan and Tinian."

Ambassador Raguliev (who had replaced Terenty Shtykov) persisted in urging a continuation of the Communist offensive, claiming that his information was that the Americans were facing total collapse. But Peng was preparing for a pause to reorganize and resupply his troops. "The Korean War can be over in one go at it," Raguliev urged. He could not see why the Chinese should stop, as Peng planned, at the 37th parallel south of Seoul.

His forces were exhausted, explained Peng. Food and ammunition were short, and air strikes had destroyed their marginal motorized capabilities. As they advanced farther south, resupply would be difficult. Also, after MacArthur's Inchon success, he worried that the enemy "could use . . . his air and sea superiority to land in our rear at any time[,] and that is extremely dangerous." Seoul, said Peng, was a very visible symbol, and he was content to pause there until the winter eased and movement became more possible. "What's more," he insisted, "the enemy is not going to make any overall withdrawal. This is a false impression that is [intended] to lure us southward. I, Peng Dehuai, am not MacArthur. I will not be taken in by this!"

His deputy, Han Xianchu, had confirmed the need for caution. The "terrible winter" had made it "a costly campaign." Due to exposure, Han had reported, "We have so far lost the backbone of our troops. . . . Many regiments and battalions are completely combat-ineffective, with some divisions only half full. . . . The [troops] are extremely tired and there are just too many difficulties: the civilians south of the 38th parallel have all fled with their houses burned down and no food left. Our troops cannot rest well nor do they have enough to eat; their strength is drained away. . . . The attacking forces need food, munitions, and boots very badly. . . . It is impossible to rely on the present manpower to continue the offensive." Rations brought down laboriously from Manchuria were inadequate, a young corps staff officer recalled: "The only food supply of the Volunteers was the earth-red grain of sorghum, washed down with cold spring water."

Still respecting MacArthur's reputation for turning things around, the Chinese People's Volunteers intelligence warned on January 8 that the enemy was no longer retreating. MacArthur might be intending to lure the CPV deep into South Korea and then surprise them with an equivalent to the Inchon flanking operation.

Peng ordered an immediate pause for his sixteen armies in Korea, each equivalent to an American corps. Many of his 400,000 men were immobilized by hunger and by winter. An inspection team from Mao's own headquarters reported early in January that the CPV lived on frozen scraps of potatoes and whatever they could scrounge locally. Further, "When the fighters bivouac on snow-covered ground their feet, socks and hands freeze together in one ice-ball; they cannot unscrew the caps on their hand grenades; the fuses will not ignite. . . . Skin from their hands sticks on shells and mortar tubes. . . ." Communist prisoners taken and sent south to hospitals suffered from pneumonia, tuberculosis and starvation more than from wounds. Peng wanted only to survive the winter in place and renew the offensive after the March thaws.

On the other side of the line, in the contagion of MacArthur's pessimism, correspondents like Maggie Higgins echoed the gloom he wanted to orchestrate in hopes of reversing Pentagon policies. On January 8, Ridgway refused to permit Higgins to file a story reporting that "American officials" and "high army sources" felt that the Korean situation was "hopeless." It did appear hopeless. She had been on the scene with Beech, the AP correspondent, and a reporter from *Time* as the capital, again in flames, was given up to the Chinese—for good, it seemed.

Ridgway charged to MacArthur, "Since she has been here Miss Higgins has not interviewed anyone authorized to speak for this headquarters. It is not known what government officials she has talked to." Her opinions, he radioed to Tokyo, unaware of her clout there, "did not reflect the views of this headquarters." In a related note to Doyle Hickey, MacArthur's acting chief of staff, Ridgway noted that Higgins was "mildly indignant" and might appeal to the Dai Ichi.

On Friday, January 26, 1951, MacArthur would become seventy-one, marking the occasion by maintaining, but for a few birthday visitors, his usual seven-days-a-week schedule. Of the 441,161 letters and cards to him from his Japanese subjects recorded at the Dai Ichi between September 1945 and April 1951, many marked his birthdays, much as the Emperor's birthday had been celebrated. Writers praised his "exalted and godlike benevolence," as if he were a monarch by divine right, and he received gifts ranging from fresh-caught fish and a dozen live hens to a brocade kimono and sash that had taken its embroiderer three years and seventy million stitches—one, according to its maker, who enclosed with it a devout Shinto prayer, for every living Japanese. Now MacArthur's great age exemplified to the vanquished populace his increase of wisdom, and the officials of Kanagawa prefecture (just south of Tokyo) arrived to present him with a bust of himself. The general was sculpted wearing the open-collared shirt he affected, and flattered by having years shaved off his jowls and strands added to his thinning pate. More and more his working day was a facade, as he left tactical decisions to Ridgway. He also left to Ridgway the housecleaning of generals, something he could never bring himself to do. Anticipating Ridgway's sackings, Ned Almond, whom Ridgway had quickly come to respect as an aggressive leader, made the first of them. At Inchon, Almond had relieved a regimental commander, perhaps for the wrong reasons. At Wonju on January 7, Major General Robert B. McClure of the 2nd Division had violated Almond's instructions about evacuating the city—the Army was still in its pre-Ridgway phase of retreating rather than making contact—by withdrawing thirteen miles south when Almond had ordered a fallback to a row of hills only a few miles away.

On grounds of poor leadership (in an interview later he called it "direct disobedience") Almond sacked McClure on the thirteenth, and Ridgway, concurring, replaced him the next day with Clark L. Ruffner, X Corps chief of staff. In an entry Almond added to his diary of that date on March 31, 1953, he noted, "A wiser move, I never made."

Ridgway had been angered at the start by command failures, writing to Collins that as early as New Year's Day "my instructions were not complied with." That night, he went on, he instructed two corps commanders "to so conduct their withdrawal[s] as to leave strong forces so positioned as to permit powerful counterattacks with armored and infantry teams during each daylight period, withdrawing those forces after dark if necessary. These orders, too, failed of execution." Ridgway warned that he would take action against offenders.

On January 15, Collins was at X Corps in Chungju and asked Almond to ride with him to the airstrip. As they jeeped there, Collins asked about the reasons for McClure's relief, and Almond bluntly described the "failure to carry out my orders." Ridgway, he said, had supported the decision, and MacArthur had a three-page "full account." Collins, whose deputy McClure had been in France in 1944, let the matter drop.

As the Eighth Army fell back below Seoul to a line running through Wonju in central Korea, Walton Walker's body was being returned for burial at Arlington. On January 2, 1951, he was interred as a four-star general. (Congress had authorized the posthumous promotion.) Among the mourners was a colleague from combat in Europe, Lieutenant General James A. Van Fleet, fifty-eight. Returned from advising the Greek government on putting down a Communist insurgency, Van Fleet was newly in command of the 2nd Army at Fort Meade, Maryland. As the group dispersed, General Collins called Van Fleet aside. Without telling him that he had been considered but passed over as Walker's replacement, Collins asked him whether he would be willing to go to Korea to replace Ridgway should that need arise.

Van Fleet agreed. The hazards of war had done in Walker; it could happen again. He never thought, then, that a replacement might be needed for MacArthur, for the shogun in Tokyo was not conceived in such terms. Still an icon, he had just been pictured on bubble-gum card number 2 in a new Cold War collectible series labeled "Children's Crusade against Communism," leading the defense against "what is believed to be part of a communist plan gradually to conquer the whole world. The United Nations pitched in to help the South Koreans, just like your dad would help the folks next door if some bad men were beating them up." At the bottom of each poster-like card was the bold injunction, "Fight the Red Menace." (Card number 1 was "Reds Invade South Korea.")

In death, Walton Walker, like his idol, George Patton, would have a new tank named for him, and he would also be celebrated on bubble-gum card number 18, which lauded his courage and closed with "His fine work had placed him in line for promotion. So he was buried as a full four-star general."

Ridgway, who would appear on card number 36 (Collins had to wait for 38), was already receiving positive press coverage in his first weeks in Korea. He employed dramatic names for small operations that instilled confidence and raised hell over dim-witted demolitions that went too far. He expected to be back. With so much to review and to oversee, and such poor staff work at EUSAK and in Tokyo, Ridgway did not learn of orders dated December 12, 1950, to blow up the complex Inchon tidal basin locks until they were demolished on January 4. Barely a month later, Eighth Army engineers were planning their enormously expensive and time-consuming rehabilitation. South of Suwon, at Osan, where Task Force Smith had engaged pathetically in the first American ground action in Korea, a 280-foot, four-span concrete bridge across the Chinwi River was destroyed under similar unrevoked orders because, said an officer in the 65th Engineer Combat Battalion, "We believed we were withdrawing from Korea and we did thorough work on our demolition."

Reacting to MacArthur's unremitting gloom about holding any part of Korea, and his recommendations to put more effort into securing Japan, the Joint Chiefs wondered early in January whether Ridgway had arrived too late. On January 10, MacArthur had responded to JCS concerns about the timetable for evacuation. Chinese military potential, MacArthur replied (later he denied saying it), "eventually will render the military position of the Command in Korea untenable. Under these conditions[,] in the absence of overriding political considerations[,] the Command should be withdrawn from the Peninsula just as rapidly as tactically feasible to do so." Unaware of MacArthur's despairing advice, Ridgway had asked his staff, inherited from Walker via MacArthur, to prepare a study as to where "major elements of the Eighth Army" could be from February through August. Ridgway's G-3, Major General F. W. Moorman, was furnished a detailed document that described a phased withdrawal to the Pusan area by April 15 with embarkation beginning the next day. Moorman warned that Ridgway would never accept it. As predicted, Ridgway gave it a glance and scrawled across it "Disapproved."

In MacArthur's top-secret C-53167, in which he warned the JCS to expect evacuation, as always he put the blame elsewhere, after declaring himself victorious:

> There is no doubt but that a beachhead line can be held by our existing forces for a limited time in Korea, but this could not be accomplished without losses. Whether such losses were regarded as "severe" or not would depend upon the connotation one gives the term. The Command was com-

mitted to the Korean campaign to fight the North Korean invasion army which in due course was effectively destroyed. It was not the intent that it engage the armies of the Chinese nation and doubtless it would not have been committed at all had there been [a] foreseeable prospect that it would find it necessary to do so in its own defense. The troops are tired from a long and difficult campaign, embittered by the shameful propaganda which has falsely condemned their courage and fighting qualities in [their] misunderstood retrograde maneuver, and their morale will become a serious threat to their battle efficiency unless the political basis upon which they are asked to trade life for time is clearly delineated, fully understood, and so impelling that the hazards of battle are cheerfully accepted.

Washington's immediate response, approved by Truman and Marshall, was: "Should it become evident in your judgment that evacuation is essential to avoid severe losses of men and materiel you will at that time withdraw from Korea to Japan." However, it was evident that MacArthur had produced a political polemic rather than a military evaluation plan, and Collins and Vandenberg immediately flew off to check the situation.

While they were en route, but presumably with their concurrence, a top-secret telex, JCS 80902, was fired off to MacArthur conceding that "Based upon all the factors known to us, including particularly those presented in your recent messages, we are forced to the conclusion that it is infeasible under existing conditions . . . to hold for a protracted period a position in Korea." What Washington wanted, however, was time for "essential diplomatic and military consultations"—in a word, negotiation. The Pentagon also wanted extreme secrecy, for instructions to prepare for evacuation were "certain to become known soon after issue" and would result—the JCS was being optimistic here—in the "partial collapse of ROK troops," further jeopardizing an outloading beachhead.

When the Army and Air Force chiefs arrived they found a situation far different from the scenario which MacArthur had dramatized without having been in Korea. The Eighth Army was in good shape and using the pause in Chinese operations at the Han River line to reorganize and go on the offensive. To instill a reversal in attitude, Ridgway would remark to his subordinates on his visits to their command posts, "Don't want to see your defense plans—want to see your attack plans." Although this was greeted skeptically at first as posturing, like Ridgway's grenade on his parachute harness, the attacks would happen.

The very limited, almost symbolic opening thrust was Operation Wolfhound, on the fifteenth, named for Mike Michaelis's 27th Infantry Wolfhounds. More a reconnaissance in force than an offensive, it sent troops up from Osan toward Suwon, enabling the visiting Collins to tell reporters the next day in Taegu, "As of now, we are going to stay and fight." Ridgway, Michaelis said, "was very forceful, very direct, very intolerant of mistakes." EUSAK was learning that on a daily basis. Collins and Vandenberg recognized that MacArthur's messages to Washington and his melodramatic defeatism in Tokyo about Dunkirk or disaster were ploys to get his way about Chiang and mainland China. Truman and the JCS were not about to test those alternatives. To MacArthur's frustration Collins and Vandenberg reported back that Ridgway would hold—and not merely a beachhead.

In support of Ridgway, a combined air-sea lift of nearly two thousand replacement Marines was authorized by Washington. By January 21 more than half of them had joined their division at Pohang, on the coast north of Pusan. Since MacArthur continued to alarm the Pentagon that the evacuation of Korea would put Japan at risk, Collins, who had refused MacArthur four newly activated National Guard divisions in December, at the height of his panic, offered two partly retrained divisions to increase the security of Japan. The 40th and 45th Infantry Divisions would begin preparing for transfer on February 24, with MacArthur specifically ordered to keep them in Japan and not to employ any of their units in Korea.

On January 25, Ridgway began Operation Thunderbolt, employing the 25th Division (which included Michaelis's regiment), the Turkish Brigade (which was learning fast) and two South Korean regiments, all from I Corps. After six days the Chinese retreated from a strategic hill near Suwon, leaving more than four thousand dead. American losses were seventy. Thunderbolt would slow down, but not before the Chinese relinquished more territory below the Han and withdrew from Inchon and Kimpo. In central Korea, Communist forces hung in tenaciously, attempted flanking ambushes after dark, and drove back the predictably vulnerable ROKs. The South Korean 8th Division broke and exposed an American artillery battery, leading to hundreds of casualties, the loss of Hoengsong and the jeopardizing of Wonju.

Pulling the strings from Beijing more now than MacArthur was able to do from Tokyo, Mao had gone into the winter with no intention of letting a stalemate develop until the spring thaws. As late as January 28 he was advising Peng that he would not contribute to peace negotiation talk floated at Lake Success until the completion of a Fourth Offensive, which he called the new operations. When they succeeded, he predicted, "conditions would be more advantageous for the Chinese/North Korean command." Stalin was finally delivering arms long promised, and even positioning Soviet fliers in new Mig-15 jets across the Yalu. Group 64 was ordered to fly in Chinese uniforms, never to engage in combat over water or close to the 38th parallel (to prevent identification if downed) and to use no Russian on their aircraft radios. The caution suggested Stalin's lack of zeal to go to war in Asia. Unconcerned, as every small Soviet step was a commitment, Mao repeated the Chinese propaganda line, which curiously paralleled MacArthur's warnings to the Pentagon, that the Americans would be "run into the sea." Mao would not let Peng settle for less.

Wondering where Peng's supposed 200,000 troops below the parallel were, Ridgway wanted to see the situation for himself and risked a flight in an AT-6 converted training plane with General Earle E. Partridge at the controls. Aerial reconnaissance photos had revealed few Chinese, or even evidence of occupation. Flying often at treetop height and into snow-covered valleys as far as twenty miles north of the UN lines, the pair would have been a tremendous catch for the Communists if brought down, but the enemy kept a low profile in daylight. As Peng put it in a memoir he wrote in prison in the 1960s (he had criticized Mao's "Cultural Revolution"), "Bombed by aircraft and shelled by long-range artillery day and night, our troops could not move about in the daytime. And they had not had a single day's good rest in three months."

"Hardly a moving creature did we spot," Ridgway writes, "not a campfire smoke, no wheel tracks, not even trampled snow to indicate the presence of a large number of troops." MacArthur was planning a flying visit, and Ridgway wanted to offer him the most current picture of enemy whereabouts. Now he knew that only ground action would expose that.

On January 20, MacArthur landed at just retaken Suwon airfield. It was his first visit to Korea since Ridgway had assumed command. MacArthur's state of mind about Korean prospects had been such that he had ordered Ridgway to issue communiqués for the press from Eighth Army headquarters in Taegu rather than have bad news emanate from the Dai Ichi.

Now he was upbeat. "This is exactly where I came in seven months ago to start this crusade," he told waiting correspondents. "The stake we fight for now, however, is more than Korea—it is a free Asia." Rebutting his own pessimism to the Pentagon he added, "There has been a lot of loose talk about the Chinese driving us into the sea, just as in the early days there was a lot of nonsense about the North Koreans driving us into the sea. This command intends to maintain a military position in Korea just as long as the statesmen of the UN decide we should do so."

The displeasure in Washington at his continuing political intrusions—the UN reference was slyly sarcastic—was enormous. His government, the direct orders of which he had again disobeyed, was not interested in ideological crusades. Its commander in East Asia was not interested in limited wars. The visit was over in little more than an hour, without the Supreme Commander offering to inspect a single unit or to see anything not visible from the airfield. MacArthur spent much of his time on the ground adjusting his scrambled eggs cap and his checked muffler for the cameras.

Ridgway suppressed his anger and stood at attention with other EUSAK officers as the *SCAP* took off for Tokyo. The flight "had served no purpose," he later wrote, "except to get photographs of MacArthur with victorious troops; and it could have warned the Chinese that a large-scale offensive was just beginning." War was serious stuff to Ridgway. To underline that, EUSAK headquarters in relatively comfortable Taegu, where Japanese-built schoolhouses had been appropriated, was abandoned to rear-area service uses. Ridgway established a forward command post which moved up with the action and consisted of two tents, one of them with cot, table and chair.

To further dramatize that he meant business, Ridgway ignored MacArthur's feelings in undertaking a wholesale rolling of heads. One—McClure in the 2nd Division—had already been relieved. Now he sacked the commanders of the 7th, 24th, 25th and 1st Cavalry Divisions, creating anguish in Washington as well as Tokyo. Years later, at eighty-nine, he explained to officers at the Army Command and General Staff College that in one case "the men just loved this man; they thought highly of him; there wasn't anything wrong with him except he was just mediocre and you don't want mediocre leadership when the lives of so many men are at stake." The Pentagon objected, vainly, that Ridgway could not claim that regular rotation of assignments was involved, for there was as yet no enlisted rotation in place, and Lieutenant General Mark Clark would get into hot water by publicly recommending it on a Korean visit.

MacArthur hadn't seen the fifty-four-year-old Clark in forty years, but he shook the younger general's hand and inquired in courtly fashion, "How's your mother? Give her my love; I'm a great admirer of hers." In 1910, when Clark's father, Major Charles C. Clark, was attending the Command and General Staff School at Fort Leavenworth, Kansas, Lieutenant MacArthur was a frequent visitor at their house. Clark was fourteen. He had come, now, to deal with training problems, his job at the Pentagon, but MacArthur quickly changed the subject to policy errors in Washington over the conduct of the war and his feud with the Joint Chiefs of Staff. (In Korea, Clark would talk with Ridgway, his West Point classmate, about training men in night fighting.) MacArthur could not understand, he insisted, why the Communists were permitted the advantage of a sanctuary in Manchuria for their base of supply and for air operations. Hitting them hard there, he insisted bitterly, would end their presence in Korea. "It can be accepted as a basic fact," he told the JCS, that unless the authority is given to strike enemy bases in Manchuria, our ground forces as presently constituted cannot with safety attempt major operations in North Korea." Yet he knew that the opportunity for major ground operations north of the parallel had evaporated with the retreat from the Yalu.

"I fully agreed," Clark wrote in a memoir, "that we should not have allowed the enemy a sanctuary north of the Yalu. I never changed my opinion." Neither general—and at the end of the war in 1953, Clark would be sitting in MacArthur's green leather armchair in the Dai Ichi—recognized that the island expanse of Japan, with its dozens of army, navy and air bases, and its recovering industrial potential so crucial to logistics in Korea, was a privileged sanctuary of enormously greater value. Both outspoken anti-Communists, they could not have accepted the parallels.

Perhaps emboldened by Clark's coincidence of views, MacArthur appealed again later in February, in a top-secret message, for Department of the Army approval to bomb the Yalu power plants, functioning fully again now that UN troops had been driven far from them. His Air Force commander, MacArthur entreated, "considers that the destruction of these facilities will hinder Communist support of the war effort, adversely affect general morale, and reduce the surplus power available to Manchuria." Since "political considerations which may have influenced previous decisions may have changed," he added hopefully, he wanted new instructions. (Action was approved on February 26, then canceled, and only in June 1952, more than a year later, were attacks made on the Suiho hydroelectric plant, the biggest in East Asia, and then for political rather than military reasons. They failed in their objectives.)

Always shooting off his mouth, Clark would have been in deeper trouble over his remarks in Korea and Japan had he not had influential colleagues at the Pentagon who had moved him up despite himself. (His far-right sympathies also helped with the Republicans in Congress.) "You were further quoted," an irate Collins cabled him, "as saying [that] the Army 'is taking advantage of the fact that we have to fight in Korea to train as many men as possible.' This used out of context is excellent material for Soviet propaganda." At the same time Washington deplored Ridgway's firings and promotions. There weren't appropriate assignments available for sacked multi-starred brass in the U.S., Collins complained; yet Ridgway was creating new generals from aggressive colonels in EUSAK like Michaelis. The pained message conceded that excuses would be made for the return of Gay, Kean, Barr and Church—"that their experience is needed in the United States."

The one general of proven incompetence whom Ridgway could not replace was MacArthur, who had seemingly aged years since the disheartening shock of Chinese intervention. Increasingly leaving the conduct of the war to Ridgway, he was moving from disregard of Washington to outright defiance, openly telling one luncheon guest in Tokyo that as "an old man of 71" he had little "to fear or lose" by risking his removal, and that he would pay no attention to Truman's gag rule. To make himself even more visible as nominal commander, he was now making flying trips to Korea, it seemed, nearly every weekend, remaining just long enough for the newsreel cameras and an informal news conference staged in a military setting. As Ridgway would sarcastically put it in a memoir, "Between the end of January, when we were in full swing forward, and February 20, General MacArthur honored my command three times with personal visits."

The second look-in had followed press accounts from Korea which MacArthur had seen (they are in his papers), announcing his irrelevancy. One was Joseph C. Harsch's story in the *Christian Science Monitor* headlined, "MacArthur Authority Sags as Staff Chiefs Take Over," which pointed to Ridgway as the effective boss. "MacArthur," the dispatch went on, "no longer is the supreme, independent, and almost sovereign viceroy of the West in the Far East." To UP's Roy Howard, MacArthur would interpret the column as part of "the drum-beating for my destruction." Soon there would also be a Drew Pearson column declaring that "Ridgway has profited from the mistakes of General MacArthur in turning a tragic defeat into Korean victory." Earl D. Johnson, an assistant secretary of the Army, would send it to Ridgway hoping, he wrote, that "such talk" would not "produce an unfavorable emotional reaction on the part of General MacArthur." Ridgway agreed that the issue was "a most delicate one, in which I must proceed very carefully." He did not want "some completely innocent act or utterance" of his "misconstrued."

Washington realized, too, that it was still essential to stroke MacArthur at every opportunity. When Dulles returned to Tokyo early in February for more discussions on the language of the draft Japanese peace treaty, he sent an acknowledgment to MacArthur immediately afterwards thanking him for his "wise counsel."

Continuing the illusion of command, MacArthur issued a press release after his February 13 visit with the familiar spin that his retreat had been a subtly devious operation. "Our field strategy," he contended, "initiated upon Communist China's entry into the war, involving a rapid withdrawal to lengthen the enemy's supply lines with resultant pyramiding of his logistical difficulties and an almost astronomical increase in the destructiveness of our air power, has worked well."

Although MacArthur would take credit for planning whatever Ridgway accomplished, he knew better and privately acknowledged as much. Receiving Ridgway's plans for a new offensive, MacArthur had responded on February 4 that he agreed on taking what could be taken without risking serious losses, particularly if "easy prey"—like Inchon for its port facilities (which EUSAK in retreat had demolished) and Kimpo for its airfield. Seoul, said MacArthur realistically, had no military usefulness but did yield psychological and diplomatic advantages. "Your performance of the last two weeks," he closed, "in concept and in execution, has been splendid and worthy of the highest traditions of a great captain."

Ridgway had followed up Operation Thunderbolt in the waning days of January with Operation Roundup on February 5, learning in both the problems of working with multi-national troops. Roundup was halted in its tracks when ROK lines were penetrated in a Chinese counterattack, forcing Ridgway to redeploy reserves. Chipyong-ni and Wonju were held by Americans augmented with a Greek and a French battalion, and supported by Corsairs from carriers off Inchon and the FEAF. The CCF lost an estimated five thousand dead. But Colonel Paul Freeman of the 23rd Regiment had run into difficulties with the much-decorated French, who fought well but lit bonfires at night to keep warm. By crank-up field phone Freeman warned Lieutenant Colonel "Ralph Monclar" (Lieutenant General Magrin-Vernerey had taken a temporary demotion to be able to command a small unit) that his men had to put their telltale fires out—a problem also common with the ROKs. "Yes, yes," said Monclar. "In the morning I will tell them."

When Freeman insisted, Monclar countered with "But, *mon colonel,* they are such little fires."

"Big fires or little fires," said the combative Freeman, "get 'em out, damn it, and do it now! You've already given away your positions to every Red within a hundred miles!"

"Ah, *mon colonel*," Monclar explained, "it is as you say, without doubt. But if they know where we are, they will attack us. Then we will kill them."

Exasperated, Freeman hung up, but the French bonfires went out.

It was just as cold for the fireless Americans and Chinese, who had launched their Fourth Phase offensive in the midst of the UN attacks, surrounding Chipyong-ni, overrunning Hoengsong and reaching Wonju. Moving up to assist the 9th Regiment (2nd Division), the 27th British Regiment, augmented by the Australian Battalion, blocked the CCF advance. Withdrawing, the Chinese released thirty American prisoners they could not take with them, but whom they could have shot, as both sides had done before, or abandoned to freeze. Other Americans had died that way. Always sensitive to press reports, and recipient of many of them from sources cultivated by Willoughby, MacArthur learned of a Toronto newspaper dispatch by a correspondent with the Canadian Princess Patricia Regiment. Bill Boss described a massacre discovered, after the Chinese retreat, at the Korean village of Kudun, four miles south of Chipyong-ni. He counted sixty-eight American bodies, "many naked, killed in flight as they struggled out of their sleeping bags and attempted to get away." They had bedded down after taking the village "and posted a solitary sentry instead of digging in and maintaining a proper watch." They were easy targets.

Most were from the segregated black L Company of the 3rd Battalion, 9th Infantry (3rd Division). Graves Registration found that many of the dead had ring fingers cut off, and winter clothing and boots removed. Their weapons were missing. A finding after Boss's dispatch noted 212 killed, wounded and missing. A report by the CCF 116th Division had claimed annihilation of two companies of what it identified as the U.S. 23rd Regiment before dawn on February 14.

MacArthur was furious. The *Globe and Mail* dispatch was embarrassing and the behavior of the troops involved no less so. He insisted that Ridgway conduct an immediate investigation, especially concerning how the story had "passed your censors." The episode was reminiscent of earlier troop failures and demonstrated that discipline had not fully returned to the Eighth Army. Chinese prisoners confessed in interrogations that they were still being told before leaving for the front that American weapons and winter gear were available for the taking.

At a conference with high ROK officers, Ridgway warned that Chinese troops were still going into battle armed with little more than grenades, and expected to capture weapons and rations. One Chinese prisoner who survived the camps as well as the war wrote afterwards that their resistance below the

Han that February was handicapped by air interdiction of their supply routes and by ice and snow. When food ran short, they thawed the snow to warm frozen fried noodles, all they had left. When ammunition ran short, they resorted, as they did for rations, "to the corpses of the enemies." Some of the Chinese abandoned their frost-jammed guns in the cold, but none their food.

Private James Cardinal, with the 5th Cav, recalled a patrol in the area on the afternoon of February 16 "not too far from the perimeter held by the 23rd," past hundreds of frozen enemy dead "and some Americans also. One in particular still stands out in my mind. . . . I knelt alongside him and turned his body to look at his dog tags. As I turned him, his brains fell out, the entire side of his head having been blown away. . . . His last name was Lombardi and the first two digits of his serial number were 42, indicating that he came from the NY area, which was where I was from."

On February 20, during MacArthur's third visit in nearly as many weeks, Ridgway showed him at Wonju an eyes-only memorandum sent that day to corps commanders and to the ROK chief of staff outlining a proposed recrossing of the Han River. To the distress of the oversensitive Pentagon, Ridgway called it Operation Killer. It was to begin the next day with preparatory air strikes and artillery bombardments. Ridgway intended it to definitively reverse the "retreat psychology that seemed to have seized every commander from the Chief on down." Later he wrote about the objections from Washington, "I did not understand why it was objectionable to acknowledge the fact that war was concerned with killing the enemy. . . . I am by nature opposed to any effort to 'sell' war to people as an only mildly unpleasant business that requires very little in the way of blood."

As was his practice, on his Wonju photo-opportunity visit, MacArthur convened the correspondents at the X Corps command post and announced to Ridgway's "surprise then and even my dismay," as if the planning had been accomplished at the Dai Ichi, "I have just ordered a resumption of the offensive." Ridgway knew that nothing in conception or planning had come from Tokyo. Almond loyally invented for his diary a ten-thirty arrival of MacArthur with his staff, and a conference at which Operation Killer was "described to CINC [commander in chief], who approved." At eleven, Almond added, as if the EUSAK commander hadn't met MacArthur's plane and been there all the time, "Ridgway joined conference." More fudging appears in MacArthur's *Reminiscences,* where he (or Whitney) wrote, "I ordered Ridgway to start north again." In Ridgway's copy of the memoir he wrote in the margin, "No such order was ever issued."

For the first time, but not the last, Ridgway intervened with MacArthur, at first diplomatically, about using Korea as a Hollywood set, "for there was a definite danger connected with it. It had long been MacArthur's habit, whenever a major offensive was about to jump off, to visit those elements of his command that were involved and figuratively to fire the starting gun. . . . The flights themselves were made with such ceremony that knowledge of them was almost certain to reach the enemy." Ridgway, "carefully choosing my words," sent a lengthy message to Tokyo, after which MacArthur postponed his next visit and looked for limelight elsewhere.

Censorship had been in force only since the disasters of December, but MacArthur's bruised vanity was getting in the way of the war. Not only had his statement suggested a belligerence that had vanished, but a role that disappointment and exhaustion had both denied him. Army censors were more concerned with his offering information of benefit to the enemy and of potential cost in casualties. Only the day before, Major General Henry I. Hodes, the EUSAK deputy chief of staff, had laid down the law to Lieutenant Colonel Melvin B. Voorhees and his staff about violation of security regulations in statements to the press. Even generals should not get away with it, Hodes said. "No matter who is quoted, your job is to safeguard the security and welfare of the army."

When reporters filed dispatches quoting MacArthur's press conference remarks, Voorhees was confronted with a no-win situation, for passing the stories endangered security, yet MacArthur was the ultimate authority in the command and had in effect authorized the dispatches by speaking on the record. Voorhees passed them, and they furnished copy for the usually newsless Washington's Birthday holiday.

MacArthur's next claim of hands-on involvement in Korea came in a radio message to the Department of the Army on March 1. He continued to claim strategic advantages for the long retreat in November and December, and reminded Washington of its refusal to let him attack enemy bases in Manchuria. "The enemy," he declared, "is finding it an entirely different problem fighting 350 miles from his base than when he had this 'sanctuary' in his immediate rear, with our air and naval forces practically zeroed out." Adopting Ridgway's moves as his own, he added, "Our strategic plan, notwithstanding the enemy's great numerical superiority, is indeed working well, and I have just directed a resumption of the initiative by our forces. All ranks of this international force are covering themselves with distinction and I again want to commend the outstanding teamwork of the three services under the skillful direction of their able field commanders, General Ridgway, Admiral Struble, and General Partridge." By labeling Ridgway's central role as "our" and linking him in a subordinate trio, MacArthur implied his continuing command supremacy when it was, in fact, now negligible.

Suggesting emphatically that he remained in charge, the next day—March 2—he submitted through Department of the Army channels his draft biweekly report to the United Nations for the second half of February, which concluded,

> While President Truman has indicated that the crossing of the parallel is a military matter to be resolved in accordance with my best judgment as a theater commander, I want to make it quite clear that if and when the issue actually arises, I shall not arbitrarily exercise that authority if cogent political reasons against crossing are then advanced and there is any reasonable possibility that a limitation is to be placed thereon.

Although his language seemed reasonable on the surface, it implied that he continued to exercise political authority with respect to the 38th parallel unless specifically reined in. Marshall and Acheson had already discussed the problems of leaving that decision to MacArthur. He was teleconned to delete the lines from his report, and complied.

Further burnishing his image, MacArthur was back in Korea on March 6, at Suwon, after which he called a press conference to deplore "our existing conditions of restraint." Unless the Pentagon furnished "major additions" to the Eighth Army, "the battle lines in the end will reach a "point of theoretical stalemate." That was, he now understood but kept to himself, what Washington wanted. What would then happen, he warned, would be an indefinite war of "savage slaughter." He had already referred unflatteringly to Ridgway's plans for limited offensives to keep the Chinese off balance as "accordion war." What Ridgway was doing, MacArthur belittled, was fighting a war in which one side pushed forward until its supply lines became attenuated, and the other side, now closer to its sources of supplies and replacements, grew stronger and reversed the process. Attrition of opposing forces leading to deadlock was the only outcome he could foresee. Even if that occurred in the vicinity of the 38th parallel, leaving no gains to the Communists, MacArthur's catastrophe below the Yalu would remain unforgotten. Only winning could compensate for that. He was for old-fashioned victory, but in the new Cold War world such absolutes were denied him.

Even the huge haul of prisoners, most of them taken after Inchon, were trouble rather than trophies of victory. More a burden than a bargaining counter, North Korean and Chinese POWs now numbered nearly 150,000. In Operation Albany, Ridgway ordered them moved from the mainland to enclosures erected on Koje-do, an island off the southern coast near Masan.

The logistical problems in feeding, clothing and policing the increasing prisoner population were enormous, as was coping with their politicization. In the compounds were militants ordered by Mao to be deliberately captured, who organized a seething second front behind the inadequate barbed wire guarded by corruptible Korean troops. Indiscipline, smuggling, conspiracy, mutiny, mock trials, murder, drug trafficking, prostitution, communication with the enemy and with other POW enclosures were all recognized and rife. What American would enter a compound with thousands of the enemy after dark? Preoccupied with the war, Ridgway paid little attention to the potential in the POW camps for explosion. MacArthur, remote in Japan, was largely uninformed.

More than in any other war, prisoners remained belligerents. Some prisoners would become combatants outside their enclosures, not by escaping but by being "turned" and spirited out of their compounds by intelligence agents to return north to organize guerrilla activity or to spy. The secret Operation Turncoat was expensive and inefficient. A top-secret memorandum of December 17, 1950, recommended supporting guerrilla activities in China but recognized that much of that activity was not pro-Chiang but "merely anti-authority." The best bets were bands south of the Yangtze, but, the document conceded, better leadership and logistical support might "accelerate the tempo" but "not greatly increase the number of [anti-Communist] personnel." Some activity was also organized in North Korea, but equally ineffectively. A political officer for Peng, Niu Chun Ren, recalled the dropping by parachute of ten alleged "fully armed" spies who killed a guard before being captured and escorted toward Pyongyang by an officer and two soldiers. "As they rested by the highway, the spies took the weapons of the People's Army, and killed the officer, wounding the two soldiers." Then they hid nearby, to ambush approaching traffic, but once they arrived in Pyongyang, Niu remembered, they were caught—and very likely executed.

Some POWs were trained to slip into China by submarines moving close to the coast, but having "died" once by spurious paper transactions at the POW Hospital, to account for their disappearances (sometimes covered by spurious "escapes"), most died in reality on capture. The intelligence operation would convince Stalin, who needed little excuse to increase his paranoia, that every POW had to be returned, regardless of personal preference, or the Americans would exploit them as spies. "The same thing happened to our POWs," he claimed, alleging that prisoners repatriated by the Americans at the end of World War II continued to reappear in Russia as agents. "Every day we capture a few of them." Despite the Geneva Convention on Treatment of Prisoners of War (which no Communist nation signed), POWs were fair game in covert war.

Although Seoul, mostly now rubble, was recaptured early in March with the Communists making no fight for it and the Americans no fuss, victory in MacArthur's terms was no longer an objective. On February 12, a month earlier, Charles Burton Marshall of the State Department Policy Planning Staff had proposed to Paul Nitze that stabilization of the front roughly along the 38th parallel would save "two sets of faces"—American and Chinese. The Chinese, he noted, had absorbed heavy materiel and manpower losses, and needed to return to the rehabilitation of their country and their economy. George Kennan suggested approaching the Russians secretly to use their clout with the Chinese to initiate informal negotiations. Stalin, however, was the wrong conduit. Hoping to bleed the United States, he saw no bargains to be negotiated. His surrogates in Asia, Stalin confided coldly, "lose nothing, except for their men."

The reoccupation of devastated and depopulated Seoul, the fourth time in nine months that it had changed hands, seemed an opportunity to suggest to the other side that no one could win the war. Peng had already told Mao as much and reinforced his messages with a risky visit to Beijing, a round trip of seven days, traveling mostly in darkness until he could cross the Yalu in safety. Opposing them in Korea to back up the 250,000-man ROK Army, he reminded Mao, were 227,000 American troops and more than 21,000 from Britain, Australia, Turkey, the Philippines, Thailand, Canada, New Zealand, Greece, France, Belgium (with Luxembourg) and the Netherlands. Unless the reluctant Soviets came in with heavy weapons and airpower, UN forces could not be driven out. Mao knew that Stalin would not risk it, and that China could only win a long war of attrition. "Win a quick victory if you can," he advised Peng; "if you can't, win a slow one."

Recognizing Ridgway's contribution to the altered outlook, which had been achieved with almost no additional personnel, a relieved MacArthur, on his next flying visit to the front, on March 6, told him with uncharacteristic effusiveness, "Matt, you do what you think is right every time, and never anything just because you may think I want it done. If you do that and make mistakes, I will back you 100 percent."

16

Courting Dismissal

ALTHOUGH THE COMMUNIST armies were far from defeated and were slipping back to prepare for Peng's spring counteroffensive, the retaking of Seoul raised optimism in the West about a truce roughly on the prewar frontier. On March 20, 1951, the JCS informed MacArthur that the State Department was preparing a presidential announcement that the UN would consider negotiating conditions of a settlement with Red China. In a few days MacArthur was to have a draft that would suggest the general lines of the 38th parallel as reasonable. Since he was already aware of a directive from Truman ordering all officials, including the military, to refrain from pronouncements on foreign policy without clearance, no one expected him to wreck the tentative moves toward peace. The front was shifting far enough to the north for a secure cease-fire line.

Having long considered himself a sovereign power rather than a field commander—wasn't he also viceroy of Japan?—MacArthur gave no heed to restrictions imposed a hemisphere away. In his area he acted as both military and civil authority, and had even ceremonially restored Rhee in Seoul as well as paid, in effect, a state visit to Taipei. In other ways, too, MacArthur was acting on his own. According to C. B. Marshall of Paul Nitze's Policy Planning Staff at the State Department, National Security Agency technicians listening in on Chinese communications from an Air Force base near Tokyo also eavesdropped occasionally on foreign embassy signals to their capitals. Anything interesting was passed along to NSA's headquarters at Arlington Hall, an Army post in the Virginia suburbs of Washington. In mid-March the President was given copies of additional intercepted messages from Spanish and Portuguese diplomats who represented the kind of Rightist dictators with whom MacArthur long had sympathies. (Earlier intercepts had surfaced as far back as October.) The reports to Madrid and Lisbon told of talks with MacArthur in which he claimed confidence that he could transform the war into a means of disposing of the "Chinese Communist question" while the Soviets remained on the sidelines unwilling to risk intervention. (Months before, MacArthur had denied a similar allegation drawn from Brazilian intercepts.)

Truman interpreted the boasts as a MacArthur strategy to push Washington gradually into a wider war, in defiance of State Department aims to bring the conflict to an end. To the President the covert talk about ideological war was treachery, yet much of what MacArthur claimed might have been a foreshadowing of post-Korea political ambitions to be the candidate of the Right in 1952. According to General Whitney much later, MacArthur by February 1951 had devised a plan to defeat the Communists in Korea without actually impinging on Chinese space by "sowing" a "defensive field of radioactive wastes" on the southern banks of the Yalu. Following that, he would trap the enemy at the upper ends of both coasts through amphibious and airborne landings, reinforcing his troops with Chiang's forbidden reserves in Formosa. "It would be Inchon all over again, except on a far larger scale."

The idea was total fantasy. Yet MacArthur was intimating to sympathetic listeners that a limited war fought to sustain a semblance of the status quo failed to justify the sacrifices already made in the field. Unburdening himself to Brigadier General Crawford F. Sams, a career service physician who had long been Military Government chief of health and welfare in Japan, and was due to become Surgeon General of the Army, MacArthur complained that he had been told, in effect, "You will not be permitted to win the Korean War." Knowing that Sams would have an audience at home, MacArthur urged, "Sams, I do not believe that the American people will permit their sons to be killed if they know that they are being killed senselessly under such a directive."

Sams had recently returned from a dangerous mission to the Wonsan area, off the east coast of Korea, where reports were coming in that enemy soldiers were dying of a plague-like disease then endemic in Manchuria. His concern was the possible spread to UN forces. In an amphibious night landing intended to be secret, his raiding party was to seize a stricken soldier—or a diseased corpse or two—and sample blood and skin eruptions. While they were examining three ailing Chinese who were killed for the investigation,

American planes materialized overhead and dropped flares and bombs, jeopardizing the mission, but Sams determined that what the "plague" seemed to be was hemorrhagic smallpox, with often fatal bleeding lesions. From an offshore destroyer he radioed the Dai Ichi that fears of a plague were groundless, but someone in public relations, assuming that the covert operation was a good story, released a sanitized version to the media. United Press transmitted a story, "U.S. General Risks Life Behind Red Lines to Probe Deadly Epidemic." It gave inadvertent backing to Chinese allegations aimed at demonizing the United States. And it was promoted by sympathizers in the West and by pro-Communist correspondents, who claimed that Americans were waging germ warfare by dropping canisters of disease-ridden fleas and flies into Korea and China. The evidence of mysterious outbreaks of disease after American raids was crude, and credible largely to true believers, but like other military powers the U.S. was secretly experimenting with bacteriological weapons and was even employing Japanese specialists who had World War II experience.

Almost every day saw another attempt by MacArthur to sabotage efforts to bargain for a compromise end to the war. On March 8 he entertained Erle Cocke, national commander of the American Legion, at lunch at the embassy and offered his routine alarmist message. On March 12 he granted an interview to Barry Faris, editor in chief of International News Service, warning that the Communist appetite for power, "without the slightest regard for geographical or political boundaries," was "insatiable." He saw the ultimate goal "of those now directing its predatory adventures" as "the universal suppression of human freedom—the springboard to world conquest. . . . They see in Asia the gateway to their nefarious purpose. They must be stopped." Korea, he explained, was only "the immediate battle area."

What MacArthur proposed was a permanent UN military command on the Korean model with forces on call to conduct "global operations," a system which could replace "bilateral or regional security pacts." Although he conceded that "unrest" in Asia was largely due to "depressed standards of living," giving "the false exaggeration of Communist propaganda . . . a real appeal," he argued that the immediate problem was "the threat of foreign aggression." Only after "checking armed aggression" could the UN deal with lifting global poverty.

Faris asked about the general's plans "with respect to a return to the United States," and MacArthur confided that he had "often" said he would return after a Japanese treaty made his post unnecessary. "That, however, was prior to the outbreak of hostilities in Korea and my assignment as the military commander. . . . Should a peace treaty for Japan be consummated prior to the conclusion of that campaign or the security of the United States be otherwise threatened in the Far East, I of course would not presume to dictate my own future moves but would be guided entirely by the wishes of the President."

The next sounding board for MacArthur, on March 15, was Hugh Baillie, chief of United Press. Since MacArthur had not been scolded for any of his recent denunciations of Washington policy, he felt confident that he could again deplore halting the Eighth Army short of "accomplishment of our mission in the unification of Korea." He ridiculed any settlement at the prewar boundary. "Specifically, with reference to the 38th parallel," MacArthur insisted, "there are no natural defense features anywhere near its immediate proximity." He did mention the line of the Imjin River, and higher, and commanding, ground to the northeast, just above the parallel. As events would prove, these were positions already eyed by Ridgway. MacArthur rejected compromise solutions.

In Foggy Bottom, Dean Acheson fumed that MacArthur "had been told over and over again that this was not [any longer] his mission," but the general was not going to let the prewar status quo be the solution to a conflict he insisted on seeing as wider than Korea.

In a remark almost as unhelpful as his A-bomb blunder in November, Truman told a reporter who asked about whether UN forces would go beyond the 38th parallel, "That is a tactical matter for the field commander. A commander-in-chief seven thousand miles away does not interfere with field operations. We are working to free the Republic of Korea. . . . That doesn't have anything to do with the 38th parallel." Truman might have meant Ridgway, who was actually in the field; but MacArthur, from whatever location, was supposed to say nothing political, and he grumbled to his palace guard about a "one-sided gag." Officials in Washington "can say what they want . . . but this old soldier cannot obtain approval on any statement more significant than a [company] morning report."

Although MacArthur's flying visits on a few hours' notice and his press releases claiming great things personally accomplished exasperated Ridgway, the proconsul set off again for Korea shortly after seeing Hugh Baillie, arriving on the morning of March 17. Canceling plans in order to greet MacArthur at an airstrip near Wonju, in central Korea, Ridgway kept his irritation to himself. He was deeply involved in what he called Operation Ripper, begun on March 7, when, not coincidentally, MacArthur had arrived on his last flying visit. Transferring at Kimpo to an L-17 liaison plane prearranged to have five stars painted on its nose, he shuttled east, poked symbolically about for photographers, held a press conference and returned to his Constellation and Japan.

A week later Ripper had begun to reach its objectives. Ridgway circumvented bad weather and rough terrain by employing, Chinese style, hundreds of Korean porters with A-frames on their backs to carry loads over ground inaccessible by vehicle. The enemy was disengaging. Sizable forces appeared to be withdrawing to positions being prepared just above the 38th parallel. Such unreliable informants as the FBI, Chiang and the British military attaché in Moscow suggested that the Soviets might intervene if the U.S. again pushed across the parallel, and Ridgway, although skeptical, conceded to MacArthur that EUSAK would withdraw, then, to positions well south.

From Tokyo, O. P. Smith learned that MacArthur, intending another visit, wanted a jeep tour of the 1st Marine Division without having to leave his vehicle. "So I took my driver and we met the plane," Smith related. MacArthur and Ridgway squeezed in with Smith. It was MacArthur's seventh fleeting trip to Korea since Ridgway had taken command, and to Smith the most memorable:

We started out on the road and I said, "Now, General, we are scattered"—I don't know how many miles we were scattered, maybe sixty miles or so up the road—"and you said you had three hours that you could spend here. We can't make the rounds in three hours." He said, "I've got the time." I said, "All right—if you've got the time."

So we went and picked up a reserve regiment of the division [5th Marines], which was the first unit we ran into—[Colonel Richard W.] Hayward was in command of it at the time—and General MacArthur didn't get out of the jeep; he shook hands with some of the staff officers. Then I said, "The 7th Marines are up the road by the Hongchon River; that's quite a distance." He said, "I've got the time." So we took off for the river. I was hoping [Colonel Homer L.] Litzenberg hadn't crossed the darn thing yet, because it was a deep and fast-flowing river that we would have to ford. But we got to the south bank of the Hongchon and Litzenberg had gone on, so we forded it in the jeep. We actually floated at times, and on the other side we got out of the jeep. We got it going again and found Litzenberg and talked to him. Then General MacArthur said, "I want to see an assault battalion." . . . We kept going up the road and found [Major] Webb Sawyer and his battalion; all the Marines crowded around. Nobody told these Marines it was General MacArthur who was coming up the road, but all of them had cameras. My God, there were a lot of cameras!

The Chinese were still being cleared from the hills above Hongchon, although they were quiet in daylight. The day before, Sawyer's battalion had taken nearby Hill 399 in a grenade attack, which he described to the visiting generals. Then the war tourists bumped over miserable roads for four hours, without a stop, back to Wonju, where MacArthur "marched majestically off to his plane and all the rest of us just disappeared." But before they scattered, Ridgway, in some discomfort, asked, "Smith, why in hell didn't you suggest we stop to take a leak?"

"Well," said Smith, "you were the senior [general], and I think it was up to you to suggest that!"

MacArthur's twelfth flying trip to Korea had been his longest. Ridgway had taken command only too well, and MacArthur wanted to appear to be in charge.

Returning to the Dai Ichi, MacArthur fielded a complaint from the Army G-3 in Washington, now General Maxwell Taylor, that the Pentagon had not received the details of Ripper in advance. For once MacArthur was innocent of bypassing the JCS. Ridgway, not wanting MacArthur to interfere, had advised Tokyo only vaguely of his plans. Claiming whatever credit he could, MacArthur replied that the operation was only a carrying out of ideas constantly exchanged between his headquarters and the Eighth Army commander, and that no formal orders had been issued by the Dai Ichi. But he did instruct Ridgway not to cross the parallel without authority from the Dai Ichi. "If [the] press forces you to discuss questions [about the 38th parallel], evade direct reply by saying matter is for my decision."

For any peace initiative to have a chance—and no one knew if the ideologues in Pyongyang and Beijing would talk seriously in any case—MacArthur had to be reined in. The MacArthur problem was a major element of discussions involving Marshall, Acheson and the JCS on March 19 as they reviewed a draft of the proposal to go out under the President's signature. From his vacation retreat at a naval station in Key West, Florida, Truman relayed his approval. It was crucial for American relations with its increasingly disenchanted allies in Korea, and with Third World nations which saw Rhee as only an extension of Western imperialism, that the offer be both pragmatic and serious.

A message requesting MacArthur's views was radioed to the Dai Ichi:

State Department planning a Presidential announcement shortly that, with clearing of bulk of South Korea of aggressors, United Nations now [is] preparing to discuss conditions of settlement. . . . United Nations feeling exists that further diplomatic efforts towards settlement should be made before any advance with major forces north of 38th parallel. Time will be required to determine diplomatic reactions and permit new negotiations that may develop. Recognizing that parallel has no military significance, State has asked JCS what authority you should have to permit sufficient freedom of action for next few weeks to provide security for the United Nations forces and maintain contact with [the] enemy. Your recommendations desired.

Immediately—it was already March 21 in Japan—MacArthur returned a response that effectively ignored the request. Again he complained about restrictions on him which made it "completely impracticable to clear North Korea or to make any appreciable effort toward that end." Yet no one anywhere but Tokyo was talking about such an end now. His existing orders, MacArthur claimed, clinging to whatever ambiguity remained to him, gave him whatever authority he needed.

Ridgway's plans required no change from Washington. He was to clear the Communists from South Korea if he could, and to cripple as much as possible their ability to mount a counteroffensive. The diplomats had to do the rest. For strategic reasons he wanted to retrieve Chunchon, in central Korea just below the parallel, and had readied the 187th Airborne Regiment for the mission. Scheduled for March 20, Operation Hawk had to be called off. The enemy had withdrawn so deeply as to make the deployment unnecessary. The 1st Cav merely moved in.

Changing the operation's site and name, Ridgway ordered Tomahawk for March 23—this time a drop at Munsan, north of Seoul and practically astride the parallel. But the day before, MacArthur reminded him who remained in charge. A top-secret "flash" warned Ridgway that he was not to cross the 38th parallel "in force" without advance authority "from me." More diplomatically he praised Ridgway's able tactics to date and closed with what was no longer an unusual concession: "If you have any suggestions let me have them."

On the morning of the movement Ridgway received another message from MacArthur, and expected it to be a cancellation of the action as politically risky. Ridgway read it in amazement. "Am in complete accord with the plan you have outlined to advance to the phase line indicated in your message. Make no announcements to this effect and allow the actual events to constitute sole press information. Further action beyond your suggested phase line will be determined by you in accordance with my previous message. Will see you at Seoul airfield Saturday." MacArthur wanted to create new facts at the parallel to outfox Washington.

With his pilot, Mike Lynch, Ridgway took off in his light plane, flying north of Seoul over enemy lines to observe the drops, one to the north of the village, one to the south. Missing a checkpoint, the lead aircraft for the southern drop aborted and headed north. Watching from five-hundred feet, Ridgway saw other planes mistakenly releasing their parachutists, and in the middle of the confusion Lynch was forced to land near a rice-paddy dike, nearly pitching the AT-6 over as its tail wheel scraped the edge of a hut. Once out of the plane, they drew small-arms fire. Ridgway, walking much too erectly, had to jump into the protection of a ditch. Paratroopers nearby asked Lynch where their road junction objective was, and he shouted, "Ten miles from here. You guys dropped in the wrong area."

With Lynch in unanticipated command of the squad, they silenced a machine-gun emplacement and returned with four prisoners. Then the GIs helped Lynch push his plane around for takeoff while mortar shells fell. At the first lull, Lynch, with Ridgway aboard, throttled the plane into the air. Later that night they learned that an armored column coming up from the south had relieved the troops left behind.

The operation was both a failure and a lesson. Although Ridgway identified with airborne warfare, sentiment and strategy were worlds apart. Korea was the wrong place for it. Its tactical day had passed.

Since MacArthur was flying in the next morning, Ridgway had to be at Kimpo at eleven for the arrival. Any other greeter would be a snub. This time, reminded cautiously by Ridgway not to tip off the enemy, MacArthur had waited until the operation had begun.

As the generals jeeped northward to Uijongbu, the 3rd Division's relocated headquarters, MacArthur warned that a collapse of the Chinese—of which there was no hint but their pullback—might bring in the Russians. Ridgway scoffed at the scenario, recognizing that if atomic war were the result, it would be suicidal for Russia, which was still grossly understrength in nuclear potential. "That would be the end of her," MacArthur agreed hopefully. In Washington, since every contingency had to be considered, Omar

Bradley, on April 5, sent a memo to Marshall from the JCS advising, "If the USSR precipitates a general war, UN forces should be withdrawn from Korea as rapidly as possible and deployed for service elsewhere. . . . The US should then mobilize in readiness for general war."

As usual MacArthur remained in Korea only a few hours, fording the Hongchon River with Ridgway in a jeep (with portable five-star license plate attached) and continuing on bumpily, attached by a chain to another vehicle, when the jeep broke down. Before departing at 2:40 p.m. MacArthur permitted correspondents reporting from the "western sector" of the front to quote him, to Washington's irritation, as saying, "Everything goes well. . . . No further comment will be necessary with reference to the 38th parallel, the status of which has been so thoroughly discussed in recent statements from Washington, London and other capitals. As a matter of fact," he dismissed, "it has never had any military significance. Our naval and air forces cross it at will and . . . ground forces have done so in the past. I have directed the Eighth Army to do so again if and when its security makes it tactically advisable."

Actually, everything had not gone well. Although the ruins of Seoul had been reoccupied on March 14, the airborne envelopment of the withdrawing enemy by the 187th Regimental Combat Team had missed its mark. Also, the North Korean 10th Division, trapped in the southwest for months and surviving as guerrillas, had found a weak spot where the ROKs were deployed, and broken through at Kangnung to link up with Communist forces.

ROK troops remained unreliable and unrestrained. Rhee enjoined them to cross the 38th parallel, which, to MacArthur's satisfaction as well, they did, on March 27 at Yangnung in the east. In the west, the ROK 1st Division crossed the Imjin River north of the parallel on the same day. American and other UN forces would follow, shortening the line from coast to coast. Ridgway would label the new front Line Kansas. It ran 116 miles from tidal lands in the west to the lower banks of the Hwachon Reservoir in the center to rugged, mountainous terrain eastward to the Sea of Japan. (It would be a close approximation to the demilitarized zone eventually negotiated.) The Chinese, however, were not retreating headlong, as after Inchon. They were mobilizing their armies for a spring offensive to regain some of the strategic initiative lost during Ridgway's three-month effort to reconstitute the Eighth Army.

Although Washington wanted to see the 38th parallel crossed, quietly, to enhance the UN negotiating position, having MacArthur brag about it seemed unhelpful. Far less helpful, as his plane was taking off from Kimpo en route to Tokyo, was a Dai Ichi release in his name that sabotaged the attempt by Truman and Acheson to issue an offer to negotiate a cease-fire. "The Unified Command," the State Department proposed to say, in cautious diplomatic language, "is prepared to enter into arrangements which would conclude the fighting and ensure against its resumption . . . including the withdrawal of foreign troops from Korea." It raised hopes that a "prompt settlement of the Korean problem" would "reduce international tension in the Far East and would open the way for the consideration of other problems in that area by the processes of peaceful settlement envisaged in the [UN] Charter." The phraseology hinted at a possible UN seat for China and resolution of the Formosa issue. "The thought behind this," Truman commented later, "was that a suggestion of our willingness to settle, without any threats or recriminations, might get a favorable reply."

Arrogantly, MacArthur derailed the initiative. Later he called his statement from Tokyo a "routine communiqué," but he knew very well that his own demand for peace was in reality an ultimatum—daring China to continue the war. Deliberately, he had released it without consultation with Washington. The tactical successes of his forces, his challenge claimed, proved that Communist China was a vastly overrated military power weak in every way but its ability to throw thousands of expendable men into battle. "Even under the inhibitions which now restrict the activity of the United Nations forces and the corresponding military advantages which accrue to Red China, it has shown its complete inability to accomplish by force of arms the conquest of Korea."

MacArthur taunted, "The enemy . . . must now be painfully aware that a decision of the UN to depart from its tolerant effort to contain the war to . . . Korea through expansion of our military operations to his coastal areas and interior bases"—and he clearly meant China itself—"would doom Red China to the risk of imminent military collapse. . . ."

He realized that everything he said intruded into foreign policy and was off-limits. Subverting the chances of a negotiated settlement, he threatened to widen the war unless the Chinese met personally with him. Yet he professed innocently that he was acting only in his military role. "Within my area of authority as military commander, however, it should be needless to say I stand ready at any time to confer in the field with the commander in chief of the enemy forces in an earnest effort to find any military means whereby the realization of the political objectives of the United Nations in Korea, to which no nation may justly take exception, might be accomplished without further bloodshed."

In Washington it was still March 23. An hour after the message was received at the Pentagon, Robert Lovett, the undersecretary of defense, was at Dean Acheson's home in Georgetown with Dean Rusk and Soviet expert Alexis Johnson. It was eleven at night, and although Truman retired and rose early, one of the exasperated conferees urged that the President be telephoned. Acheson disagreed. First, he suggested, they should each go home and sleep on the dilemma. Lovett proposed that MacArthur be removed at once. "Whom the gods destroy, they first make mad," Acheson agreed, feeling that MacArthur had "shot his face off" but that the JCS would be reluctant to sack him.

Newsweek would publish a story about MacArthur's violation of standing orders from Washington, prompting him to send the editors a dishonest message claiming, "That I had been furnished with a copy of a policy statement by the President . . . is entirely without basis in fact. I have never seen such a statement and do not know if it even exists. Please publish this in the interest of truth."

At Senate hearings later he was asked again about the December directive warning him to keep out of foreign policy. He continued to disclaim knowledge of it. He was asked (the question was rephrased) whether he knew of the March initiative being circulated to UN combatant governments. Yes, he conceded. "It had nothing to do with my statement. . . . There is nothing unusual or unorthodox or improper that I can possibly read into the statement that I made on March 24." That he again told less than the truth became evident that October when he spoke to an enthusiastic American Legion gathering and claimed that his proposal had sidetracked one of the most "disgraceful plots" in American history. Allegedly the U.S. was about to sell out Formosa and the Chinese UN seat to secure peace in Korea.

The next morning Truman awakened to the news of MacArthur's sabotage. Later he claimed that he made up his mind to get rid of MacArthur at that moment. "I could no longer tolerate his insubordination." Yet it had taken the most brazen of MacArthur's challenges to authority to reach that stage. (In his memoirs, Truman writes that after reading, on August 26, 1950, a press release about MacArthur's Veterans of Foreign Wars statement, he gave serious thought to firing the general and replacing him with Bradley, but reconsidered and asked instead for a withdrawal of the remarks, which amounted to a mild public rebuke.) As early as February 22, testing how much latitude he had, MacArthur had sent a Cold War message to the Fourth Anti-Communist Convention in New York, to be read at Carnegie

Hall by Mayor Vincent Impellitteri. It ruled out compromise. "Predatory Communist adventures must be decisively defeated," MacArthur declared. "Otherwise, all of Asia will fall to Communism." He had begun to dare Truman to relieve him and risk the domestic political consequences.

UN allies, Acheson realized, were wondering who was running the government of the United States. The order of December 6 which MacArthur had disobeyed was explicit enough to warrant court-martial proceedings. He had been building up, deliberately, it now seemed, the impetus for the anti-Communist martyrdom which might furnish him with an international forum and a renewed presidential boom. In response, Truman had given MacArthur more rope on which to hang himself, instructing the Joint Chiefs to remind the general of the December directive and to order him to report any request for an armistice in the field to the JCS "for instructions."

Set on his collision course, MacArthur looked for further opportunities to subvert Truman's policy. The next came in an interview with the military correspondent for the London *Daily Telegraph,* H. G. Martin, a retired general. His troops, MacArthur complained, were "circumscribed by a web of artificial conditions." He charged that he was fighting "without a definite objective," yet the vague intent was subject to international negotiation. For what "definite purpose," he wondered to Martin, were the six thousand to seven thousand casualties each month being incurred? (U.S. and UN battle casualties in March, aside from ROK troops, had been 728 killed in action, 4,649 wounded and 173 missing, for a total of 5,550.)

MacArthur's unusual constraints, neither he nor Martin acknowledged, were the result of something new in war, the first experiment in international peacekeeping. The other side, neither a UN member nor a signatory to the Geneva Conventions, could disclaim legal restraints on its conduct. Many of MacArthur's missing in action would never be traced. POWs could be mistreated. From the first weeks of the war, those not shot on the spot when taken prisoner were often marched, from sundown to sunup, to makeshift prison camps, most of them now in the far north. If they fell, from weakness (they had little food) or from wounds, they were abandoned. Often they had to eat their handful of corn or millet boiled in water from their cupped hands. Hundreds were taken across the Yalu to isolated camps inside China for interrogation and never accounted for. The Pentagon knew what was happening, feared for their lives if the matter became public and said nothing. Since the Chinese government was technically not a belligerent, the removal of POWs amounted to kidnapping. Admitting nothing, Mao's minions let the prisoners die miserably of malnutrition or maltreatment. They vanished from history until Defense Department intelligence records were declassified in 1998.

On March 17, Sergeant Charles Schlichter arrived at POW Camp No. 5, luckily on the Korean side of the Yalu, leading twenty lice-ridden prisoners pale with jaundice and near starvation all piled on a mule cart. There they were separated by Chinese guards into officers, NCOs and other ranks, and given some straw to lie on. He would survive. Larry Zellers, a missionary captured in Kaesong on the first day of the war, found himself at another North Korean camp, at Antung, in a mixture of civilian and military prisoners. Later in March when nine B-29s flew over and dropped bombs on the southern spans of a bridge across the Yalu, a guard angrily shot an airman POW, an F-80 pilot.

The relocation to the new camp gave Zellers a rare opportunity to glean uncensored news from more recently taken prisoners, and the appearance of the B-29s itself renewed hope. "All the news supplied by the Communists," he wrote after the war, "had to be treated as suspect. Their reports depicted a world that was totally alien to us. They told us, for example, that people all over America were rioting in the streets, that millions were starving to death, and that thousands of American soldiers in South Korea were deserting their units." From the POWs themselves he heard tales of weapons that did not work, walkie-talkie radios unusable for lack of batteries and poor-to-nonexistent intelligence. Zellers also learned that every POW camp housed both informers and collaborators, whose cooperation had been bought more with bits of tobacco or food than by brainwashing. The best strategy for staying alive until the war ended, he realized, was "to trust no one."

With the press his forum, MacArthur continued to fight his war of words while Ridgway cautiously probed above the 38th parallel. MacArthur had always welcomed press questionnaires in lieu of face-to-face interviews, and the politically conservative *Freeman* magazine published his response to a leading question about why South Korea was sending draftees home for lack of equipment which the U.S. could supply. The general's answer was that the matter "involves basic political decisions beyond my authority." Rather than have the South Koreans defend their own soil the U.S., he implied, preferred to have its own troops die. But, in fact, MacArthur had recommended on January 6 that weapons *not* be furnished to the Korean Youth Corps, which he felt was unreliable.

Just as MacArthur's apparent failure to keep to his instructions was causing consternation in Washington, Ridgway's overzealousness was creating problems with his chief in Tokyo. Whatever flexibility MacArthur said he had granted to Ridgway, the *SCAP* wanted to call the shots. He had instructed Ridgway to slow down his advance north in order to determine what the Chinese were up to, but a battalion on patrol had blundered into a firefight, called for divisional help, and before long the bulk of a corps was involved. The Chinese were turned back at their cost, but MacArthur interpreted the clash as a violation of his order and called in Hickey and Wright.

"General," explained Wright, his operations chief, "this is one of those things that just happened. . . . It wasn't an intended violation."

"Pinky," MacArthur said stubbornly, "I want you to write a letter to General Ridgway and in effect tell him that this won't [be allowed to] happen again."

Wright drafted a cautious letter for MacArthur's signature, and with Hickey, the acting chief of staff, brought it to the "Old Man's" office. MacArthur examined it with an increasingly angry look and, turning to Hickey, asked, "Doyle, have you read this?"

"Yes," said Hickey, "I've read it. I think it is very good."

"I don't like it at all. I want General Ridgway reprimanded."

Wright explained that the violation was "a sort of accident." The situation in Korea was "fine." But MacArthur declared, "All right, *I'll* write it." He drafted several pages flamboyantly. "You take this down," he ordered Wright, "and have your people type this."

Reading it on the elevator, Wright realized that the message was unnecessarily hot-tempered and called in Hickey for help. "Doyle," he appealed, "let's not let him send this." But MacArthur liked it even more when he saw the typed result and called it "what I wanted."

Summoning up his courage, Hickey ventured, "I don't think you ought to send it, General. I think you are going entirely too far."

Wright agreed, declaring the reproof "an insult. . . . He doesn't deserve it."

"Well, this is what I want," said MacArthur. He signed it and instructed Wright to deliver it personally in the *SCAP* Constellation.

By four in the afternoon the next day Wright had reached Ridgway's "tactical headquarters" just above the 38th parallel—a tent. It was raining, but Wright waited outside for the absent Ridgway. When the general returned, landing nearby in a light observation plane, Wright tendered the letter he had been "directed to deliver to you personally."

Ridgway removed it from its unsealed envelope and read it, "and his face turned white because he was so mad."

"Have you read this letter?" he asked.

"Yes, I read it."

"Who wrote this letter?"

"General MacArthur wrote the letter."

"Are you positive that he wrote this letter?"

"Yes, I am," said Wright uneasily.

"When you get back to Tokyo," Ridgway said, "you tell General Mac-Arthur that I understand the letter and I understand exactly what he meant and that he can be well assured that I will follow his directive exactly as indicated." And he asked Wright to repeat the response, as he was not going to write it down.

It was now dark, and the cold rain persisted, but Ridgway made no offer to have Wright remain until morning, referring sharply to his posh GHQ digs. "Well," Ridgway closed, "I know you are anxious to get back to the Imperial Hotel, so you can leave whenever you want to." Wright was being rebuked for his boss.

To Ridgway's exasperation, on April 3, just as he ordered a new operation (Dauntless) to advance I and IX Corps into a salient north of the 38th parallel, MacArthur flew in for what he did not know would be his last visit to Korea. Ridgway had to drop everything in order to meet the Supreme Commander at K-18 air base, near Kangnung on the east coast, and escort him by jeep north to Yangyang. The reoccupied village just above the parallel apparently had a geographical symbolism for MacArthur which he wanted for waiting cameramen. Then his party quickly returned to reboard the *SCAP* and go back to Tokyo without observing the central front above Chunchon, where the main action was taking place, or the western sector above Seoul and Uijongbu.

Even before the coverage in the press of what was no more than a photo opportunity, General Peng predicted to Beijing, "Recent inspections by Mac-Arthur and Ridgway on the eastern front [suggest that] it is most likely that the enemy will launch a frontal attack in the east coordinated by an amphibious operation on Wonsan and Tongchon. . . ."

To Truman, whose dislike of MacArthur's style was even more pronounced than his dislike of MacArthur's politics, the general in the waning days of March was replaying the conflict in 1864 between Lincoln and George McClellan. General McClellan had ignored directives as to how the Army of the Potomac should fight the Confederacy, and went on to be the presidential candidate for Lincoln's opposition. Republicans on the Right were already talking divisively of sending a congressional delegation to Tokyo, to explore with MacArthur how the war should be conducted. Long willing to cooperate with leading Republicans, MacArthur had already offered his views on running the war to Representative Joseph Martin, Minority Leader of the House of Representatives. On February 12, in a speech on the floor of the House, Martin had deplored the "sheer folly" of not using Chiang's troops in Korea, and several weeks later sent a text of his remarks to MacArthur, inviting comment.

Early in April, Martin read the general's reply to the House:

I am most grateful for your note of the eighth forwarding me a copy of your address of February 12. The latter I have read with much interest and find that with the passage of years you have certainly lost none of your old time punch.

My views and recommendations with respect to the situation created by Red China's entry into war against us in Korea have been submitted to Washington in most complete detail. Generally these views are well known and generally understood, as they follow the conventional pattern of meeting force with maximum counterforce as we have never failed to do in the past. Your view with respect to the utilization of the Chinese forces on Formosa is in conflict with neither logic nor this tradition.

It seems strangely difficult for some to realize that here in Asia where the Communist conspirators have elected to make their play for global conquest, and we have joined the issue here raised on the battlefield, that here we fight Europe's war with arms while the diplomats there still fight it with words; that if we lose this war to Communism in Asia the fall of Europe is inevitable; win it and Europe most probably would avoid war and yet preserve freedom. As you point out, we must win. There is no substitute for victory.

Although the rhetoric was familiar MacArthurese, the time and place made the language explosive. After his flight to Formosa months before he had, if reluctantly, endorsed the administration's decision to forgo the offer of Nationalist troops for Korea. At a time when the United States had to maintain deterrent strength in Europe against the Soviets, MacArthur continued to conduct his single-note symphony about his sector of the globe. As for the theatrical "no substitute for victory," MacArthur as a general did not have to deal with diplomacy, where even victories had to be masked into mutual acceptability.

Truman saw only a military commander plotting with a leader of the political opposition. "MacArthur shoots another political bomb through Joe

Martin," he wrote angrily in his diary. "This looks like the last straw. Rank insubordination. I've come to the conclusion that our Big General in the Far East must be recalled."

The Times of London called the Martin letter the "most dangerous" of an "apparently unending series of indiscretions," while a British government spokesman raged against "such irresponsible statements, without the authority of the United States or indeed of any [UN] member government." On April 9, Sir William Slim, Chief of the Imperial General Staff, told a meeting of Commonwealth chiefs of staff in London that in his opinion, "MacArthur personally wanted war with China. . . . As he had proved in November and December last year, he had few scruples about colouring both intelligence and operational reports to suit his own ends." Slim thought it "inadvisable" to delegate to the American JCS any authority to pass on to MacArthur for a "massive air attack" in the vicinity of the Yalu. "They were scared of General MacArthur; his definition of the scope of the air attack . . . might well be coloured to suit his own wishes."

Putting further pressure on Washington, the Foreign Secretary cabled his ambassador there, presumably for Dean Acheson's ears, "Our principal difficulty is General MacArthur. His policy is different from the policy of the UN. He seems to want a war with China. It is no exaggeration to say that by his public utterances, he has weakened public confidence in this country and in Western Europe in the quality of American political judgement and leadership. Here we seem to have a case of a commander publicly suggesting that his policy is not the stated policy of his government, not subject to the control of his government, and whom his own government is, nevertheless, unwilling and unable to discipline." Had Slim asked one of his Second World War colleagues, Field Marshal Bernard Montgomery, he would have found less unanimity among his more knowledgeable countrymen. Generals, the outspoken Montgomery would tell Cy Sulzberger, "are never given adequate directives. This was the case with MacArthur. First, he was told to hold on to South Korea and to drive the North Koreans out. Then, he was told to reunite Korea, which meant conquering all of North Korea. One cannot blame him for being confused. The records will show he never received any truly logical instructions." But realizing how Montgomery, like MacArthur, was wont to evade instructions, Sulzberger added in this diary, "[Montgomery] tends to bring to my mind Clemenceau's remark that war is entirely too important to be left in the hands of generals."

The predictably good words for MacArthur in the U.S. came from such domestic supporters as otherwise isolationist Senator Robert Taft, who thought it was "utterly indefensible and perfectly idiotic . . . not to let Chiang Kai-Shek's troops loose." Senator Wayne Morse, a maverick Republican from Oregon, observed that the United States had two foreign policies, "that of General MacArthur and that of the President." Foreshadowing what now seemed inevitable, Robert Kerr of Oklahoma, a Democratic power in the Senate, told a reporter about MacArthur, "I think the prolonged perform- ance of his one-man act is wearing the patience of the rest of the team pretty thin." Still, the issue of anti-Communism had split Democratic ranks while energizing the Republican right wing. Harry Truman, elected in 1948 by a minority vote, was finding himself in even more legislative weakness because of the defections of conservative members of his own party. Recognizing this, *The Washington Post* headlined, "MacArthur Recall Ruled Out. Reprimand Is Still Seen Possible." The press would have been even more skeptical about a recall had it known that the Joint Chiefs had secretly approved his request "to make a show of force" off the coast of southern China and in the Taiwan Strait, as a message to Beijing and to obtain photographs. The mission would be carried out by twenty warships and 140 planes on April 11 and 13, while newspapers were preoccupied with MacArthur himself.

In the Oval Office on the morning of April 6, Acheson, Marshall, Bradley and Harriman were closeted with the President to determine how to dispose of MacArthur. Bradley and Harriman wanted him fired forthwith. They detailed a litany of grievances against the general, going back to prewar occupation policy. Acheson was also for relief of MacArthur, but wanted una- nimity among both civilian and military advisers—"a completely unified front, with no cracks in it whatever."

Marshall, who had known MacArthur throughout their long military lives, and had cause to feel that MacArthur had held his career back in the 1920s and 1930s, warned nevertheless that Congress was practically a Mac- Arthur fan club, and that military appropriations might be held hostage. "I'm going to fire the son of a bitch *right now*," Truman insisted.

Endorsing Marshall's caution, Acheson observed that no matter how much support there was in the JCS for sacking MacArthur, to the public it would appear to be the President's impetuous action. "If you relieve Mac- Arthur," he said, "you will have the biggest fight of your administration."

That afternoon, a Friday, the group met without Truman in Acheson's office. Marshall still held out, suggesting that MacArthur only be called home for "consultation." That would leave his future up to him. The others were opposed and Marshall withdrew the suggestion.

On Saturday morning just before nine the four advisers again met with Truman at Blair House, but postponed any action until the Joint Chiefs met. Sensing Marshall's continuing reluctance to face the political repercussions from the Right, the President suggested that before they gathered on Monday for a final decision, Marshall reexamine the cable traffic between MacArthur and Washington since the start of the war.

In the exchange of cables, most of them routine, was an off-the-wall request to the Pentagon on March 10 asking for "atomic capability" to take out Manchurian airfields if that became necessary to retain air superiority north of the 38th parallel. The revived on-again, off-again nuclear exchange would continue as an ironic counterpoint to the agonized debate over relieving MacArthur—expanded war juxtaposed with realpolitik peace. Four days later, Hoyt Vandenberg had replied that the Secretary of the Air Force and the Undersecretary of Defense had gone along: "Finletter and Lovett alerted on atomic discussions. Believe everything is set." On March 31, Stratemeyer reported to MacArthur that atomic bomb loading pits at the Kadena air base on Okinawa were operational and that unassembled Mark IV bombs were on hand.

Further concern had now arisen that a "major attack" originating outside Korea from Shantung Province and Manchuria was pending to push UN forces away from the 38th parallel. Hoping to initiate the armistice negotiations which MacArthur's political intrusions had apparently torpedoed, or at worst to preemptively strike at enemy concentrations expected to escalate the war, Bradley brought a JCS recommendation to the President on April 6, authorizing MacArthur—despite his tenuous position—to initiate a preemptive nuclear strike if an attack appeared to be materializing. Between the lines was the possibility that such a nuclear warning, certain to emerge via press leakage, might have the intended persuasive effect.

Truman telephoned AEC chairman Gordon Dean, who came immediately to the White House. The Bomb, Truman confided, might be employed beyond, rather than within, Korea, but he would reserve the decision for its use until he had consulted with the National Security Council's special committee on atomic energy. Dean telephoned Vandenberg for the President, authorizing transfer of nine nuclear cores "from AEC to military custody." The next day, April 7, the 99th Medium Bomb[er] Wing in California was ordered to pick up the bombs for delivery to Guam, but not to proceed to Okinawa as originally planned. Since the deployment was only cautionary, the strike force commander would remain in Nebraska at SAC headquarters rather than fly with his B-29s to Japan.

Since MacArthur's proconsulship seemed about to terminate, JCS chairman Bradley also held up a directive, approved by Truman and Acheson, that authorized retaliatory strikes on an approved list of targets outside Korea, if necessary. Late that Sunday, April 8, the Joint Chiefs had met again to consider Truman's decision to recall MacArthur. During a transfer of command, strike orders were best held in abeyance. The likely changes in Tokyo inevitably and quickly removing a cadre of MacArthur intimates might even improve prospects for a more peaceful end to the war than activating the nuclear option suggested.

Atomic weapons secrets could not be withheld from Congress's Joint Committee on Atomic Energy. Eighteen legislators, many of them leakprone, were involved, some also likely to be critics of the relief of MacArthur. Truman might have even intended some leakage of his atomic intentions, as the show of forcefulness would demonstrate that his shake-up in the Far East meant no weakness in prosecuting the war.

In that background of tension, Truman began preparing his radio speech to the nation explaining why he had decided to replace MacArthur. Recalling the nuclear deliberations in 1960, after the history of the MacArthur months in Korea had been rewritten from the Waldorf-Astoria, MacArthur deplored the timidity of the leadership in Washington, who "lost their courage when, with our control of the air and seas, our virtual monopoly of the atom bomb, and with half a million fresh troops offered by Generalissimo Chiang Kaishek, we could have destroyed Red China's capacity for making war. . . ." He would have been less reluctant than Truman to use the bomb, he claimed. But whatever MacArthur's hindsight, it had been the Pentagon that had rattled the Bomb and even teased MacArthur with it, and that would send a second flight of never-to-be-employed nuclear-configured aircraft across the Pacific while MacArthur unpacked in New York.

On Sunday afternoon, April 8, at two, Bradley again convened the JCS. A face-saving alternative was raised—to keep MacArthur in Japan to oversee the occupation, but to replace him as military commander. When that failed on grounds that two commanders in one theater of operations were one too many, the JCS conceded that the general had to be relieved. At four they walked down the corridor to Marshall's office overlooking the Potomac and central Washington. No one welcomed what had to be done. "It was not easy," Collins conceded, "to be a party to the dismissal of such a distinguished soldier." As Collins's G-3, General Bolté, put it years later, "We were all rather scared of him. When you considered what he had been. . . ."

Each offered an opinion hedged as "from a military point of view only." Admiral Sherman saw the necessity for limiting the conflict, which required "a commander in whom we can confide and on whom we can rely." Collins felt that the President was "entitled to have a commander in the field whose views were more in consonance with the basic policies of his government and who was more responsive to the will of the President as Commander in Chief." All saw the necessity for civilian control of the military—a constitutional imperative. Marshall offered no comment but asked Bradley to report to the President on Monday morning. Touching bases, meanwhile, outside the administration, Truman telephoned Sam Rayburn, Speaker of the House, then Chief Justice Fred Vinson, both old friends from the President's years in Congress. "We talked for a long time," Truman recalled. "The Chief Justice advised caution. He said the authority of the President of the United States was at stake." Both offered no advice but "to weigh the situation very carefully and come to my own conclusion."

Anticipating MacArthur's dismissal, Marshall that Sunday, already Monday, April 9, in Japan, fired off a cryptic cable to Army Secretary Frank Pace, then in his first day in Tokyo en route to Korea on a routine inspection mission. "This is explicit. Repeat, this is explicit. You will proceed to Korea and remain there until you hear from me." However puzzled, Pace flew to Korea, where Ridgway was to escort the Pentagon party to the front and review the current situation.

When Monday morning came in Washington, Truman's crisis team was back in the White House at nine prior to a scheduled Cabinet meeting, this time with the addition of Bradley. He opened by reporting JCS unanimity on dismissal. Marshall confided that he had "gone over all those telegrams and communications . . . over the past two or three years," and had "come to the conclusion that the general should have been relieved two or three years ago."

"Thank you," said Truman. "Now will you write me the order relieving General MacArthur of his command, and I will have him brought home."

The order of relief, prepared by Paul Nitze for Acheson with Bradley's aide, Colonel Chester Clifton, would be written in Bradley's name and signed by him. It largely quoted a message to MacArthur from the President, penned by Marshall. "The only question," Truman had instructed them, "was how to do it with the least fuss."

"You will turn over your command at once," the message closed, bluntly, "to Lieutenant General Matthew B. Ridgway. You are authorized to have issued such orders as are necessary to complete desired travel to such place as you may select . . . ."

There had never been any question that Ridgway would replace Mac-Arthur, although Bradley brought up the appointment formally. The JCS also proposed Lieutenant General James Van Fleet as Ridgway's successor in the field. A means of diplomatically and confidentially notifying MacArthur was the next order of business. Using military channels, Acheson cautioned, "would be a grave humiliation and embarrassment" to the general as "almost everyone in his headquarters [would] know he was relieved before he knew." State Department code was agreed upon.

Korea was also on the mind of Judge Irving Kaufman as he passed sentence that morning, in U.S. District Court in New York, on Julius and Ethel Rosenberg, convicted atomic bomb spies. The Espionage Act of 1917 carried a maximum penalty of death. "I consider your crime worse than murder," said Kaufman to the husband-and-wife defendants, who had pleaded not guilty.

> In murder a criminal kills only his victim. Your conduct in putting into the hands of the Russians the A-bomb [several] years before our best scientists predicted Russia would perfect the bomb has already caused, in my opinion, the Communist aggression in Korea, with the resultant casualties exceeding 50,000 and who knows but that millions more of innocent people may pay the price of your treason. Indeed by your betrayal you have altered the course of history to the disadvantage of our country. We have evidence of your treachery all around us every day. . . .

The Rosenbergs were sentenced to death in the electric chair, victims not only of their political zeal but of the Korean War.

Escorted still by Ridgway, Pace on his second day in Korea was jeeped to the 936th Field Artillery Battalion, formerly a National Guard unit from his home state of Arkansas. It had just been cleared for action and Pace was invited to pull a lanyard to fire the first salvo. On the casing of the shell, Ridgway recalled, a soldier had chalked "a ribald greeting to the Chinese in the impact area." A correspondent covering the visit shouted out something to the general which sounded like, "When are you leaving for Tokyo?" Ridgway brushed it off and Pace fired his shot. As he stood back to await the results, two accompanying Pentagon generals, Ed Hull and Ted Brooks, marched solemnly up to Pace. "Don't you realize," they charged, "that as a civilian noncombatant you have no business firing that gun? If you fall into the hands of the Chinese now, you're a dead duck! "

A momentary expression of dismay crossed the Secretary's face; then he burst out laughing. It would be the last laugh of his tour. In a few hours he would learn what the newspaperman already appeared to know—that MacArthur had been dismissed, that Ridgway was ticketed to Tokyo, and that Pace was supposed to convey the news personally.

MacArthur was not unaware that his future at the Dai Ichi was under discussion at the highest levels. He had too many postgraduates of his school of military thinking, and too many partisans of his style of politics, in positions where it counted to be unaware that he now had more prospects of martyrdom than of continuing to manage the war. In March 1949 he had been called to Washington for consultation and refused to go, claiming he was needed on a day-to-day basis in Tokyo. He worried even then that he would not be returned. Loyalists in State and Defense had warned him of an alleged plot to divide his role, bringing in General Maxwell Taylor as occupation chief and a career diplomat to handle foreign relations. MacArthur sent a scorching cable to Bradley, accusing him of selling out to Acheson, and the trial balloon deflated. Still, almost no one had held a military position as long as MacArthur already had by mid-1949, and he seemed ready to remain indefinitely by something akin to divine right.

Once Representative Martin had read MacArthur's defiant letter on the floor of the House, the general's future remained on the front pages of American newspapers and crossed the Pacific into the Japanese press. Rumors burgeoned as Secretary Pace arrived, seemingly no coincidence. That Monday (April 9), General Almond stopped at MacArthur's office before returning to Korea after a week's personal leave. "I may not see you anymore, so goodbye, Ned," said MacArthur. As Almond remembered, he looked "disconsolate."

Almond was puzzled, and MacArthur explained, "I have become politically involved and may be relieved by the President."

Almond labeled the possibility "absurd." He expected further visits in Korea from the mentor whom he still called General MacArthur; the general encouraged few intimacies.

"Well, perhaps so," said MacArthur in parting.

Anticipating allegations in Washington of lack of resolve in the war effort, Truman had AEC chairman Gordon Dean brief members of the House and Senate Joint Atomic Energy Committee that Monday on the transfer of atomic bombs to military control. The next day, shipment of atomic warheads to the Pacific was scheduled to begin.

Early on the evening of the tenth, in his nationwide radio broadcast, Lowell Thomas reported that the President was planning to leave "the question" to his military high command. Any "action to curb MacArthur, [to] make him keep quiet on matters involving international politics . . . would be up to Secretary of Defense George Marshall and General Lawton Collins. . . ." They would, he went on, communicate personally with MacArthur "or through Army Secretary Frank Pace—who is now in Tokyo. We are told, however, that . . . Pace did not go to Tokyo to silence MacArthur. He took no such instructions with him when he left Washington last week."

Bad news is often bungled in delivery. (A war warning to Pearl Harbor on the morning of the Japanese attack, for example, was sent from Washington by inappropriate commercial services and the bicycle messenger in Honolulu was delayed by traffic as the air raid opening the war was already in progress.) At about three in the afternoon of Tuesday, April 10, Truman received and signed the relief and appointment orders to go to MacArthur, Ridgway and Van Fleet. A public statement from the White House to keep the expected press firestorm under control was to be released when it was certain that the proud old soldier had been duly notified. Secretary Pace was instructed through Ambassador Muccio to take decrypted cable 8743 directly to Tokyo to be delivered to MacArthur at ten in the morning of April 12— before he left the embassy compound for the Dai Ichi. (It would then be the evening of April 11 in Washington.)

Secrets, especially delicious ones, are hard to keep. There had been too many meetings over too many days mulling over the MacArthur matter, and someone had talked. No one in newspaperdom was a greater admirer of the general than crusty Colonel Robert R. McCormick, proprietor of the *Chicago Tribune* and a 1st Division veteran of France in 1918. In Walter Trohan, his Washington bureau chief, he had an indefatigable snooper, and as darkness fell on the Pentagon on the Tuesday that Truman signed the orders to be radioed to Muccio in Korea, Trohan's man, Lloyd Norman, was soliciting comment on a "major resignation" he claimed he had heard rumored from Tokyo.

Trohan bearded Truman's press secretary, Joseph Short, Charles Ross's replacement, who panicked the President into rushing his announcement. Panic even engulfed the more knowledgeable high brass. They denied everything, after which General Bradley hurried to the White House to warn that if MacArthur heard about the forthcoming orders before they reached him officially, he might resign with an extravagant, politically damaging polemic about American policy in the Far East.

"The son of a bitch isn't going to resign on me," Truman said angrily. "*I want him fired.*"

338

At ten-thirty he signed a new order for immediate conveyance to Mac-Arthur by the fastest means possible. Meanwhile the message via Ambassador Muccio, sent by State on commercial cable, was lost to a power failure in Pusan and had to be retransmitted. By the time that Pace found out about his unhappy mission, it was moot.

To keep the overreaching general in Tokyo from grandstanding on learning of his relief, Truman ordered an unprecedented White House press conference for one in the morning on Tuesday, April 10—afternoon the next day in Tokyo. "I went on to bed," Truman wrote, "knowing there would be a storm in the morning."

If "press conference" suggested the presence of the President, the eager reporters who turned up found only Joe Short and several secretaries, who distributed the announcement of MacArthur's dismissal beginning at 12:57 a.m., with copies of damage-control supporting documents. Short ducked any questions.

By 1:03, Truman's statement broke into late-night radio:

> With deep regret I have concluded that General of the Army Douglas Mac-Arthur is unable to give his wholehearted support to the policies of the United States Government and of the United Nations in matters pertaining to his official duties. In view of the specific responsibilities imposed upon me by the Constitution of the United States and the added responsibilities entrusted to me by the United Nations, I have decided that I must make a change of command in the Far East. I have, therefore, relieved General MacArthur of his commands and have designated Lieutenant General Matthew B. Ridgway as his successor.

The background papers Short distributed to reporters included the Truman directive of December 5, 1950, incorporated in a JCS message the next day to MacArthur; the message of March 20 about proposed peace feelers; MacArthur's contrary "peace" ultimatum to the Chinese Communists; the JCS memo of the same date (March 24, 1951) reminding the general of the December instructions to secure prior approval of policy statements; MacArthur's letter to Martin; and an exchange of January 5–6, 1951, asking MacArthur about arming further ROK forces and his reply advising against it (which he had denied making).

The procedure seemed a sleazy way, in the dead of night, to do in Mac-Arthur, but the system had again failed. It was "fundamental," Truman's statement read, "that military governors must be governed by the policies and directives issued to them in the manner provided by our laws and Constitution." He acknowledged that the general's "place in history as one of our greatest commanders is fully established," and he regretted "the necessity for the action I feel compelled to take in this case." All over the U.S. the headlines for the next editions of the morning papers were reset.

On the front page of *The New York Times,* just below the news of MacArthur's dismissal, would be the story that Sterling Hayden, famous for his swashbuckling film roles, had confessed to the House of Representatives Un-American Activities Committee that from June through December 1946 he had been a Communist Party member—"the stupidest and most ignorant thing I had ever done in my life." When the North Koreans had invaded South Korea the previous June, he revealed, he had his attorney contact J. Edgar Hoover at the FBI to confess and to seek a means of eliminating any prejudice to his being recalled to active duty as a Marine. But his career was as effectively over as those of the entertainment world friends he turned on and who were blacklisted. Korea continued to exact its toll remote from the war.

Secretary Pace got an inkling of impending trouble much closer to the front when roused from a nap in "Domino," the command post of the 5th Regimental Combat Team (24th Division). A call from EUSAK headquarters in Taegu for a Frank Pace was first rebuffed by a switchboard operator near Munsan, who denied the existence of any Frank Pace in the 5th RCT. Finally, as early spring hail rattled loudly on the roof of Pace's hut, his wind-up field telephone jangled in its green canvas holder. It was Major General Leven C. Allen, Eighth Army chief of staff, who read a cable that should not have been transmitted in the clear nor broadcast on an easily tapped field phone: "Disregard my cable number 8743. You will advise General Matthew Ridgway that he is now the supreme commander of the Pacific, vice General MacArthur relieved. You will proceed to Tokyo where you will assist General Ridgway in assuming . . . his command."

"You'd better read that once more, Lev," said Pace, in shock at Bradley's message. "I don't want to relieve General MacArthur on one reading."

Finding Ridgway, Pace asked him to step outside into the pinging hail. Ridgway was wearing his usual grenade on a parachute harness over his field jacket. "Matt," Pace said, "take off that damned grenade. If one of those hailstones hits that grenade, there'll be no secretary of the army and no commander in Korea."

Leading Ridgway farther from the hut, Pace told him what Allen had relayed on the phone. "I can't believe it, Mr. Secretary," said Ridgway.

Confessing that he couldn't either, Pace insisted nevertheless, "You're now the Supreme Commander. Now let's go get that cable I'm to disregard." Hours later it arrived from Ambassador Muccio. "You will proceed to Tokyo," it began, "where you will advise General Douglas MacArthur that he is relieved of his command." When back in Washington, Pace, now delivered from the embarrassment, was able to joke about how he would have accomplished the dread deed. "I'd commandeer the first plane and fly to Tokyo. Being there after hours, I would have gone directly to General MacArthur's headquarters. I would ring the bell, shove the order under the door, and run like hell!"

The eviction notice which MacArthur had been expecting—even courting—arrived in Tokyo when the White House handout was broadcast as a news flash. It reached Tokyo as quickly as it did Topeka. After his morning routine reading cables and newspapers at his Dai Ichi desk, MacArthur had returned to the embassy for a luncheon with Senator Warren Magnuson of Washington and William Sterns of Northwest Airlines. Colonel Sidney Huff, MacArthur's aide, was home preparing for Prime Minister Yoshida Shigeru's garden party to mark the first cherry blossoms. The telephone rang. It was a correspondent alerted by his home office to Joe Short's impending emergency news conference. "Be sure to listen to the three o'clock broadcast [on the Armed Forces Radio Network]," he advised. "We think President Truman is going to say something about MacArthur."

Huff did. There was nothing significant in the first few bulletins. Then the announcer interrupted his reading with a flash from Washington. Short had distributed his bombshells. Huff had already called the embassy once, just before the broadcast, to alert the MacArthurs, but they were still at lunch and he had to leave a message to call back.

Jean called, and Huff relayed what he had heard—that the general had been relieved of his commands. MacArthur accepted the unsurprising news from her impassively.

When Huff's phone rang again it proved to be the Signal Corps, asking whether he would be available to receive "an important message for the general"—Bradley's cable. The service had apparently found no one at the Dai Ichi to accept responsibility that afternoon for the brown envelope stamped in red letters "ACTION FOR MACARTHUR." Huff waited for it, then drove to the embassy compound, where he found reporters already clustering at the big gate. "What's the news?" one shouted. "Has he got the word yet?"

"This is probably it," said Huff, displaying the envelope.

MacArthur had left his guests for a walk up the stairway off the reception hall to his bedroom, but not for his customary post-prandial nap. Mrs. MacArthur was at the door when Huff arrived. "Here it is," he said falteringly, giving the envelope to her. "Anything I can do?"

She shook off the question, her eyes welling with tears. MacArthur unsealed the envelope and scanned the contents. "Jeannie," he said, "we're going home at last."

Calling Courtney Whitney at the Dai Ichi, MacArthur relayed the news and Whitney rushed to the embassy to offer his services. More reporters, and now the beginnings of a crowd, were gathering. After a quick exchange of consolatory words, Whitney left to begin the business of arranging the departure. He had been handling MacArthur's personal business all through the occupation. At the gate, reporters pressed him for an update. "I have just left the general," Whitney began. "He received the word magnificently. . . . I think this has been his finest hour."

William Sebald, informally American ambassador, called his office for confirmation of MacArthur's ouster after learning of it at the Yoshida garden party. Yoshida slipped away to receive Sebald privately. They discussed the matter quietly, with Sebald, in view of Japanese pride, expecting to have Yoshida offer to have his government resign. Anticipating that, he asked Yoshida not to consider it. Then Sebald returned to the Dai Ichi, where he found that MacArthur had stubbornly returned to his usual schedule. Stifling tears, Sebald found it difficult to offer the words of sympathy he had rehearsed en route. MacArthur smiled understandingly. "General," Sebald finally began, "you are a much better soldier in this business than I am."

Having held his tongue earlier with intimates, MacArthur's stiff upper lip was now breaking down. "Publicly humiliated after fifty-two years of service in the Army . . . ," he began.

Painfully, Sebald suggested that the general consider a statement to the Japanese people asking them to give Ridgway the support they had given his predecessor. "After all, the present state of Japan is a monument to you. . . ." All MacArthur would say was that he had never disobeyed orders, and that his dismissal was part of a plot in Washington to weaken the American position in the Far East. There was nothing further for Sebald to offer and he left MacArthur to himself.

Going Home

MACARTHUR'S ALTERNATIVES for months had been to resign dramatically while airing his policy differences with Truman and the Pentagon, or to provoke his own dismissal. Dismissing a legendary hero seemed more likely to elicit the domestic outrage he sought, to focus national attention on his agenda, and to propel his unquieted ambitions for the presidency. The initial reaction was all he could have wanted. The popular focus was upon him, and at Truman's expense, rather than upon what Ridgway described as "preventive war."

Truman could do no less than to take his case to the people, which he did by radio on Wednesday evening, April 11. "The course we have been following," he explained in his flat, unpretentious Missouri twang, "is the one best calculated to avoid an all-out war." Although he wanted to "blunt the will of the Chinese Communists to continue the struggle," he also wanted "to limit the war to Korea." General MacArthur was "one of our greatest military commanders," but since he disagreed with American policy he had to be relieved. Truman wanted no "third world war" and contended that "the cause of world peace is more important than any individual." He was ready to "negotiate for a restoration of peace in the area," but drew the line at Munich-style "appeasement." Collective action against aggression in Korea, he concluded, "may be the turning point in the world's search for a practical way of achieving peace and security."

"If what MacArthur proposed had happened—had been allowed to take place," Truman later argued, "we would have wound up being at war not only with Red China but with Russia, too, and the consequences would have been—it might have meant the destruction of a good part of the world."

Hazarding the rain and fog, Ridgway left the 24th Division zone in Pace's Constellation for a hurried flight to Tokyo. In effect he was already Supreme Commander—a fact which irritated MacArthur. To subordinates he worried privately that Ridgway, although "a good soldier," might have "sold his soul for the job." MacArthur direly predicted a purge of his loyalists in Tokyo.

In Pusan, still the temporary capital, where Syngman Rhee had taken over the residence of the governor of Kyongsang Province as his presidential mansion, Paik Sun Yup arrived on the morning of the twelfth to officially receive his major general's stars from the president. The traffic, a chaos of carts, beasts of burden, Koreans bearing A-frames on their backs and baskets of provisions on their heads, ancient American trolley cars, dilapidated auto-mobiles and frantic, honking military vehicles, was "ghastly," but Paik finally arrived to find Rhee "unsettled" by the news about MacArthur. Rhee's face was "completely enshrouded in deep shadows of disappointment." While pinning the second star on Paik's epaulets, Rhee confided, "MacArthur was a soldier who really understood my heart."

By noon on the twelfth, Ridgway was on his way to Haneda Airport, from which he was driven directly to the Dai Ichi. MacArthur, Ridgway wrote in a memoir, "received me at once, with the greatest courtesy. . . . He was entirely himself—composed, quiet, temperate, friendly, and helpful to the man who was to succeed him. He made some allusions to the fact that he had been summarily relieved, but there was no trace of bitterness or anger in his tone." Rather, Ridgway saw "the resilience of this great man that he could accept so calmly, with no outward sign of shock, what must have been a dev-astating blow. . . ." Yet that perception was not entirely accurate.

MacArthur had much more unburdening to do. He claimed later to Ridgway that Truman was emotionally unstable, a victim of "malignant hyper-tension." Allegedly the President would not live six months. MacArthur also boasted that he had been offered $300,000—then enough to buy two hun-dred Fords—to "raise hell" in a series of lectures. He still anticipated no war with the Soviets if the United States increased its pressure on China. But he predicted warmly that Ridgway would become chief of staff after his service at SCAP. "If it had been up to me to pick my successor, I would have chosen you."

The flight in Pace's plane back to Taegu, to meet briefly with Van Fleet, Ridgway recalled, "came very close to being my last. The pilot, a stranger to

Korean fields, set us down at one o'clock in the morning on a light-plane landing strip [K-37], which he mistook for the mist-wreathed K-2 field where he had been instructed to land. Through a miracle of good luck . . . , the pilot missed a mountain he never saw, a peak that rose sheer from one side of the strip, only yards from our wingtip. Then, finding himself suddenly careening down a runway intended for nothing more ambitious than an occasional C-47 landing, he had to slam on full brakes to keep from winding up tail-high in a rice paddy."

They managed to stop, but at cost to the VIP chinaware on board, and four blown tires. There were no replacement tires in Korea as the only other Lockheed Constellation in the Far East was MacArthur's personal plane, in Japan.

Ridgway remained into the next day, April 14, visiting advance command posts in a light plane, conferring with division and corps commanders, with the ROK chief of staff (still General Chung Il Kwon) and with the Fifth Air Force commander. On his final day with EUSAK he met his successor, General Van Fleet, at K-2 and ceremonially turned over command in Korea to him at Eighth Army headquarters in Taegu. After a press conference that afternoon, Ridgway flew off to Tokyo in his old B-17.

Ridgway's flurry of conferences evidence what he had learned not to do from his predecessor. "I wanted to keep always in mind," he wrote, "the clear policy decisions communicated to me by President Truman and the Joint Chiefs of Staff, the most immediate of which was to avoid any action that might result in an extension of hostilities and thus lead to a general conflagration." General Van Fleet, Admiral Joy and General Stratemeyer, as well as subordinate commanders, "were all apprised of this basic guideline and each . . . expressed his full understanding and agreement." Ridgway had established two proposed boundaries for operations above the 38th parallel, hoping to hold one or both indefinitely for military, psychological and diplomatic reasons. He charged Van Fleet "to conduct no operations in force beyond" without GHQ approval.

At Haneda, Ridgway was met at 9:15 p.m. by General Hickey and Ambassador Sebald, representing the two dimensions of his new role. Since MacArthur was entitled to his home at the embassy until he departed Tokyo, and had appointed Doyle Hickey, his deputy, as acting commander at the Dai Ichi, Ridgway was driven to the Imperial Hotel, the Frank Lloyd Wright–designed landmark that had survived the 1923 earthquake and the 1945 fire raids. From there Ridgway would operate quietly until MacArthur left, a date he moved up a day, to Monday, April 16. MacArthur would return to the Dai Ichi only twice more in the days left to him in Japan, to oversee the packing of his personal effects. Jean went herself to the Tokyo branch of the National City Bank to close out their account; photographers followed to snap prying pictures of her distraught face as she closed out her life as vicereine.

Few outsiders were permitted personal visits as MacArthur prepared to leave. Prime Minister Yoshida came to the general's embassy residence to thank him for Japan's restoration and wrote to him privately to express "shock and sorrow beyond words." Ignoring the entreaties of high courtiers, who pointed out that the general no longer had any official position in Japan and should pay a courtesy call to the palace, Emperor Hirohito made what was for him an emotional visit to MacArthur, the eleventh time he had gone to see him since the occupation began. MacArthur reciprocated the courtesy, on the Emperor's departure, by walking Hirohito to his aged limousine. The general would leave Tokyo without ever entering the serenely beautiful Imperial Palace grounds, visible from his office window in the Dai Ichi since September 1945.

His loyalists in Tokyo marveled at his poise when they came, one by one and in small groups, to offer condolences and wish him well. But the general, his hawklike, waxen face appearing serene, was angry at the way he was relieved while knowing very well he had courted dismissal and had expected it even sooner. Receiving the assembled court of Bunker, Story and Canada in his old West Point bathrobe, he told them that although he didn't know who had been on "the firing squad" in Washington, the language of the orders convinced him that "George Marshall pulled the trigger."

When he had cabled Marshall on April 6 recommending "four-star rank" for Stratemeyer, Ridgway and Joy, and three stars and two stars for others in his command on grounds that "the positions which they hold must, for maximum efficiency, be clothed with the essential authority and dignity which go with these ranks," it was almost as if he were anticipating the inevitable and arranging his going-away gifts.

MacArthur hadn't planned the logistics of a return, and now was expecting Whitney to work it out. A leisurely progress at government expense through the locales of his Pacific war glory, such as the Philippines and Australia, seemed attractive, building up momentum for a politically timed arrival in the United States, where MacArthur had not set foot since his appointment to Manila in the late 1930s. That would bring him "home" just a year before the presidential nominating conventions in 1952. Then former president

Herbert Hoover, seventy-seven and still nursing his electoral rejection nearly twenty years earlier, phoned to tell him that Republican leaders in Congress wanted the general to come "straight home as quickly as possible, before Truman and Marshall and their crowd of propagandists can smear you."

Hoover would send details, even a definition of "home." The management of the posh Waldorf-Astoria in New York, where Hoover lived, was prepared to offer MacArthur a suite, as he had no American domicile. Meeting hurriedly early on Wednesday, April 11, Republican congressional leaders agreed to urge on the Democrats, who could hardly refuse to host a hero, an invitation to address a joint session at the Capitol. (A joint resolution of Congress would direct that a gold medal be struck in MacArthur's honor, to be inscribed "Protector of Australia; Liberator of the Philippines; Conqueror of Japan; Defender of Korea.") Recently elected senator Richard M. Nixon of California announced that since the overwhelming majority of Americans were "shocked, disheartened and angered" by Truman's action, he would introduce a resolution asking the President to reconsider the dismissal and restore MacArthur to his command. Minority Leader Martin told the press that he would demand a congressional inquiry into Korean War policy, and that the issue of impeachment could come up. It was an empty threat, but an index to party hopes of exploiting MacArthur. Senator Joe McCarthy immediately offered his vote for impeachment.

To Larry Bunker, who handled most personal matters for the general, MacArthur spoke of departure from Japan the following Tuesday, April 17, flying via Hawaii and San Francisco. He told his pilot, Anthony Story, to plan the itinerary to arrive in the U.S. late in the evening, presumably to avoid any hostile demonstrations by imagined enemies. "We'll just slip into San Francisco after dark, while everybody's at dinner or the movies."

It was already apparent, however, that whatever the public thought of the clash of policy that brought about his dismissal, the crude and demeaning manner in which it was inadvertently accomplished had roused ire across America. The White House switchboard was clogged with calls, and the mail room received tens of thousands of protests daily. George Gallup's famous poll found that 69 percent of respondents of voting age sympathized with MacArthur. Truman, appearing at a Washington Senators baseball game at Griffith Park, was booed. In Ponca City, Oklahoma, a dummy of the President was burned in effigy.

In the White Oaks subdivision of State College, Pennsylvania, developer and World War I veteran Merle Homan, who had named streets for his favorite World War II heroes, Admiral Chester Nimitz, General Omar Bradley and General Douglas MacArthur, remained loyal to the President. The name of MacArthur Avenue was changed to Homan Avenue.

In New York it was publication week for Maggie Higgins's hastily stitched-together *War in Korea*. "As you have noticed from the preceding pages of this morning's paper," Charles Poore wrote in his "Books of the *Times*" column, "Miss Higgins's book is timely to a notable degree." Higgins, who had spent four postwar years as a correspondent behind the Iron Curtain, in Warsaw and East Berlin, before her posting to Japan and Korea, was militantly anti-Communist on every page. Although she faulted MacArthur for miscalculation and mismanagement in Korea, he remained a hero to her for his uncompromising rejection of Communism even if it meant facing the Soviets with the prospect of total war. "I refuse to accept the idea," she closed, "that Americans are so decadent that they prefer a life that will give them a new automobile each year rather than a way of life that will protect them from the midnight knock of the secret policeman, from the concentration camp, from slave-labor camps."

In Korea itself, where hailstorms continued and there was an unusual late snowstorm, a GI was reported by E. J. Kahn Jr. to be wondering at the wrath of the elements, "Gee, do you suppose he really is God, after all?" At K-6 air base at Pyongtaek, south of Seoul, Corporal George Hanrahan, now with a group of eighteen enlisted men, an officer and several Korean bearers in an air control squadron, heard the news of MacArthur's dismissal in his radio jeep. "We had a party," he remembered. "Our officer, Lt. Hunter Dunn (an ex-Marine) had managed to obtain certain party supplies from the Marines when we were at the Marine strip near Pusan. It was one hell of a party and it was fortunate, indeed, that we were not attacked." In Pfc. William Hayward's 6147th Tactical Control Squadron, despite their shortages of supplies and equipment, and a continuing need to cannibalize some "Mosquito" aircraft to keep others flying, none of their operational liabilities were laid to MacArthur. From commanding officer on down, air crews were irate about his sacking, which seemed to mean settling for less than victory.

Never—then or later—willing to settle for less than victory, Syngman Rhee wrote to MacArthur of his "shock" and recalled "how you told me that you would defend Korea as you would defend California in the event we were attacked and so you did. . . . I still believe, dear General, that the ultimate solution of our problems will be in accordance with your plans, for there is no other honorable result which can come from this war."

Feelings pro and con ran so high in Washington that on a radio talk show, Republican senator Homer Capehart of Indiana and Democratic senators Herbert Lehman of New York and Hubert Humphrey of Minnesota had to be separated by the moderator to prevent an unseemly brawl. Across the country, outraged veterans returned their medals, and flags were hung upside down—a traditional distress call. Truman felt obliged to cable Dwight Eisenhower, then heading NATO in Europe, that he was "sorry to have to reach a parting of the way with the big man in Asia." But, said the President, "he asked for it and I had to give it to him." Eisenhower told reporters, "When you put on a uniform there are certain inhibitions you accept."

At a naval hospital in Oakland, California, Marine Pfc. Herbert Luster, recuperating after losing his right arm at Obong-ni Ridge in North Korea in August 1950, was asked his opinion. "I recalled I had taken an oath to serve the United States and to obey the orders of my commander," he said. "Since Mac had once taken the same pledge, I was forced to agree with the president, even though I was all for going right to Moscow to bring the war to an end once and for all." To their representatives in Washington, some outraged citizens telegraphed near-obscene attacks on the President which Republicans in Congress duly inserted into the *Congressional Record.* At the White House, in a previously scheduled ceremony, the President pinned the Medal of Honor on the gutsy Tom Hudner, who had crash-landed his Corsair in the snow above the Chosin Reservoir in a vain effort to rescue his fellow-flier Jesse Brown. (Chopper pilot Charles Ward received a Silver Star.)

While most major American newspapers supported Truman's decision, the expected contrary opinions enlivened editorial pages. Colonel McCormick of the *Chicago Tribune* suggested that Truman could indeed be impeached "for usurping the power of Congress when he ordered American troops to the Korean front without a declaration of war," although the difference between the Korean action and that of previous American presidents in military interventions short of war was only a matter of scale. Many papers on the right, as well as similar-thinking officials from mayor to senator, saw the relief of MacArthur darkly as the work of a Communist conspiracy within the government. Walter Winchell spoke for them in his newspaper gossip column when he called the dismissal the "greatest scandal in American history" and asserted that MacArthur was within his constitutional rights in defying his commander in chief "if he sees the orders of his superiors in conflict [with the Constitution]." But the deed was done. Although civilian control over the military, as explicitly set out by the framers of the Constitution, had been maintained, Truman, Acheson and Marshall had to bear weeks of indignities until the emotional eruptions had run their course.

Marshall at the least had the satisfaction of seeing a striking and support-ive Herblock cartoon on the editorial page of *The Washington Post.* In it a glowering MacArthur (in five-star uniform) and a stern Marshall (in civilian clothes) are each seated before a large "globe" of the Earth. While the Defense Secretary's is the familiar sphere, MacArthur's, containing only East Asia, from Manchuria (and China) through Korea, Japan and Formosa, is square and flat. Marshall explains, "We've Been Using More of a Roundish One."

"We've Been Using More of a Roundish One"

A Herblock cartoon in the Washington Post, *April 1951, satirizing MacArthur's view of the world.*

At the next Cabinet meeting the Secretary of State, asked by Truman to sum up his impression of the final days of the MacArthur dilemma, observed that it reminded him of the family with the beautiful daughter exposed to the perils of retaining her virtue. Her mother worried incessantly about it. One day the husband found his wife weeping. The worst had happened. Their daughter had returned home to confess that she was pregnant. Mopping his brow the father said, "Thank God that's over."

In the Far East, resolutions of praise for MacArthur passed through the legislatures of the Philippines, South Korea and Japan, and in Tokyo the two leading newspapers, *Asahi Shimbun* and *Mainichi Shimbun,* paid tribute to his stewardship of postwar Japan into democracy and dignity. "Oh, General MacArthur—General, General, who saved Japan from confusion and starvation," *Mainichi* lamented, "did you see from your window the green wheat stirring in the wind? The harvest will be rich this year. That is the fruit of the general's five years and eight months—and the symbol of the Japanese people's gratitude." *Asahi* credited MacArthur for rescuing Japan from "exhaustion and despair." He "taught us the merits of democracy and pacifism and guided us with kindness along this bright path." Ignoring his almost total failure to involve himself emotionally and physically with Japan, *Asahi* went on, "As if pleased with his own children growing up, he took pleasure in the Japanese people, yesterday's enemy. . . ."

Nothing remotely equivalent appeared in Europe, where *Ce Soir* in Paris summed up feeling by observing that Truman, in sacking MacArthur, had acted under the *"volonté pacifique"* of people around the world. In awkward timing, the Labour government in Britain announced the same day that it wanted Red China associated with the Japanese peace treaty, a proposal greeted by the White House with silence. The Communist *Daily Worker* in London, the last source from which Truman needed applause, approved his "bold and courageous" action. While it condemned the general's "adventurism," Moscow radio claimed that "MacArthur did nothing that disagreed with the aggressive policy of U.S. ruling circles," and that he was removed because he "failed as supreme commander." A *Literary Gazette* article broadcast from Moscow asserted that the replacement of MacArthur did not mean abandonment of American policy in Asia, yet was evidence "of confusion in the den of American warmongers." East Berlin radio declared that Ridgway and Van Fleet were "two war criminals not a whit better than MacArthur," while the "Russian Hour" on unfree Vienna radio warned that Truman and Acheson were no different globally than MacArthur except that they thought in long-range terms. They needed "time for preparing a new aggressive war against the Soviet Union and the people's democracies. . . . MacArthur wanted to get going right away. This is the sole difference and the reason why he had to go."

While an airfield crew at Haneda painted out the no-longer-operative

SCAP on the Constellation which MacArthur's party planned to use indefinitely across the U.S. and replaced it with *Bataan,* the nervous White House staff, reading about one planned welcoming tribute after another being scheduled across the country, circulated a mock "Schedule for Welcoming General MacArthur" in Washington:

12:30	Wades ashore from Snorkel submarine
12:31	Navy Band plays "Sparrow in the Treetop" and "I'll Be Glad When You're Dead You Rascal You"
12:40	Parade to the Capitol with General MacArthur riding an elephant
12:47	Beheading of General Vaughan at the rotunda
1:00	General MacArthur addresses members of Congress
1:30–1:49	Applause for General MacArthur
1:50	Burning of the Constitution
1:55	Lynching of Secretary Acheson
2:00	21-atomic bomb salute
2:30	Nude D.A.R.s leap from Washington Monument
3:00	Basket lunch, Monument Grounds

The coverage of the actual departure ranged the gamut of political feeling. "One radio man," James Michener claimed acidly, "had to interview seventeen soldiers before he got one who would allow his voice to break and ask pathetically why they were doing this to the general. What the other sixteen said would have made better—but unwanted—stories." A newsman estimating the crowd, according to the critical Michener, guessed that "more Japanese by far appeared to welcome Marilyn Monroe into Japan than appeared to speed General MacArthur out." But the general's staff had loyally orchestrated a triumphal exit. Despite the post-dawn hour, Japanese schoolchildren, given a holiday, had been bused and trucked to street locations all the way to the airport.

A Japanese dispatch estimated vast and teary crowds. The *Asahi Shimbun* reported that of the traditional three banzais to be shouted, only the first two were voiced. "Then they saw Mrs. MacArthur weeping and the third Banzai would not come out." An elderly Japanese confided to a Tokyo reporter, "The only time I ever felt like this before was when Admiral Yamamoto died." The admiral, who had planned the attack on Pearl Harbor and was in the first rank of Japanese military heroes, had been ambushed and shot down in the South Pacific in 1943.

Before dawn on Monday, April 16, in Tokyo, throngs of genuinely sorrowful Japanese began gathering along the route from the American embassy to the airport. The MacArthur party's luggage, bulging with the desiderata of years abroad, was already aboard the *Bataan*. For those who could not be on the streets, NHK radio broadcast the account of the procession live. An announcer repeated sorrowfully (in Japanese) "Good-bye, General MacArthur" over crowd noises, while from the studio "Auld Lang Syne" was played at intervals. The convoy of cars, with MP jeeps both leading and following, began its slow course to Haneda shortly after 6:00 a.m. Many in the crowd wept as they waved farewell or unfurled homemade flags. (Authorities had provided schoolchildren—who were excused from classes—with small flags.) Some displayed banners in the Japanese which MacArthur had never learned; others waved messages of regret or gratitude in English: "Sayonara," "We Love You," "We Are Grateful to the General," "With Sincere Regret." Although aloof as a viceroy, he had filled a vacuum left when the even more remote Hirohito had been humbled by defeat, relinquishing his status as demigod.

The Japanese had another and more material reason to celebrate MacArthur's tenure in the islands. A resolution of the Japanese Diet cited the general as a leader "who helped our country out of the confusion and poverty prevailing at the time the war ended." Nothing helped more than MacArthur's unexpected *new* war, which Prime Minister Yoshida would describe as "a gift from the gods." In effect, it was an informal Marshall Plan for Japan, rejuvenating Japanese industry and commerce, and creating millions of jobs, as Japan became a logistical and manpower depot of mammoth proportions for the American (and UN) military effort. Even Red China had quiet cause to sing MacArthur's praise, although contenting itself with the usual vituperation. His miscalculation in pushing toward the Yalu had given China military credibility as a world power, international standing even beyond Asia and the impetus for industrial revival.

Margaret Almond, wife of the X Corps commander and a staunch loyalist, traveled to Haneda with the MacArthur party and was one of the relatively few Americans other than service personnel to observe the entire proceedings. To her husband, now back in Korea with his still-new lieutenant general's stars, she wrote in a tone he must have appreciated: "From the gates of the Embassy to the doors of the plane, all six miles, there was a solid line of guards, Japanese police, soldiers, sailors, and marines. And behind them thousands lined the streets the entire way. . . . Everywhere he moved, people applauded, everywhere he turned, eyes followed him, some weeping, some silent, and some, I am sure, among the followers of Acheson, relieved." She hoped that MacArthur would return someday—as President of the United States.

At Haneda an honor guard awaited the gleamingly polished old black Cadillac with its faded gray upholstery. Once it emptied, both Hickey and Ridgway accompanied MacArthur on his final review. At planeside, although it was only 7 a.m. and still bleak and chilly, the diplomatic corps, Japanese government representatives and senior occupation officials were present. Yoshida and members of his Cabinet were there, as was the Emperor's Grand Chamberlain, representing Hirohito. The leaders of both houses of the Diet represented the Japanese people. The MacArthurs shook hands with each dignitary. The Japanese returned bows. Cannon boomed a salute, and eighteen jet fighters and four B-29s flew low over the field in a further salute. In some ways the leavetaking replicated, almost in reverse, the ceremony on the deck of the battleship *Missouri* when MacArthur had taken the Japanese surrender in September 1945.

In the silence that followed, the departing members of MacArthur's circle began ascending the *Bataan*'s ramp, from Whitney and Bunker to Ah Cheu, Arthur MacArthur's amah since his birth thirteen years earlier and a veteran of the flight from the Philippines early in 1942. An Army band began playing "Auld Lang Syne" as the MacArthurs waved their farewells before the hatch of the Constellation was closed. At 7:20, Colonel Story gunned the four engines and the plane rose in the gray morning mist in a low arc toward the Pacific and its first destination, Oahu.

As William Sebald recalled, "The chilling moment was over. Officers and wives slowly trooped away, the flags were furled, the troops were dismissed—and the working day began." While Ridgway returned to the Dai Ichi, his personal belongings were being moved from the Imperial Hotel into MacArthur's house on the embassy hill. In the U.S., where MacArthur had not set foot in fourteen years, James H. Rand, president of Remington Rand, announced that within ninety days the general would become Chairman of the Board of the corporation at a salary of a hundred thousand dollars a year, his actual duties unspecified. It would be, at seventy-one, his first civilian job.

Two hours out over the Pacific, the *Bataan* flew close to another American plane, this one heading toward Tokyo. In it was John Foster Dulles, returning to continue negotiations on a peace treaty for Japan. The two chatted over aircraft radio. Dulles had been there at the beginning of MacArthur's war and, only by hours, had missed the end.

* * *

As MacArthur approached Hawaii he was still drafting, on a lined pad, his address before Congress and various shorter acceptances of anticipated welcomes to come. In New York, veteran newscaster Lowell Thomas was drafting his next broadcast, largely taken up, as his listeners would expect, with MacArthur, Truman, Acheson and Marshall. Anticipating the frenzied public outpourings to come, and the initial rage against the Truman administration, Thomas observed that in "all the huge masses of material" he had already seen on the controversy, he hadn't discovered "anything" to represent the other side. "Ever since modern diplomacy began," he wrote, "the statesmen of the West, time after time, have tried to do one particular task—to localize any small war, to keep it from becoming a big war. That has long been a habit of mind in the world of diplomacy—[to] keep a local war from spreading."

He traced the historical record, showing how some attempts failed while others succeeded. All of them "set the pattern for diplomatic thinking, the same pattern that appears in the present attempt to keep the Korean war *localized*." And for emphasis in his script he underlined the last word.

Nearly three years later, in January 1954, *The New York Times*'s Cyrus Sulzberger visited General Charles de Gaulle in Paris. The war in Korea had ended in a cease-fire six months earlier, after more than a year of bloody stalemate just north of the 38th parallel. Ridgway had succeeded Eisenhower at NATO and would soon become his Army chief of staff. General Eisenhower was President, having promised a frustrated electorate in 1952 that he would end the war, which he did on compromise terms which MacArthur would have scorned, since North Korea survived, and which the outgoing Truman politically could not have offered.

A realist, de Gaulle approved, seeing the deadlock in which the West had made costly gains as historic. The principle of forcibly resisting aggression, he told Sulzberger, had been established on an international level, and the principle of refusing to repatriate prisoners of war who did not want to be returned to a regime they found abhorrent had been upheld despite Communist embarrassment at what that implied worldwide about police-state systems.

"A détente is beginning," the shrewd de Gaulle prophesied, "a *modus vivendi*. It started already in Korea. The dangers of war at present are less and less. The decisive point in Korea was the quarrel between MacArthur and Truman. This showed that the United States did not want war. After Truman said no to MacArthur's proposal to attack China, [world] war was excluded. . . . These are the imponderables that make for a *modus vivendi* . . . ; it is an armed peace."

Privately, Eisenhower had been asked about what some saw as a battle of ideas between two generals of the same generation who had, seemingly, long been at odds—Marshall and MacArthur. "I wouldn't trade one Marshall for fifty MacArthurs," he said. Then he paused, realizing the implications. "My God!" he went on. "That would be a lousy deal. What would I do with fifty MacArthurs?"

AFTERWORD

Rɪᴅɢᴡᴀʏ ᴡᴏᴜʟᴅ ᴄᴏɴᴅᴜᴄᴛ no purge at the Dai Ichi on MacArthur's departure. Stratemeyer left the Fifth Air Force in May 1951 after a heart attack, and retired the next year. An extreme conservative in politics, he organized a failed campaign to protect Senator Joseph McCarthy from censure by the Senate in 1954. Stratemeyer died in 1969. Laurence Bunker returned with MacArthur, remained an aide, and was a founder and vice president of the ultra-Right John Birch Society. Doyle Hickey, elevated by Ridgway to chief of staff, became a lieutenant general and remained in Tokyo into 1953. He retired to raise horses and died in 1961. Edwin "Pinky" Wright remained as Ridgway's G-3. Bill Marquat, another major general (with service to MacArthur that went back to Corregidor in 1941), remained with the occupation administration. William Sebald remained chief of the SCAP Diplomatic Section until the formal end of the Occupation in April 1952. His last assignment was as ambassador to Burma.

Even Charles Willoughby was kept on as G-2. After leaving on his own in late summer 1951, he would become editor of *Foreign Intelligence Digest.* In 1954 he published a MacArthur book, mostly ghosted by John Chamberlain, *MacArthur, 1941–1951.* Courtney Whitney remained on MacArthur's staff to be his representative to the press. His biography written for Time-Life, *MacArthur: His Rendezvous with History* (1955), includes large amounts of dictation from MacArthur.

Of the Dai Ichi group, only Major General Alonzo P. Fox, *SCAP* deputy chief of staff, found his duties reduced, and left in June. Lieutenant General Edward M. Almond left Korea in July 1951 to become commandant of the Army War College, where he remained until his retirement in 1953. After taking a public relations job with an Atlanta insurance company, he became a

357

member of the Board of Advisers of Virginia Military Institute from 1961 through 1968. He died at eighty-seven in 1979.

John H. Michaelis, possibly MacArthur's favorite general officer after Almond, was posted to NATO in 1951 as special assistant to Dwight Eisenhower, then became commandant of cadets at West Point in 1952. Beginning in 1954 he held a series of senior commands, his tenure with the Army in Alaska interrupted by successful treatment for throat cancer in 1960. He returned to Korea as a lieutenant general to command forces there from 1969 through 1972, his last post before retirement. He died in 1985. James A. Van Fleet, who succeeded Ridgway at EUSAK, left at his own request in February 1953, prior to the cease-fire, in protest at the increasingly static war and the limitations on offensive operations. In retirement he wrote two long combative articles for *Life* (May 11 and 18, 1951) arguing for total victory. He was replaced in Korea by General Maxwell D. Taylor, who had succeeded Bolté as Pentagon G-3. Van Fleet died at ninety in 1992.

Marine General Oliver P. Smith, who had tussled over tactics with Almond (and, indirectly, MacArthur), became head of Marine forces in the Atlantic in 1952, earned a third star in 1953 and retired at sixty-two in 1955. He died in 1977.

Ridgway himself left Japan in 1952 to replace Eisenhower at NATO when Ike became a candidate for the Republican presidential nomination. Eisenhower as president named Ridgway Army chief of staff in 1953, a post he held only until 1955, when he retired at sixty to write his memoirs. He died at ninety-eight in 1993. His replacement in Tokyo was Mark W. Clark, who remained until an armistice in place was signed on July 27. Its terms had been politically impossible for Truman, who left the presidency in January 1953, but possible for Eisenhower, who had campaigned on a promise to make peace. Clark, who died in 1984, spent more than a decade of his retirement (1954–66) as president of The Citadel, a military college in Charleston, South Carolina.

Harry Truman, who did not stand for reelection in 1952, retired to Independence, Missouri, where he remained feisty and outspoken. He died in 1972. Syngman Rhee governed as a dictatorial and paternalistic South Korean president until he was toppled in 1960. He died at ninety, in 1965, in exile in Hawaii. Chiang Kaishek, never able to enlarge his remaining Chinese foothold beyond Taiwan but protected there by American security guarantees, died in 1975 at eighty-eight, after which his son briefly succeeded him. Democracy slowly gained ground on the island state thereafter, which prospered economically despite the diplomatic isolation forced upon it by the insistence of Beijing that nations could recognize only one China.

Kim Il Sung remained Communist Party head and de facto chief of state of the Democratic People's Republic of Korea (North Korea) until his death in 1994, keeping his hermit nation insulated from the West and maintaining its ideological rigidity. He accepted a cease-fire that did not include repatriation of prisoners of war who refused to return—a propaganda defeat even worse than relinquishing more territory above the 38th parallel than North Korea had hung onto below (in the Ongjin-Kaesong area). What made it possible was the exhaustion of China, to which North Korea had become a client state, and the death of the increasingly paranoid Stalin in March 1953. Mao Zedong remained in power in Beijing until his death in 1976, after imprisoning or executing many in his hierarchy who had fallen out of favor. One victim was his architect of victory in Korea in late 1950, Peng Dehuai, who had become defense minister from 1954 to 1959. Purged by Mao for putting military professionalism over Communist ideology, Peng was jailed and tortured, but survived to write a posthumously published memoir. He died in 1974.

John Foster Dulles, who had inadvertently made it appear in June 1950 that he was supervising the war to come, completed negotiations for a Japanese peace treaty (to which the Soviets were not a party) in 1951. It was signed in San Francisco. In 1953 he became Eisenhower's ideologically militant secretary of state, a position he held until shortly before his death in 1959. His chief aide, John M. Allison, became assistant secretary of state for Far Eastern affairs in 1952, then ambassador to Japan from 1953 through 1957. After holding other diplomatic posts he retired to teach at the University of Hawaii. He died in 1978. John Muccio left his embassy in Korea in August 1952 to become a member of the UN Trusteeship Council. From 1954 into 1961 he held ambassadorial appointments to several small nations but was then retired by the new Kennedy administration. He died in 1989.

Keyes Beech would report from the Far East for forty years, almost entirely for the *Chicago Daily News*. His last post was Bangkok, for the *Los Angeles Times*. Returning from Korea on leave in mid-1951 after sharing the Pulitzer Prize, he married (for the first time), then returned to cover the Korean cease-fire and exchange of POWs in 1953. His first book, *Tokyo and Points East* (1954), describes his early career as a correspondent; in 1971 he published *Not Without the Americans: A Personal History.* He divorced his wife, Linda, in 1969, and remarried in 1973 (Yuko, a Japanese, who survived him), covered Vietnam and Thailand, and retired to Bethesda, Maryland, in

1982. He died at seventy-six in 1990. Marguerite Higgins, the only woman to win a Pulitzer Prize for war reporting, which she shared in June 1951 with Keyes Beech and Homer Bigart, married Major General William Hall, USAF, in 1952. (Each had a previous divorce.) Settling down in Washington to write and to raise a family, she had a son in 1958 and a daughter in 1959 (another daughter had died in infancy). She returned to reporting to cover the Vietnam War, and Pakistan and India. There she acquired a rare, fatal tropical disease from which she died at forty-five in January 1966.

Following the Senate hearings on the conduct of the Korean War, at which he was the star witness at its first three days in May 1951, MacArthur and his charges faded from the newspapers. The hearings lasted for eight weeks and largely discredited MacArthur's contentions, an outcome for which the general was not prepared after his enthusiastic receptions in mid-April. It did not help him that his most outspoken admirer was Senator Joseph McCarthy, who in defending MacArthur made a three-hour attack on General George C. Marshall on the Senate floor as a man whose career was "steeped in falsehood." (Marshall, who retired as Secretary of Defense late in 1951 because of ill health, died at seventy-nine in 1959.)

Hoping that MacArthur's popular appeal would reassert itself and gain him the Republican presidential nomination in 1952, his backers arranged that he deliver the keynote address at the national convention. His oratory failed to ignite the delegates, Senator Robert Taft refused to back out and give his bloc of delegates to MacArthur, and Eisenhower gained the nomination easily.

By then MacArthur had assumed his largely honorific board chairmanship at Sperry [formerly Remington] Rand. In the summer of 1961 he returned to the Philippines for celebrations marking the fifteenth anniversary of Philippine independence, but did not go on to Japan or Korea. When nearly eighty he began his memoirs, reemploying for ghosted assistance the loyal Courtney Whitney, under a contract with Henry Luce for serialization in *Life.* The collected segments appeared as a book just before MacArthur's death at eighty-four in 1964.

Jean Faircloth MacArthur died in New York City on January 22, 2000 at the age of 101.

Sources

Four archives stand out as prime documentary sources for the Korean War. The MacArthur Memorial and Archive in Norfolk, Virginia, has assembled an immense quantity of related material, and done so without bias, although it is natural that the files of the general's longtime aides reflect loyalty to him. The National Archives Record Group 407 is especially complete on war operations and is a massive file representing all levels of command. The U.S. Army Military History Research Collection in Carlisle Barracks, Pennsylvania, includes the crucial papers of both Matthew Ridgway and Edward Almond, and exit interviews with many general officers who served at some point in their careers in wartime Korea. Also there is the Truman Presidential Library in Missouri. Some of its documentation relative to the war has now been reproduced in facsimile, as noted.

This study, which has been limited to the nearly eleven months of MacArthur's War, has sometimes necessitated going beyond April 1951, as, for example, the MacArthur-Korea hearings conducted by a joint Senate-House committee in mid-1951. Despite its status as "the forgotten war," the vast published literature belies that dismissal. Memoirs, histories and special studies continue to appear. Some drawn from in this book—dealing with the first year of the war—should be singled out for special note. In chapter citations they will be referred to in short form. For the Army they are Roy E. Appleman, *South to the Naktong, North to the Yalu* (Washington, 1961), and James F. Schnabel, *Policy and Direction: The First Year* (Washington, 1972). Billy C. Mossman's *Ebb and Flow: November 1950–July 1951* (Washington, D.C., 1990) continues the official history. For the Air Force there is Robert Frank Futrell, *The United States Air Force in Korea: 1950–1953* (Washington, rev. ed., 1983). For the Navy there is Malcolm W. Cagle and Frank A. Manson, *The Sea War in Korea* (Annapolis, 1957) and for the Marines the first four volumes of Lynn Montross and Nicholas Canzona, *The U.S. Marine Operations in Korea, 1950–1953* (Annapolis, 1954–56). For British and Commonwealth forces there is Anthony Farrar-Hockley's detailed and frank two-volume *The British Part in the Korean War* (London, 1990, 1995). Several of the authors served in Korea as young officers, adding to the dimensions they bring to their narratives. A good although thoroughly hostile general history for its time is Robert Smith's *MacArthur in Korea: The Naked Emperor* (New York, 1982). Although I have utilized some of the sources drawn upon by Smith, I have not quoted directly from his book.

Two multi-volume collections of facsimiles published only in the 1990s are crucial to my documentation. *A Documentary History of the Truman Presidency*, ed. Dennis Merrill (Washington, 1997), reproduces White House papers. (See also notes to Chapter 3.) Also valuable but small in circulation is *Collections of Historical Materials of the Republic of Korea* (Kwa Cheon City, 1996), ed. Jae-Hong Shin, Sang-Keun Lee, Kwag-Un Kim and Byung-Joon Chung, volumes 28–30 of which consist of presidential correspondence to and from Syngman Rhee from 1949 through 1951, and the diaries of his wife, Francesca, a total of nearly seven hundred documents. These include letters to MacArthur and (from Mrs. Rhee) to Mrs. MacArthur. Their contexts will make the sources apparent.

There are many volumes now that exploit Soviet and Chinese Communist documents and memoirs becoming available since the close of the Cold War in 1989. The most useful appears to be *Mao's Military Romanticism. China and the Korean War, 1950–1953*, by Shu Guang Zhang (Lawrence, Kans., 1995).

Preface

Although casualty figures here are from David Rees, *Korea: The Limited War* (New York, 1964), these vary slightly from year to year as a result of the location of remains of some MIAs. Reactions to the Korean War Memorial in Washington summarize my mail from veterans.

1. The Second Coming

The standard biographies and the newspaper press cover MacArthur's arrival in the United States and his address to Congress. Quotations from his address are from press reports. His previous use of some of its lines can be seen in a carbon copy of a letter to Col. W. E. Crist retained in MacArthur's files at the Archive in Norfolk. Congressional and national press comments, and responses in the President's mail, are recorded in the papers of Truman's secretary George M. Elsey and the White House Central Files now in the Truman Library. The *Journal-American* headline in red ink is described in James L.W. West III, *William Styron: A Life* (New York, 1998). Representative Short's revision in the *Congressional Record* of his "We heard God speak here" address in the House of Representatives can be compared with press accounts of his remarks. Truman's "damn bullshit" description of MacArthur's speech is quoted by Merle Miller in *Plain Speaking: An Oral Biography of Harry S. Truman* (New York, 1974). "Senior to everyone but God" is quoted in Robert D. Heinl, *Victory at High Tide* (Philadelphia, 1968). "Listen, darling, they're playing our song," Shelby Foote's invention to Walker Percy in a letter dated May 22, 1951, appears in Jay Tolson, ed., *Shelby Foote and Walker Percy* (New York, 1997). "The Battle Hymn of the Waldorf" is quoted by D. Clayton James in *The Years of MacArthur, III* (Boston, 1985).

2. Before the Deluge

Communist Chinese background on the beginnings of the war, refuting American revisionists, is from "Inside Story of the Korean War [to the] Cease-Fire—Secrets from the Soviet Files," by the pseudonymous Qing Shi ("clear history"), in the Chinese Red Army journal *Hundred Year Tide* 3 (1997), as translated for S.W. by Wan-Kay Li. Additional material is from Shu Guang Zhang, *Mao's Military Romanticism: China and the Korean*

War, 1950–1953 (Lawrence, KS, 1995); Ronald C. Keith, *The Diplomacy of Zhou Enlai* (London, 1989); Russell Spurr, *Enter the Dragon* (New York, 1988), and the papers of the Cold War International History Project of the Woodrow Wilson International Center for Scholars, Washington, D.C. These sources are utilized throughout this book. Some of the latter Communist accounts, particularly on Kim's connivance with Stalin and Stalin's quotes to Shtykov, appear in Vladislav Zubok and Constantine Pleshakov, *Inside the Kremlin's Cold War: From Stalin to Khrushchev* (Cambridge, 1996). Cyrus Sulzberger's interview with MacArthur, Tokyo, May 18, 1950, appears in his *A Long Row of Candles, Memoirs and Diaries* [1934–1954] (New York, 1969).

Views of Dulles are from Dean Acheson, *Present at the Creation* (New York, 1969); for Robert Loeb's "only guy who has direct contact with God," James H. Jones, *Alfred C. Kinsey* (New York, 1998). The cocktail napkin suggestion by Dulles is reported by Watanabe in his diary-memoir *Senryōka no Nihon Zaisei Oboegaki* (Tokyo, 1966), quoted in John W. Dower, *Embracing Defeat* (New York, 1999). Background on MacArthur at the Dai Ichi (the author also visited MacArthur's office—once) is from Clayton James; from William Manchester's interview with James in the MacArthur Archive and his biography *American Caesar* (Boston, 1978); and from Bunker's "Anybody want a ride?" recollection in his papers in the Archive. Also utilized are Sid Huff's *My Fifteen Years with General MacArthur* (New York, 1975), with Joe Alex Morris; Russell Brines, *MacArthur's Japan* (Philadelphia, 1948); Faubion Bowers, "The Late General MacArthur, Warts and All," *Esquire,* January 1975; and William Sebald, with Russell Brines, *With MacArthur in Japan* (New York, 1965). Also Gen. John Michaelis's 1977 interview with Clayton James, in the MacArthur Archive; and on MacArthur's rare attendance at social engagements, Gen. Edward M. Almond's interview with James. Also in the Archive are a copy of Almond's exit interview from the U.S. Army Military History Research Center, Carlisle Barracks; an interview with Dr. Crawford Sams in the Archive (Sams drew upon it for his *"Medic": The Mission of an American Military Doctor in Occupied Japan and War-torn Korea* [Armonk, N.Y., 1997]); and Douglas B. Kendrick, *Memoirs of a Twentieth-Century Army Surgeon* (Manhattan, Kans., 1976). MacArthur's "stagey" luncheon entrances and Mrs. MacArthur's complicity are also reported by Mrs. W. A. Smith, wife of an occupation officer and daughter of a general, in an interview with James, July 1971, in the Archive.

For Dulles in Japan and Korea see Townsend Hoopes, *The Devil and John Foster Dulles* (Boston, 1973), used further in the next chapter. MacArthur on Eisenhower comes from the papers of Laurence E. Bunker in the MacArthur Archive and from an oral history, July 1970, copied from the Hoover Library, also in the Archive.

3. Day One

Documents and testimony from Soviet and Chinese Communists now substantiate the fact that the war was planned by North Korea with Stalin's somewhat reluctant approval, and was by no means a global Communist conspiracy. Beyond sources cited, see Sergei N. Goncharov, John W. Lewis and Xue Litai, *Uncertain Partners: Stalin, Mao, and the Korean War* (Stanford, 1993). These, and a continuing flood of translated documents, also cloud revisionist histories which blame Syngman Rhee, who was undoubtedly provocative, and claim American connivance, which was nonexistent. Notably the South Korea-as-aggressor theory appears in books by Bruce Cumings, *The Roaring of the Cataract, 1947–1950,* vol. 2 of *The Origins of the Korean War* (Princeton, 1990), and

Korea's Place in the Sun (New York, 1997), the former of which quotes, as if authoritative, Soviet envoy Jacob Malik as claiming "an ominous and evil role . . . being played" by General MacArthur in initiating the war. T. R. Fehrenbach in *This Kind of War: A Study in Unpreparedness* (New York, 1964), still one of the best books on combat aspects of the war, notes that KMAG, the American military presence in Korea, "was not under the United States Army, or even responsible to the aloof and powerful satrap in Tokyo, General MacArthur. Because the United States was determined to show the world that its intentions in Korea were nonaggressive, KMAG was under the State Department." The quote from General Bolté about negotiating with Communists is from William Stueck, *The Korean War* (1995); Dulles's "loss to the aggressor" comment is in *Foreign Relations of the United States: Diplomatic Papers* (Washington, 1976).

A conference in Seoul after the breakup of the Soviet Union in 1990 which included reports, studies and testimony of participants in the start of the war was published as *The Truth About the Korean War,* ed. Kim Chullbaum (Seoul, 1991). It includes Chu Yong-bok's "I Translated Attack Orders Composed in Russian," quoted from in this chapter, Yu Song-chol's "I Made the Plan for the First Strike That Invaded the South on June 25th," and other firsthand accounts. Also quoted in this chapter is Yoon Seok Woo's *Korean War* (Seoul, 1987), trans. by Lee Hyung-Jin, which describes the two attempts to invade South Korea from the sea on the first day of the war.

Mike Michaelis is quoted from his interview (see Chapter 2 notes). MacArthur's serene version of how he learned of the war is from his *Reminiscences* (New York, 1964). His exchanges with Washington are in the MacArthur Archive, with many reproduced also in the multi-volume *Documentary History of the Truman Presidency,* especially volumes 18 and 19, on the Korean War. These include the Elsey and Acheson papers as well as State Department and Pentagon documents. The MacArthur Archive also includes dozens of interrogation reports of NKPA prisoners and translated orders (originally in Russian, then in Korean) for attacking specific points across the 38th parallel, often titled "Reconnaissance Orders." Col. (later Gen.) Paik Sun Yup's recollection of the first hours of the war is in his *From Pusan to Panmunjom* (Washington, 1992). Larry Zellers writes about his capture at Kaesong in *In Enemy Hands: A Prisoner in North Korea* (Lexington, Ky., 1991). Philip Crosbie's *Pencilling Prisoner* (Melbourne, 1954) also describes the first hours at Kaesong.

Truman's "By God" comment and his arrival in Washington are described by James E. Webb in a letter to former secretary of the Treasury John W. Snyder, April 25, 1975, in the Webb Papers, Truman Library. Ambassador Bruce's recollections of the reaction from Schuman in Paris are from Nelson D. Lankford, *The Last American Aristocrat* (Boston, 1996).

4. The Telecon War

Truman describes the "two typewriters and two screens" telecon system to Merle Miller in *Plain Speaking.* The description of a telecon in the predawn hours of June 30 is from General Collins's *War in Peacetime: the History and Lessons of Korea* (Boston, 1969). Documents utilized include the papers of Dean Acheson, the President's Naval Aide files, the George Elsey papers, the Acheson papers and telecon transcripts described as "Classified Teletype Conference/Top Secret." Facsimiles are in the *Truman Documentary History.* Some telecons also appear in the MacArthur Archive. Higgins tells the story of General Kim's return to Korea in her memoir. Additional material is from Antoinette May's biography of her, *Witness to War: A Biography of Marguerite Higgins* (New York, 1983). Background on Keyes Beech is from John T. McQuiston, "Keyes Beech, 76, Correspondent in Asia for Five Decades, Is Dead," *New York Times*, Feb. 16, 1990. David Douglas Duncan's description of MacArthur at Suwon is from his *This Is War!* (New York, 1951); his photographs from Korea were then regularly appearing in *Life*. The general's challenge to palace guard correspondents is from an interview with James, June 1977, in MacArthur Archive files. The general's fatalism is described to James in an interview with Edwin K. Wright, August 1971, also in the Archive.

Lowell Thomas's CBS radio broadcast transcripts, quoted here and later, are from copies supplied by Fred D. Crawford from the Thomas Archive at Bard College. Marguerite Higgins's reports are from her *War in Korea* (New York, 1951); those of Keyes Beech are from *Tokyo and Points East* (Garden City, N.Y. 1954). Harold Noble's account is *Embassy at War* (Seattle, 1974). J. W. Alsop's memoir is *I've Seen the Best of It* (New York, 1992), written with Adam Platt.

5. Bataan II

I am indebted to Col. Carl Bernard (Ret.), who arrived in Korea with Task Force Smith, for abundant letters and documents he has collected about that episode, as well as for his own recollections. Further Task Force Smith accounts are those of Uzal Ent, Robert Roy and Bob Fitzgerald in Rudy Tomedi, ed., *No Bugles, No Drums* (New York, 1993). (The "last smoke" story is from Roy.) The Bernard papers are utilized further in Chapter 6. The CIA monograph sweepingly critical of MacArthur's denigration of intelligence not in conformity with his thinking is *The Final Months of the War with Japan: Signals Intelligence, U.S. Invasion Planning, and the A-Bomb Decision,* by Douglas J. MacEachin (Washington, December 1998). Mrs. Rhee's letter to lobbyist Oliver is among the facsimiles in the Korean presidential correspondence, vol. 29 (1949–50).

MacArthur's communications with President Truman are in the MacArthur Archive and the presidential *Documentary History.* Walter Karig, Malcolm Cagle and Frank Manson, *Battle Report: The War in Korea* (New York, 1952), a semi-official history written while the war was still in progress, contains some of the most devastating descriptions of early wartime carnage. Appleman's *South to the Naktong* is the most detailed single account of the early weeks of the war. Michaelis's recollections are from his oral history. Higgins's tribulations are reported in her own memoir and in May's biography. Keyes Beech's recollections of Marguerite Higgins in Korea are from his *Not Without the Americans: A Personal History* (New York, 1971).

The recollections of Leonard Korgie and Lacy Barnett appear in Donald Knox, ed., *The Korean War: An Oral History, Pusan to Chosin* (New York, 1985). Oree Gregory's diary entries at MASH 8055 are from Otto F. Apel Jr. and Pat Apel, *MASH: An Army Surgeon in Korea* (Lexington, Ky., 1998). Jack Ben-Rubin's reminiscence is from a letter to S.W., Aug. 30, 1995. (Ben-Rubin and others who thought that Patton—and Walker, who aped him—brandished a pearl-handled pistol actually saw a bone-handled one.) Nat Wisser was interviewed by S.W. The identification of NKPA officers by their personal rice-pot is reported by Robert Rhoden in "Corsairs from Heaven," *Naval History,* July/August 1997. James Michener's comments are from the foreword to David Douglas Duncan's memoir (see Chapter 4 notes). Data on the ill-starred 24th Regiment is from the United States Army Center of Military History's volume *Black Soldier, White Army: The 24th Infantry Regiment in Korea,* by William T. Bowers, William M. Hammond and George L. MacGarrigle (Washington, 1996).

Edward R. Murrow's broadcasts, including the suppressed one, are collected in his *In Search of Light,* ed. Ed Bliss (New York, 1967). Additional details appear in Joseph E. Persico, *Edward R. Murrow: An American Original* (New York, 1988).

6. *"Stand or Die"*

Secret and confidential official documents utilized, including those of the National Security Council, come from facsimiles in the Truman *Documentary History.* Further references to the 24th Regiment are from its official history (see Chapter 5 notes) and Lyle Rishell's *With a Black Platoon in Combat: A Year in Korea* (College Station, Texas, 1993). Harry Maihafer's memoir, which includes accounts of Swett, Newman, Corley and Bernard, is *From the Hudson to the Yalu* (College Station, Texas, 1993). The conference of Communist Chinese bigwigs in Beijing is described in Spurr's *Enter the Dragon.* The Murrow accounts continue from the sources noted in Chapter 5. Rhee's war is described in Noble's *Embassy at War.* Arnold Winter is quoted from Tomedi's *No Bugles, No Drums.* Lord Tedder's cable to London is from Farrar-Hockley. Vincent Kreps and William Hayward both wrote to S.W. The Marines' story is told in detail in Montross and Canzona, *The Pusan Perimeter,* first volume in their series.

7. *Operation Chromite*

JCS 924, *Operations Against Japan Subsequent to Formosa,* a 1944 planning study that included an Inchon landing, was supplied to S.W. by Dennis M. Giangreco. Additional data—about the prewar Forney mission—came from retired Gen. Edwin Simmons in a letter to S.W., Feb. 17, 1998. Robert D. Heinl Jr.'s "The Nucleus for Victory at High Tide," *Marine Corps Gazette,* September and October 1967, a study of the invasion problems at Inchon, was the basis for his later book, *Victory at High Tide.*

The conversations of high brass in Tokyo about Inchon are reported by most of the participants with little change but for nuances of language. The best account of the dialogue may be that of Clayton James in *Refighting the Last War* (New York, 1993), in a section titled "MacArthur's Grand Obsession: Inchon." Collins's own account is in his *War in Peacetime.* The Navy and Marine perspective is best found in volume 2 of Montross and Canzona, although Admiral Burke's own version is in Oral History #21, Cineworld Productions, GG-32, in the MacArthur Archive, and Gen. Lem Shepherd's remarks are from his oral history in the Archive, Sept. 22, 1970, interviewed by Philip A. Brower. An Army summation is in Appleman. Harriman's reminiscences of his talks on Inchon with MacArthur are in an interview with Clayton James, June 1977, in the Archive; Truman's version from Washington is in his *Memoirs: Years of Trial and Hope* (Garden City, N.Y., 1956). Lt. Col. Charles R. Scherer's experiences with KATUSA troops are recalled in Chapter 3 of Rod Paschall's *Witness to War: Korea* (New York, 1995).

Air Vice Marshal Bouchier's report to London on his meeting with MacArthur is in Farrar-Hockley. A detailed White House account of the firing of Secretary of Defense Johnson, by presidential secretary Charles Ross, dated September 13, 1950, is in the Elsey papers in *Documentary History.* Copies of MacArthur's progress reports to the JCS are in the Archive.

The most detailed account of the formation and history of X Corps is Shelby L. Stanton's *America's Tenth Legion: X Corps in Korea, 1950* (Novato, Calif., 1989). Almond's more personal account is his official oral history, conducted by his grandson, an Army captain.

The Marine buildup for the invasion is reported in Montross and Canzona II, where Edwin Simmons, then a young officer, is quoted. His further recollections appear in *No Bugles, No Drums*. Marguerite Higgins and others report "Operation Common Knowledge." Alternative landing plans fill Box 103, folder 2, in the MacArthur Archive.

Rhee's undelivered message to General Walker via Captain Sim is in the Korean documentary history, dated July 26. Rhee's suggestion for a breakout from the Perimeter after a landing at Pusan is in the documentary history for Sept. 8, 1950 (it seems incredible that he would not have known of the actual operation so late in its preparation).

8. Inchon

The nuclear misunderstanding on the *Borland* is reported by James Edwin Alexander in *Inchon to Wonsan: From the Deck of a Destroyer in the Korean War* (Annapolis, 1996). The mission of the *Whitesand Bay* is in Farrar-Hockley, as are the "Bank Holiday" remarks of Admiral Andrewes. Air Force accounts except where noted are from Futrell. Larry Zellers reports hearing about Inchon in *In Enemy Hands*.

Accounts of Inchon other than those specified here or in the text are from Heinl, Stanton, and Montross and Canzona II. The recollections of Fred Davidson, Grant Sharp, David Peppin, Leonard Korgie and Merwin Perkins are in Knox, ed., *The Korean War*. Ed Simmons recalls the San Francisco truck driver in *No Bugles, No Drums*.

General Shepherd's remarks are from his oral history in the MacArthur Archive. Marguerite Higgins told her own story. Almond's version of events is from his oral history. The North Korean air attack on the invasion fleet is from Farrar-Hockley. The POW situation is from my personal records as well as accounts cited. The Collins memory of capturing female POWs is from his account to S.W., May 18, 1997.

The brief use of the *Missouri*'s big guns is described by Alexander and by Montross and Canzona II. Edwards Metcalf told me in 1997 about arranging for Japanese-made napalm. Exchanges between Washington and MacArthur are from the MacArthur Archive and from the Truman *Documentary History*. The encounter of Higgins and Beech with naked NKPA prisoners is described by Beech in *Tokyo and Points East*, as is his story of Marine Jimmie Frenchman.

Mrs. MacArthur's praise for the 1st Cav and jaundiced view of the 7th Division was reported to S.W. by 7th vet Ron Todd in September 1997. The Dutch ambassador's inquiry about the meaning of *lam* was reported by Lowell Thomas in a broadcast of Sept. 19, 1950. Richard Nixon on Korea is reported in Greg Mitchell, *Tricky Dick and the Pink Lady* (New York, 1998). Michaelis's recollection is from his oral history; Ridgway's evaluation of the aftermath of Inchon is from his *The Korean War* (Garden City, N.Y., 1967).

9. Crossing the Parallel

Sun Pin, *The Art of Warfare*, is used in the translation by D. C. Lau and Roger T. Ames (New York, 1996). Accounts by Higgins and Alsop are drawn from their memoirs and from May, *Witness to War*. POW data is from S.W. records. National Security Council and UN directives are drawn from the Truman *Documentary History*. Almond on his boss's ability to make up his mind without advice is quoted from J. Lawton Collins, *War in Peacetime*. Operations matters other than as specified are from X Corps and Eighth Army accounts by Appleman, Stanton, and Montross and Canzona II. British forces accounts are from Farrar-Hockley; Dai Ichi exchanges with Washington and commanders in Korea are from the MacArthur Archive. Ed Simmons's "What Price Glory?" comment is quoted from his letter to S.W. of January 22, 1999.

William Hayward wrote to S.W. Minesweeping operations are described in Montross and Canzona II. Harriman's account of his talks with MacArthur and with Acheson are from his oral history at the Archive.

10. Mohammed and the Mountain

Much Wake material, including meeting minutes, comes from Cabinet and White House facsimiles in the Truman *Documentary History.* Laurence Bunker's nearly parallel notes are in the MacArthur Archive. Harriman's recollections are in his oral history. Marshall's cable to MacArthur to bring Muccio along (Oct. 10, 1950) is in the Archive. Truman's policy differences with MacArthur are summed up by John W. Spanier in *The Truman-MacArthur Controversy* (Cambridge, 1959). MacArthur's *Reminiscences* rewrites 1950s history.

Bugging the Soviet embassy and the Soviet UN Mission: Although I supplied Freedom of Information Act officials with the code designations for these operations (the UN Mission code, for example, is ZF0106W), I received in 1997–98, both originally and on appeal, only deliberately erroneous documents for other dates than 1950–51 and for innocuous assignments. Even these were largely india-inked into unintelligibility. Presumably this is still too sensitive an area for access. That the ZF codes exist for these operations indicates that something happened.

Soviet-Chinese exchanges come largely from *Inside the Kremlin's Cold War, Mao's Military Romanticism* and *Enter the Dragon,* as well as Nikita Khrushchev's *Khrushchev Remembers,* ed. and trans. by Strobe Talbott (Boston, 1970). Ridgway's "on my knees" quote from MacArthur is from his *The Korean War.* William Sebald's account is *With MacArthur in Japan.* Frank Pace's oral history, January 1972, and John Muccio's oral history, December 1973, are both in the Truman Library.

A carbon copy of MacArthur's fulsome thank-you letter to Truman after Wake (Oct. 30, 1950) is in the Archive. Rosemary Foot in *The Wrong War: American Foreign Policy and the Dimensions of the Korean Conflict* (Ithaca, N.Y., 1985) includes Ambassador Panikkar's various warnings relayed from Chinese officials. Peng's memoirs, trans. by Zheng Longpu with English text edited by Sara Grimes, are *Memoirs of a Chinese Marshal: The Autobiographical Notes of Peng Dehuai* (Beijing, 1984). MacArthur's talks with the Brazilian ambassador in Japan, overheard by American intelligence when radioed to Brazil, are denied by MacArthur in a "Top Secret. Eyes Only" decrypted cable, Nov. 11, 1950, copy in the MacArthur Archive. Allegations of further MacArthur contacts of a similar nature are reported in later chapters. These were also denied.

11. To the Yalu

Peng's entry into Korea and that of his troops comes from his memoir and from the first-hand accounts by Tang Bao Yi and Qin Shu Lan in *Bombs and Fresh Flowers* (Beijing, 1983), ed. Li Zhi Min, Chao Yan and Zhang Yi Sang, translated for S.W. by Wan-Kay Li. Eighth Army accounts are, except where cited, largely from Appleman, Joseph C. Goulden, *Korea: The Untold Story of the War* (New York, 1982), and Farrar-Hockley. MacArthur's "Where's Kim Buck Tooth?" is reported by Rees in *Korea: The Limited War.* Truman's growing disenchantment with MacArthur's moves is examined in *Memoirs: Years of Trial and Hope,* and in David McCullough's biography, *Truman* (New York, 1992). For the invention of a post–Pearl Harbor Luzon landing, and its repulse, see S. Weintraub,

Long Day's Journey into War (New York, 1991); for Willoughby's concealing derogatory data about Hirohito, and about wanted war criminal Col. Tsuji, see Dower, *Embracing Defeat;* for the invention of statistics on Christianity in Japan to please MacArthur, see Faubion Bowers, "The Late General MacArthur" (full citation in Chapter 2).

Admirals Hoke and Sherman are quoted on Wonsan from a letter to the editor by Daniel A. Neuhauser in *Naval Institute Proceedings,* January 1977, on magnetic mines in Korean waters. Bob Hope's account of Wonsan is in *Have Tux, Will Travel,* as told to Pete Martin (New York, 1954). That his expenses were paid by the government despite his commercial exploitation of his service tours is reported by Lawrence J. Quirk in *Bob Hope: The Road Well-Traveled* (New York, 1998). Capt. Norman Allen's "pissing" in the Yalu forecast is from Knox's oral history, as is Pfc. Robert Harper's recollection of his Halloween patrol into Chinese lines.

Cumings in *The Origins of the Korean War* (1990) quotes People's Republic of China sources on likening their "volunteers" to the Abraham Lincoln Brigade. POW interrogation quotes appear in Almond's oral history and in General Paik Sun Yup's memoir.

O. P. Smith's long and angry message of Nov. 15, 1950, to Marine commandant Cates about the tactical blindness of Almond (and presumably his superiors in Tokyo pulling the strings) is—discreetly?—not quoted by Montross and Canzona in the official Marine history. It is filed with Smith's papers in the Marine Corps Historical Center.

12. A Turkey for Thanksgiving

MacArthur's "home for Christmas" confidence ("this movement would start before Thanksgiving") appears not only in his Wake and other voiced remarks but in his message, Oct. 21, 1950, labeled "OPERATIONAL IMMEDIATE" to Department of the Army, carbon copy in the MacArthur Archive. His messages of early November about Chinese troops pouring over the Yalu are similarly filed.

Marine accounts are largely from Montross and Canzona II, supplemented by Far-rar-Hockley. For Appleman's account of the disaster in November/December, see his *Escaping the Trap: The U.S. Army X Corps in Northeast Korea, 1950* (College Station, Tex, 1990); and for EUSAK, his *Disaster in Korea: The Chinese Confront MacArthur* (College Station, Tex., 1989). Michaelis's and Wright's recollections are from their oral histories. Appleman is detailed on the Turkish disaster. The recollections of Ole John E. (March 8, 1994) are in the Carl Bernard papers. The Chinese side is most detailed in Spurr's *Enter the Dragon.* Dolvin's incident is described in S.L.A. Marshall, *The River and the Gauntlet* (New York, 1953), one of the best sources, still, for first-person accounts of the Eighth Army after the Chinese intervention. Pfc. Lockowitz's mock-broadcast and Gen. Keiser's stumbling over a dying GI are from Martin Russ's oral history, *Breakout: The Chosin Reservoir Campaign, Korea 1950* (New York: 1999).

MacArthur's flight down the Yalu in his Constellation is described in Wright's oral history. His report to the JCS on his "personal rcn" is in the MacArthur Archive, as is the documentation on the acrimonious dispute over bombing the Yalu hydroelectric installations. Peng's "Liar!" ejaculation after MacArthur's Christmas boast is from Ye Yumeng in *Black Snow* (Beijing, 1989), memoirs of Chinese forces in the Korean War, as translated and serialized in *Chosun Ibo,* Seoul, from Aug. 3 to Dec. 3, 1989.

The atmosphere in Washington, including the White House, State and Defense Departments, is best seen, and quoted from here, in documents from the Truman *Documentary History.* MacArthur's confused and contradictory behavior at this time is well described by Goulden in *Korea,* which also reproduces intelligence documentation. The guarded *Life* interview with MacArthur or his surrogate is dated Dec. 4, 1950.

13. The Nuclear Option

An overview of the nuclear option dilemma by Daniel Calingaert, based on data available at the time, is "Nuclear Weapons and the Korean War," *Journal of Strategic Studies* 11 (June 1988). Another published at about the same time but with less detail is Rosemary Foot, "Nuclear Coercion and the Ending of the Korean Conflict," *International Security* 13 (Winter 1988/89). More valuable is Roger Dingman's "Atomic Diplomacy," *International Security* 13 (Winter 1988/89), which documents, from diary entries, telecons and filed memoranda, strategic talks and deployment orders involving nuclear-configured aircraft. Mao's risk analysis about American atomic intervention is explored by Thomas J. Christensen in "Threats, Assurances, and the Last Chance for Peace," *International Security* 17 (Summer 1992). Additional sources upon which this chapter is based are Timothy J. Botti, *Ace in the Hole: Why the United States Did Not Use Nuclear Weapons in the Cold War, 1945 to 1965* (Westport, Conn., 1997); Chuck Hansen, *U.S. Nuclear Weapons: The Secret History* (New York, 1988), and Gordon Dean's diary, ed. Roger M. Anders, *Forging the Atomic Shield* (Chapel Hill, N.C., 1987).

The JCS order dated July 31, 1950, for non-nuclear components of bombs to be shipped to Guam is no. 87570, copy in the MacArthur Archive. Most such orders are in the Archive; others are referred to in the text or in studies already referred to. The literature is voluminous.

Ridgway's contention to the Joint Chiefs that MacArthur should be fired if he would not obey orders is in Ridgway's *The Korean War.* Gold, Greenglass, Rosenberg and the loyalty oath crises appear in the national press.

14. Korea for Christmas

Lt. Sam Walker's birthday visit to his father is described in John Toland, *In Mortal Combat* (New York, 1991). Bohlen is quoted from Sulzberger's diary, December 1, 1950, in *A Long Row of Candles.* Brigadier Coad is quoted by Appleman (in *Disaster in Korea*) from Coad's "Land Campaign in Korea." General Mansergh is quoted in Farrar-Hockley.

Lt. Comdr. Lessenden is quoted in Beech, *Tokyo and Points East.* Other Marines are quoted in Montross, etc., III. Private Tyack is quoted in Farrar-Hockley; Bishop, Ransone and Killeen in Knox. General Peng is quoted from his memoirs, Brigadier Coad from Farrar-Hockley, Ridgway from his *Korean War.* Carl Youngdale's Chosin oral history is in the MacArthur Archive. (He was later a major general.) "Gimme tomorrow" is reported by David Douglas Duncan in Higgins's *War in Korea.* Conrad Johnson's "elephant feet" is from a June 1996 interview article in the *Providence Journal-Bulletin* sent to S.W. by Korean vet Wilfred Emond. Bob Hammond's Chosin reminiscence is from a long and detailed letter to S.W. of July 7, 1997. What "unfriendly" napalm fire did to Chinese POWs No Face and Half-Face was observed by the author. James Cardinal's memories were published as "Recollections of Korea—1950–51" in *Saber,* December 1993, and furnished by Carl Bernard. Maggie Higgins's recollection of the Marines at Chosin is from her *War in Korea.* Stanton B. Felzer supplied the Christmas greetings from mimeographed doggerel sent to him by S.W. from Korea.

Marine pilot Jesse Brown's end is reported in an article about Thomas Hudner in

The Boston Globe, Feb. 22, 1998. The game response to Maggie Higgins at Hagaru, and a Marine Captain's likening the lights of Hagaru to New York City are from Russ, *Breakout.* The Del Valle episode with Bedell Smith is recounted in James, *Refighting the Last War.*

MacArthur's glum end-of-year summaries to the JCS are from carbon copies in the Archive. His rollback contingency plan no. 203 to JCS, Dec. 6, 1950, is also in the Archive, as is his letter to Roy Howard of UP, Dec. 20, 1950 (Whitney file). Francesca Rhee's diary entry of Dec. 16 is from the collected Rhee correspondence (*Collections*) (1996, Seoul, Korea). Sergeant Woodruff's embarrassment about the retreat is recorded in Donald Knox and Alfred Coppel, *The Korean War: Uncertain Victory,* the concluding volume of *An Oral History* (New York, 1988).

Dean Acheson brought up the possibility of replacing MacArthur in his minutes of a State Department meeting on the crisis on Dec. 4, 1950. The facsimile is in the Truman *Documentary History,* as are all of Acheson's (and Elsey's) papers for December. General Shepherd's remark to Higgins on evacuating Chosin is in his oral history. Almond is quoted from his oral history. Vincent Kreps wrote to S.W. on Feb. 4, 1997. Erle Cocke's correspondence with MacArthur is in the Archive. The typical experience of an American POW is drawn from that of Roy Gordon as described by Joe Stuteville in "Faith Unchained," *American Legion Magazine,* May 1997. James Polk's letters are quoted from Toland.

Operational data is largely from Appleton, *Disaster in Korea,* Stanton, and Montross, etc., III. Ridgway's recollection of arriving without winter gear is from the transcript of his question-and-answer session at age eighty-nine, May 9, 1984, at the Army Command and General Staff College, Fort Leavenworth, Kansas, published in the May 1990 *Military Review.*

15. Ridgway's War

Top-secret messages between MacArthur and Ridgway, and MacArthur to the JCS, are in the MacArthur Archive. Truman's messages to MacArthur are in the *Documentary History.* Ridgway's recollections of his first weeks in Korea are in his *Korean War* and also (the ignorance of a general about local terrain and on the relief of a "mediocre" general) from his question-and-answer transcript in *Military Review,* May 1990. Going well beyond British involvement in the first months of 1951 is Farrar-Hockley's detailed and formidably cited *The British Part in the Korean War, II: An Honourable Discharge* (London, 1995).

MacArthur's 71st birthday is described in Dower, *Embracing Defeat,* which includes an illustration of the Kanagawa Prefecture officials with the gift bust of MacArthur. Rhee's appeal to arm Korean youths, denied by MacArthur, is in Rhee's *Collections,* dated Jan. 5, 1951. Copies of General Lowe's communications to Truman are in the MacArthur Archive, Whitney papers. Michaelis is quoted from his oral history, where he discusses the relief of many regimental and division commanders, and his receiving a general's star.

Peng's situation is described in his own memoirs, Appleman's quotes from additional Chinese translations, including an article in *Kunlun,* an official army publication, Shu Guang Zhang's *Mao's Military Romanticism,* Russell Spurr's *Enter the Dragon,* the recollections of Peng's interpreter ("I . . . am not MacArthur . . ."), and in a July 1997 reminiscence ("the earth-red grain of sorghum . . .") sent to S.W. by Tu Shou-peng, then a young officer.

The unnecessary destruction of infrastructure is described in detail in Appleman,

Disaster in Korea: The Chinese Confront MacArthur (College Station, Tex, 1989). Higgins's memoir does not reach this period; her activities are described from the May biography. Almond's diary is quoted from Appleman's *Ridgway Duels for Korea* (College Station, Texas, 1990), and his exit oral history from copies in the MacArthur Archive. (Both refer to his relief of General McClure.) Collins is quoted from his *War in Peacetime.* Bubble-gum-card texts are from reproductions in my files. Mark Clark is quoted from his memoir, *From the Danube to the Yalu* (New York, 1954). Clark is admonished about anticipating rotation of troops by Collins in a secret personal cable sent via MacArthur as DA 83907 on Feb. 19, 1951, in the MacArthur Archive.

Harsch's *Monitor* dispatch reporting MacArthur's loss of influence appeared on Jan. 22, 1951. William K. Hutchinson in an INS dispatch dated Jan. 27, 1951, reported flabby denials from Truman's "top advisers." Unhappiness with the wholesale removal of generals, instigated by Ridgway, is expressed in a secret message, DA 82910, Feb. 7, 1951, from Collins to MacArthur which refers to Gay, Kean, Barr and Church. (McClure's removal came separately and earlier.)

Earl D. Johnson's message to Ridgway about MacArthur is in the MacArthur Archive. The exchange of views between Freeman and "Monclar" is reported in Toland (where the pseudonym is Montclar). The massacre of sleeping Americans is reported by Bill Boss, "Pats Learn Grim Lessons from Sight of Slain GI's," *Toronto Globe and Mail,* Feb. 21, 1951. James Cardinal is quoted from his memoir in *Saber* (see Chapter 14 notes). General Hodes is quoted on censorship in the "Ridgway Takes Command" chapter of Goulden's *Korea.* Dulles thanked MacArthur for his "wise counsel" on the Japanese peace treaty draft in a letter, Feb. 11, 1951, in the Archive. Group 64 of Soviet air support over the Yalu is described by a fighter pilot, later a reserve colonel, Alexander Pavlovich Smolechkov, who participated in the squadron, in Taoka Junji's "The Soviet Air Force Participated in the War," in the Seoul-published *The Truth about the Korean War* (1991).

Communist POW hostility to prison missionaries is described in *Memoirs of the War Prisoners from the Volunteers,* by Da Ying (Beijing, 1987), a *Kun Lun* publication trans. for S.W. by Wan-Kay Li. The so-called spies captured near Pyongyang are reported in a chapter, "The Parachuted Spies Could Not Escape Capture," by Niu Chun Ren (trans. fow S.W. by Wan-Kay Li), in *Bombs and Fresh Flowers* (Beijing, 1983). Stalin's charges that the United States was sending enemy POWs as spies (". . . every day we capture a few of them") is in Zubok and Pleshakov, *Inside the Kremlin's Cold War.* The "turning" of NKPA and Chinese POWs—literally Operation Turncoat—was an operation in which S.W. was involved in the usual compartmentalized fashion in which each individual knew little more than his own role. That the U.S. was also supporting "Guerrilla Activities" in China is documented in a top-secret "sanitized copy" in the President's files dated Dec. 17, 1950 (*Documentary History*).

Future president Jimmy Carter's Navy assignment is described in Peter G. Bourne, *Jimmy Carter* (New York, 1997). Policy on stabilization of the front at the 38th parallel, suggested by C. B. Marshall to Paul Nitze, is described with source citations by Rosemary Foot in *The Wrong War.*

Ridgway's anger about MacArthur's pretending to run the war is evident in his memoir, *The Korean War,* in his chapter "Rebuilding the Fighting Spirit," and in Smith's *MacArthur in Korea,* which reports Ridgway's reaction to his staff and Almond's inventions in his diary to make it appear that Ridgway came late to his own conference after MacArthur himself announced Ridgway's Operation Killer.

16. Courting Dismissal

MacArthur's courting of Rightist diplomats in Tokyo is documented by Goulden in his *Korea*. Courtney Whitney is quoted from his *MacArthur: His Rendezvous with History* (New York, 1956). Crawford Sams's adventure into North Korea is drawn from his oral history in the MacArthur Archive, from which the account of his memoir, *"Medic,"* was drawn. *The United States and Biological Warfare: Secrets from the Early Cold War and Korea* (Bloomington, Ind., 1999), by Stephen Endicott and Edward Hagerman, discusses American interest in the occupation period in the Japanese World War II bacteriological warfare program and alleges a CIA cover-up, but the authors can make no persuasive connection to the alleged germ warfare in Korea. MacArthur's mention to Sams that American boys were being killed "senselessly" is drawn from his interview with James in the Archive. MacArthur's relations in early March with Erle Cocke, Barry Faris, H. G. Martin and Hugh Baillie are also documented in the Archive. Ridgway's irritation with MacArthur's photo-opportunity visits is documented in Ridgway's *The Korean War*, in Appleman, *Ridgway Duels for Korea,* and Goulden. MacArthur's relatively long jeep tour with the Marines is reported in Montross and Canzona IV from Gen. O. P. Smith's oral history. The full interview, from which the MacArthur visit is also extracted in Knox and Coppel, *The Korean War: Uncertain Victory,* is in the Oral History Collection, Marine Corps Historical Center, Washington, D.C.

MacArthur's exchanges with the Pentagon and with State are in the Archive; those with the White House are in *Documentary History.* His exchanges with Ridgway, including his self-invitations to visit the front, are also in the Archive.

MacArthur's statements to Mayor Impellitieri and to Representative Martin are documented in the Archive and reported at length in the press. His *Freeman* magazine questionnaire is in the Archive. His sabotage of peace feelers is described by Truman in *Memoirs,* in McCullough's *Truman,* in Acheson's memoir and in dozens of secondary volumes as well as in the press.

Sgt. Charles Schlichter's arrival at POW Camp No. 5 at Pyoktong on the Yalu on March 17, 1951, is described by T. R. Fehrenbach in an excellent chapter on the prisoner-of-war situation on both sides in his *This Kind of War.* Larry Zellers writes about the POW camp at Antung in his memoir (see Chapter 3 notes). That American POWs were slipped into a clandestine network of Chinese camps for interrogation and indocrination and were never accounted for thereafter was revealed by declassified reports in the files of the Army's assistant chief of staff for intelligence only on Feb. 16, 1998 (AP dispatch). These vanished POWs are among the 8,100 missing in the war.

MacArthur's cranky insistence to his staff generals Wright and Doyle that Ridgway be given—in person—a letter of reprimand is described in detail in Wright's oral history (with James), August 1971, in the Archive. MacArthur's claim to *Newsweek* (March 31, 1951) to have never received a gag order on policy from Washington is in the Archive. The JCS reminder that he did is JCS 86736, March 24, 1951, referring to JCS 98134 of Dec. 6, 1950. The "Top Secret Priority" message is in the MacArthur Archive.

Sir William Slim's report to Commonwealth chiefs of staff, April 9, 1951, and the Foreign Secretary's cable to Acheson, are in Farrar-Hockley II. Sulzberger's report of Montogomery's reaction is from *A Long Row of Candles,* diary entry for May 12, 1951.

Much of the record on the dismissal of MacArthur is in *Documentary History*—Truman's secretary's notes, for example, drafts of orders and Truman's White House diary. Marshall's confession to Truman that MacArthur should have been relieved two years earlier comes from Truman's reminiscence in a letter, Nov. 30, 1962, to Brig. Gen. S.L.A. Marshall, also in *Documentary History.* Other documents range from the memoir and war literature to Truman himself through members of his crisis teams, such as Dean Acheson, Gordon Dean and Lawton Collins. Mossman, in *Ebb and Flow,* chronicles the sequence of events well. How Ridgway responded is described in his own memoir. How *Chicago Tribune* reporters discovered the potential scoop is best described in Richard Norton Smith's *The Colonel: The Life and Legend of Robert R. McCormick* (Boston, 1997); a copy of a letter on the firing from Washington correspondent Walter Trohan on *Tribune* letterhead, June 5, 1964, to Bonner Fellers, a general who had become a Republican Party division chief for veterans, is in the Archive.

How MacArthur received and took the dismissal order is described by Huff, Manchester, Sebald and Whitney.

17. Going Home

General sources for both Truman and MacArthur are the same as in the previous chapter. Notes on Ridgway's first (April 12) meeting with a "composed" MacArthur after his dismissal, as Ridgway arrived in Japan, are from Ridgway's *Soldier* (New York, 1956), as told to Harold H. Martin. MacArthur's allegation to Ridgway that Truman was suffering from "malignant hypertension" is in Ridgway's memoir. MacArthur's anticipatory—if not parting—request to Marshall, C-59497, April 6, 1951, to promote (in the order in the message) Stratemeyer, Ridgway, Joy, Hoge, Allen Hickey and Wright each one rank is in the Archive. Ridgway reports his own first experiences of Japan and Korea in both *Soldier* (where he is more cautious) and *The Korean War,* and Appleman, in *Ridgway Duels for Korea,* furnished additional detail.

Mrs. Almond is quoted on the popular pro-MacArthur motorcade to Haneda in *MacArthur in Korea,* and Manchester gives an equally positive account. A sour account— that Marilyn Monroe would have drawn larger crowds—appears in Michener's foreword to David Douglas Duncan's *This Is War!* Niles W. Bond of MacArthur's staff is quoted in an interview by James, June 1977 (Archive), as viewing "a triumphal exit" (and a "sincere" one), although the Army and Japanese government "orchestrated" the crowd.

Lowell Thomas's radio scripts are from the Bard collection. George Hanrahan e-mailed to S.W. on June 17, 1998. Herbert Luster is quoted in Knox and Coppel, *The Korean War.* Walter Winchell is quoted from Neal Gabler, *Winchell* (New York, 1994). Merle Homan's changing the name of MacArthur Avenue is taken from Jo Chesworth, *Story of the Century: The Borough of State College, Pennsylvania, 1896–1996* (State College, 1996). Press and public responses to the dismissal are drawn from press accounts and such biographies and war histories as James, Perret (Geoffry Perret, *Old Soldiers Never Die,* New York, 1996), Manchester, Goulden, and the Truman *Documentary History,* which also contain such Truman diary entries as "Quite an explosion" on April 10, 1951. Even letters from children are in the Truman collection, as well as summaries of domestic and international reaction, one document quoting "Soviet Bloc" comments. Acheson's "Thank God that's over" anecdote is repeated in many books. I have quoted here from Toland and Goulden. The mock White House schedule for welcoming MacArthur is in many accounts. I have quoted here from Michael Schaller, *MacArthur: Far Eastern General* (New York, 1989).

Paik describes learning of the dismissal from Rhee in *From Pusan to Panmunjom.* Rhee's letter to MacArthur, April 12, 1951, is in the collected Rhee correspondence.

Eisenhower's "I wouldn't trade . . ." is quoted by Herbert S. Parmet in *Eisenhower and the American Crusades* (New York, 1972).

Acknowledgments

I AM INDEBTED TO the people identified below for their memories, their good offices and their access to materials relevant to my research. Interviews, oral histories, letters and documents are also cited in my source notes and, often, in the text itself. As always, too, I owe a special debt to the Institute for the Arts and Humanistic Studies at Penn State, my research "home"—and to the staff of the Pattee Library at Penn State, my other research home. At the head of my Source Notes I have also acknowledged the indispensable resources of the MacArthur Memorial and Archive, and its helpful and knowledgeable staff.

My gratitude goes also to Lucy B. Addington, Edgar A. Aufill, Erica W. Austin, Larry Barulli, Jack Ben-Rubin, Carl Bernard, the late Charles T. Butler, Harry P. Clark, Sam Cohen, William T. Collins, John Cook, the late Fred D. Crawford, Robert C. Doyle, Robert S. Elegant, Wilfred Emond, Bonny Farmer, Stanton B. Felzer, Dan Freedberg, Dennis M. Giangreco, Bob Hammond, George Hanrahan, William Hayward, Seong-Kon Kim, Donaldson Koons, Vincent Kreps, Hyung-Jin Lee, Wan-Kay Li, Val Limburg, Kang Liu, Bonnie McEwen, Harry Maihafer, the late Charles W. Mann Jr., Edwards H. Metcalf, Bruce Nichols, Michel Pharand, Richard Posey, Carol A. Reardon, Sue Rieghard, Barbara Ryan, Edwin H. Simmons, Sandra Stelts, Mike Stinnett, Mary Anne Sutphin, Ron Todd, Rudy Tomedi, Tu Shou-peng, Horace G. Underwood, Elliot S. Vesell, Herbert H. Weintraub, Mark Weintraub, Rodelle Weintraub, Claudia Stone Weissberg, M. G. Wiebe, Richard E. Winslow III, Nat Wisser, Peter Zimmerman and James Zobel.

Index